D1452996

Music as Philosophy

MUSICAL MEANING AND INTERPRETATION
Robert S. Hatten, editor

MICHAEL SPITZER

Music as Philosophy

Adorno and Beethoven's Late Style

INDIANA UNIVERSITY PRESS
Bloomington and Indianapolis

This book is a publication of

Indiana University Press
601 North Morton Street
Bloomington, IN 47404-3797 USA

http://iupress.indiana.edu

Telephone orders 800-842-6796
Fax orders 812-855-7931
Orders by e-mail iuporder@indiana.edu

The paper used in this publication meets the minimum requirements of American National Standard for Informa-tion Sciences—Permanence of Paper for Printed Library Materials, ANSI Z39.48-1984.

Manufactured in the United States of America

Library of Congress Cataloging-in-Publication Data

Spitzer, Michael.
   Music as Philosophy: Adorno and Beethoven's late style / Michael Spitzer.
      p. cm. — (Musical meaning and interpretation)
   Includes bibliographical references and index.
   ISBN 0-253-34724-6 (cloth : alk. paper) 1. Beethoven, Ludwig van, 1770–1827—Criticism and interpretation.
2. Music—Philosophy and aesthetics. 3. Adorno, Theodor W., 1903–1969. I. Title. II. Series.
   ML410.B4S686 2006
   780.92—dc22

                                                                                                2005029958

1 2 3 4 5   11 10 09 08 07 06

For Karen and Emily, and in memory of Lilli Spitzer (1928–1966)

There can be no concept of a style.
—Schleiermacher

Contents

Acknowledgments

This book originates in an ambitious Ph.D. thesis I once submitted in youthful confidence. A lot older, and a little wiser, I now realize that Ph.D.'s are beginnings, not endings. This, then, is another go, although if the philosopher is correct, books about style are not even possible at all. What have I learnt since 1991? The insights that my supervisor Bill Drabkin planted in my Southampton days continue to grow. Max Paddison's arrival at Durham helped give my hazy notions of Adorno new critical focus, and I have drawn inspiration from the clarity and depth of Max's writings. Meeting the semiotics crowd at the big Edinburgh conference of 1992—Naomi Cumming, Robert Hatten, David Lidov, Raymond Monelle, Eero Tarasti, and other friends too numerous to name—transformed my attitude to music theory and enriched my life. I owe Robert Hatten particular gratitude for the example of his own book on Beethoven, for kick-starting this project with his invitation to contribute to his series, and for being an unstinting support and guide during the book's genesis. Thanks also to Donna Wilson and David Anderson at Indiana University Press, and to Jürgen Selk for processing my examples so beautifully. A generous subvention from the Music & Letters Trust helped pay for these. A grant from the U. K. Arts and Humanities Research Board extended my research leave from Durham University. I wrote this book at a wonderfully happy time, beginning soon after my marriage to Karen, and completing it just before the birth of our daughter, Emily. It is dedicated to Karen and Emily, with much love, and to the memory of my mother, Lilli Spitzer. I never knew Lilli, but I'm told she had a passion for Beethoven, and I like to think she would have approved.

Music as Philosophy

1 Away with All Rules?

Schein—Artistic illumination; the sheen of natural beauty; surface semblance; illusion; veil; husk; the quivering of life; the flicker of aesthetic categories; an image of freedom; the promise of reconciliation; harmony.

"As soon as the feeling opens up a path to us, then away with all rules" (*Sobald das Gefühl uns einen Weg eröffnet, fort mit allen Regeln*). Never take composers at face value. Beethoven's comment, from his letter of 6 July 1825 to Prince Galitzin, seems to propound the commonplace that expression is achieved by breaking rules (see Lockwood 2002: 89–91). The trope certainly accords with the reception of his last works by his contemporaries, who had difficulty understanding them in terms of the forms, or "rules," of Classical convention. It fits the perception, popular in the nineteenth century, and still with us today in concert program notes, that, as Carl Dalhaus puts it, "Beethoven's forms 'shattered' under the force of expression" (1989: 86). Yet Beethoven embeds his remark in the context of his discussion of voice leading and functional harmonic progression, explaining to Galitzin a distinction between $\frac{6}{4}$ and $\frac{6}{3}$ chords. As Lockwood observes, Beethoven's letter, in which he demonstrates an analytical preoccupation with details of motivic working, voice leading, and harmony, is a "rare jewel" in Beethoven scholarship (90). "Away with all rules" must thus be taken with a good pinch of salt; on the level of technical grammaticality, Beethoven is anxious to appear to keep within convention.

More broadly, Beethoven's innocent remark to Galitzin, so straightforward in itself, surely misrepresents the apparent normalcy of much of his late music. Take the *Arietta* from his last piano sonata, Op. 111 in C, which seems merely to reiterate tonics and dominants—the very building blocks of the language (ex. 1.1). If the harmony is stereotypical, then the melody is a cliché, closely resembling the workaday tune which the publisher Diabelli supplied Beethoven for another variation set. Rather than subverting these conventions, the *Arietta* projects them with newfound clarity, so that they shine. It is this very directness, even nakedness, of expression which gives the *Arietta* its quality of a "little song" without words. What a shock, then, to discover that the *Arietta*'s normalcy is predicated on utter contradiction at a foundational level of its syntax. Scrutinized more carefully, the tonics and dominants projected by the melody are disposed in such a way that it is impossible to decide which comes first: that is, whether the melodic G's of mm. 1 and 2 express chords I or V. The ambiguity turns on the nature of upbeats. A basic knowledge of the Classical style tells us that upbeats, when they begin a movement, are conventionally unharmonized, as in Diabelli's waltz. The job of an upbeat is to

Arietta

Adagio molto semplice e cantabile

Example 1.1. Piano Sonata in C, Op. 111, second movement, mm. 1–4

impart a metrical accent, a "kick," to the first beat of the measure, the point where the bass comes in and the piece properly starts. Grounding the upbeat with a bass note in the left hand, as Beethoven does in the *Arietta,* cuts across the bar line and short-circuits the anacrusis. Beethoven's opening gambit profoundly shapes how we hear the harmony—and, of course, the subsequent variations built upon it. Ordinarily, the first bass note of m. 1 would sound like an accented neighbor to the D, so that the prevailing harmony in the measure is in fact a *dominant,* rather than a tonic (this effect is enhanced when the C is sharpened in variation I, m. 17; even more so with the $^6_4$ inversion of variation II, m. 33). But grounding the upbeat with a deep C anchors the C of m. 1 and tilts the harmonic center of gravity from the dominant toward the tonic. Thus *neither* harmony—dominant nor tonic—ultimately prevails; instead, the two are locked into a delicate equipoise. To grasp what is so distinctive about this equilibrium, one need only compare it with the so-called "bitonal" harmony of twentieth-century composers such as Stravinsky, by which chords or keys were stacked above each other. The *Arietta* is not "bitonal" in this respect, since the chords never properly clash. We hear, rather, a flicker of interpretive perspectives, as in the famous rabbit/duck illusion: now the chord is a tonic, now it is a dominant, but never both at once. Because this "flicker" is in principle endless, never susceptible to a definitive interpretation, Beethoven's harmony is notionally beyond analysis—an enterprise which depends on synchronic "snapshots" of musical structure, such as Schenkerian graphs. In his profound analytical study of the sketches (1976), William Drabkin plausibly graphs the *Arietta* as a Schenkerian initial ascent from C to G (or Î to 5̂), albeit with some distinctive gaps seminal for the theme's subsequent career in the variations. He also reviews how the genesis of the piece oscillated between tonic and dominant beginnings, as if Beethoven couldn't make up his mind whether to start the theme with a I or a V. Example 1.2a indicates that Beethoven's upbeat had originated as a full tonic measure. Example 1.2b, conversely, shows a sketch closer to the final version, with a tonic upbeat to a full measure of dominant, yet missing the crucial tonic suspension in the bass. It is the introduction of this suspension which affects the final version's tonic/dominant ambiguity. The ambiguity could be said to absorb the *Arietta*'s dynamic genesis into the music's fabric. Analysis is powerless to model this continuity be-

Example 1.2. Beethoven's sketches for his *Arietta* (transcribed and numbered by Drabkin)
    a. No. 37, mm. 1–4
    b. No. 51, mm. 1–2

tween genesis and structure. If traditional methods are unable to account for the *Arietta*'s harmonic "flicker," what can?

The *Arietta*, normative at one level, paradoxical at another, exemplifies procedures which Beethoven developed in the last decade of his life. In the late style, musical categories which we blithely take for granted—"rules," "expression," "convention," "coherence," "process"—are thrown dramatically into doubt. Whereas innovative art is often held to elaborate, subvert, or deconstruct convention, Beethoven's late style enshrines rules at their most fundamental. When musical conventions are subsumed within an original artistic process, we draw the irresistible analogy with language, in which words are transparent to the sense they express. By contrast, Beethoven's conventions cloud over, looked *at*, not *through*, so that process unfolds *within* musical material, not *across* it, in a weird mixture of external rigidity and internal tension. He is not the first, or the last, artist to foreground the materiality of his idiom, a device better known in painting than in music. The bricks in De Hooch's seventeenth-century courtyards are often more richly grained and "alive" than the human subjects who populate them. And much has been written about Van Gogh's famous peasant shoes, whose expressiveness transcends their utilitarian function (see Heidegger 1975: 36; Derrida 1987). To some extent, Beethoven's self-reflexivity—his "music about music"—follows in this tradition, except that music is *abstract*. To render *musical* material concrete, to even think of music *as* "material," is a radical step. A chord, clearly, is not a brick or a pair of boots. Beethoven objectifies a *rule*, rather than a physical object proper, and that is far more disturbing.

Such observations are not obviously captured by music theory. If we are to unravel the significance of Beethoven's achievement, and reactivate the metaphors sleeping within his casual references to the "rules" and "feeling" of music, we must stake out a broader interpretive context. A *philosophy* of Beethoven's style makes the basic assumption that musical rules correlate both with *social* convention and with *conceptual* reason and are underpinned by certain *natural* categories of perception—in short, that musical material bears the imprint of society, mind, and nature. "Music as philosophy" is predicated also on the historical drama of modernism and the emergence of the autonomy principle in the late eighteenth century. According to this story, the formally abstract and self-contained ("autonomous") Classical style of Haydn, Mozart, and Beethoven is celebrated as the benchmark for rationality in music, as well as the ideal balance of this rationality with the individual and societal dimensions of human subjectivity. With Beethoven's late style, this utopian high-water mark in Western music encounters its catastrophe: a repertory which critically reflects upon the foundations of musical Classicism, while at the same time reconstructing them from a quite different position. Beethoven's object, therefore, is nothing less than the foundation and limit of human reason itself. This, in a nutshell, is the gist of Theodor Adorno's reading of the late style, the most influential and intellectually sophisticated interpretation we have. As well as a front-rank philosopher and cultural critic, Adorno was arguably the sharpest writer on music of the twentieth century. Anybody at all familiar with his writings will have recognized my account of the *Arietta* as surreptitiously Adornian in its focus on stylistic contradiction and formal disunity. Adornian also is my emphasis on the unresolved tension between convention and play, registered in the processual dynamic of our artistic cognition. What I informally term a "flicker" actually has a name in the Adornian tradition: *Schein*, a Hegelian concept which mixes the notion of artistic "semblance" with the glimmer of the numinous in the Romantic symbol. In his fragmentary essay on *Schein*, Walter Benjamin, a key influence on Adorno, talks of the vital "quivering" of aesthetic beauty:

> No work of art may appear completely alive without becoming mere semblance [*Schein*], and ceasing to be a work of art. The life quivering in it must appear petrified and as if spellbound in a single moment. The life quivering within it is beauty, the harmony that flows through chaos and—that only appears to tremble. What arrests this semblance, what holds life spellbound and disrupts the harmony, is the expressionless [*das Ausdruckslose*]. That quivering is what constitutes the beauty of the work; the paralysis is what defines its truth. (2002: vol. 1, 224)

As regards the music, *Schein*—an attribute of beauty in all art, and hence a background foundational quality—is objectified in late Beethoven on the level of grammatical contradiction. As regards the theory, the trembling which *Schein* describes besets the identity of the concept itself—the interplay between its various aspects of "illumination," "semblance," "surface," and "harmony" (see the epigraph which begins this chapter), as well as its relationship within a family of cognate, yet distinct notions, including *Erscheinung, Apparition*, phenomenon, and phantasmagoria (extending ultimately to complex questions from the philosophy of consciousness and Marxist ideology critique). Furthermore, the stylistic contradictions which Benjamin describes as arresting or paralyzing the harmony of *Schein* seem in late Beethoven to be just another, more dramatic, expression of this same "quivering." Strangely, the late style's oppositional flicker appears to embrace the very interruptions of this flicker, so that the music's "beauty" and "truth" are thrown into a dialectical dance, becoming, as Adorno discovered, far less separable from each other than Benjamin suggests. In short, the ambiguity which I hear as being the late style's most beguiling aspect spreads out from the music to encompass both philosophical categories such as *Schein* and the very relationship between these categories and the music: between music and philosophy.

Beethoven and Adorno

The title of my book nods at the title of the Beethoven monograph Adorno labored on for much of his life, and which he left unfinished at his death. The publication of *Beethoven: Philosophie der Musik* in 1993, edited by Rolf Tiedemann, called for a response on a larger scale than the still-continuing spate of review articles. Given that Adorno is best known to musicians as a critic of twentieth-century music, a theorist of musical modernism centered around the Second Viennese School, here is a chance to nudge the "center" of critical theory back to its true origin—the musical enlightenment of the Classical style, and the Classical composer who occupies the highest plinth in Adorno's pantheon: Beethoven. This book is basically an extended reflection on the significance of Adorno's critical theory to tonal music. In some ways, I attempt a mediation of Adorno's insights within a musicological and music-theoretical culture he did not live to see. Such an exercise begs the question of method. What, precisely, *are* musical conventions, and *how*, exactly, do we analyze them? The analytical portions of Adorno's *Beethoven* are primitive, and he had a limited historical grasp of Beethoven's roots in eighteenth-century style—an irony, given his emphasis on the role convention plays in the late style. The work of Classical scholars such as Allanbrook, Ratner, Rosen, Webster, and many others has enormously enriched our understanding of the facts of the Classical style: the normativity underlying Haydn, Mozart, and Beethoven's individual genius. Likewise, we have benefited from theories which study style from the perspective of musical perception and cognition, particularly the work of Leonard Meyer and Eugene Narmour. These facts and theories were simply unavailable to Adorno. Likewise, Adorno had a problem, practical as well as philosophical, with music analysis. Not only did he misunderstand Schenker, he also mistrusted the hermeneutic side of critical enquiry—its dependence on conventional frameworks of interpretation. One can make too much of the conflict between philosophy and music analysis, caricaturing it as an opposition between the negativity of thought and the positivism of facts. Much recent work in the philosophy and history of music theory has helped bridge this gap. As quickly as I write this, however, I hasten to add that Adorno cannot be translated into music without missing the entire point of philosophy's critical autonomy as a perspective *onto* music "from the outside." And vice versa: eliding or assimilating the two removes music's viewpoint on philosophy. Their reciprocal, yet independent, relationship is at the heart of Adorno's vision of music's place in the world. I employ the facts of modern musicology and analysis rather as an *illumination* of Adorno's ideas. Conversely, Adorno's ideas illuminated my *own*, many of which were gained before I read a word of his writings. Some of these ideas are developed in my previous book on music and metaphor (2004). It is interesting that Adorno's key concept in his discussion of late Beethoven is allegory, metaphor's dark twin. In this respect, the present book is essentially about allegory in music, and thus a (critical) complement to my (hermeneutic) study of metaphor.

If Adorno cannot be simply cross-checked against the score, then a parallel and even greater danger is to misrepresent the complexity of his thought as a series of slogans or "buzzwords." Adorno does utilize an identifiable array, or, to use Walter Benjamin's term (1998: 34), a "constellation" (1998: 34), of concepts—"mimesis," "ratio," "mediation," "material," "language character," "concept character," "apparition," "caesura," "breakthrough," *Schein*, etc. But these terms draw their meaning from their position and interaction within the entire constellation; it is extraordinarily difficult both to extract a single term from the network and to pin it down with a stable definition. Benjamin's analogy that "Ideas are to objects as constellations are to stars" (34) is a good way of imagining the loose and mobile relationship between general and particular (as in Wittgenstein's comparable notion of the crisscrossing "family relationships" which connect "language games").[1] According to Adorno's very German notion of thought (i.e., *philosophy*), categories are kept constantly in motion within the process of reflection. It is particularly hard to separate the spirit from the letter of Adorno's writings (by which they resemble music), and many musicologists who claim to be broadly influenced by Adorno end up just extracting the jargon from the context. This includes a recent study of the late quartets purporting to be a "translation of Adorno's philosophy of music into actual analysis" (Chua 1995: 6). Another symptom of this syndrome is the co-option of Adorno as an outrider for postmodernism, a New Musicologist *avant la lettre*. Adorno was actually profoundly hostile toward the various tendencies which have coalesced into a "postmodern theory," not least in his commitment to the principle of musical autonomy. Autonomy, a bankrupt concept for postmodernism, continues nevertheless to hold sway in a parallel tradition of German social thought, in which the Enlightenment Project is alive and well. The writings of post-Adorno critical theorists such as Jürgen Habermas, Karl-Otto Apel, and Albrecht Wellmer suggest that the New Musicological consensus that we live in a post-Enlightenment world is both negotiable and contestable.[2] The defense of musical autonomy does not mark out Adorno as a desiccated formalist—how could it, since no writer has done more to contextualize musical form socially, culturally, and historically? At issue for him is a point so simple as to be breathtaking: the instant we consider music as a document (of a theoretical model, a semiotic code, a hermeneutic window, a cultural unit, a social practice) it ceases to be music. We appreciate music *as* music precisely because it is *music* and *not* the many things with which it can be compared. To be sure, models and contexts are revealing, but only as staging posts on the path back to the tones. Musical meaning can never be captured by analytical systems or hermeneutic readings. Hermeneutics errs when it assumes that there is a meaning reachable at the end of a long relay of interpretations. Music just isn't like that. Hermeneutic models, nevertheless, have an important function to play as a necessary moment within the cycle of musical reflection. The tension between hermeneutics and critical theory turns out to be the intractable problem at the heart of Adorno studies. One can insist that Adorno's texts remain resistant to interpretation in their difficulty, just like complex music is. Yet every book needs its reader, every theory its student. Even Schoenberg, one of Adorno's major influences, recognized the heuristic efficacy of simplification in his American pedagogical works. Adorno would have been horrified if his key concepts were tabled in a glossary, as I have attempted to do at the end of chapter 3. Better a problematic attempt than no attempt at all. Otherwise, Adorno commentary would remain an endless prolegomenon to future research.

Musicology is playing out this tension between hermeneutics and critical theory in the current sea change in Beethoven studies, evidenced by two distinguished additions to the literature on the late style. Both Maynard Solomon's *Late Beethoven* (2003) and Stephen Rumph's *Beethoven after Napoleon* (2004) contextualize Beethoven in the politics and cultural values of early Romanticism, correcting a deficit which they ascribe to the long-established, yet fallacious, view of him as a Classical artist. Both authors credit the founding of this view to Arnold Schmitz's *Das romantische Beethovenbild* of 1927, the consensus sealed for Anglo-American readers by Rosen's *The Classical Style* (1972) and *Sonata Forms* (1980), which treat "Beethoven throughout as if he were a late eighteenth-century composer" (Rosen 1980: 354). By reevaluating Beethoven as a Romantic, Solomon and Rumph seek to rescue the late style from "conservative German cultural criticism" (Solomon, 33) and reassert its radical and hermeneutic dimensions. My own belief is that, on the primary level of musical syntax, Rosen was right. We cannot caricature the Classical style as either formalist or conservative, whatever the agendas of early-twentieth-century German historiography. Ironically, it is Beethoven himself who emerges from Rumph's study as the conservative, even reactionary figure, begging the question of why we value the music at all. Either we ignore his politics altogether, in which case we return to old-fashioned musicology, or we hear his music as critical of those politics, leading us ineluctably from hermeneutics to critical theory. Either way, critical theory wins. The problem with hermeneutics, at least in its raw state, is that one-to-one correlations between style traits and cultural tropes are always undone by the fact of *context dependence*. Context dependence is a term much discussed in the annals of analytic-philosophical studies of style, as we shall presently see.[3] Its analogue in the German idealist tradition is Adorno's concept of *mediation,* as in the part's mediation in the whole, and the whole in its various social and cultural contexts (see Paddison 1997: 108–48). In other words, just as the technical meaning of a chord depends on how it is used (its "context dependence"), so the cultural meaning of an idiom is always mobile or dialectical. Take the case of the possible "objectivity" or "subjectivity" of Beethoven's late counterpoint. Notwithstanding Beethoven's image of "archaic counterpoint as a symbol of orthodoxy and ancien régime" (Rumph, 110), his actual use of this idiom challenges any clean-cut distinction between discipline and expression (or "rules" and "feeling"). And it is misleading of Rumph to impute such a simple object/subject distinction to Adorno:

> Adorno viewed the archaic counterpoint of the *Missa Solemnis* and late quartets as signs of retreat from middle-period subjectivity. Yet, as this study has labored to show, Beethoven integrated counterpoint into his late style with the same rigor as sonata

form or motivic development in his heroic works. Subjective presence is stronger than ever throughout his late works. (243)

In fact, Adorno said no such thing. Adorno always stresses the interplay of forces within all musical materials. On the one hand, counterpoint is "objective" because it represents a material particularity not compromised by the schematization of Classical convention. On the other hand, it is also "subjective" by very virtue of this freedom from convention. The counterpart to this ambiguity is a similar split in Adorno's estimation of the Classical style as a whole, which is both the best and the worst thing to have happened in the history of Western music. Adorno is not interested in pinning down the meaning of music to socialist-realist objective correlatives in economic or political history. While recognizing the horizon of these factors, Adorno finds meaning rather in the mobility of categories, which he compares to the dynamic of human thought itself. Curiously, the closest analogue to Adorno's notion of musical material as a micrological force field is as far away as possible from critical theory on the spectrum of style study: Narmour's theory of musical style as an interplay of subatomic intervallic tendencies (Narmour 1992; Spitzer 1998b). As Adorno would put it, critical theory enjoys a "pseudo-morphosis" to cognitive science. It is surely significant that the historical fulcrum for both Adorno and style study is the Classical style. Adorno would fully concur with Rosen that Beethoven is a Classical composer, yet with the proviso that the Classical style is already modernist in its tensions. Webster's designation of the Classical style as "the First Viennese Modern School" (1991: 367) is thus extremely helpful in this matter; as the Adornian critic Martin Zenck points out: "Webster's thesis thus has the advantage of positioning Beethoven as a modern, without thereby identifying him as an anti-classical romantic, or cutting him off from Viennese classicism" (Zenck 2002: 6). Seeing Beethoven as both Classical *and* modernist cuts the ground beneath the Classical/Romantic dispute of periodization.

If my position is to staunchly reaffirm Beethoven's Classicism, it is also to defend Adorno from his devotees in sociology. It probably takes a music sociologist to write a book called *After Adorno* (DeNora 2003), since it is from a social perspective that Adorno's analysis is most obviously dated. His was a mind-set formed in the struggle against fascism of the 1930s and 1940s, and then the Cold War of the 1950s and 1960s. His preoccupations with art music's battle against commodification by the culture industry spoke to us more loudly when the centrality of the canon, the relevance of new music, and the viability of formalism, with its attendant culture of "structural listening," seemed less problematic. Nevertheless, Adorno's thought is a complex constellation of many disciplines, and it is a mistake to focus on the social strand at the expense of his aesthetics and philosophy. It is here, in the supple and rich thinker of *Aesthetic Theory* and *Negative Dialectics,* that we find the "other" Adorno, free of the hectoring polemic of over-familiar texts such as *Philosophy of New Music,* with their untenable critique of Stravinsky and jazz. Leppert's compendium of translations has thrown the net much wider than that, of course. But I would argue, polemically, that musicology is even *better* served by circumventing the musical texts altogether, and extrapolating directly from the aesthetic and philosophical writings—domains where Adorno was more competent. This, then, is the main tactic of my book: to rewire the circuit between Adorno and music, bypassing most of his writings on music itself. I do so, paradoxically, by maintaining my focus on his monograph *Beethoven: Philosophie der Musik*. This oblique enterprise is an exercise in speculative reconstruction, requiring many intuitive leaps. For instance, I construct my own theory of style "inspired by Adorno," based on a dialectic of language, reason, and nature. And I fill out Adorno's sketchy comparison between Beethoven and Hölderlin (the composer's historical *Doppelgänger*), surmise links between Adorno and musicologists such as Guido Adler, and ground his critical project in the early-twentieth-century discourse on literary "style." In fact, this lost discourse of style is my starting point.

Recuperating Style: Context Dependence and Mediation

The concept of style was especially current in German literary criticism in the 1930s–40s, among scholars such as Erich Auerbach, Ernst Robert Curtius, and Leo Spitzer. Each of these critics worked in the middleground between linguistics and comparative literature, and "style" was a versatile tool for mediating language's general and particular aspects. A typical gambit was to seize upon a peculiarity of a writer's syntax and extrapolate observations about his or her intellectual environment, finally returning to the text with a deepened understanding of the writer's "soul" or "center." For example, Spitzer's essay "The Style of Diderot" begins with the personal observation "I had often been struck, in reading Diderot, by a rhythmic pattern in which I seemed to hear the echo of Diderot's speaking voice: a self-accentuating rhythm, suggesting that the 'speaker' is swept away by a wave of passion which tends to flood all limits" (1948: 135). After a detailed analysis of Diderot's idiosyncratic syntax, Spitzer makes connections with themes of "psychophysical disharmonies" in works such as *La religieuse* (which features a homosexual Mother Superior), as well as tensions between the attested "mobility" of Diderot's character and his "respect for scientific data" (165); an understanding of "*style coupé*, the style of nervousness," allows Spitzer to glean new insights from a well-worn text such as *Neveu de Rameau*. The enterprise involves a shuttling from detail to whole and back again, with the whole comprehending not just the entirety of the text, but the world and the "soul" of the artist. Again and again, Spitzer talks of an artist's ethos having a "center." Spitzer's "center" inevitably invokes the famous "hermeneutic circle" of Schleiermacher, by which "the detail can be understood only by the whole and any explanation of detail presupposes the understanding of the whole" (in Spitzer, 19; see also 33–35).

A preoccupation with "style" continued with the New Criticism of the 1950s and the Zurich School of the 1960s, especially in the work of Emil Staiger. It parallels ideas developed independently by the Russian Formalists and anticipates many of the themes of structuralism and deconstruction. In some ways, our notion of *écriture* or "semiosis" is simply style in modern parlance. Nevertheless, the progressive focus on the signs and mechanisms of language departs from style analysis in one crucial respect: an out-and-out rejection of the psychologism of early-twentieth-century critics, whose talk of "souls" and "centers" makes us un-comfortable today. The "death of the author" taught us that the meaning of works always exceeds artistic intention and is a product of preexisting contexts. And yet with the demise of authorial subjectivity came the loss of historical consciousness, and one wonders whether the price was worth paying. Recent Germanists such as Manfred Frank (1997) and Andrew Bowie (1997) lay much of the blame for this on misreadings of Schleiermacher, a philosopher who actually anticipated and even "overcame" our problems with subjectivity and history. Peter Szondi (2003), perhaps the most gifted German critic after Adorno, placed particular guilt at the door of the founders of modern hermeneutics, Dilthey and Gadamer, for neglect-ing the aesthetic character of interpretation, and caricaturing Schleiermacher's nu-anced notion of the "psychological" as crude "intention." On the contrary, Szondi stressed that Schleiermacher was interested only in the artist's "life" as it was in-scribed within linguistic material, as part of his distinction between a personal, aesthetic, use of language and language as a body of declarative statements:

> It is true that in technical-psychological interpretation attention is directed at man, at his individuality, just as in grammatical interpretation it is directed at language and its individual modifications. But even in the Academy addresses, Schleiermacher's charac-terization of the object of psychological interpretation as "the original psychic process of generating and combining ideas and images" implies the objective aspect of lan-guage as a medium of this generation and combination. This is even clearer in the ear-lier drafts and in the concept of technical interpretation *and its central category, style, which of course relates directly to the use of language.* (131, my emphasis)

Style, then, is always more than just language; with style, Schleiermacher states that "thought and language merge with each other" (in Szondi, 131).

Adorno seldom talks about style or Schleiermacher and appears to have no links with the world of Auerbach, Curtius, or Spitzer. Nevertheless, when he writes an essay called "Beethoven's Late Style," his intellectual hinterland shows. Adorno connects Beethoven's syntax with his cultural milieu, moving backwards and for-wards between musical detail and philosophical ideas in complex circles. Just as style for Schleiermacher is a fusion of thought and language, Beethoven's style, by Adorno's lights, is both a musical language and a philosophical system. The differ-ence turns, as I will argue, on a flicking of the switch from positive to negative, on the opposition between hermeneutics proper and its modernist cousin, critical the-ory. Adorno, like Spitzer et al., is drawn to the stylistically peculiar or dissonant. But unlike the critics of the thirties, he shies away from centers or closure, keeping the process of interpretation open and self-critical to the last. In fact, he even states, in a passing observation from *Dialectic of Enlightenment*, that the very possibility of "style" is historically limited to Classicism, because after Beethoven style turns into *stylization*—pastiche. Since the quality of style ought to be "discrepancy" rather than "harmony," he calls the culture industry "the most rigid of all styles" (Adorno and Horkheimer 1989: 131).

Rigidity is antithetical to the part/whole dynamic of the hermeneutic circle. Al-though this circle applies to all artistic media, it is arguably epitomized by the context dependence, or mediation, of musical processes: that is, the identity and significance of any musical detail (be it a motive or a chord) is utterly dependent on its function and position in the artistic whole. Context dependence is the chief reason why music was taken up by Romantic philosophy (and Adorno) as the paradigm for the processual character of thought.[4] Adorno's mixed fortunes in the English-speaking world are thus due as much to the ascent of analytic philosophy (after Wittgenstein) as to the paradigm shift from music to painting as a model for thought. Analytic critics who write about style, such as Nelson Goodman (1978), Arthur Danto (1981), or Richard Wollheim (1979; 1995), focus largely on the visual arts, since the philosophy of mind is more directly amenable to questions of representation than to matters of musical form.[5] A contributory factor to the neglect of music is that understanding harmonic process requires specialized technical training, more so, perhaps, than the criticism of a picture. This neglect is certainly the impression gained from Stephanie Ross's chapter on "style" from the *Oxford Handbook of Aesthetics* (2003), a good recent survey. Ross's critics stem mostly from the analytic tradition; they focus on the visual arts; and Adorno's name is characteristically entirely absent. Within their terms of reference, analytic critics make useful distinctions between the form and content of style (Danto's "medium and matter" [1981: 159]), while recognizing that style embraces both categories: "Style comprises certain characteristic features both of what is said and of how it is said, both of subject and of wording, both of content and of form" (Goodman 1978: 27). They distinguish "individual" from "general" style (Wollheim 1979; 1995), akin to the difference between "style" proper and "manner" (Danto 1981: 200). For Danto, "A style is a gift" whereas "a manner can be learned" (200); similarly, Wollheim thinks that "general style" manipulates rules and schemata and can therefore be taught, whereas "individual style" can only be "formed" (1979: 142). All are agreed that the individual pole of style expresses the artist's identity; perhaps her way of seeing the world (Danto), or even her actual bodily gestures (Sircello 1975), albeit mindful of the intentional fallacy—the proviso that the artist's identity or "body" is artistically constructed, what Kendall Walton calls "the apparent artist" (Walton 1979: 60). Nevertheless, Ross's critics come unstuck, finally, on the fact of context dependence, the paradox that, notwithstanding the analytic search for clear categories, "No fixed catalogue of the elementary properties of style can be compiled . . . we normally come to grasp a style without being able to analyse it into component features" (Goodman 1978: 34). Style features are defined by use, so style ultimately evades necessary or sufficient conditions. The problem of context dependence afflicts Danto's oddly "subtractive" definition of style as that which is left when we take away the "transparency" of representation (1981: 156–64). If this were truly the case, it is hard to see why style would exceed mere "expression," or how it might concern "content" at all. It cuts against Goodman's claim for the importance of style, the belief that, "The discernment of style is an integral aspect of the understanding of works of art and the worlds they present" (1978: 40). Of course, context dependence is for music not an impasse but a starting point. But the aesthetic model music predicates would seriously undermine the propositional, declarative theory of knowledge which underpins the entire analytic project. For this reason, analytic critics of style hesitate on the threshold of a proper engagement with musical form or a theory of context dependence.

The case of Leonard B. Meyer reveals just how much can be achieved in music analysis without actually crossing that threshold. Meyer's definition of musical style is stringently behaviorist: "Style is a replication of patterning, whether in human behavior or in the artifacts produced by human behavior, that results from a series of choices made within some set of constraints" (1997: 3). Like Danto's account of individual "manner," a composer's style for Meyer is "adverbial" (see Ross 2003: 234), in that it focuses on the "how" (the inflection of the pattern) rather than the "what" (the origin or the status of the pattern itself). Despite Meyer's intellectual debt to early-twentieth-century pragmatist philosophers such as Mead and Dewey (see Cumming 1991), his approach to style is even more "painterly" than the critics discussed by Ross. By assimilating the principles of gestalt psychology into style analysis, Meyer is in step with art critics like Rudolph Arnheim and Ernst Gombrich, who similarly drew on research in visual perception (see Spitzer 1997). In fact, by bringing forward the role of psychology so prominently, Meyer adds, or at least enhances, a "third term" which is only implicit in the work of the "painterly" critics: nature. Perhaps Meyer's signal contribution is a ternary model of style, triangulating individual style and general style with *natural* (i.e., psychological) style. This ternary scheme has a considerable influence on the model of style I propose in chapter 2. Without wishing to detract from the remarkable analytical power of Meyer's theory, I should nevertheless state that it also entails a variety of problems. We may nowadays question Meyer's analogy between artistic originality and scientific innovation (2000: 18); his denial that aesthetic objects have a truth content (23); his reduction of cultural "ideology" to a pressure point acting externally on musical material, rather than a force immanent to material (247); his overly rigid dichotomy between "critical analysis" and "style analysis" (1973: 6–7) and normative "rules" and individual "strategies" (13–14); his comparison of aesthetic understanding with the enjoyment of a "game," which downgrades art's broader significance (2000: 193); and finally, Meyer's tendency to reify "nature" and "convention" into schematic categories, in the shape of gestalt principles (such as gap-fill motion) on the one hand, and melodic archetypes (such as "axial" melodies) on the other (1997: 241). Meyer claimed, in 1973, that "Understanding music is simply a matter of attending to and comprehending tonal-temporal relationships" (1973: 109). Such a formalist conception of musical style would be unthinkable today.

This is not the place for a full evaluation of Meyer's complex, and extremely positive, contribution to style theory. I will simply stress that his rigid separation of music's nature and culture errs equally in relation to both terms. From the former standpoint, our understanding of music's nature is subject to disciplines in an evolving state of empirical research, as is seen in the annals of journals such as *Music Perception*. For example, Meyer never countenances the possibility that musical processes may "naturally" embody either human gestures (see Cumming 2000; Hatten 2004) or metaphorical schemata (Spitzer 2004). From the standpoint of "culture," Meyer's theory sins against context dependence by imposing unrealistic limits on composers' freedom. Context dependence entails flips between natural and conventional use of musical material. A composer like Beethoven may express a convention as natural, or objectify a natural gestalt, like a gesture or "image schema." Meyer's cardinal insight is that musical originality may result through "exploiting limits" rather than through "transcending" them (Meyer 2000: 189–225). Yet his theory is not supple (i.e., dialectical) enough to show that limits may be transcended *in the course of being exploited*. Such is the case, I argue, with Beethoven's *Arietta*. The objectifying of a convention may be posited by Beethoven as a subjective act of compositional will. Meyer's emphasis on the projection ("exploitation") of convention converges with a key motif of Danto's and Goodman's theory of style. Danto talks of "the transfiguration of the commonplace" (1981); Goodman, of art "exemplifying" simple categories (1978). This might be adequate to the stasis of a painting, but not to the musical processuality exemplified in what I have termed the *Arietta*'s "trembling," its *Schein*. A fully dialectical model of style, doing justice to context dependence, heightens the horizon of *time*—in both its phenomenal and historical dimensions. A temporal horizon profiles the fragility of the *Arietta*'s conventions, and the heroism with which it upholds them in the face of historical decay and human mortality. It discovers nature *within* convention. Style, then, becomes properly critical when it illuminates music's quotidian facticity—the everyday and the normal.

To repeat, such an approach is hardly a wholesale rejection of Meyer in particular, or of music theory in general. It would be a mistake to renounce the resources of normative style analysis in the name of some utopian, poststructuralist future. This would serve only to perpetuate the rifts between the two perspectives on style I have identified. By contrast, the normative and the critical are mutually supportive; the one affording priceless analytical *aperçus* on musical details; the other exposing "false consciousness" in how we evaluate them. An example of "false consciousness" is Meyer's contradictory account of Classical convention as both "natural" and "ideological," in his essay "Nature, Nurture, and Convention" (in Meyer 2000: 244–47). First, Classical music is esteemed for its "clarity, order, and perhaps naturalness" (244); and yet Meyer writes that Romantic music's "valuing of the 'natural' . . . involved the repudiation of whatever was deemed artificial and arbitrary—that is, whatever seemed *conventional*" (247). The role of critical style analysis is not to tidy up or gloss over such contradictions but to recruit them; to understand, for instance, how the Classical style's *simultaneous* tendencies toward nature and convention were a driving force of stylistic development.

Another way of looking at normative stylistic systems is as analytical tools, with the status of what Wittgenstein called "language games" (1984: 5), that is, social practices conducted within a professionalized academic community. To counter the threat of relativism, the role of critical theory is not merely to take its place as one "language game" among many, but rather to assume the status of a regulative meta-theory. The existence of such a meta-theory is fiercely disputed by analytic philosophy and French poststructuralism alike.[6] Nevertheless, Apel points out (1998: 21) the "performative self-contradiction" of philosophers who deny the possibility of philosophy while practicing this discipline (e.g., Wittgenstein strangely avoided reflecting on the language game of philosophy itself).[7] Apel, together with Habermas and Wellmer, is a leader of critical theory's so-called "second generation." These thinkers attempt to reconcile Adorno's German tradition with the more productive outlook on language and society typical of the new "communication model." They discover emancipatory energies within the intersubjective consensus of liberal democracy—in Meyer's terms, not "transcending limits" but "exploiting" them (2000: 189). According to Wellmer, the role of the aesthetic is precisely to "light up" social norms: to see nature *within* culture. In his beautiful phrase, art "fires the finite world of communicative meaning with excitement and makes its colors glow" (Wellmer 1998: 177). A powerful example of intersubjective debate is the dialogue between music theorists. Just as some of the best work in contemporary philosophy is conducted "between" the analytic and critical schools, there is need for a similar conversation between normative and critical approaches to musical style.[8] Or simply a requirement for a recuperation of *style* itself, since Manfred Frank reminds us that Schleiermacher's concept of style already encompasses these normative and critical dimensions (Frank 1997: 1–22). To this unitary, normative/critical notion of style I would like to add the concrete example of *Beethoven's late style*. Viewing his late style in terms of "music as philosophy" suggests an Archimedean point from which to appraise the current intellectual situation: the search for "feeling within rules."

The Plan of the Book

Inspired by the mobility and context dependence of the music, I have sought to develop a ternary model of musical style based on the interactions of nature, convention, and subjectivity. Since these terms are impulses which defy rigid definition, their exposition in this book is deliberately gradual, and embedded within musical examples. Chapter 2 explains my ternary theory of style as an interaction of three fields I call S1, S2, and S3. Chapter 3 is an explication of Adorno's Beethoven monograph. Chapters 4–6 analyze the music. Chapter 4 gives an overview of the late style; chapter 5 looks at the late sonata forms; and chapter 6 considers the way Beethoven's works project ideas, materials, and natural categories. Chapter 7 moves on to history, looking at contemporary discourses of old and new. It is here that I compare Beethoven to Hölderlin's own late style. Chapter 8 puts the late style in the context of Viennese Classicism, particularly Haydn. Chapter 9 gives a summary of critical theory and music.

At the head of each chapter, I table a definition of one of the key concepts which steer my exploration of the late style: *Schein, mimesis, mediation, Durchbruch, allegory, Apparition, parataxis, caesura,* and *critique.* As well as being extrapolations from Adorno's writing, these concepts identify real musical effects which otherwise have no name: the flicker of music's ambiguity; the eruption of repressed forces; the dawning of recognition in the listener; the compaction of musical ideas within superdense points; a methodology geared to contradiction, etc. I would hope that these concepts offer a useful contribution to style analysis, in addition to illuminating the late style in particular. While forming a constellation as a group, the concepts are also constellations in themselves, in that each rubric gathers together seemingly conflicting impulses, so that the successive definitions within each family broadly traverse a circle.

Thus three chapters on style, three on the music, three on history, governed by a constellation of nine concepts. For my many triplicities, I make no apologies, like Kant, who observes in passing that:

> It has been thought somewhat suspicious that my divisions in pure philosophy should almost always come out threefold. But it is due to the nature of the case. (1989: 39)

2　Styles

THE FIRST MOVEMENT OF OP. 132

Mimesis—Nature; immediacy; expression; miming; mimicry; imitation; metaphor; identifying; reconciliation; withstanding; overcoming; abstraction.

The works of Beethoven's last decade are among the richest and deepest of Western art music. As well as being extraordinary in themselves, they force us to rethink that enigmatic hybrid of language and worldview which musicians call *style*. Whereas a musical phrase can seem both to express an utterance and to unfold a train of thought, Beethoven's late style takes instrumental music further into these spheres of language and thought than it had ever gone before, and arguably since. The present book explores the dual metaphor of "music as language and thought," summarized under the rubric "music as philosophy," in the context of the scores. This extra-musical aspect of (musical) style throws our problem wide open in two directions: how to define the border between music and nonmusic (language and thought); and how to circumscribe the technical attributes of a repertory on its own terms. These questions can be caricatured, respectively, as "Can the 'meaning' of music be translated into nonmusical terms?" and "Can whatever Beethoven's late works have in common be summarized into a predictable grammar or generative code?" The answer to both questions, of course, is no, since if music really could be translated, it would cease to be music, and if it could be predicted, it would forfeit its creativity. But it is a strangely qualified "no." Music does, in fact, mimic the grammar and thought patterns of the world: a musical "phrase," like a phrase in language, has lexicon, syntax, punctuation, semantics, even affective inflection; it can also be structured "rationally" into part-whole relationships, unfold "logically," or develop a motivic "idea." Moreover, as regards predictability, even the most original "genius" has to work with handed-down formulae and conventions. It becomes apparent that the truth lies somewhere in the middle, in the shape of a dynamic and open-ended oscillation between a "no" and a "maybe," as we track the way this most playful of all art forms toys and flirts with the world. Actually, the contour of this dynamic mimes the dialectic of human consciousness itself, the ability of subjects to reflect at ever increasing levels both on themselves and on the objects of their attention. Music is like thought, it invites thought, it resists thought. Such an approach appears to fly in the face of the positivism inherent to music theory and musicology, which prefers to pin musical meaning down to identifiable units of structure or reference. It would be a mistake, however, to ascribe this method to an unreconstructed Romanticism, a nostalgia for immediacy. On the contrary, the "maybe" of our dilemma brings to bear practically the entirety of music-theoretical and musicological knowledge as grist to the mill—all the rich social and intellectual contexts in which musical practice is grounded. But this knowledge is underscored by a huge qualification: that musical experience is distinct, and forever in excess of all we can say about it. The uniqueness of music, and its context dependence, belong together and reflect upon each other as moments of a common process.

So why Beethoven? It is simply a fact of style history that a composer of enormous specific gravity—what the Germans call *das Schwere* (Kropfinger 2003)—happened to enter the fray at a time when musical material was uniquely conventionalized. Like an astral singularity, Beethoven is so heavy that he bends light. Beethoven inherited the ready-made forms and genres of Haydn and Mozart and could be said merely to have inflected them with his personal voice. At no time, before or after, was the clash between music's normative and individual aspects more dramatic. The accident of Beethoven's late style lights up and magnifies a more general attribute of musical experience. "Music as philosophy," in general, can be read off the late style of this particular composer. An arresting feature of Theodor Adorno's interpretation of Beethoven is that the late style sits at the center of all centers in the grand narrative of Western civilization: the peak of our cultural Himalayas. A tall claim indeed, and the stakes could hardly be higher. At the foothills of this approach, we are best served with a concrete example, and a basic question: Does Beethoven's late style itself have a "center"?

Beginning in the Middle: Op. 132 in A Minor

If we were to indulge a fantasy that we could put our finger on the solar plexus of Beethoven's late style, then a prime candidate would be the passage which breaks out in the middle of the A-minor quartet's opening movement at m. 92 (ex. A.1, see appendix). After the first wave of the development comes to a head with a C minor cadence and a portentous pause, a jaunty tune, scored oddly in bare octaves, enters with crashing incongruity, interrupting the quartet's prevailing gloom and seemingly shattering its unity. No sooner come than it is gone—the cadence is repeated in E minor, and the development picks up where it left off, with the melancholy material presented in the exposition. Totally unprepared by anything in the score, the listener is puzzled. It is as if an absurd creature—an elephant, perhaps—were suddenly to wander across the stage of a Shakespearean tragedy.[1] Hermeneutically speaking, the absurdity of m. 92 throws down a gauntlet to interpretation, challenging us literally to "make sense" of it.[2]

Listeners make sense of music through a knowledge of style, which functions roughly like the rules of a language. A listener attuned to the syntax of the Classical style will hear the interruption of m. 92 as a manipulation of convention, and specifically as a flouting of formal decorum, because although it is embedded in the center of the movement, it actually flaunts signs of *opening*. Knowledge of the repertoire will invoke two venerable precedents of C-major quartets which also resolve to the diatonic major after chromatic introductions: the third of Beethoven's

"Rasumovsky" Quartets, Op. 59, no. 3, and Mozart's "Dissonance," K. 387 (one thinks also of Haydn's *Creation,* the C-major blaze of *Licht* after the "Representation of Chaos"). In all these pieces, the texture is scrubbed clean of black notes, so that when the tune enters it is as if the sun comes out. There is the sense of what Heidegger calls a "clearing" and Adorno terms a "breakthrough": the music opens up a space so as to discharge a suppressed force. Now, the Classical style conventionally stages this procedure as the birth of the main theme out of a nebulous introduction. The normative placement of this theme would be at the start of the sonata-form exposition. For Op. 132 to displace this moment to its development section marks an outrageous breach of protocol. The question, to repeat, is why? Of course, the quartet cannot possibly be said to "begin" at m. 92, given that it has a fully realized exposition in A minor, mm. 1–74. Knowledge of style may have sharpened the problem of the interruption, but it gets us no nearer to making sense of it.

Paradoxically, the notion of style once again comes to the rescue, because in addition to conventional code, style carries the opposite sense of individual manner, akin to literary discourse. Schleiermacher argued that "style" comprises an "individual manner of combining" elements which intimates "the essence of individuality." Manner and syntax both rely on combination, but whereas syntactic rules can be codified, stylistic manner is as resistant to theoretical modeling as the peculiar identity of a human subject. As Schleiermacher maintains, "There can be no concept of a style" (in Frank 1997: 19). Even so, the particularity of stylistic manner, which we can now call Style 2, is accessible only via the generality of stylistic convention, Style 1. Style 2 supervenes upon and is mediated through Style 1, and the dialectic between them animates Beethoven's musical texts, the compositions of the *late style.* This interaction is paralleled by Hatten's model of a "methodological dialectic" between "the stylistic and the strategic," although without Schleiermacher's critical dimension (Hatten 1994: 29–30). Reversing our standpoint from the general to the particular, we can also consider Op. 132 as a unique sui generis structure. This affords us a quite different interpretational context, by which local-level irregularities are justified by the coherence of the whole. We embark on a process of analysis, and the story which unfolds is simple yet compelling.

The C-major tune is based on a rising scale implicit at the end of the A-minor introduction, which in the first instance went on to generate the first subject of the exposition. This relationship between introduction and tonic-group material is absolutely normative for Classical music. Introductions conventionally adumbrate ideas which the exposition crystallizes. It is the sheer tightness of the introduction's grip on the exposition which is surprising. This is evinced most overtly by the underpinning of the tonic group by a chromatic tetrachord derived from the opening motet: G♯–A–F–E, interwoven with its dominant answer, D♯–E–C–B. But the shadow of the introduction is present also in the very key of the Allegro: minor-mode introductions more generally resolve to major-mode expositions in Classical music, and one might have expected the quartet to ensue in the key of A or C major. Much of the A-minor Allegro's air of tragedy flows from the suppression of these more likely keys. Nor is C major permitted for the second group—the norma-

Example 2.1. Op. 132, finale, new melody

tive key in a minor-mode sonata form. Beethoven chooses instead the unusual sub-mediant key of F, thereby highlighting a pitch that had figured particularly strongly in the introduction as the apex of the tonic tetrachord and the climax at m. 9. Given that the shadow of the introduction extends well beyond its normal bounds to cover the entire exposition, and the start of the development, the intuition that the C-major sunburst at m. 92 represents a displaced "beginning" gains support. Note the sudden lightening of texture and quickening of tempo here: with its rather odd octave doublings, the tune shakes off the counterpoint which has thickened this movement; and it moves briskly at two steps a measure, twice as fast as the first subject, each measure of which had staked out a single step of the cantus firmus. There is an exhilarating air of freedom here, all the more tragic since after a mere eleven measures, the tune is snuffed out by a premature reprise of the exposition, in the key of the dominant. Again, there are precedents in Classical convention in the witty device of interrupting a development with a "false recapitulation" (a gambit especially beloved of Haydn). But false recapitulations never last more than a few measures. The E-minor reprise, by contrast, is literal and total; we know it is "false" because it is duly followed by the "correct" reprise in the tonic. We have, then, the makings of an answer for the meaning of the jaunty tune in Op. 132. It is the relic of a putative string quartet in *C major* Op. 132, squeezed onto an out-crop of the development by the outlandish expansion, on either side, of two Clas-sical conventions—a slow introduction and a false recapitulation. Despite and *be-cause* of its brevity, the passage is dazzling enough to dominate the surrounding gloom as a beacon of hope. Its rays arc across the entire quartet and hit their target at the last possible moment in the coda of the finale. Against all the odds, this ob-sessive dance of death is overtaken by an eleventh-hour rescue, when A minor yields to the major, and the cello soars into its stratosphere with a heartbreakingly beautiful melody (ex. 2.1).

Out of nowhere, the quartet is given a happy ending.[3] For shock value alone, this intervention is the precise analogue of m. 92 in the first movement, although it achieves the opposite effect—resolution rather than interruption. The two melo-dies are motivically similar, being both based on the rising-scale figure derived from the introduction. But it is overwhelmingly their dramatic incongruity as in-terventions seemingly "from without" (like a deus ex machina) which connects these two outbursts together across the span of the quartet. Like two structural pillars, these moments prop up the quartet according to the quintessentially comic rhetoric of the Classical style, which Evan Bonds aptly characterizes as "disconfirmation followed by a consonance" (1991: 190). As with the question-answer dynamic of a musical phrase, or a "false reprise" corrected by the real one, m. 92 is put right and explained by the coda of the finale. And yet this pattern turns Classical rhetoric on its head, since the two passages are only obliquely related to the quartet as a whole, being interventions from beyond its conceptual space. Adorno's term for this effect, which he uses sporadically through his writings about Beethoven, is "extraterritoriality." For example, in his own essay on the quartet, which I will discuss at the end of this chapter, he observes that "the first entry of the main theme in the cello [m. 11] is 'extraterritorial,' a 'motto'; only then, on the first violin, is it 'in' the piece [m. 13]" (1998a, 133). One could say, hyperbolically, that Op. 132 is framed by "extraterritorial" pillars which don't even belong to the piece (they belong, perhaps, to putative quartets in C major and A major).

Having appealed to the "style" of the quartet considered as a whole, we now find that foundational categories of "in" and "out" are turned literally inside out. This is the peculiar logic of Beethoven's late style—an eccentric manner of disposing Classical convention. Beethoven's discourse does indeed make sense of syntactic anomalies, but only so as to raise even deeper questions about the nature of musical language. Some of these questions don't bear on convention at all, but rather on more basic experiential categories of space and time. The outbreak at m. 92 suggests a depth model of musical process, as if something were literally erupting from the center of the work out to the surface. As an interruption, it also invokes a formal sense of boundary, as if the passage were "outside" the container of the work, like a parenthesis or cadenza. Most striking, perhaps, is the sense of motion through a gravitational field, with the contour's dramatic plummet from the violin's top D at m. 91, followed by the gradual ascent back to the cadence of m. 102. It is often remarked that the profundity of Beethoven is that he cuts through the Classical game with convention to these basic dimensions of life: depth, contrast, motion, contour. Yet the ultimate mystery of the late style is how Beethoven submits these aspects of human experience to the logic of artistic discourse, to the extent that our notions of space and time are turned inside out, reversed, exploded. To reckon with this joint negotiation with convention and nature, we need to throw open our definition of style in a further direction.

A Ternary Model of Musical Style

Style, as I have so far argued, constitutes two kinds of musical economy: the rules of the language ("Style 1"), and the way the composer configures these rules within the internal relations of the work ("Style 2"). Simply put, a dialectical notion of style describes the interaction of the compositional subject with inherited conventions. But we may also speak, with Peter Schleuning (1998), both of and in a "language of nature," a "Sprache der Natur," a Style 3. Even more than convention or subjectivity, "nature" is an elusive, volatile concept. There is no shortage of perceptual or cognitive perspectives on musical nature, for instance, looking at the implications of pattern (Narmour 1992), or of "musical forces" (Lerdahl 2001), or even of "conceptual blending" (Zbikowski 2002). But what of the human nature which selects such diverging theoretical premises as Narmour's, Lerdahl's, or Zbikowski's, and which suggests that any definite formulation is at best relative and contingent? Or the subjective nature of expressive immediacy? Or, for that matter, the materiality of musical convention, which could also be deemed "natural"? A similar openness besets how Styles 1, 2, and 3 relate to each other. From one standpoint, a natural Style 3 is the cognitive or bodily underpinning of Styles 1 and 2. But the underlying order of things could also be construed as conventional (Style 1), or alternatively subjective (Style 2). There are at least three ways of experiencing the "natural" quality of m. 92 in Beethoven's quartet: (1) a "thickening" of musical convention, so that is becomes naturally expressive; (2) an outbreak of subjective immediacy, hitherto suppressed by convention; and (3) a disclosure of music's foundational first principles of space and gesture. There is also a difference of modality: nature as a steady horizon of time and history, supported by the constant foundation of perceptual categories versus nature according to the modality of the instantaneous. Drawn to the Romantic hermeneutics of the moment (see Hoeckner 2002), Schleiermacher viewed "individual expression as a 'moment of life breaking forth,' as an 'act'" (Szondi 2003: 116). It is from Schleiermacher's tradition that Adorno drew his crucial notion of *Durchbruch,* breakthrough. In his Mahler study, Adorno gives *Durchbruch* an almost biological complexion: it is "an influx of reality, of blood" (1992a: 10). By Adorno's lights, the event at m. 92 of the quartet is a *Durchbruch:* the eruption of suppressed musical forces engendering a new spark of life.

This ternary model of style is inspired, as I have said, by Meyer's triangulation of conventional rules with individual strategy and psychological constants, which could be seen to roughly correspond respectively to Styles 1, 2, and 3. Much is lost by forgoing Meyer's precise definitions of musical pattern in favor of a mobile and open model of style. But even more is gained by assimilating analytical tools such as Meyer's into a fully dialectical model commensurate with music's context dependence. The concept which comes closest to the deliberate indeterminacy of this model is Adorno's notion of "mimesis." Mimesis is a term which is notoriously underdefined in Adorno's writings; it basically functions as a placeholder for all the various perspectives on "nature" which I have listed above. Despite its shadowy nature, the concept of mimesis functions no less than as "the obscure operator," in Michael Taussig's words, "of [Adorno's] entire system" (Taussig 1993: 45). Punning on senses of imitation and mediation, Adorno wants "mimesis" to convey both the immediacy of artistic expression and its miming of external forces such as physical gesture, form, and vocal contour. For instance, just when music seems most immediate, when it becomes language-like in its expressivity, it is actually miming something nonmusical, that is, language, so it is in fact mediated. That is the paradox of music's "language character" (Adorno 1992b). A similar dynamic obtains in music's imitation of *anything* in the world, particularly our physical experience of space, motion, and time. Music also imitates reason, philosophy. Crucially, this link between mimesis and mediation keeps the channels open between critical theory and "objectifying" theories such as music psychology and cognitive science.

It is thus a mistake to over-interpret Adorno's hostility toward the empirical sciences. Music's mimesis of the rational is closely related to those "metaphorical" processes I explored in my previous book, but with a critical twist (Spitzer 2004). Adorno's critical theory of mimesis teaches us that musical style's various analogies with language, thought, and the body are "metaphorical" in a peculiarly mobile and tensive sense of the term. It also places the metaphorical, or mimetic, faculty as a whole in a historical context: against the horizon of its archaic origin and its compulsion to return in modernity, as a figure of the utopian. Benjamin's essay "On the Mimetic Faculty" traces mimesis to mimicry, man's "gift for seeing similarity," which he argues is "a rudiment of the once powerful compulsion to become similar and to behave mimetically" (Benjamin 2002, vol. 2: 720). This gift is pervasive in the magical identity thinking of astrology, which seeks affinities between the microcosm and macrocosm (see Spitzer 2004: 150–54). Paradoxically, archaic mimesis flairs up "like a flame" in modern language and aesthetics at moment of fleeting immediacy, so that the concept is inscribed within a historical loop (Benjamin, 722). This joint archaic/utopian aspect, linked to Adorno's powerful notion of "breakthrough" (*Durchbruch*), confirms mimesis as a concept in dialectical motion. How might mimesis, in this dialectical sense, be accommodated within a cognitive theory of metaphor?

In my *Metaphor and Musical Thought*, I developed the thesis that music's "nature" partially corresponds to elemental categories of human bodily experience, such as our concepts of motion, dimensionality, balance, etc. Like a physical body in the world, a musical phrase can be imagined to have surface and depth, part/whole relationships, rising and falling contour; it can also appear to balance in a gravitational field, submit to or generate physical forces, traverse spatial coordinates or undertake a journey. According to cognitive semantics, these experiences are enshrined as well-formed categories called "image schemata." Image schemata are projected onto the "epistemic" world of concepts—including abstract reasoning, language, and social behavior in general—through the process of *metaphorical mapping*. Furthermore, each of these schemata motivates correlations between musical material and prototypical cultural metaphors, such as "music as language," "music as thought," and "music as organism." I showed that the isomorphism between bodily schemata and cultural metaphors goes a long way to explaining the intimate fit between musical structure and extra-musical meaning. In our musings on Op. 132, we were drawn ineluctably from the domain of the score out into the wider world of categorical experience, pertaining to concepts of "in" and "out," "front" and "back," "up" and "down." Until recently, this wider dimension of musical experience has tended to be dismissed or overlooked by musicology. Yet it is foundational to *all* music, not just Beethoven's. Extending Adorno's concept of mimesis to include bodily image schemata is another way of fostering a dialogue between critical theory and Anglo-American pragmatist orientations in philosophy.[4] The crucial qualification is that cognitive metaphorical thought, insofar as it is a pragmatist variant of mimesis, is also cast in an archaic/utopian light relative to critical theory.

Considering now the three styles together, it is tempting to label Style 1 "music as language" (musical convention), Style 2 "music as thought" (the individual ideas which speak through convention), and Style 3 "music as body" (the prelinguistic and preconceptual realm of bodily experience), and to call them metaphors. This would be misleading for a number of reasons. First, separating them out into discrete metaphors discounts the interaction *between* them: the thought of a work is defined in the context of language, and on the basis of a bodily (image-schematic) ground. Second, the linguistic, the rational, and the bodily interact with infinite complexity, in that there are rational aspects to language, social constraints to thought, a communicative dimension to gesture, etc. Last and not least, even assuming that language, thought, and the body could be reified into ideal types, it still begs the question of the flow of the metaphorical transaction. Why should music be compared to these other domains, rather than the other way round? A venerable philosophical tradition, from Plato through Rousseau and Schopenhauer to Adornian aesthetics today, holds that music constitutes a primal language, an essential level of thought, and the most concrete and corporeal mode of being. Rather than music following behind as the junior partner, it is language, reason, and the body which are compared to music and found wanting. And so metaphor must undertake a self-reflective critical twist, whereby music kicks back so as to structure and interpret its contexts. Music, then, is not simply a blank screen—an object—for metaphorical projections; it functions also as the *subject* of these transactions, leading to what I previously called a "bidirectional" model of musical metaphor (Spitzer 2004: 54). Nominalist accounts of semiotics are familiar with the recalcitrance intrinsic to metaphors and attribute it to moments of resistance on the path to eventual conventionalization. Nelson Goodman memorably defined metaphor as "an affair between a predicate with a past and an object that yields while protesting" and conceded that "metaphor requires attraction as well as resistance" (Goodman 1976: 69). A *critical* view of metaphor, by contrast, shifts the emphasis onto difference and resistance, so that interest now falls, say, on how music is *not* like a language more than on its similarities, while keeping both terms in motion. Otherwise put, although difference and similarity are very much kept in play, the process is weighted *asymmetrically* toward the left pole of difference, according to what Hatten terms a "markedness" effect (1994: 34–38). Similarity, then, is marked against the ground of difference. On the broadest level, this privileging of difference is germane to an approach predicated on the distinctiveness of music, particularly Beethoven's, vis-à-vis everything with which it compares. To grasp this dynamic aspect of style, it is best to think of Styles 1, 2, and 3 not as fixed and well-defined categories, but as place holders or nodes of attraction within a force field. Benjamin's notion of "constellation" has proved very popular to describe this sort of model, so long as one remembers that the stars don't stand still, but dance around each other in interlocking and erratic orbits.

Style 1

An obvious symptom of this dynamism is the plurality of style. The rules of a musical language (S1) do not constitute some monolithic block marked "convention," but are highly variegated according to historical, social, even geographical parameters. Historically, the Classical style embraces aspects of Baroque, *galant,* "high" Classical, and proto-Romantic; socially, it reflects "high" and "low," secular and sacred registers; geographically, it may refer to civic, pastoral, and exotic idioms. Furthermore, a distinctive aspect of musical material, in strong contradistinction to real language, is a permeability between feature and procedure, whereby what a stylistic trait *is* gets defined by what it *does* or how it is *used.* The prime example is counterpoint, which despite its Baroque provenance, can be used Classically, or signify as a marker of Romanticism. But the same applies practically to every aspect of a style, reminding us of Rosen's persuasive definition of the Classical style as a general sensibility, rather than as a checklist of features. In other words, the configurative, relational, dimension, S2, drifts across the diagram to become a constitutive moment of S1. And by reciprocal echo, elements of S1 cross over to S2, since personal styles can be objectified and referenced, as in Haydn, Mozart, and Beethoven's frequent parodies of each other. Finally, the element of nature (S3) has a role in the gradation of stylistic material according to degrees of artifice. Lyrical idioms, for example, were valued by Classicism as tokens of a quasi-natural immediacy, at the opposite extreme to a comic rhetoric articulated through layer upon layer of conventional coding. The fundamental issue here is the origin and foundation of convention. As well as functioning as an external underpinning and support, "Nature" circulates within the economy of the material.

Style 2

A similar plurality informs the identity of a composer's personal style. One often assumes that this style is unitary; in fact, any unified identity (S2) exists in tension with a variety of manners or voices mediated through all the possibilities of S1. A composer may work differently in different periods of his life, and in response to varying materials and genres. Moreover, the composer can objectify and reflect upon elements of his own style, past and present. Finally, the natural expression (S3) which insinuates itself as a moment of S1 becomes mediated through compositional process, with the result that the unlikeliest of materials can be rendered "natural." Expressive immediacy can be elicited from anything.

Style 3

Musical nature also splits into the nature which can be schematized into patterns or rules (S1) and the elusive remainder which can't even be represented (S3). In the middle comes the nature which emerges through composition. The contours, gestures, and dynamics of music (S2) are emergent phenomena which accrue their properties through being fashioned by artifice (Cumming 2000; Hatten 2004). Composition *changes* nature, reminding us of the profound interpenetration of music's natural and historical aspects. Musical material is constructed to the same extent that it is naturalized. The dialectic between nature and history in music complements that between material and composer. Rather than being an abstract "stuff" (object) upon which the composer (subject) works externally, musical material is always precomposed; it enshrines layers of subjectivity sedimented by composers of the past, to be thawed out and utilized by the present. The subject/object continuum between composer and material resembles that between water and ice; or better, to use Adorno's favored geological metaphor, between molten and cooling rock.

A Model of Beethoven's Late Style

Over nearly two centuries of reception, Beethoven's late style has been caricatured as heterogeneous, disunified, and unnatural. Reading this traditional portrait against the template of our ternary model allows us to see the late style more clearly as an extension, rather than rejection, of Classical principles, albeit raised now to a higher power. The plurality of Classical rules (S1) is heightened by Beethoven, making it harder to hear how they might be accommodated by any overarching principle or sensibility. In other words, stylistic heterogeneity is relegated from a surface phenomenon to a governing principle. Regarding the individual manner of the style (S2), there is a corresponding sense that Beethoven loses himself in this wealth of material, rather than blending the conventions into a unified voice. Instead of speaking *through* these conventions, Beethoven lets them stand freely and discovers expression *within* them. Finally, while Beethoven reduces musical material to its archetypal shapes and contours (S3), he does so in order to compose *against the grain* of its natural properties. His music at times resists nature heroically. This, then, is a model of the late style; properly speaking, the late style as a whole comprises the interaction of all three components (S1–3) in a particular way. Given the intricately systemic quality of this interaction, traditional attempts to characterize Beethoven's late style in terms of simple rubrics such as "dissociation" or "abstraction" fall wide of the mark. Lazy ascriptions of "disunity" for any style are virtually meaningless without a theoretical framework which explicates criteria for "unity" in the first place. Conversely, the theory will be empty without empirical content. So let us return to the A minor quartet, freshly armed with our theoretical model.

Style 1: A Universe of Particulars

The first page alone unfolds a spectrum of styles. At one level, Beethoven avails himself of the eighteenth-century "universe of topic" (Agawu 1991): a vocabulary of textural and metrical idioms such as "Learned Style," "Alla Breve counterpoint," and "Fantasy" (all in mm. 1–8); "Cadenza" (mm. 9–10); "March" (mm. 11 ff.); and "Fanfare" (mm. 18–19). More striking is the historical spread of the styles, from Baroque through *galant,* high and late Classical, giving the quartet an encyclopedically retrospective purview.[5] Beethoven's blend of genealogy with grammar moves the quartet beyond the sphere of structuralist approaches to language. Rather than sticking to the most contemporary language available to him in 1825, Beethoven looks down beneath the "glass floor" of his immediate horizon and X-rays strata after strata of musical material. This backwards glance also incorporates the three main phases of Beethoven's own development—the playfulness of his early years, the heroic rhetoric of the middle period, as well as the enigmatic quality of lateness. The movement begins with a starkly archaic motet texture, with fugal imitation at the fifth of a chromatic tetrachord. Shifting forward in history, the tonic subject at m. 11 elaborates an archetypal *galant* melodic schema based around the scale steps 1̂–7̂ . . . 4̂–3̂. Robert Gjerdingen's statistical survey pinpoints the popularity of this cliché to 1772 (1988). According to Gjerdingen, such patterns are the epitome of artifice, since the appoggiaturas which punctuate, or "cue," each subphrase (here A–G♯ and F–E) recur in thousands of different contexts in the late eighteenth and early nineteenth centuries. The incipit of Mozart's Piano Sonata in G major, K. 283, is perhaps the schema's prototype (ex. 2.2):

Example 2.2. Mozart, Piano Sonata in G, K. 283, first movement, mm. 1–4

It is this very indifference to content which enables the schema to function as an aid to cognition, helping the listener to recognize, process, and predict unfamiliar material. The schema epitomizes the abstraction and transparency of musical convention.

The juxtaposition of Baroque and *galant* idioms on the first page is dramatic enough. But they are framed within high Classicism's table of functions. Thus the motet assumes the function of slow introduction, after which its contrapuntal material is rationalized by symmetrical phrase rhythms. The phrase beginning m. 11 displays what would later be called a "sentence" structure (Schoenberg 1984: 20) and traces the typical sentence's acceleration from a stable four-measure phrase (2 + 2) through an ever faster sequence up to a cadential apex at m. 18. The four-measure appendix at this point, extending the phrase from the normative eight measures to twelve (mm. 19–22), is a procedure Beethoven would have learned from Haydn and Mozart. The music's high-Classical aspect, incepted by Haydn and Mozart in the 1780s, and developed by middle-period Beethoven in the 1800s, is its motivic drive and harmonic richness. The passage is generated "top down" from its phrase structure as much as "bottom up" from its thematic units; this balance is a particular hallmark of the Classical style in its heyday. So too is the functional integration of augmented sixth (m. 13) and Neapolitan (mm. 18–19) harmonies within a clear diatonic framework of tonic-dominant relationships.

What distinguishes styles from static referential counters such as topics is, as I have said, a permeability between feature and procedure. Baroque, *galant,* and Classical styles comprise both well-formed materials and regulative modalities which structure how we hear these materials. Like the children's game where paper wraps stone, stone blunts scissors, and scissors cut paper, Baroque, *galant,* and Classical procedures all seek to circumscribe each other. From a Classical standpoint, the music's Baroque and *galant* materials are subsumed within Classical sonata form. From another standpoint, the permeation of the motet tetrachord throughout the Allegro gives the piece the additive, variational form and linear texture associated with Baroque music. Last, the very disjunction between these Baroque and Classical elements is highly characteristic of the mosaic-like *galant* style of the early 1770s, only more so.

If the interpenetration of these three styles bespeaks a relativity of perspective, then it implicates the listener in questions both of musical value and of historical consciousness. The questions devolve, first, to a reflection on the value of convention *in itself,* second, to a consideration of its historical grounding. Insofar as convention is a social compact, it is anchored in a particular historical time and place; given that Classical convention by its nature predicates an abstract relationship toward musical material, it necessarily evolves through the active bracketing of specific material, namely, *the Baroque.* The turn from Baroque to *galant* at m. 11 enshrines the trace of a key step in style history—the onset of a kind of formal faculty which was simply unavailable to Baroque musical thought. The essence of Classical convention is, texturally, a quasi-linguistic arbitrary relationship between form and content; structurally, it is a recursive differentiation of formal functions into beginnings, middles, and endings.[6] This is what makes the Classical style, among the myriad of styles in music history, uniquely transparent to musical cognition. The spectrum of styles, and the notion of stylistic "center" which we have been playing with, is thereby given a wholly new cast. We can now recognize the *galant* $\hat{1}$–$\hat{7}$ . . . $\hat{4}$–$\hat{3}$ schema, the pattern at the heart of Beethoven's theme, as the center of the spectrum, hedged on either side by a "preconventional" and a "postconventional" style. On the "left" side, the schema brackets the through-composed materiality of Baroque counterpoint, the motet introduction. On the "right" side, the schema is quickly drawn into an organic Classical discourse, which closes the gap between form and content by assimilating convention into an idiosyncratic developmental discourse. The historical narrative inscribed within the music is thus played out in three episodes: a time before convention, the inception of convention, the critique of convention. We should not confuse the succession of these three paradigms with the compositional discourse which we have called Style 2. The fact that they happen to follow each other in such a way in the music is fitting, of course. But the narrative testifies, rather, to the fact that subjectivity inheres as much within musical material as in the compositional subject who receives it. The *galant* style was created by individuals, partially in response to the growing impression that the Baroque was too complex and obscure to be audible or enjoyed. Conversely, high Classicism and Romanticism sought to attenuate the artificiality of the *galant* and imbue it with greater personal feeling.

Style 1 is shot through, then, with an appeal to musical nature, Style 3. Nevertheless, the identity of this nature can be neither fixed nor correlated with a particular style. From one standpoint, the *galant*-Classical period marks an interregnum of artifice between the more "natural" Baroque and Romantic periods, so that nature is first repressed, then recuperated. We can easily imagine that Beethoven's $\hat{1}$–$\hat{7}$ . . . $\hat{4}$–$\hat{3}$ schema is "laid over" the Baroque counterpoint, which then reemerges to "cover" the schema in the subsequent discourse. From another standpoint, however, no style was more commonly identified in the eighteenth century with pastoralism than the *galant*. Its limpid textures and square forms came to convey a rustic simplicity, as in the musette-like trio of Op. 132's second movement (a correspondent of the *AMZ* refers to the trio's *naiven Natürlichkeit* [27/840]). This effect is part of the broader consensus, still active today, that simple diatonic melodies sound "natural," and that certain idioms by Mozart are psychologically normative. We are led ineluctably to the antinomy that convention is both natural and unnatural. The difficulty of pinning nature down to any fixed parameters reminds us that whatever people call "nature" is by definition represented and constructed, and therefore subject to historical change. Conversely, the very nature of convention is contradictory, in that it serves to facilitate communication just as much as it may block more personal expression as a mechanical constraint. The same move which may liberate us from brute nature by controlling it also coerces our own inner nature. We see how reflection on the dynamic interactions of style engenders speculations on the limits and grounds of thought itself, which brings us now to Style 2.

Style 2: Subjectivities

Despite its multiple styles, the quartet's juxtapositions of tempo, topic, and harmony are presumably mediated—and *unified*—within a single stylistic manner, Style 2. Nevertheless, countless critics have pointed to the quartet's broken surface as a paradigm of the late style's disunity. By the same token, the music's apparent dissociation begs the question of what kind of unifying intelligence holds the pieces together into a well-formed style at all. The most extreme solution would be to claim that such a stylistic manner, into which all the contrasts can be accommodated, doesn't actually exist, and that late Beethoven thereby evinces the fractured subjectivity of the postmodern condition (McClary 2000: 119–33, critiqued in Hatten 2004: 267–68). But to resort to this gambit is both to give up on the notion of compositional identity and to walk away from the problem of *how* the structure is dissociated. A more fruitful position is to hold that the plurality of

Beethoven's language simply entails a higher notion of stylistic manner: not con-figuration of rules, but configuration of types of configuration (of rules). Simply put, Beethoven manipulates not rules but styles; the late style is a "meta-style." And these styles, as we have seen, comprise the three historical paradigms of Baroque, *galant,* and high Classical, each of which provides a different interpretive pathway through the mosaic. The Baroque counterpoint spreads out "subthematically" be-neath the Allegro, unifying the music with a web of semitones (see Dahlhaus 1991: 204–18). Against this, the view from the center affords the playful discontinuities typical of *galant,* in which case the Baroque unifying web is redundant: the con-trasts aren't dissociative at all, but rhetorical, according to the eighteenth-century comedy of manners. Third, the music is shaped by a high-Classical discursive logic which Beethoven learnt in his middle period, and which he harnessed toward the projection of an underlying compositional "idea." Although discredited as apocry-phal, Louis Schlösser's report of Beethoven's own account of how he composes ac-cording to a "zugrunde liegende Idee" is compelling: "the underlying idea never deserts me. It rises, it grows tall, I hear and see the image in my mind in its entire extent, as if cast in a single mould, and all that remains is the task of writing it down" (Dahlhaus 1991: 143). Even if its roots are historically shaky, the notion that Beethoven's music is unified by a basic shape or principle gave rise to a formidable theoretical tradition, culminating with Schoenberg's theory of *Grundgestalt* and those writers who sought to explicate it analytically, such as Rudolph Réti (1967) and David Epstein (1987). Since it is by nature both an abstract and holistic phe-nomenon, the "basic shape" can hardly be captured by empirical models. But it may have much in common with the growing role in the nineteenth century of what Meyer terms the "secondary" or "statistical" parameters of rhythm, register, tex-ture, and dynamics. In fact, mm. 1–10 afford a perfect example of Meyer's "statis-tical climax," an extremely common pattern in Romantic music: "gradual increase in the intensity of the more physical attributes of sound, the arrival at a tensional 'highpoint,' followed by a usually rapid decline in activity" (Meyer 1997: 207). The melodic arch from the cello's opening at m. 1 to the first violin's F apex at m. 8 is thus a trace of a general intensity curve, embracing harmonic dissonance, rhyth-mic and tempo changes, textural density, and dynamic crescendo. This arch, there-fore is the *shape* of the music, and it is underscored by the topical modulation from strict Learned Style of mm. 1–8 to the free cadenza of mm. 9–10; that is, a growth in subjectivity. Tonally, the shape is associated with a climax on the submediant scale step, F in A minor. The same shape controls the micro- and macrolevels of the structure—the arch of the opening tetrachord from base (G#–A) to apex (F–E), and the first wave of the exposition up to the cascade at m. 18 from the first violin's top F.

The late style's manner, then, is the interaction of all three formal procedures—contrapuntal web, *galant* play, and high-Classical gestalt—in a way which leaves none of them unscathed, but which "problematizes" them in a general interference pattern. There is nothing straightforward about the introduction's counterpoint; by masking the second half of the cello's tetrachord (F–E) with a retrograde of its first half in the viola (A–G♯), Beethoven suggests that the generative event of the piece is a *two*-note rather than a four-note motive. And even before the viola gets to play its G♯, the second violin covers that with a B. What might have been a stately exchange of a fugal theme, imitated at the fifth, thus dissolves into a pointillist constellation of one-note motivic cells. Through succumbing to *galant* fragmentation, the counterpoint is assimilated into the sweep of the arch. The effect is even more pronounced in the Allegro, where the constituents of the tonic and dominant tetrachords are scattered in free permutations (e.g., mm. 11–12, A–G♯; mm. 13–14, F–E interlocking with C–B and D♯–E). The middle tier of Beethoven's complex, the Classical game with convention, incorporates this Baroque analysis of pitch into a framework of formal functions, beginning with the perceived role of the introduction. The single-measure Adagio at m. 21 is sufficient to suggest a ritornello of the Assai sostenuto, and aspects of the introduction recur at varying strength throughout the movement. Beethoven plays with our sense of an opening, since the Allegro figurations at m. 9 can be heard either as the end of the introduction or the beginning of the movement proper. If the latter, then initiating a sonata allegro with a cadenza is marked against the convention that the movement begin with a strong tonic chord—a requirement further undermined by the pointed quarter-note rest on the first beat of m. 11 (corrected in the coda) and the atypically high cello entry. The topical realm deepens the reference of these games, so that the missing first beat amputates the right foot of the March, and the sixteenth-note cascade, like cadenzas in concertos, is parenthetical to the "real time" of the structure. Most cleverly, the descending Neapolitan fanfare at m. 18 reverses the convention that trumpet fanfares rise through a tonic triad. And the syntactical placement of the fanfare at the climax of the phrase reminds us of the F apex of the introduction at mm. 9–10 and clarifies the link with the sixteenth-note cadenza, which had also descended in thirds. Despite the fact that the harmony is different (Neapolitan instead of diminished seventh), and that the actual cadenza recurs, slightly varied, at m. 22, the formal rhyme suffices to splice the two topics together (this is explicated at m. 38, where the descending fanfare is decorated with sixteenth notes). Beethoven thereby splits the features of the original apex of m. 9 in two, giving its pitch, F, and its aspect of climax to the fanfare, and allocating the diminished-seventh harmony and its opening function to the cadenza of m. 22. This noncongruence (Meyer 1973: 85) of pitch, harmony, and phrase rhythm is a historical throwback to early Classicism, a time before musical parameters had coalesced into the feature bundles we call "conventions." Surprisingly, the fission of Beethoven's material follows through a twist in his gestalt, the third strand of this process. As befits the Assai sostenuto's fugal gambit, the movement is driven not by one arch shape, but *two*—a tonic form with its dominant answer. Actually, the first apex in the introduction is the top C of m. 7, the submediant of E minor; the dominant peak is thus higher than the tonic version, the F of m. 9, and this imbalance goes on to unsettle the movement. We now recognize the fanfare climax at m. 18 as a representative of the tonic gestalt (F–E crux), and the cadenza at mm. 21–22 as the dominant answer (C–B crux). This tonic/dominant alternation is quasi-fugal. On the architectonic level of the movement, it generates the peculiar gambit of turning most of the development into a dominant ritornello of the exposition.

Style 3: Varieties of Nature (Schema, Mimesis, Schein, Durchbruch, Apparition, Caesura, Allegory, Parataxis)

"Nature is founded on Art and, again, Art is founded on Nature," says Beethoven in his letter to Galitzin (Anderson 1986: 1224). The composer's view on the mediated character of musical nature is healthily dialectical. Despite his rhetorical appeals to the true paths of "feeling," he actually leads Galitzin through the more sober paths of technical music theory. The dialectic of nature in Op. 132 breaks up into a panoply of types: patterns versus gestures; materiality versus abstraction. Apart from schema, these effects are given names by Adorno: *Schein, Durchbruch, Apparition,* Caesura, Parataxis, etc. They elaborate Adorno's concept of mimesis, while keeping its fluid, floating quality. For this reason, it seems best to introduce them in the context of musical analysis, indeed, as extrapolations of musical observations. Part 1 of this chapter therefore closes by eliding an analysis of Beethoven's "nature" with a concise and of course selective glossary of Adorno's terminology, albeit starting with a non-Adornian concept borrowed from cognitive semantics: schema. This glossary should be treated as provisional to the evolving discussion (it will be supplemented by a further glossary at the end of chapter 3).

SCHEMA: Op. 132 mimes a suite of contours and gestures projecting the dimensionality of bodily experience. The arches move up and down (the "UP-DOWN" schema); the miniature cadenzas are moments of interiority interpolated into musical structure (the "IN-OUT" schema); m. 92 erupts out of the depths of the music (the "SURFACE-DEPTH" schema). Far from constraining the music, these schemata follow a trajectory of reversal. The arches exchange the functions of base and apex; cadenzas displace their frames; the repressed rises up to dominate the surface. All three transformations converge, in the first instance, on the lyrical second group. By tonicizing F, the new key installs the erstwhile apex as, quite literally, the new bass/base. Lyrical intensity, previously a crisis in the gestalt, is leveled out into a group. This lyrical group also represents an "externalization" of a parenthesis. It follows in the wake of the reversal in mm. 37–47, where a contrapuntal D-minor gavotte finds itself framed by two cadenza-like passages. And there is the sense also of sustained subjectivity finally being allowed to rise to the "surface." In each case, then, Beethoven schematizes his material into natural patterns only to reverse these patterns. Schematization, far from defeating "Art," in fact permits Beethoven to transcend "Nature" even more efficiently than in the heroic middle style.

MIMESIS: The music mimics the world, via schemata, but also transcends such mediations in its expressive immediacy. As an aesthetic object, the work can hardly be subsumed by schematic categories. Mimesis is channeled into a variety of effects, which may even imitate schemata. Thus *Schein* and *Durchbruch* mime SURFACE-DEPTH, *Apparition* imitates UP-DOWN, while caesura mimics IN-OUT.

SCHEIN: The sheen of natural beauty; the surface semblance covering an underlying reality; the flicker of structural play: all of these aspects are covered by Adorno's rich concept of *Schein*. Measure 92 displays *Schein* in its luminosity. Yet the underlying reality of much of the music is the cantus firmus. The kaleidoscopic mixing of Baroque, *galant*, and Classical materials creates the iridescence of *Schein*. This interplay is also focalized around oppositions, engaging the schematic reversals themselves. When Beethoven gridlocks schematic categories, this is also *Schein*.

DURCHBRUCH: The music proceeds as a series of stylistic breakthroughs. Broadly, these are eruptions of subjectivity, which cannot be identified with any particular type of material. Rather, each and every kind of style and category can break through the other: counterpoint through homophony; lyricism through form; S2 through S1; schema through *Schein;* etc. The defining factor is the modality of breakthrough, by which it chiefly differs from *Schein's* homeostatic flicker. Namely, a modality of the moment: localized, forceful, evanescent, vectored.

APPARITION: Adorno compares the artwork's magical aura to that of a celestial vision, albeit one which explodes with the fleeting quality of a fireworks display (1999: 81). *Apparition* is related to Kant and Hegel's notion of Appearance (*Erscheinung*), and hence cognate with *Schein*. *Erscheinung* means a dynamic process of "coming *into* appearance," by which the listener grasps continuities between the many stylistic categories. We hear surface emerging from depth, mimesis from schemata, S2 from S1, along a dynamic curve analogous to the UP-DOWN arches. *Apparition* discloses *Erscheinung's* momentary modality of a flash of insight.[7]

CAESURA: The surface breaches which fragment the music are caesuras. These are interventions of natural violence, thunderbolts. But they are also, paradoxically, the normative phrase endings which articulate Classical syntax. Indeed, the *Apparition* of caesuras moves, "allegorically," between these two extremes: rendering conventional punctuation expressive, and ossifying expression into bone-dry relics. This happens to the semitone appoggiaturas on the first page of Op. 132. They begin as expressive chromatic *pianti* (sighing figures), lapse into markers of Classical articulation in the Allegro, and wax lyrical in the second group.

ALLEGORY: This is the principle by which a detail, normally subsumed into syntax, is liberated and rendered materially concrete. By "thickening" convention in this way, Beethoven turns it into nature. "Seeing" the materiality of convention is a kind of *Apparition*.

PARATAXIS: Adorno sees natural discourse as additive, chainlike, and open-ended: "paratactic." He associates it with the archaic, in particular, with the Baroque idioms of counterpoint, variation, and ritornello, but also with looser Classical forms such as rondo. Parataxis in Op. 132 is discovered in the contrapuntal textures, the varied ritornellos in the first group, the stop-go discontinuities of the flow. Globally, the ritornello of the exposition in the development gives the sonata form an additive A^1–A^2–A^3 structure. Nature is elicited also through the sparks created when parataxis grates against hypotactic sonata form.

These various categories of musical nature are permeable to each other. *Apparitions* dawn with the force of a *Durchbruch,* inducing *caesura,* creating *parataxis,* fostering the play of *Schein,* which engages transformations of schemata, and so on, in infinite combinations. The kaleidoscope of musical nature is itself paradigmatic for the interpenetration of all categories in Styles 1, 2, and 3. We will see much later, at the end of chapter 7, how this combinatorial model of style chimes with an extraordinary system proposed by Hölderlin, called the *Wechsel der Töne.*

The Rochlitz Circle

A review of Op. 132 appearing in the December 1825 edition of the Leipzig *Allgemeine Musikalische Zeitung* (henceforth *AMZ*) is typically double-edged. Despite hailing the quartet as "great, marvelous, unusual, surprising and original," the reviewer adds that to be fully grasped, "it must not only be heard more frequently, but also studied" (vol. 27, col. 840). Even so, he tactfully blames "the unbearable heat in the packed low-ceilinged concert-room" for the work's failure to make the sort of sensation which it is reported to have produced in earlier private performances. Giving the work every benefit of the doubt, the writer confidently points to the fate of its older sister quartet, Op. 127 in Eb, which had likewise divided its public in a performance earlier that year, but which went on to become fully appreciated as a masterpiece (see *AMZ*, April 1825, vol. 27, col. 246). The reviewer predicts that the A-minor quartet would follow in the earlier work's footsteps to a similar belated recognition. And sure enough, after a second performance, the same reviewer concedes that Op. 132 was "this time grasped much better and received incomparably more warmly" (col. 843).

This pattern of initial incomprehension followed by ultimate recognition cleaves to the heroic struggle-to-triumph narrative of Beethoven's most celebrated music, especially middle-period works such as the Third and Fifth Symphonies. The fit between the heroic style and its pattern of reception exemplifies how the very qualities of Beethoven's music shaped the tools of its own criticism. This circular aspect of Beethoven criticism features prominently in the reception histories of Eggebrecht (1972), Burnham (1995), and Sipe (1992; 1998). More broadly, it instantiates the hermeneutic circle between a text and its interpreter, whereby the qualities imparted onto criticism by the text feed back to structure the text, which in turn projects new aspects onto our critical apparatus, and so on. Even if text and critic spring from distantly opposed "horizons," the object-subject feedback loops of interpretation can weave them into a single hermeneutic tradition. Such a tradition arose very quickly around the *topos* of Beethoven's heroic style, and the commensurately heroic demands it required of its audience. It is therefore understandable that critics of the late style sought to assimilate it into the same tradition, whereby its comprehension was held to be merely a matter of time. Yet over time, understanding obstinately refused to come. Three years after this pair of reviews, an *AMZ* report of May 1828 suggests that the work had made little real progress with the public since then (*AMZ*, vol. 30, col. 363). The reviewer refers to "the difficult, new quartet by Beethoven" and states that "despite the many individual beauties of thought, [it] did not on the whole go down well, the blame lying mostly on the tiring length of the movements, and the rhapsodic nature of the developments." Incomprehension of late Beethoven, of course, would never go away; indeed, it would increase rather than lessen over the passage of time. The first writer to draw explicit links between Beethovenian heroism, the heroic responsibilities of reception, and the recalcitrance of the late style was Friedrich Rochlitz, editor of the *AMZ,* in an essay written to mark the publication of Op. 131 in C♯ minor (July 1828). A verbose and unfocused critic, Rochlitz nonetheless rams home the point that Beethoven "the hero of the musical world" (490) demands a correspondingly heroic act of interpretation in his listeners. Rochlitz assumes an intimate mode of involvement between listener and music which parallels the hermeneutic circle described by his contemporary Schleiermacher. Indeed, the nub of the listener's hermeneutic responsibilities toward the *musical* text is captured in an aphorism Rochlitz uses as the punch line to a lengthy footnote: "If a work doesn't appeal to you, it is at least possible that it is not the work's fault but your own. Or as Lichtenberg bluntly puts it: When a book and a head clash making a hollow sound, must that sound always be in the book"?[8] Beethoven hermeneutics could thus be said to be exemplified by the "Rochlitz circle."

Rochlitz begins: "It is a difficult and serious matter to write about Beethoven's last, great works." The problem is only partially due to the specific qualities of the late style, which Rochlitz summarizes as follows:

> The richness of his harmony, since we are not familiar with it, will not be visible, still less audible to us. His miraculous combinations are often obscure, striking the contemporary listener as unclear and incoherent. The architecture of his through-composed melodies, with their constantly changing instruments and ever-varying figuration, can hardly, even with some effort, be heard through and grasped, still less enjoyed, without our being distracted by the excess of contents. (494)

Surprisingly, Rochlitz assimilates the difficulty of the late style to the *general* problem of understanding *all* challenging works, and not just Beethoven's. He reminds us of the bumpy reception of Beethoven's very first opus number, the three piano trios, and of Spazier's notorious review of the Second Symphony, where he compares it to the writhings of a monstrous dragon (*Lindwurm*) in its death agony. He notes that Reichardt urges us to allow any work bearing the signs of genius the benefit of the passing of time—"to grant such works time and space" (489). With time, and good performances, Adam Hiller changed his mind about Handel's *Messiah,* and Reichardt reversed his initially hostile opinion about the Mozart operas. So why shouldn't Beethoven's late works be the same? Since Beethoven the hero "stints at nothing" (490), the critics should emulate his heroism, "although this will drive even the most capable spirits to fits of despair" (495). Rochlitz had used this gambit before, in his review of the *Eroica* of 18 February 1807. Whereas a previous review had complained that "in this composition [the reviewer] finds too much that is glaring and bizarre, which hinders one's grasp of the whole" (in Sipe 1998: 55)," Rochlitz praises the work's unity and, crucially, puts the onus on the audience to accommodate themselves to it: "this symphony must have an audience that is capable of giving and sustaining serious attention to it" (Sipe, 57–58). Rochlitz's 1828 essay on the late style, then, faces in two directions. From one side, it is couched within a reception pattern which Rochlitz had framed two decades earlier. From the other, it leaves the late style poised on the edge of an ethical imperative, pointing to the future: one *ought* to understand the music, given the moral necessity of trusting this tried-and-tested genius.

Styles 4 and 5

This book is not a reception history. In fact, it doesn't even begin to do justice to the countless things which have been said about late Beethoven during his lifetime and since his death. But I will hazard one generalization: that for most of the nineteenth century, readings of late Beethoven were *hermeneutic*, whereas since then they have been *critical*. Let me lay out the terms of this argument. Although the idea that Beethoven's music fell into three periods became popularized in such influential texts as Schindler's 1840 biography and Lenz's *Beethoven et ses trois styles* of 1852, the consensus formed that its recalcitrance differed from the general difficulty of his music only by a matter of degree. Hence understanding of the late style, like that of the heroic middle style, was susceptible to *hermeneutic closure*, the end result of this process being the reader/listener's divining of the author/composer's intention (Schleiermacher), or the "fusion" of the receiver's "horizon" with that of the artist (Gadamer). The idea that a style can be grasped, that after struggle comes resolution and understanding, denotes, in our own terms, that Styles 1, 2, and 3 can be harmoniously reconciled. We can call this stable, final, and synoptic notion of musical understanding "Style 4."

Conversely, the approach which denies the possibility of stylistic "harmony," which asserts that the resistance of Beethoven's late style to interpretation is non-contingent and part of its nature, will be called "Style 5." Style 5 is Adorno's style, the style of critical theory. By contrast, Style 4 is the style of Romantic reception. The hermeneutic project to understand the particular subjectivity of an artwork on its own terms was congruent with the historical drift from Classicism to Romanticism. As the century wore on and the conventions which Beethoven subverts themselves faded from public awareness, it became easier to appreciate the music, however mistakenly, as sui generis in a Romantic light. Rochlitz's promissory note was met, as it were, in Romantic coin. This became harder to do, ironically, with the advent of modernism and the development of a historical consciousness of past musical practice. Style 5 is predicated on a renewed understanding of historical convention, a paradox which is overlooked if we focus solely on modernism's negative or dissociative aspects. On the plus side, a bonus of modernism is that critical distance on the past allows us to survey aspects of eighteenth-century style which would not have been so clear to Beethoven's contemporaries. We probably know more about Haydn and Mozart (not to mention C. P. E. Bach, Sammartini, and Stamitz) than the early Beethoven critics; moreover, the entire theoretical enterprise, of which this book itself partakes, reflects the same historicist progress. The paradox is that recuperating the conventional background to Beethoven's late style serves actually to heighten, rather than lessen, its problematic aspects, since it widens the perceived distance between convention and subjectivity. This is a gap which Style 4 attempts to close, and which Style 5 prefers to keep open.

From the Hermeneutic to the Critical

The move from Style 4 to Style 5 was both a historical fact and a function of a new sense for history. Musical historicism was already in full swing at mid-century in works such as Karl Franz Brendel's *Geschichte der Musik* (1852) and Eduard Hanslick's *Vom Musikalisch-Schönen* (1854). Nevertheless, the shift became exponential in the late nineteenth century with the writings of Ambros, Chrysander, Riemann, and Spitta, while 1911 can be considered something of a watershed. This year marked the publication of both Schoenberg's *Harmonielehre* and Guido Adler's *Der Stil in der Musik,* epoch-making texts followed shortly by August Halm's *Von zwei Kulturen der Musik* (1913) and Ernst Bloch's *Geist der Utopie* (1918). Paddison argues convincingly for the seminal importance of Schoenberg's work for Adorno, particularly his notion of musical "material" as a historically evolving network of conventions in tension with the composer's formal faculty (Paddison 1997: 71–78). Adler invents our notion of style as an overarching historical framework, analogous to an organically developing language. The web of style weaves together "the style of an epoch, of a school, of an artist, of a work"; it encompasses leaps, transitions, influences, and mixtures, "the "objectivity of the genre" and the "subjectivity of the artist" (1911: 240), in a Hegelian-Goethian "law of becoming, of the rise and fall of an organic process" (13). Although the teleological aspects of this organic model fell into disrepute, Adler's concept of style made it easier to position a work within an interpretive context—to evaluate it *critically.* Two responses to Beethoven's Op. 132, respectively by Theodor Helm and Adorno, written before and after the 1911 watershed, capture this shift from a hermeneutic to a critical perspective. Thus the object in Helm's 1885 analysis is the quartet in itself, considered as "a profoundly individual and miraculously unified work" (in Bent 1994: 243). By contrast, Adorno evaluates the piece as a document of the Classical style, using specific passages to expose the style's contradictions and show how Beethoven bursts "classicity into fragments" (1998a: 134).

Style 4: Helm

Helm's analysis of Op. 132, appearing in his *Beethoven's String Quartets,* is a quintessentially hermeneutic reading, as much for its attention to formal coherence as to its ascription of this coherence to a unifying dramatic image. Taking his cue from the "Canzona di ringraziamente," Helm explains the music narratologically as a progression from sickness to recovery, in terms much indebted to a previous analysis by A. B. Marx (1884). The quartet is accordingly a picture of "the passionate, agonizingly slow striving of a great soul," while the first movement "is a heart-wrenching depiction of night, wrapped in nameless darkness despite isolated flashes of light and moments of vigor, with all the fevered overwroughtness of a sick man" (in Bent 1994: 243). Helm tells this story in tandem with a straight-forward structural analysis, faithful to Marx's theory of sonata form: "What is distinctive about the formal shaping of this movement is that Beethoven instinctively adheres to sonata form" (244). Nevertheless, Helm clearly doesn't know, or care, enough about the basics of sonata form to notice Beethoven's games with convention. He thus misidentifies the enormous dominant restatement of mm. 119–87 as the "recapitulation" ("section III" in Marxian terms), whereas it is actually a grotesquely inflated false reprise to the correct tonic reprise of m. 193 (misidentified as "a wonderfully expressive coda," 248). A typical Romantic, Helm is sensitive more to thematic than tonal parameters; a historically informed modern critic would care more about the ritornello being in the wrong key than its thematic correspondence with the exposition. Curiously, Helm holds up this correspondence as proof of the work's "strictest, most consistent musical logic . . . in the midst of this most spontaneous, most individual outpouring of the soul" (248). He compares this organic blend of symmetry with expression to Wagner's *Faust* Overture and *Tristan* Prelude; indeed, Helm's practice of tracking Beethoven's drama through the interaction of a set of labeled motifs (chiefly, the motive "a" of lament, 244) recalls Hans von Wolzogen's leitmotif tours through the Wagner operas a few years earlier.[9] Helm's hermeneutic requires the harmonious subjectification of form. On the one hand, "Beethoven instinctively adheres to sonata form . . . On the other hand, Beethoven has thrown all of that into flux by causing the various themes to take over turns of phrase from one another in spontaneous fashion," that is, as a "melodic discourse" (244–45). Helm sees no contradiction between these two claims; they represent two aspects of the same phenomenon.

Despite a lack of stylistic sophistication, Helm does pick up on the movement's most striking event, what I have called the central moment of the late style—the C-major interruption of m. 92. This is what he has to say about it:

> As if the confused imagination of the unhappy sufferer can no longer endure such a painful *ideé fixe* (those selfsame half-notes of the introduction), the passage is precipitously broken off [m. 91] by a restatement of the staccato figure c, now hammered out wildly. The first time, the abrupt cessation on the dominant of C minor is followed by an apparently new episode, though motivically derived from a, playing on ambiguities between C major and A minor in a unison which speaks almost in recitative. This quickly and urgently spreads through the upper instruments [mm. 94–96] in imitative fashion and brings all four parts together [m. 97] in a somewhat modified version of figure b, as if a more cheerful image had momentarily entered the sufferer's soul, as a smile may shine through tears. Thereupon, however, the motif of the introduction in the three upper parts brings back the cello lament [mm. 99–101]. And after the staccato figure c [m. 102] (in E minor), which with its wild hammering now causes the melody to break off, the introduction motif re-enters with truly fearful violence [m. 103], all four parts *ff* unison. It is as if warring demons had just achieved some mighty victory, or as if some terrible nightmare had invaded the composer's mind and built up to annihilating proportions. (in Bent 1994: 247–48)

The language is informal, yet it is remarkable how many aspects of the episode Helm communicates: The emancipation from the introduction's obsessive grip ("can no longer endure such a painful *ideé fixe*"); its derivation from the lament, "motive a," despite its apparent novelty; its vocal quality ("speaks almost in recitative"); "As a smile may shine through tears" suggests a depth model, a breakout of underlying subjectivity; the promise of the episode is tragically defeated ("It is as if warring demons had just achieved some mighty victory"). Helms's narrative is vivid and urgent, and it is full of analytical content. Far from being a mark of technical deficiency, as twentieth-century music theory often supposed, the Romantic penchant for couching analytical observations in the form of programs held true to the phenomenal unity of musical experience. Hermeneutic criticism partakes of the holistic quality of the music itself, whereas modern theory thrives in the gap opened up by abstraction. The beauty of Helm's physiological narrative is that it brings together the formal, subjective, and bodily aspects of organicism as a unified image; it melds Styles 1, 2, and 3 into the hermeneutic Style 4. But Helm pays for this unity by simplifying convention, thereby making it impossible to determine how Beethoven's materials (Style 1) can be interesting enough to engender artistic complexity. Since Beethoven "adheres to sonata form" (244), the particularity of the work is relegated to a quasi-religious "realm of feeling" (242), inaccessible to technical analysis. Feeling, the watchword of Romantic aesthetics, functions here as an index of ineffability. Helm is not saying that Beethoven's late style is incomprehensible; on the contrary, the meaning of Op. 132 seems to be transparent enough. The music is ineffable only from the point of view of technical analysis. By contrast, its "feeling" communicates effortlessly from composer to listener, perhaps in the spirit of Beethoven's famous entreaty, on the title page of the *Missa Solemnis,* that "from the heart, may it return to the heart!" The immediacy of this suggested bond between composer and listener is in line with the value Romantic hermeneutics placed on personal experience. Twentieth-century style consciousness turns this orientation literally 180 degrees, not abolishing the subject so much as emphasizing how subjective experience is socially mediated through technical material.

The signal irony of style consciousness is that style as a compositional category had to die for it to be born as a critical tool. This is a paradox epitomized in the gap between Schoenberg's theoretical writings, with their normative slant, and his radical compositional practice; by the time of *Harmonielehre,* the conventionality which had given the Classical style its language character had long gone, to be replaced by what Adorno in the *Aesthetic Theory* calls "the immanent lawfulness of the individual work" (1999: 207). At a fundamental level, Adorno identifies style *proper,* "the quintessence of all language in art" (207), with the music of the late eighteenth century. Given that "immanent lawfulness"—what we defined as S2— had been inherent to style from the outset, the dissolution of style is understood to be driven by its internal tensions. The interaction between Style 1 and Style 2 thus acquires a historical dimension. It has to be said, however, that Adorno reserves the term "style" for its Classical prototype and subsumes its broader dialectical aspects into his overarching concept of "musical material." Nevertheless, as is clear from Paddison's exposition of this concept, Adorno's notion of musical material as "dual level" does in fact parallel the dialectic between S1 and S2. On one level,

> The material is already "formed" and is not "natural"—genres, forms and schemata themselves being "material," as well as tuning systems, compositional techniques and stylistic norms. On another level, these conventional meanings—as musical gestures, figurations, formulae—are dismantled, deconstructed and re-contextualized within the new complex of meaning represented by the "immanent law of form" of the particular musical work. (Paddison 1997: 150)

The dual level operates both synchronically, within any timeframe of musical material, and historically, with the weighting gradually shifting from level one to level two. The concept of style/material thus affords a historical perspective in two ways: first, as sheer musical knowledge laid out across a historical canvas; second, as an explanation for change. Unlike the crudely teleological models of the nineteenth century, change for Adorno takes the form of a spiral rather than a line. Since he views style as an accommodation between compositional acts and social forces which are on the whole hostile to originality, technical advances become backward-facing reckonings with previous compromise. The archetypal example, which sends shock waves throughout music history, is the Classical style's accommodation with the social demands of entertainment. The (socially driven) need to be popular induced greater variety and simplicity than Baroque music, a step which in many ways represents a loss. Adorno's spiral model of history sees what happens next, from Haydn through Mozart to late Beethoven, as successive attempts to recuperate this loss by rethinking the relationship between Baroque and Classical materials. The object at the center of Adorno's target, the central preoccupation of his late-style critique, is the questionable nature of this original compromise between the Classical style and the Baroque. Turning now to Adorno's own essay on Op. 132, we see that the referent is not a programmatic image, nor the piece considered as a whole, but *style*.

Adorno: Style 5

Adorno's "On the First Movement of the A-Minor String Quartet"—fragment no. 269 in Tiedemann's edition, dated 9 November 1948—is not so much an essay as a two-page bundle of disconnected notes. The most arresting feature of the text is its fixation with the interruption at m. 92; Adorno begins and ends with this passage, and treats the opening of the movement in the middle. The text thus plays out the concepts of framing and interruption intrinsic to the music itself. This sort of synergy between the content and medium of representation, whereby criticism mimics qualities of its object, is absolutely typical of Adorno's philosophical aesthetics. Here Adorno's procedure is most pronounced in the late-Beethovenian fragmentation of his argument, which unfolds as cryptically as the actual quartet.

Adorno's opening observation is "Extraordinary treatment of form and its harmonic correlates." He is more aware than Helm of the development section's anomalous character, measured against a normative formal and tonal template. Adorno notes that the section is actually not very developmental at all, being mostly dedicated to repetition of the exposition in the dominant: "the development is hinted at" (*die Durchführung ist angedeutet*). It is thus a first reprise, and Adorno calls the final section both a "seventy-measure long coda" and a "second reprise" wherein "the principal key is restored." Lack of thematic elaboration is focused for Adorno around the passage at mm. 92 ff., what he terms the development's "second intonation." The "second intonation" begins "with a model derived from the main theme, which one expects to be elaborated. This, however, does not happen." For Adorno, then, the C-major episode's significance consists as much in its novelty as in its suggestion of a development which is frustrated. As if mimicking this interruption, Adorno returns to consider the meaning of the gambit only at the end of his essay, after looking at the recapitulation and exposition. This second pass over the C-major episode—akin, perhaps, to a second reprise—is far more substantial. It fixes not on form per se but on texture: the juxtaposition of monody and polyphony in the late style, epitomized by the episode's "bare two-part structure." The end of the essay is a particularly rich example of Adorno's enigmatic and elliptical prose style, and is given here in full:

> The bare two-part structure in the second intonation of the development.—The analysis of the movement leads me to the technical explanation of the bareness of the late Beethoven, from which the philosophical interpretation must follow. The so-called thematic work, which Beethoven had established, for example, in Op. 18, is usually a dividing up and rupturing [*Durchbrechung*] of something unified—of a melody. Not genuine polyphony, but the *appearance* [*Schein*] of it within harmonic-homophonic composition. To the late Beethoven this seems [*erscheint*] uneconomical, superfluous. Where there is only one thing, where the *essence* is a melody, only one should appear, at the expense of harmonic balance. The late Beethoven is the first great rebellion of music against the ornamental, that which is not necessitated purely by the matter itself. He presents, as it were, the essence always *intended* by diaphonic work, as a phenomenon. No "beating about the bush" [*Keine Umstände machen*]. In this way, through the assertion of the *concept* proper to the music itself, the "classical" element, fullness, roundness, closedness, are lost. The late style, the splitting up into monody and polyphony, is inherent in the classical Beethoven. To be purely the matter itself, to be "classical" without adjuncts, classicity burst into fragments. This is one of the decisive tenets of my interpretation. (1998a: 133–34)

Unlike Helm, Adorno interprets the episode not motivically or programmatically, but as an extreme case of a stylistic tension fundamental to musical Classicism. Adorno's highly condensed argument makes sense only against the background of a historical-stylistic narrative. This narrative turns on the shift from contrapuntal to homophonic textures at the birth of the Classical style, a move which at first entailed an impoverishment of musical resource. According to Adorno's spiral model of history, the loss was restored when composers such as Haydn and Mozart fortified Classical homophony with a rigorous voice leading reminiscent of Baroque linear thinking. The paradigm of this homophonic-polyphonic fusion was the democratic part writing of the string quartet (and especially fugal quartet finales, such as Haydn's Op. 20, Mozart's K. 387, and Beethoven's Op. 59, no. 3). Adorno's critique of the Classical style centers on the dubious appearance of *harmony*, punning on the dual sense of this word as both triadic verticality and harmonious reconciliation. An ear cocked critically to the tensions of the style will hear that the lines of a string quartet, epitomized by the independent cello voice, actually *conflict* with the triadic dimension. The friction between line and harmony is especially loud in Beethoven's Op. 18 quartets, works which Adorno frequently cites as strong precursors to the late style. As well as his critique of pseudo-harmony, Adorno is equally dismissive of the illusory appearance of polyphony. He calls the "so-called thematic work . . . a dividing up and rupturing of something unified" in the Op. 18 quartets a case of "not genuine polyphony, but the *appearance* [*Schein*] of it within harmonic-homophonic composition." Classical texture, a compound of pseudo-harmony and apparent polyphony, is thus rejected by Adorno as a dubious hybrid which dissolves stylistic tensions into a lazy mélange rather than confronting them directly. Beethoven's late style is superior by virtue of its rigor and intellectual honesty, manifest in an uncompromising attitude toward these tensions. A texture which is left loosely hybrid in the music of Haydn, Mozart, and early Beethoven is radicalized and rationalized into a clean-cut opposition between extremes—unmediated juxtapositions of polyphony and monody. The "bare, two-voiced texture" of the passage at m. 92 of Op. 132 is monodic and is wedged between two contrapuntal episodes based on the introductory motet. This large-scale alternation of polyphony and monody highlights a process underway at lower levels too, since the entire texture of the movement is fractured by weird octave pairings (e.g., m. 23) and pointillist figures (e.g., "the broken accompaniment of the first violin to the second subject group," m. 49). And so we reach the nub of Adorno's paradox: "The late style, the splitting up into monody and polyphony, is inherent in the classical Beethoven" (i.e., as in Op. 18). Beethoven's late style is more Classical than the Classics, because it demonstrates the quintessential Classical virtue of uncompromising self-consistency ("no beating about the bush," p. 133). Adorno's paradox is achieved by splitting common notions of Classicism into two, and turning one side against the other. On the one side, unity ("the classical element, fullness, roundedness, closedness," p. 134). On the other, a reductionist rigor (eschewing the lax "appearance" of counterpoint; rejecting the "uneconomical, superfluous," p. 133). Unity is sacrificed for the sake of a deeper Classical principle of intellectual stringency. In this way, then, late Beethoven is both Classical and non-Classical: "To be purely the matter itself, to be 'classical' without adjuncts, classicity burst into fragments" (134).

Style 6: Lateness

Near the top of the above passage, Adorno makes the extraordinary claim that an entire philosophy flows from his musings on the texture of m. 92: "The analysis of the movement leads me to the technical explanation of the bareness of the late Beethoven, from which the philosophical interpretation must follow." Adorno's philosophical project was inspired by reflection on late Beethoven. Indeed, the bones of his *Aesthetic Theory,* his own late masterwork, are detectable beneath the skin of his early essay on the late style, the *Spätstil Beethovens* of 1934. This flow from the music to the philosophy reverses the expected pattern, where conceptual reason is held to have priority over a supposedly "conceptless" art such as music in the great scheme of things. One might have thus expected the art of musical interpretation to be a matter simply of joining sounds to concepts, with concepts falling squarely on the side of philosophy. But Adorno's notion, in the cited passage, of the "*concept* proper to the music itself" deconstructs this opposition by suggesting that musical thought can be intrinsic to music, can even be more fundamental than philosophical thought. Thus music not only engenders reflection, it also gives rise to a philosophical system. And yet Adorno never did manage to explicate these much-mooted links between the two—between Beethoven and philosophy. The projected Beethoven monograph was left in fragmentary form. Given the "shattered quality" which Adorno identifies in this music (133), and given the fragmentary state of his own work, thinking about Adorno's Beethoven distances us at two removes from the music, as reflection about (philosophical) fragments about (musical) fragments. The goal of this enterprise is ultimately to understand gnomic pronouncements such as those which fill fragment 269. It would be unfair to treat this passage as fully representative of Adorno in any way, since it is the philosophical equivalent of a Beethoven sketch—a memorandum to oneself, never intended for publication. Nevertheless, it does epitomize, in highly caricatured form, some of the qualities often attributed to Adorno's finished prose: elliptical syntax; paratactic, chain-like, clauses; sudden leaps from observation to inference; a penchant for poetic mysticism. In other words, it is rather like late Beethoven, as Adorno describes it, evincing the same dissociation and disjunction he imputes to *Spätstil.* This synergy between composer and philosopher, as well as affording an extreme solution to the perennial problem of how to capture tones with words, also takes the self-reflexivity of the hermeneutic circle to a new level. Because the circle is now tilted toward dissonance rather than harmonious closure, it draws into itself the further dimension of how the actual critique is written and understood. Style 5 is the dissonance between S1–3; Style 6 is the dissonance of the language in which we represent this relationship. Late Beethoven is hard to understand (S5), and therefore Adorno is hard to understand (S6). Styles 1–3 can as little be subsumed into a Style 4 as Adorno's knotty prose style be simplified or paraphrased.

A premise of Adorno's critical theory is that "objects do not go into their concepts without leaving a remainder" (1990: 5). Just as Beethoven's music doesn't go into any concept we might frame of it, Adorno's insight was that Classical content doesn't go into form, and Baroque texture doesn't go into the Classical style. Adorno's method is *critical* (as opposed to hermeneutic) insofar as its difficulty reminds the reader of the contingent and open status of all representations of music. In some ways, Schleiermacher got there a century earlier with his brutally skeptical slogan, cited at the head of this book: "There can be no concept of a style." *There can be no concept of Beethoven's late style,* and his music cannot go into any book. Nevertheless, the moral of Style 6—that musical structure is implicated in the way we represent it; that the subsumption of material into convention becomes the subsumption of music into our concept of music—is not necessarily a pessimistic one. In this respect, we can draw our hopeful prognosis from the present health of Adorno exegesis, as seen in books by Jameson (1990) and Nicholsen (1997) for philosophy, and Paddison (1997) and Leppert (in Adorno 2002) for music. Shierry Weber Nicholsen puts her finger on the problem, not only recognizing the rapport between Beethoven's late style and Adorno's own "late style," but by admitting that the import of late texts such as *Aesthetic Theory* will take time to unpack:

> As an attempt to grasp these "late" phenomena and to give form to the discontinuities between subject and object, Adorno's own work is late work as well, and its difficulties are consonant with its enterprise . . . Within Adorno's oeuvre, *Aesthetic Theory* is the paradigmatic late work in a late style, and if, as Adorno says in "Beethoven's Late Style," late works are the catastrophes in the history of art, embodying that radical discontinuity, then surely *Aesthetic Theory* has been the catastrophe in our reception of Adorno. (8)

Although Beethoven's is the extreme case, "lateness" is in fact a much broader phenomenon, closely associated with the modernist aesthetic of the inorganic and the fragmentary. Many of the greatest composers *other* than Beethoven (including Bach, Schubert, Mahler, Schoenberg) also reveal lateness. Lateness is evinced in Adorno's writings, as well as in its belated reception. Lateness is performed even in our grappling with Adorno's ideas in the context of this book. Style 6—the name I give this phenomenon—might well be the last of the styles I consider. But there is in principle no limit to the circles of style, which are after all just the spiraling circles of context—including the reader's reception of Beethoven-Adorno. What follows, in the rest of this book, is successive layers of context which, as in Adorno's condensed argument, are in the present chapter merely "hinted at" (*angedeutet*), just as in m. 92 of the Beethoven quartet.

3   Adorno's Beethoven

Mediation—Context dependence; holism; immanence; embodiment; grounding; transition; reflection; spirit; argument and exemplification through extremes; interaction; interrelationship of part and whole, individual and general, reason and society, music and philosophy.

Beethoven: Philosophie der Musik is a book which was left incomplete at the author's death. The work edited by Rolf Tiedemann includes those few finished texts published in Adorno's lifetime, such as the early *Spätstil Beethoven* (1934) and the mature essay on the *Missa Solemnis, Verfremdetes Hauptwerk* (1957). It also assembles a large quantity of fragments that Adorno composed throughout his lifelong Beethoven project. As Tiedemann wisely warns us: "None of the notes on Beethoven were written for a reader; they were all intended for the author himself, as *aide-mémoire* for the time when he would apply himself to the final composition, a task he never began" (1998a: ix).[1] A comparison with Beethoven's own sketches, also *aide-mémoire*, is tempting. One must resist, therefore, glib analogies with the aphoristic or paratactic style of the "finished" Adorno, or even the posthumously published *Aesthetic Theory*, which was left as a torso. All these works were composed for a reader, whereas the Beethoven "book" is fragmentary in the most vulnerable sense. A commentary on these fragments must be as cautious as, say, an analysis of the disputed "Tenth Symphony." Tiedemann's caveat aside, however, the problem is not as bad as it looks. First, Adorno's views on Beethoven changed remarkably little over the course of his career, an intellectual consistency which informs his body of work as a whole. One can easily slot the fragments into overarching themes and preoccupations. Second, the book is a treasure trove of analytical aperçus, displaying a degree of technical detail which is so signally lacking in Adorno's general writing about tonal music. These scattered observations on virtually every genre that Beethoven mastered—from the violin sonatas to the early Mass in C—can help the critic put analytical flesh on the philosophical bones. More generally, it facilitates the conversation between style study and critical theory, drawing out Adorno's alluring notion of Beethoven's late style as an "allegorical" style.

Tiedemann arranges the materials specifically concerning the late style in three (out of twelve) chapters. "The Late Style (I)" (chapter 9) and "The Late Style (II)" (chapter 11) are sandwiched around a chapter intriguingly entitled "Late Work without Late Style." Nevertheless, these three chapters can be understood only in the context of Adorno's discussion of early and middle Beethoven in chapters 1–8. Moreover, this initial phase of the book sets up Adorno's fundamental analogy between Beethoven's musical thought and Hegelian logic. The title of chapter 2—the book's exposition, after the "prelude" of chapter 1—is "Music and Concept." In a letter to his friend, the violinist Rudolph Kolisch, dated 16 November 1943 (appended on pp. 179–81), Adorno declares that his priority after the war would be finally to begin his long-planned Beethoven book. "I will work it out," claims Adorno, "in the context of Hegelian logic" (179). Adorno planned to begin his study with a discussion of "music and concept," and central to this enterprise was an identification (rather than analogy) between Beethoven and Hegel. Fragment 24 (1998a: 10) gives "In a similar sense in which there is only Hegelian philosophy, in the history of western music there is only Beethoven" (10). Tiedemann notes (202) that this jotting is prefixed by a "?". Adorno's question mark can probably stand as both stumbling block and epitaph for the entire project. Of course, the identification of Beethoven and Hegel is immediately problematic, given the opposition between metaphysics, which is directed toward universality, and aesthetics, which values particularity. Adorno's argument sets up a tension which is played out in the relationship between the middle and late periods. If middle Beethoven is Hegelian, then late Beethoven is anti-Hegelian, just as modern philosophy critiques metaphysics. Late Beethoven's modernity is thus the vengeance of the aesthetic upon the conceptual, or, in Freudian terms, the return of the repressed.

This dialectic of the metaphysical and the aesthetic is embedded within the "nuts and bolts" of the language. Adorno sees even Beethoven's middle style as a compact between conceptual logic and an expressive, or "mimetic," dimension: within works, *between* works, and also between the middle style and the early style. Hence the alternation of the symphonies between discursive and lyrical: nos. 3 and 4, 5 and 6, 7 and 8: "The configuration of Beethoven's oeuvre in pairs of works assists interpretation as an external sign of its dialectical nature" (21). But this dialectic is immanent within works as well. Thus Adorno hears the origin of the late style in the "mimetic" material subsumed within the conceptual, which breaks out in junctures such as the second halves of development sections. Further, he considers the early style to be a kind of "false dawn," provisionally bracketed by the middle style only to reemerge triumphantly in the late style. On a broad level, the dialectic of the late style embraces Beethoven's relationship to Haydn and Mozart, and, broader still, the Classical style's to the Baroque. Adorno's model of the late style is a multitiered spiral. But we have to begin somewhere, and the most natural place is Adorno's conceptual analysis of the heroic style. Given Adorno's claim that Beethoven's late style originates within expressive moments contained by musical logic, I will review his critique from two angles—first the "conceptual," then the "mimetic" which concepts seem to suppress.

Concepts

Adorno discovers Hegel's "Beethovenian" quality in his very style of writing, which has Beethoven's "floating element" (1998a: 12). In fragment 27 he states: "[Hegel's] ideas, like those of [Beethoven's] music, are explained only by each other" (12), a claim which is amplified in the second Hegel study, "Skoteinos, or How to Read Hegel": "Nothing can be understood in isolation, everything is to be understood only in the context of the whole" (1993b: 91). Reading Hegel or listening to Beethoven,

> One has to know a whole movement and be aware retrospectively at every moment of what has come before. The individual passages have to be grasped as consequences of what has come before, the meaning of a divergent repetition has to be perceived not merely as architectonic correspondence but as something that has evolved with necessity. (136–37)

Beethoven is nevertheless credited with authorship of this style, since it is "a law of artistic form transposed into the philosophical domain" (137).

Crucially, the Beethoven/Hegel affinity is a matter not of superficial style or rhetoric, but of conceptual substance. So what, precisely, *is* a concept? Adorno ascribes to Beethoven both the Kantian and Hegelian senses of "concept," although he overall favors the latter. First the Kantian, which corresponds to the traditional or modern sense of concepts as fixed mental categories which we hold up to experience. Judgments are accordingly produced from the fit between a concept and an intuition. In music, concept is form, and Beethoven's forms are "Kantian" because they are "regenerated from the subject" (1998a: 61); this, says Adorno, is Beethoven's "Copernican revolution" (61). Tonality also "is 'reproduced' by Beethoven as *a priori* synthetic judgments are reproduced by Kant" (17). The Hegelian concept, which Adorno upholds far more consistently, is quite different. From being a tool for grasping reality (Kant), the concept becomes the creative principle underlying and constituting reality. It is dynamic, holistic, and expressive. Hegel's concept abrogates the Kantian split between form and content by *generating content out of itself.* So too, Beethoven appears to generate formal conventions freely from the thematic discourse. Beethoven's forms are not static jelly molds, but contextually defined logical functions, such as "statement, identity, similarity, contradiction, the whole and the part" (11). Individual details—pitches, harmonies, thematic ideas—are defined by their function within the whole: not by what they *are,* but what they *do.* Divorced from its "work," musical material "is insignificant in itself" (22). For Adorno, the supreme example of this "nullity of the particular" is the opening of the recapitulation of the "Appassionata," which on paper looks like a mere descending triad over a pedal: "In isolation it is in no way striking. In conjunction with the development it is one of the great moments in music" (23).

Just as Hegel "completes" Kant in negating him, Adorno's Hegelian reading of Beethoven's holistic style builds on, rather than displaces, his Kantian notion that Beethoven "subjectifies" the concept. From a Hegelian standpoint, Kant's concept is not empty or wrong, but incomplete, requiring a supplement. The Kantian concept is worked into the Hegelian as a moment in its path. Thus the system is driven by a fruitful tension between static and dynamic levels of conceptuality: "Contradiction itself—the contradiction between the fixed concept and the concept in motion—becomes the agent of philosophizing" (1993b: 70). The assimilation of Kant into Hegel is mirrored by the wholesale assimilation of Haydn and Mozart's forms into Beethoven's discourse. Adorno's stress on wholeness and process might suggest that individual themes do not exist in Beethoven. But of course they *do* exist, albeit only to be negated:

> The concept of *negation* as that which drives a process forward can be very precisely grasped. It involves a *breaking off* of melodic lines before they have evolved into something complete and rounded, in order to impel them into the next figure. (1998a: 18–19)

Contradiction as the basic experience of life is one of the key insights that Adorno would retain from Hegel. Another insight is that thought is driven *through the extremes*, in marked contrast to the Aristotelian logical principle of noncontradiction. Thus Adorno's notion of "mediation" does not mean that oppositions are resolved by finding a middle term: "For Hegel mediation is never a middle element between extremes, . . . instead, mediation takes place in and through the extremes, in the extremes themselves" (1993b: 8–9).[2] These thoughts transfer well to our experience of Beethoven's musical drama, the exhilarating jostle of ideas against each other. We *hear* "dialectical logic" at the opening of the *Eroica* as a dramatic opposition between "the force making the music proceed" and the "obstruction" of the C♯ (1998a: 19).

But logic, surely, is not just a play of forms; it is also worked out in relation to the world. The difficulty is that one of the things which distinguishes musical from philosophical concepts is a lack of reference or predication: "Music is the logic of the judgment-less synthesis" (11). Music *mimics* the synthesizing, unifying, role of thought, but without the kind of content that might support a judgment. Adorno's solution is to invoke the social and historical character of musical material: the "true synthesis" (60) in music is played out between musical logic and convention, or the subjectivity of artistic play with the objectivity of inherited forms. The synthesis arises "as the product of a combining of pre-ordained schemata with the specific idea of each particular work" (60). Thus the formal schemata which Beethoven inherits from Haydn and Mozart are not just "abstract framework[s] 'within' which the specific formal concept is realized; the latter arise from the collision between the act of composing and the pre-existing schema[ta]" (60). Adorno's examples are two masterworks of the middle period: the "Waldstein" and "Appassionata" sonatas. Both these pieces stay within the sonata-form convention while recasting the roles of the development and coda. We are thus dealing with two, interdependent, subject/object dialectics. *Internal:* between theme and developmental process (respectively, fixed and mobile concepts). *External:* between theme/development considered as an abstract and self-enclosed economy on the one hand, and as inherited conventions on the other. This double axis is described in Adorno's account of a "typical" development, in terms of a subject/object dynamic of "mind" borrowed from Hegel's *Phenomenology of Spirit*:

> The theme of the development is mind, that is, the recognition of self in the other. The "other," the theme, the inspired idea, is, to begin with, left to itself in these developments and observed; it moves *in itself.* Only later, with the *forte* entry, comes the *intervention* of the subject, as if anticipating an identity unattained. It is only this intervention which creates the actual *model* of the development through a *resolution,*

that is, only the subjective moment of spirit brings about its objective movement, the actual content of the development. The subject-object dialectic is therefore to be traced in the development. (62)

Adorno's account presumes the perspectival mobility of a self-reflecting subject, a mobility which implicates the listener. Which is the object, which is the subject? From the perspective of the whole, the theme is the object of the developmental process. It is its "other." But the theme fulfills its destiny as a *subject* when it returns in the reprise, an entry which of course clinches the integrity of this very "whole." At this moment of reprise, the subject "returns to itself," as if in the course of self-reflection. Hence the recapitulation's affinity with those great Hegelian moments of synthesis, as at the end of *Phenomenology of Spirit,* where Hegel's climactic reprise reviews the very path which has led up to this point of elevation.

The other kind of "object," apart from the developed theme, is convention. The recapitulation effects synthesis of (subjective) expression and (objective) convention. Paradoxically, the "intervention" of the subject at the end of the development creates the very form which prescribes its entry; although the reprise is conventional, it seems to issue logically from the development. The "double axis" of reflection thereby engineers two paradoxes: (1) that the theme is both mover (subject) and moved (object); and (2) that the form is both free (subjective) and conventionally ordained (objective). In other words, "reflection" for Beethoven means both developing a theme (internal) and subjectivizing a convention (external). Since Beethoven's "double axis" renders his forms both logically unified and conventionally real, we see how Hegel's dictum that "the true is the real" can be true for Beethoven, if false for Hegel. The "true" means artistic authenticity; the "real" denotes the social reality of conventional language. Their coincidence in Beethoven is for Adorno historically unique: "Beethoven 'is' tonality" (and tonality "is" *Geist*) (21).

Beethoven's Logic

Adorno's letter to Kolisch envisages translating Beethoven's style specifically into the terms of Hegelian *logic.* This was never accomplished, despite one isolated analysis of the "Waldstein" sonata, which I will cite in full below. To get the most from this passage, however, we need a quick overview of the *Logic.* It is from Hegel that Adorno gets his crucial concepts of *Apparition, Schein,* idea, mediation, positing, and of course dialectic itself. Furthermore, the overall course of the logic—from the immediacy of "Being" to the mediated subjectivity of "Concept"—inaugurates one of the great narratives of Western philosophy.

Next to the *Phenomenology of Spirit,* the *Logic* is Hegel's central text. (It exists in two versions: the *Science of Logic,* 1812–1816, and the first volume of the *Encyclopaedia,* 1817. I will lean mostly on the former, often called "the Greater Logic.") The *Phenomenology* is a historical narrative of the evolution of consciousness, from ancient times to Hegel's present day. The *Logic* presupposes, and builds upon, the level of consciousness attained at the end of the *Phenomenology*. At this position of rest, Hegel's philosophy crystallizes into a system with an explicit set of categories. One way of looking at the difference between these two treatises is in terms of the ever present tension in Hegel between politically progressive ("left") and conservative ("right") tendencies. Hegel's orientation depends upon whether one regards the dialectic from the position of negation or synthesis. The negativity of the *Phenomenology* engendered both the Marxist and critical-theoretical traditions. The positivity of the *Logic*, oriented toward the closure of "the true is the real," yielded a repertory of categories such as "being," "essence," "existence," "appearance," "reality," "concept," and "idea." Categorizing cognitive behavior in this way looks forward to the Hegelianism of American Pragmatists such as Dewey and Peirce. For example, Hegel's triadic categories of "being"-"nothing"-"becoming," and "being"-"essence"-"concept," strikingly anticipate the Peircean categories which are so influential in music semiotics today—the triads of "icon," "index," and "symbol," and "firstness," "secondness," and "thirdness." Despite its forbidding difficulty, then, Hegel's *Logic* lies at the root of many modern orientations in philosophy and semiotics. My account below draws upon A. V. Miller's translation of the *Science of Logic* (1998), and also Charles Taylor's *Hegel* (1999), which is a reliable and accessible guide.

Hegel's most radical departure from traditional formal logic is his infringement of the laws of "the excluded middle" and contradiction (see the section on "Contradiction," book II/chapter 2/C; 1998: 431–43). This is encapsulated in Hegel's "Unity of Positive and Negative" (435–38), or his principle of the "identity of the identical and nonidentical," summarized in the formula $A = A$, $A = $ not-A. The principle reflects Hegel's philosophy that life and art entail overcoming and mediating oppositions. In music, the formula runs as follows: A piece is identical with itself insofar as it can reflect on itself and return to itself. But, given that this journey subsumes moments of difference and contrast, it renders these moments of nonidentity *identical* with the whole, so that *content* is subsumed within *form*. This is the musical instantiation of the dialectic. It is time now to confront the issue of the "dialectic" head-on.

"Dialectic" is one of the great misnomers of Hegelian reception. This is probably the fault of postwar Marxists who sought to freeze and codify Hegel into dogma. Adorno rejects this approach absolutely. Regarding "dialectic," Adorno states that "there is no definition that fits it" (1993b: 9). He dismisses as "claptrap" the notion that it could be simplified into a "methodological schema" of the "triplicity of thesis, antithesis, and synthesis" (75). That being said, of course, Adorno contradicts himself. He thus finds Beethoven's sonata Op. 101 "eminently *Hegelian*" because the first movement is "the subject," the second is "alienated," while the third, "were one not ashamed to write it down, the synthesis, sprung from the force of an objectivity which, in the process, proves identical to the subject, the lyrical core" (1998a: 128). But this is just the exception which proves the *Logic*'s rather more supple rule. It is best, then, to grasp the following account as "dialectic" in its approach, rather than its form.

The *Science of Logic* concerns categories of consciousness. It progresses from immediate perception to mediated reflection, with "mediation" conceived in an increasingly systemic and embodied way. The process culminates with the notion of the Concept, which Hegel identifies with the "I" of human subjectivity. The overall shift, then, is from reality "in itself" to reality "for" a subject. The process is "logical" in that the successive steps are driven by internal contradictions which become apparent through reflection, with advanced categories brought forth by inadequacies in preceding steps. This is epitomized in the famous argument of the opening lines, where Being turns into its opposite, Nothing, and this Being/Nothing opposition engenders a third category of Becoming. On reflection, this perverse formulation seems utterly reasonable. Percepts may seem at first to be real, but since they have *quality,* they turn out actually to be functions of some determination—such as color, shape, or number. What we first took for *Being* thus turns out to be *Nothing.* Furthermore, since determinations are conceived negatively—in reaction to other determinations—reality ends up as a dynamic process, *Becoming.* Take the example of the concept "wood." One progresses from a simple notion of wood (Being); to wood's determinate qualities of size, shape, etc. (Nothing); to situating these determinations negatively within opposed categories such as "forest" and "tree" (Becoming).[3] The next stage is to enrich our understanding of negativity itself. In addition to being a contrastive principle, negativity can be interactive and dynamic, as when a quality endures against the negation of opposite forces. A wood maintains itself against inhospitable elements, such as fire, water, and soil erosion. Pushed far enough, moreover, the negative reverts to the positive. Maintenance becomes *endurance*—the negation of the negation. This leads us to positively reassess the otherwise tragic notion of human finitude, with its correlative of mortality. Rather than being hopelessly negative, finitude is celebrated as a positive achievement in the face of possible destruction: a returning to itself. Mere Being, *Dasein,* turns into Something, *Etwas.* Certainly, on one level everything which comes into being passes away. Yet the pattern which *underlies* this transience is itself stable, leading to an abiding process which Hegel terms "infinity." Hegel's pun of "going to ground" manages to suggest the "grounding" rationale underpinning all change—the "identity in difference." Having developed a notion of the finite and dependent, the *Logic* is next compelled toward the complementary idea of the infinite and autonomous whole—a whole not as a static collective, but mediated through its parts and emergent from logical necessity. This notion of the whole prefigures, *in nuce,* the goal of the *Logic:* the Concept, or Idea, as a system which is both universal and embodied in finite things. Hegel identifies this Concept with the subjectivity of the "I." The trajectory of the *Logic* is thus toward the inwardness and self-sufficiency of the human subject. It is a circular, recursive, trajectory, which completes its elementary circle at the end of book I, "Being." It will unfold in greater arcs through book II, "Essence," and book III, "Concept."

One way of viewing the turn from "Being" to "Essence" is in terms of a shuttling between finitude and infinity. The course of Being had flowed from finite to infinite. Now, with Essence, Hegel shifts back to the finite, but from a higher vantage point, treating it as something *posited (gesetzt)* by the human subject: by thought

(Hegel: "This is *posited being* or *positedness,* immediacy purely and simply as *de-terminateness* or as self-reflecting. This immediacy which *is* only as *return* of the negative to itself, is that immediacy which constitutes the determinateness of illu-sory being and which previously seemed to be the starting point of the reflective moment" [book II, section 1, chapter 1/A, 1998: 401]). This subject is the "infinite," now conceived as an underlying rationale, a systematic web of relations which ex-plains something as a moment within a process. Essence, then, is revealed as Being's substrate. The ultimate Essence is the human subject, who "posits" reality by grasp-ing it as an extension of internal reflection. We are most familiar with this principle in aesthetic terms, as when we comprehend a passage of music not as an object in itself, but as posited by a compositional idea.

The path from Essence to Hegel's goal, the Concept, also involves a "shuttling." This time we move from *contingent* causes to *necessary* ones conceived in the con-text of a closed system. More importantly, we shuttle back from the infinite and abstract to the finite and embodied: namely, *reality.* But this is reality radically dif-ferent from Being, as is captured in Hegel's subtle term "Appearance" (*Ersche-inung*), a close cousin to Adorno's *Apparition.* Appearance, unlike Kant's "phenom-ena," does not describe the hiddenness of the real but, on the contrary, reality's "manifest-ness," its dynamic *coming into being* (book II, section 2, 1998: 479–528). Hence not "appearance" so much as the process of *appearing.* Hegel's dialectical concept of Appearance rejects the misleading notion that "ground" or Essence is something "behind" reality, since this harks back to Kant's dualism. Rather, ground finds its fullest expression within external reality, so that Essence is not hidden but manifest. This is how Hegel can view reality (Concept) as the dialectical synthesis of Being and Essence.

Following Hegel's *Science of Logic,* Adorno reads mm. 1–13 of the "Waldstein" as a story of developing consciousness, but one conceived in terms of *tonality* (see ex. A.11, in appendix). Adorno considers the passage's emergent sense of tonal cen-ter from the point of view of a listening subject interpreting—and retrospectively *reinterpreting*—each moment in time. His analysis is "dialectical," first, because re-interpretation is described in terms of negation and negation of the negation; and second, insofar as it considers tonality equally as presupposition and result:

> The working-out of tonality—a system which is at once prescribed and freely
> elaborated—can be demonstrated, perhaps, by the opening of the "Waldstein" So-
> nata. The *pre-existing,* "abstract" aspect of tonality is contained in the first m., C I.
> But at the same time, in reflecting on itself—through movement (*all* musical elements,
> including rhythm and harmony, are functionally interrelated)—this harmony reveals
> itself to be, *not* C I, but G IV, through the theme's tendency to move both forwards
> and upwards. It thus leads to G I, but because of the ambivalence of the first m. this
> G, too, is not definitive: hence the sixth. The following B♭ [m. 5] is thus not merely a
> "descending chromatic bass." It is the negation of the negation. In that it belongs to
> the subdominant region, it implies that the dominant is not a final result (it is actually
> just another reflection of itself, a possible aspect of the chord of G, not something
> "new." But since, unlike the opening, it does not manifest itself as self-reflection, but
> as something *posited,* as a quality bringing about a fundamental change, it is empha-

sized by the structure both metrically [first note of the half-period] and by its harmonic isolation). The dominant of the dominant is thereby negated; but so, too, retrospectively, is the opening: it is not only IV of G, but also V of F, and only through this double negation does it become concretely that which, through its concept, it was from the first, namely C major. (1998a: 55–56)

Adorno's tonal drama unfolds in three acts. C major is presented (Being), negated (Nothing), and then reconstituted as process (Becoming), thus returning to itself at a deeper level. The C-major triad at m. 1 presents a "pre-existing, abstract" aspect of tonality which is akin to pure Being. The immediacy of this Being is relativized negatively at m. 3 when C is reinterpreted as a subdominant of G, rather than a tonic. It becomes a *determinate* quality. If G major negates C, then G is itself negated by the B♭ of m. 5, which is "the negation of the negation." This double negation is not yet a return—that will come later, when C major is confirmed. Rather, it is the realization of an underlying *process* or pattern which makes sense of the apparent evanescence of C major. Although C had "gone to ground" as a finite moment, negated by G, its "finite-ness" is redeemed by the "infinity" of an overarching tonal progression. In other words, the B♭ triggers a shift in perspective from a local, static, view of harmony, to a systemic, dynamic one. With this switch from the Being of Beethoven's harmony to its underlying Essence comes another dialectical reversal from Essence to Appearance: presupposing a systematic rationale in the music allows us to understand the B♭ as "something *posited*," as issuing into Reality out of Essence—as coming into Being. That is to say, there is a palpable sense at m. 5 of a subjective compositional intervention; the figure of Beethoven as the governing subjectivity begins to step forward. Finally, C major returns, all the more secure for having been tested: "only through this double negation does it become concretely that which, through its concept, it was from the first, namely C major."

Adorno's reading, however interesting, is still hopelessly labored from the standpoint of modern analytical approaches. (When I return to the "Waldstein" in chapter 8, I will imagine an Adornian analysis from the perspective of the "Beethoven-Hegelian" tradition of music analysis.) On the plus side, Adorno's phenomenological perspective is salutary, in that it puts into the spotlight a temporality which is masked by more synchronic analytical models, such as a Schenkerian graph. On the negative side, Hegelianism as explicit as this serves Adorno, paradoxically, as a negative example of what to *avoid*, and it is instructive that Adorno never follows up his "Waldstein" experiment. In other words, such a reading casts an oblique light on how Beethoven's Hegelianism is always more supple than Hegel's own: "In this he is really more Hegelian than Hegel, who in applying the *concept* of the dialectic, proceeds far more rigidly, in the manner of all-embracing logic, than the theory itself teaches" (1998a: 160). To slough off rigid Hegelianism is, ironically, to mimic the trajectory of the Logic itself, which moves, in volume 3, toward a much more dynamic, holistic, and *human* notion of the "Concept": concept as human subject. This is the heart of the Beethoven/Hegel dialectic: that Beethoven becomes all the more like Hegel by resisting and transcending him. Hence Adorno's "Wald-stein" analysis remains within the purview of volumes 1 and 2 of the *Logic;* to reach volume 3 means giving up on Hegel altogether. This path takes Adorno toward his key notion of expressive *mimesis.* But "mimesis"—surely Adorno's *most* dialectical tool—also means an expressive miming (mimicking, imitation) of conceptuality. As we saw in chapter 2, the concept blends immediacy and logic, the archaic and the utopian, the cognitive (metaphorical) and the mimetic (critical), into a highly unstable alloy.

Mimesis

Beethoven's "analogy" with Hegelian philosophy cuts both ways for Adorno, in a dialectical mixture of identity and difference. It is both more than analogy ("the thing itself" [1998a: 11], an "analogue . . . that transcends mere analogy" [1993b: 136]), and *less* ("Beethoven's music . . . is truer than that philosophy" [1998a: 14]). The music/philosophy analogy is dialectical because music becomes more similar to the spirit of dialectic to the extent that it resists its letter. This is the key to understanding "mimesis," one of Adorno's most potentially confusing, yet central, ideas. Although music's ultimate philosophical truth is that it exemplifies a mode of "conceptless cognition"—a kind of rationality which transcends concepts—it nonetheless mimics the workings of concepts and language: the artwork is "deter-mined 'critically' as music's mimesis of judgment" (1998a: 11). The music/philosophy "analogy" must be grasped, then, "in terms both of the ineluctability of this mimesis and of music's attempt to escape it" (11). But why *is* music's mimesis of concepts so ineluctable? Surprisingly, the answer leads to the basis of Adorno's term in zoology. Paddison, following Michael Cahn (1984), explains that "mimesis could be understood as a form of copying, or identifying with, the outside world in order to protect oneself from a threatening environment, as a means of survival" (Pad-dison 1997: 140).[4] The "threat," from art's point of view, is "the process of ration-alization which characterizes the outside world, means-end rationality itself" (141). An astonishing fragment (no. 347) from the Beethoven monograph links this pro-tective sense of mimetic adaptation to the final stage of the Hegelian *Logic,* that of becoming human:

> Bring together the idea of music's *standing fast* with that of its *becoming corporeal.* Does not music perhaps stand firm against fate precisely in *becoming* fate? Is not imita-tion the canon of resistance? I have said that the Fifth and Ninth stand firm through looking-in-the-eye. Is that not still too little? Does not the Fifth stand firm through taking-into-itself? Does not gaining-power-over-oneself, freedom, lie only in imitation, in making-oneself-similar? Is not that the meaning of the Fifth, rather than the feeble *per aspera ad astra?* Is this not altogether the theory of the "poetic idea," and at the same time the law of the connection between *technique* and idea? Is not new light shed from here on programme music? To explain why the first movement of the Fifth is bet-ter than the rest. (169)

The "poetic idea" of the Fifth, popularly interpreted as the composer shaking his fist at Fate, resists an external threat by imitating it. At the highest artistic level, the symphony embodies the same sense of defiance and endurance Adorno detected, at a much lower level, in the double negations of his "Waldstein" analysis. C major "stands firm" against the threat of evanescence; the music "resists" translation into Hegelian language.

This notion of "resistance through mimicry" will take us, step by step, to understanding how the late style can critique Classicism while at the same time adopting its *clichés* more rigidly than ever before. The dialectical split within mimesis enables Adorno to treat it from two opposite viewpoints—the expressive and the allegorical—which he identifies, in turn, with the middle and late styles. As we shall see, late-style mimesis turns the middle-style version inside out: "subjectivity" is twisted into the "subjectivity of objectivity." Or, to borrow a phrase from Adorno's friend Benjamin, from whom he lifted the entire concept of allegory, "allegory . . . is not convention of expression, but expression of convention" (Benjamin 1998: 176).

Mimesis as Expression

Mimetic expression is not opposed to reason; it is a type of rationality which transcends the rigidity of conceptual logic. From one angle, mimesis is archaic, in that it suggests the preverbal expressive immediacy of intonation and gesture associated with primitive magical thinking. In this respect, Habermas thinks that Adorno's concept is simply a "placeholder for [a] primordial reason that was diverted from the intention of truth" (in Jameson 1990: 256). Given that "primordial reason" reckoned on controlling the environment by imitating it, music can be defined as *second-order imitation:* it imitates not reality as such, but *imitation itself,* that is, a primitive form of (mimetic) thinking. Mimesis, then, is imitation of imitation.

From a different angle, mimesis is not archaic but utopian. In escaping the constraints of conceptual logic, musical expression points to a utopian reconciliation of nature and reason. The mimesis of artistic expression is thus an enclave, or lifeboat, for our alienated subjectivity. It is here that mimesis flips over into its opposite, "construction" (or *ratio*). Only by miming logic as musical form, and using form to discipline mimesis, can music shield itself from the twin dangers of means-end rationality and regression into inarticulate emotion. Mimesis and construction, or expression and form, are therefore mediated in each other. In middle Beethoven, mimesis is of course mediated through the utmost formal sophistication. Nevertheless, even at this level of construction, a counterflow between archaic and utopian tendencies survives. Adorno hears intimations of "lateness" in the two critical junctures of Beethoven's sonata forms: the exposition's modulation to the new key, and the climax of the development section. These are "mimetic" in contrary ways: the former by relaxing formal logic; the latter by intensifying it to the point of sheer *will*. These extremes engender two important elements of Adorno's late-style critique: the concepts, respectively, of *Rückung* and *caesura*.

Rückung

Adorno hears the "secret of the late style" in what he terms the "extensive" temporality of certain works of the "later middle period" such as the Violin Sonata in G, Op. 96, and the "Archduke" Trio, Op. 97. These works display a retreat from a dynamic, teleological, type of temporality—the "intensive type"—in favor of "a renunciation of the symphonic mastery of time" (90). In the "Archduke," for example, "time is set free," with "scarcely any mediation" (89). These works have a lyrical, expansive, even epic, quality kindred with much of Schubert, as in his great B♭ piano sonata. Another feature which "later middle" works share with Schubert is the favoring of abrupt harmonic shifts over coherent modulations. A long analytical essay on the "Archduke" (91–97), entitled "Elements of a Theory of the Extensive Type," draws attention to "the *abrupt shift* [*Rückung*]—instead of a modulation—from B♭ major to D major in the transition group" (93). The harmonic rupture of *Rückung* subverts the principle of tonal transition, which is fundamental to Beethoven's (Hegelian) musical logic. It fosters a formal fragmentation which will emerge more fully in the late style. Adorno compares the *Rückung* in the "Archduke" to similar shifts in the *Hammerklavier* (the same key), and in the song cycle *An die ferne Geliebte*. Hence *Rückung* comprises the "origin of the late Beethoven."

In a remarkable dialectic twist, Adorno argues that it is not *Rückung* which is strange but *normal modulation,* which seems "fussy," "academic," and "over-ceremonious" by comparison (93). Pragmatically, Adorno wonders whether the incorrectness of *Rückung* would trouble anybody but theorists: "the great composers never went in much for modulation—that was left to the harmony teachers and the Regers" (93). This is exactly how the lateness of the "extensive type" can be heard to critique "the classical Beethoven" (90). From the vantage point of *Rückung,* "modulation's fussiness appears especially as a *veiling* (yet another aspect of *Schein*), a tendency which lays it open to criticism by the older Beethoven" (93). *Rückung,* therefore, reveals and critiques the contingency of musical logic.

Interestingly, Adorno's reinterpretation of *Rückung* is actually consistent with the term's evolving tradition in German music theory. Although nineteenth-century theorists talked of it exclusively as a harmonic device, its origins were actually *rhythmic.* It meant a rhythmic shift, synonymous with what we nowadays call syncopation, and what the eighteenth-century termed "imbroglio." Thus the entry *Rückung* in Heinrich Koch's *Musikalische Lexicon* (1802) lists the following features: (1) ties arising from nonessential dissonances, or suspensions; (2) *imbroglio;* (3) syncopations produced by agogic (durational) or dynamic accents.[5] It is only in the fourth and shortest section of his entry that Koch refers to the modern harmonic sense of *Rückung* as "enharmonische Ausweichung." Perhaps one way of reconciling *Rückung*'s rhythmic and tonal perspectives is to focus on Adorno's usage of the device as an expression of "extensive temporality." The "shift" is thus tantamount to what he calls "the renunciation of the symphonic mastery of time." Poetically, we remember also Schoenberg's expressive direction on the final movement of his Second String Quartet: "Entrückung," meaning transported with rapture. Rupture is literally an agent of rapture.

Caesura

Beethoven's music is "truer" than philosophy in moments that are difficult to explain formally, and which consequently seem purely inspirational, such as the E-minor theme in the second half of the *Eroica*'s development. Characteristically, Adorno can only "explain" such moments in Hegelian terms, even if their point is that they transcend Hegelian logic. Hence the E-minor theme obeys no formal rationale, but rather marks "a decisive act of *will*, a turning point: it *must* be so" (65). For Adorno, "this comes extraordinarily close to Hegel's concept of the subjective moment in truth as the condition of its objectivity" (65). The theme is *posited* as a forceful compositional act: "The whole, Being, can only exist as an act of the subject, that is, of freedom. This principle is raised to a self-conscious level in the new theme of the *Eroica*" (66). The outbreak of subjectivity at "turning points" in the structure, or "caesuras," is identified by Adorno with the modernism of late Beethoven: "here lies the secret of the decomposition of the late style" (66). This notion of "caesura," with its overtones of rupture and fragmentation, is seminal for the late style. Despite its suggestion of formal collapse, "caesura" must be understood in the context of a Hegelian narrative of consciousness; with those dialectical "turning points" in the story when mind turns round to examine itself, turning back again to "posit" reality as a subjective act.

Despite the caesura's intrinsic freedom, Adorno uncovers an underlying normativity with his theory of the "two-part structure" of sonata-form development. In the "Appassionata," "Waldstein," "Kreutzer," *Eroica*, and Op. 59, no. 1, the first part is "more vacillating, fantasizing," while the second part is "firm, built on a model, objectified, but with the character of a decisive act of *will*" (65). Moreover, he attributes the notion of caesura, together with the two-part model, to Hölderlin's "calculable law of tragedy" (64). For Hölderlin, the "caesura" marks the turning point between the "descending" and "ascending" curves of the drama, "the moment where subjectivity intervenes in the formal structure" (64). Inevitably, Adorno relates the subjectivism of such moments to the famous "Difficult Decision" of the last quartet, Op. 135: the mimetic positing of "Es muss sein!"

Allegorical Mimesis

Another root of Beethoven's late style is the subversive effect of comedy, as in the comic idioms of his early period. Adorno finds premonitions of lateness in the Op. 18 quartets, the comic finale of the G-major Violin Sonata Op. 30, no. 3, and that of the F♯-major Piano Sonata Op. 78 (1998a: 98). If mimesis is deviation from rules, than comedy takes this principle in quite another direction. Expression is found, rather, *in the rules themselves,* which are made to sound absurd. In this sense, Classical play does not *break* conventions, it *foregrounds* them.

The notion of rendering logic expressive is fundamental even to Adorno's philosophical idiom. A collateral effect of Adorno's "Waldstein" analysis is that it makes reason absurd. So much jargon applied to so few measures may seem faintly ridiculous, especially to Anglo-Saxon ears. Yet this impression plays straight into Adorno's argument that music critiques logic by underscoring its inadequacy. The "Waldstein" analysis is an extreme case, not only of music theory in general, but of *all* theory. "Regular mimesis," if I may call it that, is expression mediated by construction—the condition general to artworks. "Reverse mimesis" is the expression *of* construction: turning "structure" into an expressive quality in itself. This is the particular quality of late works. An unusually gnomic remark, inserted parenthetically within fragment 363, gives:

> The question how the formula can come alive, a problem very closely related to the late style (in which it is inverted: How can the living become a formula, its own concept? The late style corresponds to Hegel's subjective logic). (174)

In simple terms: middle Beethoven takes convention ("formula") and fills it with subjectivity; late Beethoven begins with subjectivity and ossifies it into convention. The middle style *symbolically* unifies music and concept; the late style *allegorically* keeps music and concept apart, *and rings an expressive note out of this separation.*

Adorno's argument that late Beethoven is prototypical of allegory seems to conflict with his later tendency, epitomized by his magnum opus *Aesthetic Theory,* to ascribe allegorical expression to *all* authentic art. *Aesthetic Theory* hardly mentions "allegory" per se, but it absorbs it into a thorough-going critique of aesthetic "harmony"—the artwork's double-edged claim to be a seamless, harmonious whole. To caricature this critique into a crude celebration of "disunity"—as is so often done in Adorno reception—is to miss its dialectical core: "harmony" is both a truth and a lie, and its ultimate truth (art's residual *truth content*) depends on this antinomy being maintained. *Aesthetic Theory* elaborates this antinomy by demonstrating that art's illusory character—its *Scheincharakter*—is reciprocally related to the figural, "as if" quality of logic.

Adorno and Hegel's notion of *Schein* punningly combines opposite meanings. *Schein* blends illusion or semblance with the notion of a veil covering an underlying reality. But there is a sense also of this veil being redeemed by its aesthetic luminosity, recalling Hegel's concept of art as the Absolute shining forth into corporeal substance. This is why art can be at the same time aesthetically "true" yet cognitively false: "it shines black," as it were. Its falseness is never clearer than when art mimes rationality, as in so-called "musical logic." The logicality of musical processes in a Bach fugue or a Classical development is "figurative" rather than actual (1999: 137) and is only "*analogous* to the logic of experience" (136). Musical form tolerates a far greater degree of latitude than actual logic, as in, for example, the improvisatory element underlying eighteenth-century style. In artworks, "everything only appears as if it must be as it is and could not be otherwise" (136). In practice, Bach or Beethoven could easily have found another solution to their compositional problem, without prejudicing the illusion of logical "inevitability." Their structures do not *really* fall apart if one changes a note here and there.

Ironically, the figural quality of artistic "logic" kicks back to undermine the assumption that the logic of the world is in principle any more absolute than the aesthetic kind: "the more the artwork's own organization assimilates to a logical order by virtue of its inner exactitude, the more obviously the difference between the artwork's logicity and the logicity that governs empirically becomes the parody of the latter" (119). What artistic "logic" parodies is our tendency to forget that the rationality supporting social praxis, rather than remaining a means toward a social end, is frequently reified into an end itself. This parody gains aesthetic expression in Haydn's comic procedure, in which the pretensions of "logic" are rendered ridiculous. Haydn's developments expose the ostensible "harmony" of the self-regulating bourgeois economy as comic intrigue:

> The individual activity of the motifs as they pursue their separate interests, all the while assured by a sort of residual ontology that through this activity they serve the harmony of the whole, is unmistakably reminiscent of the zealous, shrewd, and narrow-minded demeanor of intrigants, the descendants of the dumb devil; his dumbness infiltrates even the emphatic works of dynamic classicism, just as it lingers on in capitalism. (223)

The "as if" character of musical logic unmasks reason as a commedia dell'arte. Crucially, it is not Haydn's music which is absurd, but reason itself. The true intent of *Aesthetic Theory* is thus to "aestheticize theory," rather than the more prosaic object of a "theory of aesthetics." Like Adorno, but following the model of his great precursor Haydn, late Beethoven aestheticizes logic by thawing out the subjectivity congealed within it.

Late Style

The essay *Spätstil Beethovens* was written in 1934 and was published in the 1964 collection *Moments musicaux*. Although an early text, it contains *in nuce* nearly all the motifs that will preoccupy Adorno for the rest of his life. Moreover, it couches them in an enigmatic tone which recalls the Jewish mysticism of Kafka and Benjamin. Of the many quotable (and much-quoted) aphorisms in the piece, the opening and closing remarks are especially effective:

> The maturity of the late works of important artists is not like the ripeness of fruit. As a rule, these works are not well rounded, but wrinkled, even fissured. (1998a: 123)

> In the history of art, late works are the catastrophes. (126)

Adorno's poetry certainly does justice to his notion of the "puzzle-character" (*Rätselcharakter*) of authentic art, and also to his desire to imbue philosophical aesthetics with the quality of the art it is describing. But it should not distract from the essential clarity of the essay's ternary scheme, which reviews three types in "the relationship between conventions and subjectivity" (125), or, construction and mimesis: (1) Subjectivity deviates from convention; (2) Convention is subjectivized; (3) Convention "becomes expression" (125). Adorno argues that only the third model is adequate to the peculiar "disharmony" of Beethoven's late style.

Late works are "fissured," Adorno begins, because they "lack all that harmony which the classicist aesthetic is accustomed to demand from the work of art" (123). Adorno immediately dismisses the standard view that late Beethoven's "disharmony" is due to "expressive" factors—the venerable explanation of artistic license as rhetorical "deviation" from conventional rules. Such a model is often imputed, for example, to the Classical "play" of Haydn and Mozart, where it works fairly well. The second model which Adorno rejects is the "subjectivist procedure" (124) of middle-period works such as the "Appassionata." Here, "the effect of subjectivity . . . was not so much to disintegrate form as to produce it" (124). The "subjectivist procedure" is "to tolerate no conventions, and to recast the unavoidable ones in keeping with the urge of expression" (124). Thus works such as the Fifth Symphony appear to generate convention out of their "thematic substance." The use of convention in the late style is quite different. According to Adorno's third model, "convention is often made visible in unconcealed, untransformed bareness" (124); "hence the conventions no longer imbued and mastered by subjectivity, but left standing" (125). Adorno points to the many "conventional formulae" of the five last piano sonatas. For example, "the first theme of the Piano Sonata Op. 110 has an ingenuously simple semiquaver accompaniment which the middle style would hardly have tolerated" (124). Adorno associates this procedure with allegory's historical materiality, with a "reflection on death" (125).

The essence of Adorno's critique thus concerns "the role of conventions" (124). It is unfortunate, therefore, that so much of Adorno-inspired criticism of late Beethoven has dwelt on its fragmentary or "dissociated" (Kerman 1967) character. To be sure, this is not helped by the conclusion of Adorno's essay, which invokes apocalyptic images of "fissures and rifts" (125) in a "fragmentary landscape," torn apart by Beethoven's "dissociative force" (126). Nor, on the technical side, by Adorno's focus on textural breaches: "caesurae" and "abrupt stops," unmediated juxtapositions of textural extremes such as unisons and polyphony (126). This stress on textural dissociation may well fit a work such as the first movement of Op. 132, a locus classicus of late-Beethoven analysis. But it fails to capture the lateness of a piece as superficially seamless as Op. 110, or, indeed, the first phrase of the *Arietta*. We will see in the next chapter that there *are* in fact ways of accommodating even this "seamless" aspect of late Beethoven into Adorno's image of a fractured landscape. Nevertheless, to focus on the fragmentary in an overly literal way is to slip back into Adorno's rejected "first model" of subjectivity: the commonplace that expression breaks (breaches) rules. Adorno's punning notion of "harmony" encourages this confusion by conflating a sense of musical coherence in particular with the broader concept of *aesthetic* harmony. Aesthetic harmony is not an attribute of structure but a category of cognition, akin to the understanding achieved in the Hegelian synthesis. By the same token, *Aesthetic Theory*'s mantra that "dissonance is the truth of harmony" contends that aesthetic cognition is processual and open-ended, endlessly deferring the closure of synthesis. Menke (1999) defines this as "aesthetic negativity"—the aesthetic analogue of Adorno's "negative dialectic." The late Adorno of *Aesthetic Theory* and *Negative Dialectics* reformulates subjectivity negatively as an active resistance to grounding and closure. This entails the paradoxical notion of the "flight of the subject," where subjectivity is registered no longer in the plenitude of an accomplished subject position, but in the dynamic trajectory of withdrawal itself: of negation. If subjectivity were denied completely, it would entail a regression to pre-Kantian (i.e., precritical) dogmatism, of the kind that Adorno ascribes to Heideggerian ontology (1990: 61–128): an immediate identification with the "Being" of objects. Rather, "objectivity" is attained through an active negation of reason, *and in the context of reason*. In the famous words of *Negative Dialectics*, philosophy "must strive, by way of the concept, to transcend the concept" (15).

Amazingly, Adorno's late philosophy is already implicit within the Beethoven essay of 1934. Subjectivity is withdrawn from Beethoven's material, which is "expression-less" and "dispassionate" (1998a: 124). It is registered, instead, in the very contour—the "gesture"—of withdrawal:

> The force of subjectivity in late works is the irascible gesture with which it leaves them. It bursts them asunder, not in order to express itself but, expressionlessly, to cast off the illusion [*Schein*] of art. (125)

The "caesurae" which in the *Eroica* marked turning points of subjective *positing* are inverted in the late style into exit holes of escape—"the caesurae are . . . moments of breaking free" (126). The position of "development" is also reversed. In the middle style, development takes place within the musical material and is grasped as an accomplished whole. In the late style, processuality is withdrawn from the material, which ossifies into unmediated extremes or antinomies. Processuality is relegated instead to the understanding, compelled now to flicker endlessly between antinomies: "His late work still remains a process, but not as a development; its process is an ignition between extremes which no longer tolerate a safe mean or a spontaneous harmony" (126). In short, immanent development is abstracted into *Schein*'s cognitive flicker.

The rigidity of convention and the processuality of aesthetic cognition mark the extreme poles of Beethoven's late style, according to Adorno's essay. In the language of late Adorno, these poles are the analogues of a philosophical antinomy between the *positivity* of material and the *negativity* of reason; between the particularity of the nonidentical and the universality of the concept. These antinomies are locked into a single category which Adorno felicitously christens *Floskel* (1993a: 184). In the tradition of Hegel's multivalent neologisms, *Floskel* usefully combines the senses both of cliché and flourish: connotations of both rigid convention and subjectivity *as contour*.[6] "The cliché/flourish is set in place as a monument to what has been—a monument in which subjectivity is petrified" (*Die Floskel einsetz als Denkmal des Gewesenen, worin versteint Subjektivität selber eingeht*) (184).

Contrapuntal Elaborations

Adorno's later writings on late Beethoven are, in the main, elaborations of motifs adumbrated in the 1934 essay, although with one great exception. The exception is a motif entirely absent from *Spätstil Beethovens:* the Baroque. "Dogmatic" or "strict" Baroque idioms such as counterpoint, cantus firmus, and variation are antithetical to the free and developmental character of sonata form. The antithesis is used by Adorno to throw the contingency of musical Classicism into historical relief: far from being "natural," "inevitable," or "transparent," the Classical style actively displaces and suppresses a previous style. The "historical suppressed" *returns* in late Beethoven's Baroque turn: the extraordinary series of fugal and variation movements in the sonatas and quartets. To be sure, this return is partially driven by Beethoven's conscious choice to pursue a *Kunstvereinigung,* or "unification of the arts," as we will see in chapter 7. Nevertheless, from Adorno's perspective, compositional choices, however voluntary, are undertaken with responsibility to the properties, even dictates, of the musical material. Adorno thus temporalizes (historicizes) his philosophical project of recuperating particularity or nonidentity: "To change this direction of conceptuality, to give it a turn toward nonidentity, is the hinge of negative dialectics" (1990: 12). The "objectivity" of Baroque material is the historical analogue of the sensory data subsumed by the Concept, of the mimesis mediated in construction. It is as if late Beethoven discovers the ghost of contrapuntal texture lurking in the hollow spaces of Classical form. The *Grosse Fuge* explodes out of the formulaic *galant* language of the Op. 130 quartet. The elegance of Adorno's own Baroque turn is that it brings out a historicism buried all along in his original notion of allegory. The "home" of allegory is seventeenth-century Baroque German literature, and allegory was given its critical-theoretical stamp in Walter Benjamin's 1925 *Ursprung des deutschen Trauerspiels* (1998).

Underlying Adorno's interest in the objectivity of archaism is his increasingly bitter debate with Heidegger over ontology, registered in the polemical tract *Jargon of Authenticity* (1964), but also in vast swathes of *Negative Dialectics.* The quarrel with Heidegger maps almost directly onto Adorno's critique of Stravinsky in *Philosophy of New Music.* The Baroque/Classical fusions of Stravinsky's neoclassicism reflect late Beethoven in a distorting mirror. Despite superficial similarities, Stravinsky is a "bad" Beethoven, just as the "unmediated immediacy" (see Paddison 1997: 29) of Heideggerian ontology is a travesty of negative dialectic. The Beethoven text which picks up the Heidegger polemic most directly is the great essay on the *Missa Solemnis, Verfremdetes Hauptwerk.* Beethoven's refractory and seemingly hopeless compact in the mass between Classical idealism and the dogmatic faith of Baroque theology raises the stakes of his musical philosophy into a worldview. In Adorno's words, "What is at issue for him, expressed in later terminology, is whether ontology, the subjective spiritual order of Being, is still possible at all" (1998a: 149).

Between *Spätstil Beethovens* and *Verfremdetes Hauptwerk*—the two corner-stones of Adorno's late-style critique—come a constellation of fascinating frag-ments. The scattered remarks on the late style fill in the outlines with some stimu-lating details. "Constellation" seems the appropriate format in which to present these ideas, and I accordingly arrange them under the four rubrics of "lateness," "retreat from harmony," "allegory," and "Baroque," spinning the motifs in a series of contrapuntal elaborations.

"Lateness"

What is it, exactly, which qualifies a Beethoven work as "late"? The nearest Adorno gets to a checklist of features is in fragment 286, pertaining to the mass. Adorno here lists seven criteria by which the mass is "late": "there are no tangible 'themes'—and therefore no development" (139), the music is neither properly poly-phonic nor melodic, it is inimical to sonata form, etc. The notion of a checklist is of course highly dubious, since it essentializes the style into a closed set of features. Yet, for Adorno, whether or not a piece is truly "late" is tantamount to a judging whether or not it qualifies as authentic art. In this, he echoes the aesthetic reduc-tionism of Romantic philosophers such as Novalis, for whom "Criticism of litera-ture is an absurdity" and thus "the only possible decision [is] whether something is literature or not" (in Bowie 1997: 279). Hence Adorno's inveterate sorting of the sheep and goats. The irony is that he can never decide, and draws the line in at least four or five different places. Fragment 282 claims "the boundary is doubtless marked by the Piano Sonata Op. 101" (136). Elsewhere Adorno is absurdly exclu-sive, and discounts *all* the sonatas: "strictly *only* the last string quartets, perhaps the Diabelli Variations and the last Bagatelles" (158). Most disturbing is his disen-franchising of the Ninth Symphony itself: "The Ninth Symphony is not a late work, but a reconstruction of the *classical* Beethoven" (97); "The ninth symphony falls outside the late style altogether" (144). And yet this oft-repeated claim is flatly con-tradicted by fragment 262, which gives the most technically penetrating analysis of "late" polyphony in the entire book:

> Critique: the problematic character of Beethoven's polyphony can be shown, for
> example, in a passage at the start of the development of the Ninth Symphony, m. 180.
> It concerns the relations between voices, between first violins and solo bassoon. They
> enter in octaves . . . But one has to decide: either octave doubling, or independent
> voices. And yet the matter is not so simple. For the ambiguous character of the pas-
> sage, suspended between stasis and development, is emphasized precisely by the
> "impurity" of the passage, that is, its *technical* indeterminacy . . . It has the character
> of alienation—of a subjective, but violent, transition to objectivity. (115–16)

So is the Ninth late or not? The *Missa*, worse, is both late and not-late: it is a "late work without late style." And then there is the anticipatory lateness of the Op. 18 quartets: "The rendering indifferent of the material, the stepping back from ap-pearance which characterizes the late style, applies much earlier to the *chamber music*—and only to it" (136). The Op. 18 quartets "often have an angular, unpolished element running counter to sensuous balance." Moreover, early comic works, such as the sonatas Op. 30, no. 3, and Op. 78, which avoid (i.e., *negate*) fully formed subjects, are called "late style in disguise" (98). Lateness is everywhere and nowhere. Perhaps, then, it can only be pinned down as a *philosophical* category: a "stepping back from appearance," or retreat from "harmony."

Retreat from Harmony and *Schein*

"Beethoven's late style . . . is essentially critical" (97). What it critiques is the semblance (*Schein*) of aesthetic unity, of "harmony." Adorno exploits to the full his pun between aesthetic harmony and literal, *musical,* harmony. Philosophically, "harmony" is the "illusion of unity," the "identity of precondition and result" and of "subject and object" (157). Musically, the semblance of "harmony" is epitomized by the middle style. When Beethoven critiqued this style, "he saw through the classic as classicism" (151). The joints of the middle style seem to creak: "Sometimes, if one listens closely to its idiom, his music has something contrived" (77). For example, one often senses that a recapitulation's inevitability is forced: "aesthetically dubious in the same fundamental way as the thesis of identity in Hegel" (17).

The late style's critique of harmony abrogates mediation, resulting in "a splitting into extremes" and "a dissociation of the middle." This has both a horizontal and vertical dimension. Horizontally, the breakdown of mediation between steps of a harmonic process, as in the concept of Rückung. Vertically, the objectification of harmony from a process to a structure, leading to a notion of stratification or layering:

> But harmony itself . . . takes on something mask-like or husk-like. It becomes a convention keeping things upright, but largely drained of substance . . . In the last string quartets, at least, one can hardly speak any longer of the construction of tonality. It no longer has an autonomous law of motion, but remains behind as a sound veil, and it is not harmonic proportion but the individual harmonic effect. (156)

Ossified into a "veil," musical harmony becomes *Schein,* semblance. The late style's *Scheincharakter* is highly paradoxical. On the one hand, it suggests that the "masklike" or "husklike" harmony overlays an underlying authenticity, waiting to burst out or rip through the veil as *Durchbruch.* In fact, Adorno describes *Durchbruch,* in his *Mahler,* as "the rending of the veil" (1992a: 5). On the other hand, by very virtue of being dissociated, late harmony is already "beyond the veil," denoting "Beethoven's stepping back from appearance" (157). The late style, then, is a retreat from harmony in the guise of a *Durchbruch,* so that surface and depth collapse into each other. By folding over the spatial coordinates of "surface" and "depth," Adorno simply radicalizes the dual sense of *Schein* as both semblance and luminosity. This conflation, nevertheless, is tensile, not settled: it is *allegorical.*

Late Allegory

"One must start with the allegorical, and in an important sense fractured, nature of these pieces" (Adorno 1998a: 158). Or even better, simply: "Allegorical rather than symbolic" (155). This terse formulation at the end of fragment 308 refers to a venerable opposition of Romantic aesthetics (see Todorov 1982). The defense of allegory over symbol follows Benjamin's polemic against the nineteenth-century aesthetics of organic unity, epitomized in the symbolic theories of Goethe, August Schlegel, and Friedrich Creuzer (Benjamin 1998: 159–235). Beethoven's allegorical character is thus anti-organic: "The bareness of the very late Beethoven's music is connected to the *inorganic* element" (Adorno 1998a: 154–55). According to Menke (1999: 16–19, 21–22), allegory for Adorno is a metonym for literal, as in Adorno's writings on Kafka. In Kafka's fiction, extraordinary meaning is ascribed to very ordinary events and rendered in language which is absolutely plain and unadorned. Because of this combination of the allegorical and the literal, Kafka both invites and resists interpretation. Kafka's "stony" plainness of expression, with its unmediated split between (mundane) signifier and (metaphysical) signified, is captured by Adorno's favorite image of fractured petrification: "the abyss" (= a breach in a rocky landscape). Hence the striking similarity between the following statement on Kafka's allegorical style, and the climactic image from *Spätstil Beethovens:*

> Each sentence is literal and each signifies. The two moments are not merged, as the symbol would have it, but yawn apart and out of the abyss between them blinds the glaring ray of fascination. (1997: 245)

> He no longer draws together the landscape, now deserted and alienated, into an image. He illuminates it with the fire ignited by subjectivity as it strikes the walls of the work in breaking free, true to the idea of the dynamic. (1998a: 126)

There are plenty of references in Adorno's Beethoven fragments to the bareness of late-style harmony. Of the quartet Op. 127, Adorno writes: "The musical language is displayed here nakedly and—as compared to the middle style—*directly*," or: "Beethoven looks the bare language of music, purified of all individual expression, in the eye" (154).

Adorno's remarks point to the possibility of a tonal semiotic based on the concept of allegorical harmony. "Symbolic" harmony merges part and whole into a coherent tonal structure, just as, according to Adorno, the "individual moments" of Goethe's symbolic play *Pandora* "point beyond themselves by virtue of their interrelationships [so that] their totality coalesces into meaning" (1997: 245). Although Adorno's notion of middle Beethoven's "motivic kernels" as "formulas of tonality, reduced to nothingness as things of their own and preshaped by the totality" (1998a: 43) is couched in Hegelian language, it also parallels Schenker's theory of prolongation. By the same token, "allegorical" harmony is *anti*-Schenkerian, in that it questions the functional assimilation of individual chords within the tonal process. Hence Adorno's concept of "subsumption" has a *tonal* referent, in addition to the better-known philosophical and social meanings: "Beethoven's stepping back from appearance, the withering of harmony in the widest sense, stems from *resistance to subsumption* by the unchanging" (157). When tonal harmony "withers," it shrinks from a process to a sum of *chords:*

Tonality shrinks to the bare chord. Its substantiality passes from the whole to the single chord, which "signifies" tonality; the chord as allegory replaces the key as process. (129)

The fragment (no. 267) ends with an enigmatic "Reference to complementary harmony," which suggests that Adorno's shift from the linear to the vertical is in line with his Schoenbergian orientation. "Complementary harmony" refers to the vertical, blocklike, dimension of twelve-tone harmony. Adorno tentatively illustrates these comments with a passage from the slow movement of the *Hammerklavier* (mm. 69–73). "Tonality speaks" (129) in Beethoven's unmediated juxtaposition of pure triads. Adorno also detects "a curious rocking between degrees, especially I and V" (128) in the Adagio, a "suspension effect" at odds with tonal *process.*

Adorno addresses Schenker in a radio lecture, "The Problem of Musical Analysis," which he gave a few months before his death (Adorno 1982). Although he clearly misunderstands Schenker's notion of *Ursatz,* ascribing to it a rigid reductionism and an aesthetic disregard for thematic detail ("features which, for Schenker, are of mere secondary importance but which make all the difference" [174]), it is striking that the two theorists drew diametrically opposed conclusions from similar ingredients. These ingredients are (1) a concept of tonal stratification, and (2) a renewed interest in the unfashionable tradition of counterpoint (Blasius 1996: 13–35). Unlike Schenker, Adorno thinks that the metrical/formal "foreground" and contrapuntal "background" of a late-Beethoven texture are not mediated by any "middleground." On the contrary, Adorno's concept of "layering" takes after the two-tier surface/depth model of Schoenbergian serialism. As in Schoenberg, the rigid neoclassical phraseology of late Beethoven supervenes upon a "subcutaneous" (or "subthematic," in Dahlhaus's phrase) contrapuntal web. Another difference is that a Schenkerian structure is generative (or reductive) in a single direction, whereas "surface" and "depth" for Adorno are dialectical. As with *Scheincharakter,* the extremes of surface "veil" or "husk" (*Schein*) and background "reality" turn into each other, subject to a dialectical "flip." Beethoven's foreground metrical articulation is expressive *because* it is "ossified" (in Schenkerian terms, *because* it is nonreducible); Beethoven's background counterpoint is authentically linear (in Schenkerian terms, it is recalcitrantly foreground and cannot be prolonged into scale steps). Put simply, allegorical harmony is expressed along a "formal" (horizontal) and "textural" (vertical) axis: "formal" disharmony redeems articulation (which Schenker disparages as *merely* "foreground"); "textural" disharmony redeems the foreground reality of counterpoint (which Schenker commutes to an imaginary model of a "middleground"). Simpler still, Adorno's "splitting into extremes" is the polarization of Beethoven's late style into Classicizing form and archaic polyphony.

Compared to Schenker, Adorno lacked the analytical skill to synthesize form and counterpoint within a single (anti-)systemic model. He was therefore obliged to lay out his claims paratactically, with no indication of how Beethoven mediates formal and contrapuntal dissociation in single pieces. All Adorno can do, therefore, is to impute "the secret of the late style" to *both* varieties of allegory in turn, switch-

ing endlessly between them, just as late Beethoven himself revels in "abrupt, unmediated juxtapositions of bare axiomatic motifs and polyphonic complexes"
(152). On the one hand, speaking of form, Adorno maintains that

> to say that the tonal material is ossified into a convention is only a half-truth. In its
> estrangement from the process and identity, it juts out bare and cold, like rock. In
> having become subjectively expressionless, it takes on an objective, allegorical expres-
> sion. (129)

On the other hand, switching to counterpoint, he writes:

> The latest Beethoven represents an attempt to reconstruct the *cantus firmus* from sub-
> jectivity. The starting point of the entire style is connected to this. All else can be de-
> rived from the problem of this *cantus firmus* and from the question of the compulsion
> towards counterpoint. (159)

Baroque

The burden for music of Benjamin's *Ursprung des deutschen Trauerspiels* is
that the Classical style is illegitimate. This comes as something of a shock, in view
of Haydn, Mozart, and middle-period Beethoven's status as the central planks of
our musical canon. Taking the historical long view, Benjamin regards the Enlightenment rule of the symbol (which continues through most of Romanticism) as a
hiatus or interregnum between the Baroque and modernity—periods of allegorical
disunity. Or rather, the modern age actually starts in the seventeenth century, is
interrupted by the Enlightenment, and resumes in the twentieth century. Benjamin's
ternary historical model more or less matches Schoenberg's view in his 1931 essay
(in Schoenberg 1984), "National Music" (although his "Brahms the Progressive"
of 1947 is more circumspect, and acknowledges that Classical periodicity has its
own virtues of "comprehensibility"). For the earlier Schoenberg at least, Haydn
and Mozart's "un-German" periodic style, based on phrase repetition, intervenes
between Bach and Beethoven's (or Bach and Brahms's) more authentic thematic-
developmental idioms. Adorno's dialectical perspective finds a way of melding the
ternary model with an appreciation of the Classical style's centrality in Western
music. He portrays the return of counterpoint in the late style as a grand historical
da capo, and he gives Baroque idioms a philosophical gloss. "Baroque" thereby becomes a placeholder for all those archaic, precritical tendencies which Beethovenian subjectivity negated. Philosophically, late Beethoven's confrontation with the
presubjective Baroque is an attempt to redeem objective ontology. Characteristically, this move entails a dialectical reversal of "subject" and "object" slots. The os-
sification of Classical form indicates a renunciation of subjectivity; the objectivity
of counterpoint is subjectified in movements such as the *Heiliger Dankgesang*. The
text which deals most frankly with these issues is Adorno's late essay (1957), "The
Alienated *Magnum Opus:* On the *Missa Solemnis.*"

The *Missa Solemnis,* according to the essay, is a work "of permanent renunciation" (151) in which Beethoven, rather than asserting his subjective intention, is

concerned with "eliminating it" (151). Much of the *Missa*'s anti-Classical character is of course intrinsic to the problematic genre of the Classical mass in general, as witness Rosen's pejorative assessment of Haydn and Mozart's church music (1972: 366–75) and Adorno's own verdict on Beethoven's early C-major Mass Op. 86 as "an entirely uninspired" failure (1998a: 139: see also fragment 19: "To come closer to understanding the *Missa*, it is doubtless necessary to study the Mass in C major," p. 9). More than the contrapuntal textures themselves, however, the mass's liturgical text imposes a paratactic formal aesthetic deeply alien to the Classical style. And this is without mentioning the spiritual content of the text, which is so antithetical to the "humanity and demythologization" (142) upon which Beethoven's power is founded. For Adorno, then, Beethoven's problem is to redeem ontology. Reconciling faith and idealism is, on a theological level, linked to late Beethoven's aesthetic project of safeguarding artistic particularity, and to late Adorno's recuperation of the object from the concept:

> He is concerned with saving ontology musically in a state of subjectivism, and his recourse to liturgy is meant to achieve this in the same way as invocation of the ideas of God, freedom and immortality was to do for the critic Kant. In its aesthetic form the work asks what can be sung without deception about the Absolute, and how it can be sung. (149)

We arrive, finally, at the point where Beethoven's "problem" is arguably *Adorno's* problem: the reason why Adorno ultimately proved incapable of subsuming Beethoven's style into theory and finishing his *Beethoven* book. Adorno's "problem" in late texts such as *Negative Dialectics* was how to balance a philosophy of subjective renunciation with a critique of "unmediated immediacy"—the retrogressive move he identified with Heideggerian ontology. In Jameson's summary: "*Negative Dialectics* can in many ways be read as his attempt to deal productively with the historical dilemma of immanence and transcendence" (Jameson 1991: 191–92). Heidegger's "philosophy of Being" is impugned by Adorno, in his *Negative Dialectics,* as "Unsuccessful Realism": "When we believe we are, so to speak, subjectlessly clinging to the phenomenality of things, are original and neo-realistic and at the same time doing justice to the material, we are in fact eliminating all definitions from our thought, as Kant once eliminated them from the transcendental thing-in-itself" (1990: 79). Realist ontology is thus an invalid, retrogressive, and counter-Enlightenment step behind Kant. In musical terms, there must remain a degree of subjective mediation in the *Missa*, otherwise the work of art would degenerate into a pile of fragments. The problem, for Adorno the musicologist, was how to prove this analytically.

More than anywhere else, the *Missa* essay is the place where Adorno is confronted and defeated by the problem of music analysis. He has something to prove: that Beethoven's ontology is not as unmediated as he thinks it is in Heidegger (and Stravinsky), yet this is a claim which remains for Adorno, with deep irony, *a pledge of faith.* The "puzzle," for Adorno, is that the *Missa Solemnis* is "enigmatic" and "incomprehensible" (142), yet it is largely in a "traditional musical idiom [which] does not fall within the stylistic category of the late Beethoven." Unlike the authentically "late" quartets, for example, the mass does not have "edges and fissures" (144). Since the "lateness" of the mass is not apparent in its technical detail, Adorno surmises that it is buried in its "content." If this "lateness" is spiritual, rather than technical, how can it ever be analyzed, demonstrated? Perhaps Adorno means that, rather than being the great exception, the *Missa Solemnis* is really the extreme case which proves the "nonanalyzability," as it were, of Beethoven's *entire* late style (and, if pushed, of all music too)?

And yet Adorno is adamant that the *Missa Solemnis,* despite "appearances" (in the loaded sense of that word) really *does* promise the possibility of "salvation" (148). The fact that such "salvation" can neither be envisaged politically nor demonstrated analytically opens Adorno to the accusation—standard with "second-generation" critical theorists—that his aesthetics really amounts to a negative theology (see Geuss 1998: 314).

How to Read Adorno for Musicology

"The real problem," surmises Adorno in fragment 282, "is to resolve this allegorical element. The complex precedes all technical and stylistic questions, which have to be determined and solved with reference to it" (136). Adorno means that aesthetic insights precede, and guide, analysis, a claim hardly objectionable in itself. The "real problem," surely, is Adorno's "take" on analysis, or, more broadly, hermeneutics. Hermeneutics seeks enlightenment within rather than against historical tradition and interpretational frameworks, positivities which critical theory likes to transcend or negate. And yet, even when we avail ourselves of the enormous advances in Classical scholarship and analytical method since Adorno's day, his ideas cannot be simply "translated" point against point into empirical data, for reasons identified in chapter 1. A more circumspect approach is required, respecting the protocols of each space. The following three chapters, in many ways the heart, *Durchbruch,* and "center" of my book, provide three broadly Adornian illuminations of Beethoven's late works. The approach is Adornian because it draws together the following concepts, concerns, and insights from his writings:

1. Aesthetic categories such as *Schein, Durchbruch,* caesura, and parataxis;
2. A historical model of musical style directed to the tensions of material;
3. A dialectical perspective on thought, oriented toward the circulation of categories rather than their synthesis;
4. A ternary model of style as an interaction of music's semblance to language, reason, and nature.

My major gambit will be to raise Styles 1, 2, and 3, the categories considered in chapter 2, to a level of systemic conceptual metaphor. Chapter 4 gives an overview of the late style by mapping it as a "landscape"—Adorno's main metaphor in his *Spätstil Beethovens* essay. Viewing the music as a landscape generalizes the natural categories of Style 3. Chapter 5 moves on to the "invisible cities" of the late sonata forms, focusing on the systematic and dialectical contexts afforded by complete single movements. In its emphasis on sonata convention, the chapter builds on Style 1. Finally, chapter 6 expands the range to consider whole works, to explore how cyclical unity projects compositional ideas. Its ideational focus is in the spirit of Style 2. This nesting of ideas within forms within nature also follows the venerable footsteps of Hegel's *Logic,* in its spiraling journey from immediacy through mediation to completed subjectivity; from Being through Essence to the Concept. Of course, this apparatus is never more than a heuristic; Hegel and Adorno retreat into the roles of guides in the spirit world, letting music go her own way. And it may be useful to refer occasionally to this abbreviated glossary of Adornian terms:

Allegory: Objectification of musical material, releasing expressive attributes of convention. A critique of symbolic "harmony" results in a breaching of textural unity and formal continuity.

Apparition: The flash of insight when we grasp the mediated character of musical events, understand the continuity between structure and genesis, or "see" particularity hitherto subsumed in convention. Also the dynamic modality of *Schein:* a coming *into* appearance.

Caesura: Intervention of the composer's subjectivity or of extreme "natural" expression. A formal turning point, but also a normative punctuation mark for Classical phrasing. Caesuras are agents of fragmentation, cutting musical reality at the joints.

Constellation: The loose and dynamic arrangement of ideas, concepts, objects or musical materials as a mobile. Beethoven's late works are a constellation.

Dialectic: Not a rigid ternary schema, but a mode of argument based on oppositional thinking and self-reflection. It entails negation, a process geared to reversing starting points, overcoming resistance, and subsuming both natural and conventional categories within a holistic process. The epitome of dialectic is the Classical sonata.

Durchbruch: A breakthrough, or eruption, of the repressed, which can be subjectivity, nature, particularity, or the historically archaic (Baroque parataxis, Classical articulation, heroic rhetoric).

Floskel: An ossified cliché; also a dynamic gesture/contour of subjective withdrawal.

Mediation: Not the reconciliation of opposites, but the grounding of style in cultural and historical forces, the dynamic interrelation of part and whole in musical structure, and the mediation (*Vermittlung*) of abstract ideas through concrete musical material.

Mimesis: On the one hand, natural or immediate expression, a world of gestures, contours, intonations, and dimensional schemata. On the other, a mimicking of its opposite: rationality and language, respectively as musical argument ("concept character") and articulation ("language character"). Stylistically, Baroque, Classical, and heroic can be mimetic relative to each other.

Moment: A temporal instant or a part of an argument. An aesthetic of the moment is geared to the instantaneous or explosive detail. Although fragmentary, moments mediate, and often summarize, the whole.

Negative dialectic: A suspension of synthesis, yet within a system oriented toward synthesis. With the withdrawal of the middle, material is polarized into categorical extremes, which interact without closure. Associated with the critique of the Classical style, and its deconstruction into oppositional parameters.

Parataxis: An umbrella term for repetitive, chainlike, nondialectical discourse. Both archaic and utopian in outlook, it is associated with Baroque idioms of counterpoint, ritornello, and variation.

Rückung: A harmonic shift or pivot progression in place of a functional modulation or resolution, common in Beethoven's late music.

Schein: The surface illumination of a musical work, and the irreality (semblance) of this surface, eliciting a *Durchbruch* or *Apparition* of depth. Yet also the collapse of surface and depth into each other. This oscillation of surface and depth is the model for the "flicker" of all aesthetic oppositions, and the interplay of all categories, including all the above.

4 Late Landscapes

OVERVIEW OF THE MUSIC

Durchbruch—Breakthrough; eruption; return of the repressed; resurgence of - subjectivity, nature, the particular, the archaic, the utopian; a structural breach; broken texture; impulse to obbligato style; catastrophe; revolution.

Beethoven wrote his last bagatelle, according to Adorno, "in the midst of the hardest rock strata of the multivocal landscape" (Adorno 1998a: 124–25). The *Spätstil Beethovens* essay paints a bracing picture of the music as a barren, volcanic world, pitted with abysses and craters, a metaphor he actually introduced nearly a decade earlier (1928) in his youthful essay on Schubert, where it is obviously inspired by the lyrics of *Winterreise* and famous settings of Goethe poems such as *Grenzen der Menschheit*.[1] Adorno's traveler steps out "from an extruded, still-cooling crater, becoming aware of skeletal shadows of vegetation in the midst of lava formations in these exposed, broad peaks" (Adorno 1998b, vol. 17: 18). The music-as-landscape metaphor was a Romantic stock in trade (see Rosen 1996: 116–237; Hoeckner 2002: 51–114); currently, music theory models the piece as a journey through tonal or formal "space," configured as a lattice of key relations or structural functions. In the present chapter, viewing the late style as a landscape is principally an expository conceit to help sketch out the topography of Beethoven's music prior to homing in on complete movements in chapter 5. Looming over this landscape is the biggest work Beethoven composed, and the one he thought was his best—"l'oeuvre le plus accompli" (in Adorno 1998a: 143). The *Missa Solemnis* dominates the early part of his late period, as much as its companion piece, the Ninth Symphony, casts its light over the music after 1824. This is why it is customary to divide up the late style into two periods; the first, 1816–1823, encompassing the mass, the last five sonatas, the bagatelles Op. 119, and the *Diabelli* Variations; the second, 1824–1827, embracing the symphony, the bagatelles Op. 126, and the last five quartets. There is the question of whether these two periods belong to a single style at all. And there is Adorno's vexing charge that the mass and the symphony fall out of the late style altogether, as "late work without late style" (1998a), as pastiches of dead languages, respectively the archaic and the revolutionary-heroic. Adorno seldom discusses the concept of "style" proper, but he speaks in the *Missa* essay of "stylization," and of authentic style as an idiom which retreats inwards or into the distance. In the *Missa Solemnis*, "the style and tone, *despite all the stylization*, withdraws toward something unexpressed, undefined" (149, my emphasis); the work has "a distanced, silhouettish character" (153). Landscape is defined negatively, as a surface of petrified stylization, out of which true style occasionally erupts, like magma. The cycle of style and stylization is imagined like that of molten and cooling rock.

We should take Adorno's notion of "late work without late style" in its full context, and in the spirit of his frequent dictum that the truth lies in the extremes, rather than in the middle. The extremes of the style are staked out by the mass at one end, and the piano miniature, or bagatelle, at the other. It was at these extremes that Beethoven touched the *Zeitgeist* most directly, rather than with the Classical genres of the sonata, quartet, or symphony. By the 1820s, these genres were already dated. On the other hand, the lyric piano piece would become the favored idiom of Schumann, Chopin, and Liszt, and the oratorio enjoyed a new currency on the back of several developments: the rediscovery of ancient music (the Bach and Palestrina revival), the awakening of nationalist feeling around institutionalized choral singing, and the peculiar role historicism played in the German Romantic imagination (see Garratt 2002). So the extremes meet, and allowing for absolute differences of scale and genre, the futuristic bagatelle and the archaic mass entail surprisingly similar formal strategies. Both the bagatelle set and mass are loosely constructed hybrids, being suites of movements which are self-contained yet co-dependent. With this looseness, the technical entailments of the landscape metaphor come into focus. These works have a decentered quality, suggesting a rolling horizon and the act of wandering from one staging post to the next, after the prototype of Beethoven's song cycle *An die ferne Geliebte*. To wander is not to develop, but to view the same scene through changing, or shifting, perspectives. Conversely, composition approaches the Baroque ethos of *inventio*, by which creativity consists not so much in the creation as the *discovery* of material with properties which can be presented from various angles (see Dreyfus 1998). Late Beethoven's Baroque turn consequently extends not just to his fugues and variations, but to his habit of repeating his material, modified, as wholesale chunks or ritornellos. To compose is to explore the hidden spaces and interstices of the material. Musical material is simply "out there," like an object of nature, to be picked up as an *objet trouvé*. Baroque also is the way this material is objectified—*stylized*—into living fossils, from which subjectivity periodically breaks through, recalling Benjamin's theory of allegorical expression as "the conflict between the cold, facile technique and eruptive expression" (1998: 175). Adorno's seminal notion of *Durchbruch* is thus a corollary of his landscape metaphor.

The metaphor of landscape also illuminates the loose connections *between* the works, and even the fuzzy identity of the work concept itself. The late works cluster as constellations with family resemblances, although Deryck Cooke (1963) probably goes too far in calling the last five quartets a unified cycle. Finally, we can think of a huge work like the mass as a kind of landscape in its own right, with many of the concurrent works nestling in its enclaves. This is not entirely a conceit: turning to page 35 of Kinderman's transcription of the sketchbook Artaria 195, we see that Beethoven interrupted work on the Credo of the mass to sketch what became his E-major Piano Sonata, Op. 109 (Kinderman 2003). The sonata is dominated by a "technique of parenthetical enclosure" (Kinderman 1995: 233), the formal isolation of a lyrical interlude by faster outer sections, which Kinderman discovers in many of the late works. The sketch for Op. 109 is interpolated into the start of a draft of the Incarnatus, itself a "parenthetical enclosure" between the Allegro panels of the Credo. The three-fold homology is irresistible—a sonata "about" parenthesis, parenthetical within the mass, at the parenthetical Incarnatus.

More broadly, the mass is a quarry for those metaphorical image schemata we began to explore in chapter 2. The eruptive *Durchbruch* predicates a SURFACE-DEPTH schema, while "parenthetical enclosure" is based on a schema of IN-OUT. Third, the mass is bursting with UP-DOWN schemata of musical contour allied to the theological dialogue between God and man, soaring to "coelum" and plummeting to "terra." Recent critics of the mass such as Birgit Lodes have paid particular attention to how Beethoven harnesses the liturgical imagery in order to dramatize these dimensional concepts (Lodes 1998). We can turn on its head Adorno's criticism of the mass as being an archaic anomaly, and recognize it as a progressively free realm of archetypes, an idealized landscape in which Beethoven could rehearse schematic oppositions of space and motion. The mass establishes late landscape as a generalized Style 3, a style of petrified, allegorical nature. These schemata are particularly prominent in the Credo, in conjunction with the text setting's tone pictures.

A SURFACE-DEPTH schema is suggested by the occasional breakthrough of the mass's broad D-major tonality through the Credo's "surface" key of Bb. For instance, the collapse of the Eb-major "visibilium omnium" into the D-minor "et in visibilium" (mm. 28–33), immediately followed by the Eb head motif, correlates the visible/invisible opposition with a suggestion of D being a hidden key, or the global tonic. An IN-OUT schema is borne out by the Credo's ternary form, with the central section (the incarnation, crucifixion, and burial) unfolding three tonalities of D-Dorian, major, and minor. As well as confirming the breakthrough of this "background" tonic, the central Adagio also conveys the sense of journeying "inwards" to witness the mystery of Christ's earthly story. The parenthesis is framed by two F-major chords, at mm. 123 and 200; the common tone A becomes the pivot into D-Dorian at m. 124, and the orchestral sonority is recaptured at "coelum" at m. 200. Finally, liturgical metaphors of contour are the most venerable of all, as Kirkendale has shown (1970). This central section is flanked by the traditional falling and rising scales, indicating a descent to earth followed by a rise to heaven. As we saw for Op. 132, Beethoven reduces musical material to its conceptual fundamentals only as a means of then challenging them—turning our notions of time and space literally inside out and upside down. Of all the late works, the mass does this the most frankly. Is the central section really only a parenthesis? After the Incarnatus's hazy modal beginnings, the crystallization of D major with "et homo factus est" is tonally the first arrival point of the movement, and humanistically the most sympathetic. Regarding contour, there are intrinsic contradictions in our received associations of descending lines with resolutions, and ascending progressions with mounting tension—a gravitational metaphor enshrined in so much Western theory. After all, the drama pivots on the turn from the snaky chromatic

Example 4.1. Melodic cruxes in *Missa Solemnis,* Credo
    a. Opening, mm. 1–3
    b. Mixolydian ascent, mm. 17–22

descent of "et sepultus" to the joyous ascent "in coelum." Which is our goal, earth or heaven? The theological choice underpins the most characteristic gesture of the Credo, an oft-repeated rising scale to a top Bb, usually in conjunction with a Mixolydian seventh (Ab) or a local modulation to Eb—both of which confirm the piece's subdominant orientation (see Fink 2001: 108–13). Late Beethoven favors scale degree 6̂ for his melodic cruxes; a climax on an upper octave creates the paradox of a closure which is extremely tense, because so hard to sing. At its outer boundaries, the Credo is framed by a variant of this pun, which becomes especially characteristic in many of the late works, involving the identification of scale degrees 6̂ and 3̂, or the melodic crux and the primary note (ex. 4.1a, b, c).

The movement's first climax, at m. 21, is in Eb, with a new melody pivoting on a G (see ex. 4.1b). Beethoven has tonicized the subdominant flourish which opened the Credo (ex. 4.1a), converting the high G from a tense 6̂ to a stable 3̂. The same illusion haunts the Credo's ultimate climax, the overwhelming blaze of Eb sonority at the end of the fugue, mm. 420–24, which trumpets the G on "saeculi," stabilized

Example 4.1. Melodic cruxes in *Missa Solemnis,* Credo
   c. Climax of "et vitam venturi" fugue, mm. 416–22

as a $\hat{3}$ above a tonicized subdominant (ex. 4.1c). The earth tilts to the subdominant, up-ends the crux, we float free, curiously weightless, and then the coda's scales run up and down like a Jacob's ladder.

The Agencies and Dimensions of Landscape

If Beethoven's late music is a landscape, what then is the subject which navigates it? In accord with late allegory, a curious inversion occurs, by which it is the landscape which moves, while the subject becomes reified. Benjamin writes that the function of "allegorical personification" is "not the personification of things, but rather to give the concrete a more imposing form by getting it up as a person." Ultimately, this "thing" is the natural world: "The whole of nature is personalized, not so as to be made more inward, but, on the contrary—so as to be deprived of a soul" (Benjamin 1998: 187). On the one hand, the compositional idea of a work can be a chunk of tonality, such an interval cycle or a cadential model.

For example, one of late Beethoven's favorite thematic types is simply an alternation of thirds and fourths, the building blocks of a harmonic progression, as in the opening of Op. 110 (ex. 4.2):

Example 4.2. Piano Sonata in A♭, Op. 110, first movement, mm. 1–4

On the other hand, the music's ideational level becomes objectified into palpable gestalts. A developmental process which, in the heroic style, can hardly be pinned down congeals into archetypal contours and gestures, such as late Beethoven's favorite melodic shape: the arch. The subject consequently splits into a "material" and "ideational" dimension; in Op. 110 it is as much an interval cycle as a schematic arch contour. Contours exist in all music, of course, and Beethoven's arches reflect a tendency in Romantic music toward gross formal and textural contrasts (see Meyer 1997). The difference is that Beethoven's contours rhyme with, and distil the essence of, the Classical tonal progressions on which they supervene. For instance, it is no accident that Beethoven's arches typically apex on the sixth degree (F in Op. 110), because the submediant plays a special role in the tonal landscape, both on the level of the phrase and the movement as a whole (which often modulates to the submediant *key*). In fact, I shall argue, following Daniel Harrison's dualist harmonic theory, that scale step 6̂ is an "agent" (i.e., representative) of the *subdominant,* chord IV (1994: 45).

One might well think of contours as the "ghosts" of tonality, so that the ideational is the ghost of the material. Other materials have their own ghosts, again following trends in nineteenth-century music. Beethoven objectifies harmony into tonal models, such as the I–IV–V–I cadential pattern. Materially, the progression is manipulated as a neoclassical shell, frequently with its pitches abstracted and played against each other. Ideationally, Beethoven gets beneath the skin to the shape of the model as an alternation between stability and tension. For example, chord IV can be treated less as a harmony in itself than as a functional auxiliary to the dominant, in which case it is substitutable with other auxiliaries, such as II⁷ and VI. The same with form. Materially, Beethoven keeps faith with the structures and genres of the Classical style, most importantly sonata form. From an ideational standpoint, however, these forms are reduced into schematic ABA ternary or ritornello patterns, typically an alternation of dynamic and lyrical materials (Kinderman's "parenthetical enclosures"). As with form, so with texture. Beethoven preserves the stratified Classical scheme based on a functional differentiation of melody, bass, and inner parts. Conversely, texture is treated as "contrapuntal" in the broadest sense, meaning a free interplay not just of polyphonic voices, but of the musical parameters themselves—absolute pitch, melodic interval, scale step, rhythmic duration, etc. Hence parameters or dissonances which are normally subsumed within the Classical scheme break through to the surface, or foreground. Beethoven's ghosts thus float within the material landscape in three directions. Contours arch; forms wax into lyrical parentheses; textures are overcome by contrapuntal breakthroughs. Curiously, the marked term in all three of these processes tends to be associated with the expressive or archaic, even with the subdominant. Music theory has traditionally had difficulty explaining IV as anything other than an adjunct to V, given the priority of the I–V–I tonal model. Chord IV thus becomes a token of the irrational or the archaic, which is why it exerts such a strong gravitational pull on late works like the mass. As Lodes argues, in the mass the subdominant, often allied with modality (e.g., the Mixolydian), is a symbol for the Deity or the Absolute (see also Kinderman 1985). Taken together, the material and ideational subjects can be listed as follows:

Melody: a. *Interval cycles.* Melodies are polarized into mechanical interval
           cycles, which map out cross-sections of tonality.
           b. *Contour.* Beethoven likes to polarize melodic contour into an
           arch peaking on scale degree 6̂.
Harmony: a. *Cadential models.* Beethoven reduces harmonic material to its
           essential oppositions, typically between chords I, IV, and V.
           b. *Dynamic functions.* A reduction of harmony to the alternation
           of stability and tension.
Texture: a. *Stratified.* The melody/bass frame is enshrined.
           b. *Parametric.* Texture is atomized into a free "counterpoint" of
           musical parameters.
Form: a. *Generic.* Beethoven reifies Classical and Baroque schemes such
           as sonata and fugue.
           b. *Absolute.* Musical form is simplified into ABA ternary or paratactic chain forms such as variation and ritornello.

Transformations

A late work ends up revisiting its starting point with its premises transformed. These circular, or spiral-like, journeys through late landscape turn change into a matter of shifting perception: the illuminating *Apparition.* Late transformations are as schematic as their objects. Given that Beethoven polarizes his material into oppositions, the oppositions can be reversed. And since each of the processes is cyclic, reversal is achieved simply by displacing the cycle so as to foreground the marked, rather than the unmarked, stable term. An interval cycle can be parsed in several ways. In Op. 110 the opening theme stresses falling thirds, while the finale fugue brings out the rising fourths. A melodic arch can be displaced so as to oscillate between two apexes, rather than two bases; that is, ending on a peak rather than a trough, as happens at m. 4 of Op. 110. A cadential model can stress the tense or auxiliary harmonies, rather than the tonic, as obtains again in Op. 110, which is weighted toward the cluster-like sonorities of m. 4. The II^7/IV auxiliaries overflow into the cadence, telescoping subdominant and dominant chords into each other as a dominant-ninth complex. Formally, late Beethoven likes to lift out the parenthetical lyric moment and place it center stage, as in the theme of Op. 110, which is weighted toward its climactic cadenza. The triumph of lyricism on the final page of this sonata is hinted at here. Texturally, the phrase flows from homophony to more independent part writing, from limpid consonance to luxurious dissonance. Although the end of the phrase is technically unstable, the trajectory of a late work celebrates such dissonances as ends in themselves.

The course of a late work is thus elegantly simple. After reducing musical material to its basic oppositions, it then reverses the relationship between these oppositions, turning black into white, negative into positive, marked into unmarked. In schematic terms, the three dimensions of the musical landscape are interchanged: up becomes down, inside becomes out, under becomes over. We thus come to the third of Beethoven's dialectical flips: that of natural categories themselves. Having "subjectivized" landscape, so that it seems to move, and "objectivized" subjectivity, so that it appears to stand still, he then transforms the categories of musical space into each other. In this way, late Beethoven keeps true to the Enlightenment doctrine of human freedom hard won through transcendence of nature, yet also *within* nature. Beethoven ultimately overcomes his landscapes, paradoxically by seeming to yield to them through spiritual abnegation (see Hatten 1994: 59–63). This *fantastic* nature of Beethoven's landscape, its transcendence of the physical laws of space, time, and gravity, is in line with the magical worlds of much early-nineteenth-century literature and philosophy, such as the novels and fairy tales of Novalis (see Birrell 1979), the plays of Tieck (see Szondi 1986), and the Romantic irony of Friedrich Schlegel (see Behler 1993; Longyear 1970). A further analogue is the dialectical twists of Hegelian logic itself, particularly the ins and outs of *Schein* and *Erscheinung*. Finally, schematic reversal is a token not only of Beethoven's freedom—of how to compose material—but also of our own—how to *hear* it, and this brings me back to the notion of metaphorical "hearing as" which I developed in my earlier book (Spitzer 2004). Beethoven teaches us how to hear an apex "as" a base, a subdominant "as" a tonic, a parenthesis "as" a frame, and a dissonance "as" a consonance. The act of musical perception is thereby endowed with an almost theological dimension, so that a technical gestalt shift becomes a transfigurative act, a source of revelation: *Apparition*.

Melody

Arch Contours

In the nineteenth and early twentieth centuries, the notion of musical contour was associated with Goethe's biological theory of *Steigerung*, with its blended connotations of "intensification," "ascent," "growth," and "spiritual development" (Spitzer 2004: 294–95). While the life of a plant was in principle cyclical, oscillating between the seeds in the ground and the seeds in the blossom, *Steigerung* is in practice a one-way process; that is, a rise is *not* balanced by a symmetrical descent, *pace* the gravitational metaphor enshrined in Schenker's *Urlinie*. The asymmetry of arches cannot be emphasized too strongly. It tallies with Meyer's theory of a "statistical climax," where "the arrival at a tensional 'highpoint' [is] followed by a usually rapid decline in activity" (1972: 119), and with Zohar Eitan's empirical experiments. Eitan finds that up is not quite the opposite of down in musical space, since each stresses different kinetic and spatial associations:

> Pitch "descent" is more strongly associated with vertical direction than pitch "ascent." Pitch ascent, however, is significantly related to change in distance (moving away) and velocity, while pitch descent is significantly associated with neither. (Eitan and Granot 2003)

Melodic rises, then, are more richly coded than falls, perhaps in compensation for their weaker association with verticality. Whatever the reason, this asymmetry is borne out by the "sawn-off" nature of Beethoven's arches. The introductions to the three "Galitzin" Quartets all begin with such melodies. Op. 127 in E♭ rises to a fermata on C; Op. 130 in B♭ ascends to G; Op. 132 in A minor climbs to F. Moreover, in each case the arch to $\hat{6}$ is projected onto the movement's tonal architecture. Although the second group of Op. 127 is ostensibly in G, Beethoven actually defers arrival to the middle of the development, to a ritornello in C. Op. 130 modulates more frankly to its flat submediant, G♭, and Op. 132 is equally clearly directed to F major. Nevertheless, by no means all, or even the majority, of the late works begin with an arch to $\hat{6}$, or modulate to the submediant. In many cases, arches are disguised.

The $\hat{3} = \hat{6}$ Arch

The most concise example of such disguised arches occurs in Op. 109. Many critics interpret the piece as an arch to $\hat{5}$, the dominant. In this respect, the work is a perfect example of an asymmetrical, "sawn off," arch. The first movement rises from its opening G♯ to an A♯ at m. 8, on the way to the B of the dominant key. This B is interrupted by the cadenza-like "parenthetical enclosure" of the Adagio espressivo, before being realized at m. 16 with the resumption of the Vivace material. The development gradually raises the B a further octave to a climax at m. 42. This top B covers the reprise at m. 48, and although the register collapses to its original octave four measures later, the B is implicitly suspended in midair. Beethoven never resolves it back to the original G♯ by step via the requisite A♮ passing note. The movement ends, in m. 97, emphasizing B, not G♯. We have known, since Allen Forte's *A Compositional Matrix* (1961), that the G♯–A♯–B–A♮–G♯ arch figures in Beethoven's sketches. Nicholas Marston observed that Beethoven had originally experimented with resolving the arch with a complementary A–G♯ descent in the reprise and coda, and then decided to leave the movement open-ended (Marston

1995: 75–80). The top B famously returns at the climax of the variations finale, m. 175, drops to the seventh of the dominant, and is resolved by the G♯'s of the Thema on its da capo. Nevertheless, this resolution happens far too late to alter the shape of the sonata, which is dominated by a suspended B arching across the entire work.

A crucial subtlety of the arch is that it has not one but two apexes. Although the Adagio espressivo interrupts the rise to B at m. 9, this section cannot be simply disregarded (as in Marston). Rather, the Adagio pivots on a reinterpretation of the G♯ primary note as a 6̂ of the new key (ex. 4.3):

Example 4.3. Piano Sonata in E, Op. 109, first movement, mm. 1–16
Continues on the next page

Example 4.3. Piano Sonata in E, Op. 109, first movement, mm. 1–16

The diminished-seventh chord at m. 9 substitutes for VI (G♯) of B major, as part of a VI–II–V–I cadential pattern; the melodic A♮ really covers for a G♯, to which it resolves. In short, the peak of the arch is G♯, the submediant of B major. The music rises, paradoxically, from one G♯ (m. 1) to another (m. 10), from G♯ as $\hat{3}$ to G♯ as $\hat{6}$. The reinterpretation of the primary note as $\hat{6}$ of the new key ($\hat{3} = \hat{6}$) is a common device in Haydn and Mozart, where it helps to mediate the transition to the second group in sonata-form expositions. Thus Beethoven's procedure is grounded in convention. But Beethoven bends it to his late agenda, where the convention serves some radical purposes. The G♯ ($\hat{3}$) to G♯ ($\hat{6}$) arch suggests an interchange of base and apex, of "up" and "down," of modulation and return. And since the G♯ apex actively interrupts (via A♮) the expected climax on B, the music projects a collision between $\hat{6}$ and $\hat{5}$. It is better, then, to speak of a "counterpoint" of arches, as we saw in the introduction to Op. 132, where a tonic arch, flexing to F, alternates with a dominant arch, peaking on C—the primary note. Another spectacular example of the $\hat{3} = \hat{6}$ interchange is the transition of Op. 110, which elaborates the arching contour of mm. 1–4, except that it pushes up to the stratosphere of Beethoven's piano, the top C of m. 20. This C initiates the descent of the second group and is a transparent analogue of the F at m. 4, while also representing, in voice-leading terms, a massive registral transfer of the piece's opening C. Even more clearly than Op. 109, the modulation stakes out a rise between the same pitches at different octaves, disposed as $\hat{3}$ and $\hat{6}$.

Intervals

Underlying many of the late melodies are mechanical intervallic cycles. Beethoven exploits the structural as well as affective properties of the different intervals: fifths are the most open and consonant; minor seconds the most dissonant; cycles alternating thirds and fourths the most dynamic and sequential; third cycles potentially the most disruptive.

Fifths and Seconds

The *Arietta* melody captures a simplicity emblematic of one extreme of Beethoven's language, a quality it owes to the fourths and fifths of its opening. The melody is kindred with the theme of the "Diabelli" Variations, and both correspond to a type Meyer calls the "Adeste Fidelis" schema, after the hymn tune (Meyer 1997: 266).

At the other extreme, Beethoven fashions melodies from minor seconds to create a melancholy or tragic mood reminiscent of the Baroque mourning topos. Seconds would appear distant from fifths, yet they are generally disposed as neighbors to $\hat{1}$ and $\hat{5}$, that is, as $\hat{7}$–$\hat{1}$ and $\hat{6}$–$\hat{5}$. Dualistic harmonic theory offers a reason for this complementarity: in a minor key, the descending semitone from the flat submediant to the dominant functions as a kind of leading note (Harrison 1994). More simply, Beethoven plays with the four semitones at the top of the descending harmonic minor scale. These are often arranged so as to profile the flat $\hat{6}$ as a melodic crux. The Adagio of Op. 110 does this by registrally isolating the G♭, dropping a diminished seventh to the A♮. In the introduction to Op. 132, the $\hat{6}$ is simply the highest note. The fugue subject of Op. 131 places the $\hat{6}$ below, but gives it durational and dynamic emphasis. The subject of the *Grosse Fuge*, unusually, is based not on this tetrachord but on the pitches of B–A–C–H. Even here, however, the contour pivots on the A♭–G crux.

Thirds and Fourths

The fugues from the Gloria and the Op. 110 sonata are the most sustained examples of a theme type which alternates thirds and fourths. Nevertheless, the cycle crops up in many other places, often disguised by passing notes. For instance, in the Dona of the mass (mm. 107–10), the cycle is completely scalar; the theme of the Finale of Op. 135 begins with four measures of the cycle presented intervalically, answered by a filled-in consequent phrase. Sometimes the cycle is irregular: the Maestoso of Op. 127 is broken by the rogue intervals of a sixth and a second (B♭–G–F).

Thirds and Sixths

A family of pieces in B♭ feature subjects based on descending-third cycles: the *Hammerklavier* fugue, the fugue on "et vitam venturi" from the Credo, and the first movement of Op. 130. Of all Beethoven's thematic patterns, the third cycle is the most mechanical, since it involves only a single interval (the "minor-seconds" cycle includes intervening intervals such as diminished sevenths [Op. 110], augmented seconds [Op. 131], and sixths [Op. 132]). Descending-third cycles are a common feature of the Classical style, as in the finales of Mozart's "Hunt" Quartet, K. 458, and Haydn's Symphony no. 88 (see Rosen 1972: 407–8). Late Beethoven is particularly drawn toward their *moto perpetuo* character as a driving force. Moreover, it is no accident that Beethoven's third cycles nearly always descend, since this is in line with the subdominant pull of the late style (the descent B♭–G–E♭ moves from I to IV). But thirds can also be a source of tension. Three consecutive major thirds trisect the octave into an augmented triad; although Beethoven rarely does this thematically, he clearly means us to hear the B♭–G♭–D–B♭ tonal scheme of Op. 130/I as related to the (mixed, i.e., major-minor) third cycles of the Allegro semiquaver figurations. The thirds of the *Hammerklavier* fugue are unstable in a different way. In descending from the B♭ (B♭–G–E♭–C–A–F), the subject (mm. 17–20) enchains an implicit subdominant harmony with a dominant seventh, both of which are dissonant; that is, the quarter notes B♭, G, and E♭ stake out chord IV, and the E♭ is then reinterpreted as the seventh of V. Paradoxically, although the subject *begins* on a tonic note, tonic harmony is consistently withheld. By contrast, the third cycle of the "et vitam venturi" fugue is shaped into a harmonious I–IV–V–[I] cadential model, as befits its stabilizing role at the end of the Credo.

Melodic Transformations

The A♭ fugue subject in Op. 110 discloses the intervallic cycle underlying the first movement and is itself inverted in its companion G-major fugue ("L'inversione della Fuga"). Beethoven prefers to transform his thematic patterns wholesale as blocks, rather than develop piecemeal motivic fragments, in a manner kindred with Baroque fugal practice. But the Baroque analogy is misleading, because the melodic profile in a fugue tends to be fairly consistent, whereas Beethoven transforms his patterns with a plasticity which foreshadows Liszt, Wagner, even Schoenberg. In fact, it was Schoenbergian acolytes such as Rudolph Réti and Hans Keller who first made us aware of the systematic nature of Beethoven's melodic practice: that is to say, cyclic transformation is just as striking in the *non*fugal movements. The process in Op. 110 is particularly rich, and could be chronicled exhaustively, but a couple of examples suffice. The archlike theme in mm. 1–4 of the first movement zigzags between falling thirds and rising fourths, and then descends by step. The second subject, from m. 20, reverses this pattern. It *begins* with a linear descent from a 6̂ of the new key, repeated, and then rises in a pattern of linear ascents and disjunct drops. From m. 28, the derivation from mm. 1–4 becomes transparent: a cycle of filled-in rising sixths (inverting the falling thirds) and falling fourths or fifths, G–E♭–B♭; D–B♭–E♭; E♭–C–F (inverting the rising fourths). The middle theme of the scherzo (an allusion to the folk song *Ich bin lüderlich*) transforms the pattern again into filled-in descending fourths and leaps of a sixth.

Contour and character, then, play an equally important role in the pattern; the narrative is driven just as much by whether the progressions are disjunct or linear, and by the ordering of the arch. Beethoven is endlessly resourceful in exchanging the functions of base and apex, flattening them out, inverting and retrograding the order. Clearly, a pattern which begins on a low point and rises to a climax outlines a different "drama" to one which *begins* on an apex and descends to a nadir. We can speak, therefore, of transformations of gesture as much as of interval cycle. Namely, we can track the story of a work such as Op. 110 in terms of whether sections or movements end with a "high point" or a "low point," and according to their scale-degree affiliations. For instance, the top C at m. 20 is an extreme dissonance, because a submediant, whereas the same pitch, at the very end of the sonata, is a transfiguring tonic culmination. Conversely, the protracted descent in the course of the first-movement development leads to the satisfying resolution of the reprise, whereas the sonata as a whole "bottoms out" in the tragic Adagios. Of course, intervallic and gestural transformations can often come together, as they do wonderfully at the climax of the Finale. At m. 201, Beethoven creates two gestalt shifts. The sforzatos on the first dotted quarter note of each measure displace the previous parsing of the cycle as a sequence of rising fourths (with the thirds as dead intervals). The pattern now switches to a cycle of falling thirds—the scheme, in fact, in the cycle's first-movement version—thus enabling the final C–A♭ gesture of mm. 209–13 to spark off an anagnoresis (dramatic recognition) of the sonata's falling-third incipit. At the same time, the passage diverts the natural, gravitational tendency of arches to descend. Through an act of sheer compositional will, Beethoven bends gravity so as to soar to "coelum." Something very similar happens with the third cycle of the Credo fugue (see ex. 4.1c above). At m. 402 (and again at 416), the cycle is liberated from its I–IV–V–I cadential straitjacket, so that it overshoots its target to climax on a resplendent subdominant. The blazing G at m. 406 is an apotheosis of the $\hat{6}$ apex which starts the Credo, reinterpreted now *as $\hat{3}$ of E♭*, in much the same way as the end of Op. 110 transfigures the submediant C apex of its first movement. Intervallic *Verklärung* is just the earthly face of gestural change.

Transformations may be staged as sudden illuminations—*Apparitions*—which let us "see" something in the material or the piece for the first time. Just as often, however, Beethoven may pace them as fluid transitions, as in the fugue from Op. 131, which takes its time reinterpreting the leading-note-to-tonic head motif as a homophonic appoggiatura. The exposition supports the neighbor note as a V–I cadence, a harmonic dynamic which is ultimately suspended at the A-major plateau of m. 63, where the G♯–A sounds against a tonic pedal. One can speak, if not of tragedy, then at least of "fate," insofar as the destiny of the fugue is wired as a trait of character into the subject: the head motif foretells a trajectory from counterpoint to homophony, and the sforzato crux on A predicts that the plateau will level off on the key of $\hat{6}$. In the fugue, this destiny unfurls seamlessly; in the sonata-form finale, it erupts as a *Durchbruch*.

Harmony

The tonal landscape may be navigated in two circles—the circle of fifths (C–G–D–A etc.) and the circle of thirds (C–A–F♯–D etc.). By conflating the two cycles as two axes of a lattice, it is possible to conceptualize the tonal universe as a grid of "tonal pitch space," an idea first proposed in 1739 by the mathematician L. Euler (see Lerdahl 2001: 43). Other grids are possible; for example, Lerdahl creates a chart of "chordal space" (57) by combining the "chord circle" (the diatonic circle of fifths) with the "common-tone circle" (chords a third apart sharing two common tones: e.g., C major and A minor share C and E). Lerdahl's chart reflects the venerable thesis that chord progressions be restricted by those intervals present in the major triad (Rameau's *corps sonore*), namely, the fifth and the third. Of these, the fifth is more important, because "root motion by fifths is basic to cadences and pervasive at all levels of tonal organization" (54).

It is against the background of pitch space that Beethoven's own tonal landscapes can be gauged, except that the late style, as we have seen, is unusual in absorbing harmonic cycles into its own language. We are witnessing not a figure against a landscape, but the landscape itself. Beethoven's objectification of tonal models is epitomized by the opening progression in the Kyrie of his mass (ex. 4.4). Riezler identified it as the mass's "germinal motive" (*thematischen Keim*) (Riezler 1936: 203), and Joel Lester's study of the sketches confirmed that this "Urmotif" was seminal in the work's compositional process (Lester 1970: 428–29). The Kyrie progression is unusually rich in blending at least three of Beethoven's favorite har-

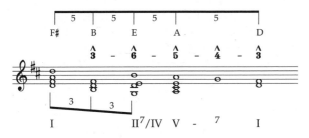

Example 4.4. Tonal model of Kyrie opening

monic schemes. Broadly speaking, it outlines a I–IV–V–I cadential pattern, with the E♮ at m. 5 giving the subdominant a supertonic seventh inflection, and the bass step D–G staked out as a third cycle D–B–G. Although these three strands are fused, they actually pull in different directions. The I–IV–V–I cadence is a well-formed tonal utterance, which projects the strong role of the subdominant in the mass. It is this IV which gets the 6̂ apex of the arch, the B, a note which is further emphasized by being approached by an F♯. Conversely, if we read the chord at m. 5 as a II⁷ rather than a IV, then this F♯ initiates a fifth cycle which pushes toward the A in m. 6—the real climax of the phrase. Either the phrase is directed toward the B or the A, a parallel to, and possibly even a source of, the 5̂/6̂ ambiguity we saw in Op. 109. Third, we can interpret the progression as a descending cycle of thirds: D–B–G, implicitly continuing to the E-minor harmony of m. 5, resolving into the A–D cadence. Although this cycle is cut short by the fifth step of the cadence, it is in principle open-ended and dynamic, as is realized in the many derived third progressions of the mass. As the work unfolds, these various tendencies go their separate ways, like branches radiating from a trunk. A more germane analogy, perhaps, is pathways splitting off from a central junction: the Kyrie progression sets up the harmonic landscape of the mass as a complex network of intersecting spaces. The progression charts the space of the mass, one could even say of the late style as a whole.

What the Kyrie progression does is throw up a set of ambiguities implicit within tonal relations, and which are arguably papered over when we seek to simplify the tonal landscape into grids and lattices. Ambiguities include the relationships between chords IV and II⁷, between I and VI, between IV and VI, between IV and V—all of which relate to the deeper tensions between the parameters of pitch and function. A late work explores the cracks and interstices of these harmonic relations. Beethoven's tonal journeys don't fly across the landscape, but prospect underground, as if with an infinitesimal microscope.

The "I–IV–V–I" Model

Looking again at the opening phrase of Op. 110, we see how it flows from the Kyrie's "source set." At first glance, it seems a straightforward I–IV–V progression. Nevertheless, as in the Kyrie, the subdominant is actually a II⁷ (the tenor-voice

Bb of m. 3), and the C–F (– [Bb]–Eb) in the bass suggests a similar fifths cycle. Mapping the model in terms of Classical pitch-space theory is problematic; whether we interpret the chord in m. 3 as a IV or a II^7, we are left with a tonal "seam" (see Lewin 1984) which contravenes the rule of root bass motion by fifths. If IV, then we have the step of IV–V; if II^7, then the equally problematic seam between I and II. Rameau's concept of "supposition" (underlying a hypothetical bass a third below the fundamental) was designed to get us out of this aporia (Christensen 1993). But reading the opening I as a VI, while setting up a satisfying fifths cycle VI–II–V, just shunts the problem left of field, for how then do we account for the work's off-tonic opening? Either way, we encounter an infinite regress. A similar set of questions arise when we consider the contour, or shape, of the harmony. The apex of the melody is the F of m. 3, yet how does this square with the common perception of subdominants as relaxing, compared to the tension of the dominant? Given that the Eb chord of m. 4 is the goal of the phrase, shouldn't the apex fall there? If mm.1–4 are a "tonal arch," flexing to a cadenza, then pitch and function aren't congruent with each other. The basic problem with 6̂, as we saw with Op. 132, is that it is a migrant step, capable of sounding against a range of harmonies—I, V, VII, VI, as well as IV.

Of course, what appear to be aporias for the theorist are just grist for the composer's mill. Beethoven exploits these very tensions for aesthetic effect; he even projects them onto the architecture of the movement. As IV–V, the progression initiates the arch contour which will peak at the climax of the modulation, m. 20. It enables Beethoven to rhyme the arch of the theme with the arch of the movement as a whole. As II^7–V, the progression encapsulates the modulation itself, insofar as the supertonic functions as a secondary dominant to Eb (the actual modulation, at m. 17, elaborates the melodic rise from C to Eb, but raises the passing note to a D♮, as part of a Bb^7 chord). The ambiguity thereby enables the theme to undertake precisely the two roles which seem irreconcilable: to prefigure both tonal motion and musical contour. Last, the affinity of I with VI is realized when F minor arrives at the start of the development section, confirming a gravitational pull toward the submediant which afflicts so many of Beethoven's late works (so, too, the F♯–B progression tucked within the Kyrie theme points to the keys of the Christe section). It is almost as if a VI–II–V–I fifth cycle lurks within the I–IV–V–I cadence as a kind of "shadow."

The "VI–II–V–I" Model

Compared to the I–IV–V–I model, the VI–II–V–I is unstable, both because of its cyclic nature and its off-tonic beginning. As a cycle, it threatens to tip over the tonic and continue to IV and VII, as it does in the recapitulation of Op. 130/I. The development of this movement is built upon a fifths cycle, which continues into the reprise, shunting it from Bb into Eb, Ab, and Db. The model's off-tonic beginning makes it particularly congenial to the open-endedness of Beethoven's late forms. Both finales of Op. 130 begin with this model, the *Grosse Fuge* and the rondo which Beethoven substituted for it. Tonally, the introduction to the fugue cycles from G major through C and F to the tonic B♭; the fugue subject itself enshrines this G–C–F–B♭ progression in its harmonies. Since Beethoven also begins the rondo replacement with this progression, the model was clearly of thematic importance in his mind. Interestingly, the rondo follows its opening statement of the model with a version as I⁷–IV–V–I (mm. 25–32), indicating the complementarity between the two progressions, as "stable" and "unstable" journeys through the same tonal space.

Harmonic Transformations

Transformations of a tonal model can take one or both of two interlinked paths. The progression may be displaced so as to reverse the functions of the initial and goal chord; or the pitches and tonal functions of the chord sequence may be abstracted from each other, and then thrown into conflict. Again, Op. 110 affords an excellent example of both. Taken as a group of pitches, the three chords which constitute mm. 1–4 (A♭, B♭⁷, E♭⁹) recur, in order, at the climax of the second group, mm. 31–32, but with the functions reversed (ex. 4.5):

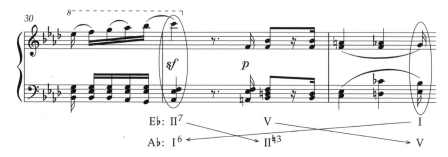

Example 4.5. Displaced tonal model in Op. 110, mm. 30–32

A♭ is transformed from a tonic to a II⁷ of the new key, and from a base to an apex: it supports the top C in the melody. Conversely, E♭ is tonicized (the harmonies on the first two beats of m. 32 are taken as passing from the dominant of the previous measure). And the B♭ chord of m. 31 gets a D♮ and loses its seventh. The reversal is achieved simply by transferring the F♮ from the end to the beginning—from the ninth of E♭ (as at m. 4) to sixth of A♭, turning this chord into an F-minor seventh. Beethoven means us to hear mm. 31–32 as a transformation of mm. 1–4 by planting unmistakable references to the dotted rhythms and semitone slide of the first subject. In this case, the transformation of the base chord into an apex harmony consists in a progressive darkening of the A♭ triad with "F-ness." The process unfolds in three main stages: at m. 20, A♭ becomes chord IV of E♭; at m. 31, chord II⁷; and the journey is completed at m. 40 of the development, when F is tonicized, and the theme is reinterpreted fully in F minor (the recapitulation takes things further, with an episode in F♭ major [= E major]).

Obviously, when a work *begins* with an unstable tonal model, such as the VI–II–V–I, the process has an opposite outcome—one of stabilization. Thus, in the first movement of Op. 130, the model which crystallizes in its two finales is only sketchily adumbrated in the Adagio introduction. It emerges into the light of day in the second half of the introduction, mm. 7 ff., and is reinforced in the development section, which consists of a mechanical fifths cycle, D–G–C–F–B♭. As we shall see in chapter 5, this "development" is, strangely, a point of stability, since Beethoven converts the cycle into a lyrical plateau. In any case, the development section is the VI–II–V–I model's rightful place, since by starting with it, Beethoven is recalling Haydn's favorite trick of beginning movements with a retransition (e.g., the VI–II–V–I of the Vivace assai of the "Surprise" Symphony, no. 94 in D).

The recurrence of pitch collections against the grain of a modulation or key change is implicit in Schoenberg's notion of "monotonality" ("According to this principle, every digression from the tonic is considered to be still within the tonality" [1969, 19]). This conflict between dynamic and static use of tonality is of absolutely central importance in Beethoven's late style—a tonal analogue of the interpenetration of sonata and variation. Nevertheless, Beethoven's most systematic analysis of a tonal model occurs without any modulation at all, in his "Diabelli" Variations. Measures 9–12 of the theme trace two fifth progressions a tone apart, C to F and then D to G, a harmonic cliché known as a *Schusterfleck* or "cobbler's patch" (ex. 4.6a–d):

Example 4.6. *Schusterfleck,* with transformations, in *Diabelli* Variations
    a. Theme, mm. 8–16

Example 4.6. *Schusterfleck,* with transformations, in *Diabelli* Variations
    b. Variation 4, mm. 7–15
    c. Variation 7, mm. 8–16
Continues on the next page

Example 4.6. *Schusterfleck,* with transformations, in *Diabelli* Variations
d. Variation 20, mm. 8–16

In the course of the variations, this model (ex. 4.6a) is dismantled and reassembled in bewildering permutations. In variation 4 (ex. 4.6b), the harmonic sequence is retrograded, descending from A minor to F major, and yet with the melody still rising from E to A, as in the original theme. This abstraction of pitch and contour from harmonic function is even more drastic in variation 7 (ex. 4.6c). Although the variation as a whole remains in C major, the *Schusterfleck* is raised a third, E–A–F#–B. Yet in spite of this transposition, the melody notes E–F–A and F#–G–B return, reordered, at original pitch in the bass. Variation 20 is the most abstract of all and achieves the seemingly impossible feat of transforming the original G-major triad of mm. 11–12 into a C major (ex. 4.6d). How can a dominant become a tonic? Moreover, this tonic—outwardly an utterly reasonable root-position C-major triad—is quite alienated, sounding stranger, and in some ways more "dissonant," than the diminished-seventh chord which precedes it.

Disregarding the content of the chords for the moment, the passage does make sense according to the linear logic of the bass's rise from the G of m. 9 to the D of m. 13. Surprising as it may be, by deferring the G-major resolution to m. 16, the variation is more coherent than the theme, which reaches G prematurely as part of its *Schusterfleck.* This had been one of the principal kinks in Diabelli's often-criticized theme, and the reason why earlier variations, such as 4 and 7, had absorbed the premature G into A minor. The G of m. 16 isn't just a tonal resolution; it marks the return of tonality itself, after six measures of quasi-atonal obfuscation. Remarkably, this process is staked out, *in nuce,* by the *Schusterfleck* itself. The first chords of mm. 9 and 10 are functionally deadened by their B♭'s but resolve to dominant sevenths of A minor; likewise, the first, chromatic, chords of 11 and 12 resolve to the dominant of F; the D of m. 13 supplies the last of the *Schusterfleck's* three dominants, of G. The three tonics of the *Schusterfleck's* sequence had been rearranged in previous variations (variation 4 ordered them as A–G–F); variation 20 merely takes things further, by representing the chords by their dominants alone, and by deadening the intervening steps.

Harmonic abstraction reaches its limit when the identity of a chord is defined entirely by context. Beethoven proves that in C major, a C triad can substitute for a G and be made to sound like an extreme dissonance. The broadest context for Beethoven is an overarching opposition between tonality and "nontonality." At the level of the measure (the pairs of chords in each of mm. 9–12), the phrase (the arrival of G at m. 16), and the piece (the return of diatonicism in Variation 21), harmony seems to "die" and then be "reborn." The metaphor is explicit in the central section of the Credo, from the "Crucifixus" and "Et sepultus est," which contains some of the late style's most dissonant harmonies (ex. 4.7).

The affinity with mm. 9–16 of variation 20 is striking. Although the section is broadly in D minor, the transition from the chromatic "Et sepultus" to the radiant G-major (Mixolydian) "Et resurrexit," mm. 182–88, is built on a descending fifth progression D–Db–C–Bb–Ab–G (a *rising* fifth G–D in the variation), and the local tonic is the C major of "Et ascendit." The music thus "falls" into chromatic abstraction before "rising" into functional harmony. Variation 20, the natural turning point of the set in most performances, is the "Et sepultus" of the *Diabelli,* marking the "burial" of harmony. In this respect, it is simplistic to associate abstraction solely with metaphorical elevation. Solomon, noting that "upward motion is present in virtually every variation," sees the cycle as "a metaphorical ascent from lower to higher [toward] an increasingly rarefied sphere" (2003: 189). While this might suit the very end of the cycle, in the case of variation 20 Solomon hits the mark with his analogy of "the landscape through which the Virgilian composer-performer-guide is escorting us" (186). The circles, or cycles, of abstraction must be *subterranean* in Adorno's Dantean volcanic landscape, prior to the ascent of any Purgatorial mountain.

Texture

The texture of the late landscape is cracked and fissured along the many fault lines of the style. What erupts, or breaks through, this carapace is *counterpoint,* defined in the broadest sense as interplay of parameters which fail to be subsumed by Classical function. It would be unhelpful to define "homophony" and "counterpoint" too rigidly, and to claim that the texture splits cleanly between the two, since these are gross terms for complex alloys which are subject to a seemingly ceaseless process of fission and fusion. On the one side, Beethoven certainly reifies the categories of Classical homophony, in the same way that he objectifies melodic and harmonic cycles. He enshrines the textural division of labor between melody, bass, and inner parts, articulated by a phrase structure organized by an equally conventionalized syntax of beginning, middle, and ending. Nevertheless, he "darkens" and "thickens" these categories, so that we look "at," rather than "through," Classical convention. Textural and cadential clichés which are normally so transparent that we seldom notice them are ossified into material which itself becomes the-

Example 4.7. *Missa Solemnis,* Credo, mm. 182–93
Continues on the next page

Example 4.7. *Missa Solemnis,* Credo, mm. 182–93

matic in the discourse. Beethoven achieves this through categorical displacements analogous to the cyclical displacements we reviewed earlier. For example, the functional and motivic dimensions of a line, typically a bass line, which normally coexist perfectly harmoniously in the "mixed" (or obbligato) textures of Haydn or Mozart, are thrown into interference patterns. Paradoxically, the outcome of such interference patterns is to objectify Classical categories even more powerfully—to "darken the glass," as it were. One might have expected the outcome to be not reification but a *dissolution* of Classical texture into the kind of mélange we see in much of Schumann's piano music (as in the opening of his *Fantasie,* Op. 17). Such textural entropy, however, marks the opposite, *ideational,* boundary of Beethoven's landscape, parallel with the tropics of melodic contour and harmonic abstraction. Just as melody rises, and harmony sinks into the cracks, texture sublimates into the ether. The lyrical/fugal mélange at the apotheosis of Op. 110 is emblematic for the trajectory of late textures. Technically speaking, it is a process of displaced "congruence," to borrow a term of Meyer's (1973: 81). When parameters such as pitch, harmony, and rhythm march in step to articulate a conventional device such as a Classical cadence, they are in a state of *congruence.* When a cadence is interrupted, harmony is *noncongruent* with pitch and rhythm. In line with the arch of the music, the many parameters which build up a theme or model gradually drift apart.

What, then, is "counterpoint"? The dramatic return of counterpoint in the late style actually figures in three separate guises. As a *material* texture, counterpoint is objectified in the same way as Classical textures. As an *ideational* texture, counterpoint is found in the "polyphonic," kaleidoscopic interplay of noncongruent parameters, in both fugal and Classical contexts. Third and most radical, "contrapuntal" describes the linear, heterogeneous quality of both fugal and Classical conventions when these are materially "thickened." When texture becomes linear, it resists assimilation into harmony, leading to a "counterpoint" of tonal perspectives. I call this effect "bifocality," and it comes in a textural and tonal form. Textural, as well as tonal, bifocality engage both Classical and Baroque categories. Bifocality is a dynamic oscillation, rather than a fixed state; it composes out *Schein*'s flicker.

Textural Bifocality

With its limpid textures and crisp phrasing, Op. 135 is an almost neoclassical exercise in reconstructing the idiom of Haydn and Mozart. The most interesting detail in the opening phrase is the eighth-note rest at measure 9, which interrupts an otherwise normative approach to the cadence, the I^6–IV–I^6_4–V progression (ex. 4.8). The cello is often the principal player in the Classical comedy, given its dual role as both bass and participant in the dialogue. The dialogue here is the swift exchange of the rising-third motive A–B♭–C between the upper instruments in mm. 5–8. When the cello enters at m. 8, it ostensibly carries the last entry of this dialogue, augmented into eighth notes. If the imitation had been literal, and if it had not been interrupted by the rest, then the texture would have been a perfect example of the Classical fusion of melodic and accompanimental roles in one voice, as in many of Haydn's quartets (e.g., Op. 33). However, the interruption, together with the slight rhythmic discrepancy, is enough to throw the two categories out of kilter, creating an interference pattern, so that the progression is neither melody nor bass, but an open-ended oscillation between the two. Equally dramatic is the effect on the I–IV–I^6_4–V progression itself, a cliché which is so conventional as to be transparent, even invisible. The interference pattern clouds it over, so that it suddenly becomes visible as distinctive material in its own right. Merely playing the convention loudly, or repeating it, would not have projected it so effectively. The illusion Beethoven discovers is that a convention becomes more noticeable, more "real," through being broken.

Beethoven applies bifocality also to Baroque textures. The textural drift toward noncongruence is intrinsic to the Baroque device of *Fortspinnung*, the florid tail which conventionally rounds off a theme. A fugue subject normally starts with a sharply profiled head and tails off into progressive diminutions and freer dissonances, which are then cut short by the next entry of the subject, and so on. This cycle of gradual entropy followed by sudden reclamation cleaves to the same contour as the fore-shortened arches of *Steigerung;* indeed, critics of *Steigerung,* such as Ernst Kurth, detected it as much in Baroque as in Romantic music (although much less so in Classic). The question is whether the *Fortspinnung* is indeed reassimilated. In late Beethoven it is not, leading to a problematic relation between the texture's linear and harmonic dimensions. This dissonance creates "linearity" of a higher order.

The tensions of the *Hammerklavier* fugue necessarily flow from the nature of its

Example 4.8. String Quartet in F, Op. 135, first movement, mm. 1–14

Example 4.9. Piano Sonata in B♭, Op. 106 (*Hammerklavier*), finale, mm. 16–49
Continues on the next page

subject (ex. 4.9). From a Baroque perspective, the subject is most anomalous on account of its overly long *Fortspinnung*. We know from the sketchbooks that Beethoven devised the subject in conjunction with those from the two B♭ fugues from Bach's *Das wohltempierte Klavier* (see Küthen 1980). Basically, Beethoven seems to have spliced the descending-third structure of the subject from book 2 (B♭–G–E♭–C) with the semiquaver *Fortspinnung* idea of the subject from book 1. Yet whereas

Example 4.9. Piano Sonata in B♭, Op. 106 (*Hammerklavier*), finale, mm. 16–49
Continues on the next page

Example 4.9. Piano Sonata in B♭, Op. 106 (*Hammerklavier*), finale, mm. 16–49

Bach's *Fortspinnung* is structurally and harmonically balanced (two measures to the second opening, and with a repeated V⁷–I progression resolving onto the answer of m. 5), Beethoven's trips into a different meter (a $\frac{2}{4}$ pattern starts from the stressed second beat of m. 20, ultimately suggesting a $\frac{6}{4}$ hemiola cross-meter to the fugue's $\frac{3}{4}$) and then trails off into eccentrically chromatic figuration. The upshot of the comparison is that Beethoven's subject is more dissonant than Bach's; it is harder to subsume the semiquavers into a harmonic region. This is curious, since the head of the subject, climaxing with the stressed F of m. 20, emphatically sets up a V⁷ harmony (the descent from the E♭ in the previous measure outlines this chord). Perversely, although the *Fortspinnung* is introduced as a perfectly normal elaboration of a V⁷ progression (as in Bach's), it *fails* to keep to this frame. The misfit between figure and frame, or counterpoint and harmony, widens in future entries. At m. 31, the eighth notes of the countersubject can be heard as outlining either a tonic or a dominant, depending on where we infer the stress. If we hear the stress on the first eighth note of each pair, the figures continue the V⁷ established in the preceding measure; alternately, we can take them as accented passing notes within a tonic harmony. With the next entry of m. 36, the *Fortspinnung* is elaborated even further, almost doubling its length from six to eleven measures. Although it clearly begins (m. 39) and ends (m. 49) on a V⁷, it is difficult to hear the intervening passing chromatic harmonies in this context. Beethoven takes the definition of the subject to the brink of collapse and uses the *Fortspinnung* as a growth point for the fugue's centrifugal, entropic, tendency. It is the nature of fugue that this tendency is repeatedly reined in by reentries of the subject, creating a rhythm of successive dissolution and clarification across the work. This cycle is compounded by the affinity between the subject and the Largo introduction which created it; Beethoven has married the Baroque genre of toccata and fugue with the Haydnesque slow introduction (where the materials of the subsequent movement are adumbrated). As a result, the "rhythm" of the fugue endlessly rehearses its own genesis in the episodes between the entries.

Tonal Bifocality

The congruence between harmony and meter is often deeply ambiguous, meaning that it can be parsed from opposite tonal standpoints, depending on where one draws the grouping boundary. On the surface, the texture of the opening phrase in Op. 130 looks straightforwardly Classical: an antecedent-consequent pair (mm. 1–4), the first subphrase cadencing on V (D–C), the second on I (A–B♭), extending into a modulation to the dominant (mm. 5–7) (ex. 4.10):

Example 4.10. String Quartet in B♭, Op. 130, first movement, mm. 1–7

Nevertheless, according to how one hears the upbeat B♭ to m. 1, in the context of the two caesuras, the phrase can be interpreted harmonically as either tonic or dominant. If B♭ is an upbeat, and the D of m. 2 is an accented appoggiatura to the C, then mm. 1–2 sit on the dominant; moreover, the rising scale of appoggiaturas through mm. 4–7 absorbs the A–B♭ cadence of m. 4, subsuming the entire consequent into a dominant phrase (a linear unfolding from the A of m. 4 to the F of

m. 7). Measures 1–7 are thus entirely *dominant*. Conversely, with no textural or harmonic cues to guide us through the unison opening, there is reason to interpret the first B♭ as a downbeat; one can also hear the violin's C at m. 2 as a passing note between the D and the B♭, thus gluing the two subphrases into a tonic prolongation. Choosing to halt on the A–B♭ caesura of m. 4, we can thus regard the phrase as firmly anchored on the *tonic*. There is no "right" or "wrong" interpretation. Beethoven has calibrated the metrical and harmonic equipoise in order to lock the texture into *Schein*'s "counterpoint" of perspectives. As with the *Arietta*, the bifocal flicker engages the counterpoles of tonic and dominant. Calling this process "subthematic abstraction" (Dahlhaus 1991: 202–18) does little justice to the dynamic, polar, and diatonic nature of this counterpoint.

By definition, linear textures resist being subsumed into a harmony governed by a bass note. Late Beethoven often enhances the independence of his lines by endowing them with conflicting tonal profiles: that is, irrespective of the accompanying voices, a line may suggest a harmonic progression in itself. In the *Grosse Fuge*, the subject outlines a I–VI–II–V–[I] progression, whereas the countersubject outlines I^7–IV–V–[I] (ex. 4.11). The first violin's A♭ at m. 30 nudges the line into the subdominant E♭, whereas the viola's B♮ in the next measure moves into the supertonic C minor. The bifocal clash is focalized around the diminished fourth B–E♭, and the augmented triad sonority (completed with the G) is responsible for much of the fugue's rebarbative *tinta*. Nevertheless, this is a delicate, gentle, form of bifocality, since Beethoven is combining not two keys or triads, but two tonal perspectives on the same material. Here, we should note that the flicker engages the two rival tonal models we examined earlier, and which are presented in the substitute rondo *consecutively*, rather than simultaneously. Slightly adjusted, they are also given in the fugue's introductory *Meno mosso*, mm. 17–21.

The fugal Presto from the Dona of the mass also disposes its voices bifocally. The violins trace a subject-answer progression in G major, the lower strings in D. In Drabkin's interpretation: "the upper line of the subject is answered a fourth higher, the lower line a fourth lower, so that the original interval of an octave, on the tonic, is answered by a seventh on the dominant" [1991a: 93–94]). Since the development gravitates flatwards, shifting the bifocal frame a fifth down to G/C major at m. 284, the ambiguity has a form-generating role in the movement.

Textural Transformations

The pointillist, shattered, textures at the start of Op. 135 would appear to leave the music little space to go. But actually they prove to be the premise for even more extreme transformations, and I shall focus on the first phase of the development section, mm. 62–80, prior to the B♭ false reprise of m. 81 (ex. 4.12). The development's opening gambit is to put together two ideas that seemed far apart: the viola theme (henceforth "theme") of mm. 1–2, and the bare cantus firmus, played unisono at mm. 10–14 (henceforth "cantus"). These Classical and archaic textures are themselves combined in a sort of meta-counterpoint from m. 62, revealing that they had belonged together all along, as keys to each other's puzzle

Example 4.11. *Grosse Fuge,* Op. 133, mm. 30–36

Example 4.12. String Quartet in F, Op. 135, first movement, mm. 59–81
Continues on the next page

Example 4.12. String Quartet in F, Op. 135, first movement, mm. 59–81

character. If so, then this begs the question of surface and depth: does the cantus implicitly underlie the theme, or does the theme displace the cantus? The dialogue between them sets in motion a chain reaction through which Beethoven deconstructs all manner of textural oppositions: between bass line and melody, subject and countersubject, motives and chords, releasing the parameters (pitch, interval, scale step, rhythm) only to recombine them in kaleidoscopic permutations, until the ideas' original profiles are pushed very much into the background. Let us consider their harmonic dimension first, then the melodic.

The theme of mm. 1–2 outlines a "Tristan chord," Bb–Db–F–G (a step down from the opera's G#–B–D#–F). Functionally ambiguous as a chord—between II and IV—the idea also treads the textural line between motif and harmony, the pointillism dissolving into harmonic fields. The theme is in search of a proper answering phrase, a V–I to its IV (or II)–V. Measures 5–9 won't quite do, and it finds its answer only at mm. 65–66, yet ironically by *losing itself* (note the enigmatic silence over the first half of the cantus, mm. 62–63). The reason for this withdrawal relates to the harmonic profile of the cantus, overtly a classic instance of Beethoven's favored VI–II–V–I model. This model is outlined, independently of the cantus, in the codetta figures of mm. 58–60, as A–D–G–C, and so the cantus's E–A takes the cycle up a fifth. Despite the texture being so bare, the implicit harmony in mm. 63–64 is thus a cadence in A minor; if Beethoven had left the theme in, we would have had a bifocal clash of A and D, II and V. Of course, this comes to pass in the next phrase, mm. 67–70, when theme and cantus are combined complete. Nevertheless, although the voices in mm. 67–68 seem to fit perfectly well, each line retains its distinct tonal profile, which strains against the union. Why, then, has Beethoven omitted the theme's antecedent phrase at mm. 63–64? All the better to point up the tangential cross-relationships with the cantus. First, the cantus is not a *complete* II–VI–V–I model, since E–A is followed by a rise to F#–C rather than the requisite fall to D–G. In this light, *the theme completes the cantus;* the theme is really a bass line. A further ambiguity in the cantus is its strange upbeat phrasing, which cuts across the tonal model: the falling seventh D–E sounds like a cadence but of course cannot be. Here and elsewhere in the movement, Beethoven abstracts the gestural profile of a cadence from the functional (see also the related G–C cadence of mm. 24–25, which should really be a C–F).

The motivic relationships between the two ideas are equally oblique, pivoting on a split between contour and intervallic profile. If we ignore the two grace notes, the theme's four pitches, D–A–B–G, echo the contour of the cantus's first half, D–E–B–A. The intervals are quite different, the B is only a thirty-second note, and the meter is displaced by a beat, but the contour is similar. Conversely, if we retain the C grace note, and drop the B *echappé*, then, in real pitch terms, and allowing for intervallic inversion, the theme is a sequential repetition of the cantus, a step down (C–D–A–G). There isn't a name for this kind of ambiguity—"bifocal" doesn't suit. Nor is there a term for the "give-and-take" of the negotiations at mm. 62–70, where the theme gains its "answer," via losing itself, and the cantus finds its true bass line in the theme, but by ultimately compromising its VI–II tonal orientation. This is "counterpoint" in the broadest sense of dialectical dialogue. All the same, the transformations are not achieved through development proper or substantive change, but through shifting the perspective, and letting the materials cast fresh light—as well as new shadows—on each other.

From m. 70 on to the climax at m. 80, the elements are increasingly scrambled. At m. 75, the pitch and rhythm of the theme are split between the cello (D♭–A♭) and viola (dotted note); at m. 77, the theme in the first violin is ironed out into straight quarter notes and inverted into a rising fifth, transforming it into an aspect of the cantus. Theme and cantus have exchanged "genes," and all their elements become compressed in the unison arpeggio gesture of m. 80—the rising fifth, the four-note contour, the dotted rhythm. This brusque, dismissive gesture of "Nicht diese Töne" marks a point of merger, dissolution, and collapse, appropriate to signposting the next juncture of the development, the false reprise. The paradox is that Beethoven presents this crisis in the most consonant texture possible in his language—a tonic, F-major triad. Yet this tonic triad is as mediated by context as the C-major triad at m. 11 of the twentieth "Diabelli" variation. Beethoven has led us ineluctably into hearing a simple arpeggio as the climax of a contrapuntal stretto. He folds "textural space" just as he interchanges contours and harmonies. In this regard, the outcome of the late style's "drift toward the linear" is not exactly a triumph of counterpoint or free dissonance treatment. Rather, it is a richer, more mediated, conception of Classical homophony itself. The glorious rising triad at the very end of Op. 135's finale is a product, not a premise, as much as a long-range "answer" to its "question" at m. 80 as the framing melodic apexes in Opp. 109, 110, and the Credo. Triadic homophony isn't merged with counterpoint, nor does it supersede it. Rather, Beethoven teaches us to metaphorically *hear* homophony "as" counterpoint. In this dialectical fashion, *Durchbruch* can be Classical. What breaks through is convention "as" counterpoint.

From this standpoint, the "last-minute turn to the homophonic"—a stock gambit of several late fugal finales—looks rather different. For instance, the broken-chord accompaniment to the lyrical apotheosis in Op. 110 isn't what it seems. Beethoven derives it through the progressive acceleration of the fugue subject, so the texture really suggests a mensuration fugue, with the theme stated in two simultaneous time values: both in its original dotted quarter notes and speeded up into sixteenth notes. A similar effect is produced in the Presto of the Gloria fugue, which brings back the opening ritornello in the role of stretto, thereby telescoping the extremes of the movement into an explosive contradiction (the subjects of the Gloria and Op. 110 fugues are both based on the "thirds and fourths cycle"). Extreme speed, as in the latter halves of both the Gloria and Credo fugues, takes counterpoint to the borders of its identity, where it threatens to collapse into the kind of undifferentiated "noise" which might be mistaken for homophony. The *Grosse Fuge* ostensibly has the most confirmed homophonic turn, with an Allegro molto "reprise" which dresses up the violent subject as a $\frac{6}{8}$ dance. The countersubject is replaced with a *galant* $\hat{3}$–$\hat{4}$–$\hat{4}$–$\hat{3}$ cadential figure in the first violin, and the I–V V–I harmony is grounded by viola F's. Nevertheless, the fugue subject doesn't quite fit this cadential pattern, particularly with the clash between the viola F and the cello G, which replaces the original bifocal flicker—between II and IV—with one between II *and* V. Simply refashioning the fugue as a dance, and squeezing it into a cadential corset, doesn't remove its intrinsic tensions. If anything, it reveals the fakeness of the cheerful *denouément*. Tagging a resolution at the end of a fiercely dissonant piece doesn't necessarily mean that these tensions are contained, just as Schoenberg's ironic E♭ cadence in his *Ode to Napoleon* really concludes nothing.

On the surface, Op. 135 looks like a creative throwback, and is formally much more conventional than the "Galitzin" Quartets or Op. 131. Nevertheless, its experimental ambitions are evident on the level of texture, bearing out the argument, more common among German than Anglo-American critics (as we shall see in chapter 7), that the late style was in general *more a matter of texture than of form*. Put more gnomically, in terms of Adorno's landscape metaphor, thinking of textural *style* underlying a carapace of formal *stylization* itself predicates a textural model—of surface and depth.

Form

The most striking aspect of the terrain Beethoven inherited from Haydn and Mozart is that it can be navigated according to familiar landmarks and well-prepared signposts. Again and again in this book, I will emphasize that the Classical style was more conventionalized than any musical idiom before or since, and that this enabled the listener to mentally map a work according to a predictable pathway of beginning-middle-end, what Lakoff and Johnson term a *source-path-goal* schema. To know the style is to know exactly where one stands in a phrase or a sonata, in a consequent phrase, in a second group, in a coda, etc. By contrast, a Baroque or Romantic work can be navigated with nothing like the same certainty or precision. Nevertheless, the Classical map contained lacunae, which emerged when nineteenth-century theorists like A. B. Marx attempted to simplify the musical journey into gross oppositions between "motion" (*Bewegung*) and "rest" (*Ruhe*). An ideational motion-rest-motion schema is a powerful presence in the late style, as a formal analogue of the arch contours. And yet understanding a sonata-form development as a "restful" interlude between exposition and reprise is counterintuitive (even Marx calls the *Durchführung* "the motion-oriented part"; see Burnham 1997: 146). Conversely, the most obvious interlude in a sonata form comes in the second group, whose character was often more lyrical than the first group. A powerful example of such "parenthetical enclosures" is the second subject of Op. 111, mm. 50–55, a melody which foreshadows the *Arietta,* and which constitutes an island of lyrical contemplation in the midst of a developmental torrent. As points of shelter in the storm, lyrical interludes open up an axis of "inner" and "outer" space in the landscape. At the same time, lyrical interiority is not necessarily stable or static: the Op. 111 interlude sits on a dominant E♭, while the cadenza-like interruption in Op. 109, mm. 9–15, is chromatically migrant. These aporias reflect the complexity of the Classical map itself, which issues from a counterpoint of tonal and thematic processes. For instance, a second group in the dominant may be lyrical in character, but it is also tonally tense. A sonata form is tonally binary, dividing at the double-bar sign at the end of the exposition; but it is also thematically ternary, splitting into exposition, development, and reprise. Beethoven's practice, therefore, is to exacerbate tensions which are already implicit both within and *between* the material landscape, and the ideational motion/rest schema.

As before, transformations can be "material" and "ideational." Beethoven abstracts the signposts of the map, so that functions of beginning, middle, and end are shifted from their regular position. As with intervallic and harmonic patterns, however, these functions tend to be displaced one position, rather than radically permuted. For instance, an introduction may be shunted into the first-group slot; or Beethoven may cloud the central landmark of the form—the double-bar division at the end of the exposition—so that the development floats either side of it. I accordingly term this device "functional rubato," and it results in what I call "functional multitasking," when material fulfils simultaneous roles, such as second-group and development, or development and reprise. Ideational transformations, as with arch contours, displace the motion schema so as to end with material hitherto enclosed parenthetically. A prototypical formal gambit in late Beethoven is to shift the marginal center stage, with an apotheosis of "inner space." In Op. 111, for example, the *Arietta* turns the lyrical interlude of the opening Allegro into the substance of an entire movement, transforming the parenthesis into a frame.

Phrase

Formally, the opening phrase of Op. 135 is inside-out: an off-tonic introduction (mm. 1–4) and a cadence (mm. 9–10) framing a short tonic statement (mm. 5–6, echoed m. 8). As a "parenthetical enclosure," mm. 5–6 stake out the G–A–B♭ grace-note figure of the incipit—the epitome of the decoratively marginal—and stabilize it as a tonic F–G–A. By turning a decoration into structure, and placing the tonic in the middle, the phrase does things the wrong way round (compare with mm. 1–4 of Op. 110, which *end* with an ornament summarizing the contour). The relationship between the "tonic interlude" and the introductory phrase is even stranger, since it is not clear whether the middle phrase answers and resolves the opening, or if it compounds the question. In short, are mm. 5 ff. a consequent to 1–4, or a disguised repetition?

Superficially, Beethoven indulges Haydn's favorite trick of beginning with a cadence, a token of ending, which is put right by being reworked at the end of the phrase, mm. 8–10, commuted from an imperfect to a perfect cadence (compare with Haydn's Op. 33, no. 5 in G). The transformation is motivically intricate: the viola's B♭–F–G–E is elaborated into the first-violin figures at m. 9, so as to resolve onto the F; but the motive also interlocks with a transposed and filled-in version in the previous bar, F–C–D–B♭. More subtly still, the opening cadence even casts its influence over the intervening material in mm. 5–8, due to its ambiguity of harmony and contour. Taken as an approach to V, mm. 1–4 prepare the answering resolution to I, which "arrives" when the prolonged B♭ (m. 2, violin 1, then mm. 3–4, violin 2 in successive octaves; finally, m. 5, violin 1) finally falls to the A of m. 6. But note how Beethoven does his best to rhythmically deflect this A to the C, which is the real goal of the phrase. If C, then we focus on the suggested voice leading in mm. 1–2 from the viola's B♭ to the cello's C, and the rising B♭–C motive becomes seminal for the violins in mm. 6 and 8, and the cello in mm. 7 and 9 (this strange, falling-sevenths motive also generates the "cantus" melody of m. 10). The B♭–C progression keeps alive the dominant "feel" of bars 5–9, as an expansion of the opening cadence and a preparation for the closing one. We thus have an example of "functional multitasking." If the B♭ *falls* to the A of m. 6, then the middle phrase *resolves* the opening; if the B♭ *rises* to the C, then it *compounds* (i.e., repeats) the opening.

It is extremely typical of late Beethoven that these broader formal questions turn upon an infinitesimal motivic detail—the A♮–B♭–C figure, itself derived from the ostensibly "marginal" grace-note decoration. It is also typical that the crisis of this figure, as we have seen in an earlier discussion, is pinpointed at the exact climax of the phrase, at the goal of a structural acceleration, m. 8, where it also intersects with the deconstruction of textural categories (motive and bass line). Fantastic as it is, Beethoven's phrase is a finely calibrated piece of musical engineering.

Sonata

Mass and bagatelle—the outer poles of late landscape—are free of the historical baggage of sonata form, *and for this very reason* epitomize the freedom of late sonata form. Much of this freedom inheres in the functional multitasking of formal juncture, as I shall show at length in chapter 5. I close the present chapter by approaching sonata—arguably the center of the style—from the extremes.

Beethoven's manner, as we shall see in the next chapter, is to problematize the "counterpoint" between sonata's binary and ternary dimensions. Tonally, the form divides in two between the exposition and the development. Yet this binary scheme plays against the ternary exposition-development-recapitulation structure. The *Missa*'s Credo seems to reference the ternary sonata with its ABA form. Nevertheless, the central section does equal service as a lyrical parenthesis (a *quasi* second group) and a development section. It thus distils the sonata's binary/ternary "counterpoint" into paradox. This multitasking is especially intricate with the elision of the "development" and the "reprise." Drabkin points out that the recapitulation is diffused across as many as five junctures (1991a: 55). After the central section reaches its dramatic nadir with the "et sepultus est," the third and final section may be heard to begin with (1) the *a capella* Mixolydian "Et resurrexit"; (2) the "et ascendit," Allegro but in F major; (3) the F-major chord at "coelum," m. 200, which rhymes with the chord immediately preceding the Incarnatus; (4) the return of the main Credo theme at m. 264, albeit still in F; and (5) the return of the B♭ tonic in the closing fugue. While resurrection may be the programmatic analogue of recapitulation, Beethoven still has a lot of text to get through, so he needs to blend the functions of development and reprise as he does in much of his late instrumental music. In this respect, Beethoven's procedure in the mass proves to be not the exception but the rule of the late style, which is to mix the signs of Classical form in radical combinations.

On the surface, the miniature eighth bagatelle in a set of eleven, Op. 119, seems a straightforward example of sonata form (ex. 4.13):

Example 4.13. Bagatelle Op. 119, no. 8

It modulates conventionally to the dominant rather than to the mediant, and the repeat marks at m. 8 supply the requisite caesura between the two halves of the form, dividing the exposition from the development. Four measures of development, wandering through harmonies of B♭, F, and G minor, lead to four of retransition (13–16) and four more of tonic resolution (17–20) by way of an abbreviated reprise. The thematic correspondences are there, if artfully oblique. The first phrase climbs, via a sequence of yearning appoggiaturas, up to the E of m. 7, which initiates the descent to the cadence in the secondary key of G. The line may *seem* to peak on the G of m. 6, but this note is really a cover for an E-minor chord, and the voice leading runs from the F♯ half note to the E half note of m. 7. The melody is a skip of a third, D–F♯, followed by a fall of a sixth, E–D–C–[B]–A–G, which is answered a fifth below in the second half. The very last note at m. 8 doubles as the first of the answering progression, G–B♭–A–G–F–E–D–C. In short, the piece elaborates two cadences, in G and C, worked out in complementary $\hat{6}$–$\hat{1}$ descents, from E and A, respectively.

And yet there is nothing straightforward about this unfeasibly condensed structure. The clue lies in the question of where exactly the return begins. Is it the very head of the second half, in proper binary fashion, with the onset of the answering descent (which of course *starts with the last note of the first half*)? Is it the disguised motivic reprise at mm. 13–16, which recalls the A/G neighbor-note figures of the opening, with their diatonic/chromatic mixtures? Or is it the return of tonic harmony at m. 17? From yet another standpoint, mm. 13–18, ostensibly the retransition and reprise, even comprise two successive variations on the development's falling-triad idea, the arpeggiation of an octave between an upper and lower dominant (the F's in mm. 10 and 13; the G's in mm. 14 and 15, and 17 and 18). Even more ingeniously, the last phrase, mm. 17–20, does three jobs. Against the descending arpeggio in the right hand (reprising the development), the left hand recapitulates the rising bass line of mm. 1–4, filled in, wiped clean of chromatics, and condensed from four measures to one and a half. The right-hand part of mm. 1–4 is then referenced in the second half of this phrase: the rising figures in mm. 19–20 clarify the implication in mm. 1–6 of an elaborated dominant seventh, "correcting" the jarring F♯ of m. 6 into a cadential seventh.

The mixture of developmental and recapitulatory functions in the second half of the bagatelle recalls the Credo after the Resurrexit. Indeed, the shocking B♭ of m. 9, as jarring as the F♯ of m. 6 which it parallels (the two leaps of a third, prior to the sixth descent), is in the spirit of the mass's well-placed tonal ruptures; particularly the equally dramatic shift to A♭ in the Credo at "Judicare," m. 221 (also a flat seventh). The developmental phrase, mm. 9–12, seems to float either side of the caesura, to group also with the exposition, as a *minore* extension to the second group. From the vantage point of m. 8's G major, what comes next is not actually in B♭, but rather is an elaboration of a G-minor seventh chord. This sonority is prefigured in m.1, when the sixth chord on C (C–E–G–A) is read as A min^7 (A–C–E–G). Famously, the second group of Op. 127 will also turn on a G major/minor ambiguity (although in reverse, running minor/major), with implications for where we hear the start of the development. In this light, the second half, the journey home, begins only when the B♭ is naturalized at m. 13, eliciting a V^7 against the F. The astonishing fact about this piece—perhaps the most remarkable—is the harmonic bifocality engendered by the repeat, for the B♭ of m. 9 sounds differently the second time around. Heard after the final tonic cadence of m. 20, it becomes a seventh of a dominant to F, swinging up a fifth to B♭ in m. 10. Measures 9–12 are now transformed into a IV–V sequence typical of developments in dance movements. Thus the passage multitasks as second group the first time round, and development the second, with its harmonic function switching from dominant to subdominant. This switch is entirely appropriate for the course of the music, with V sustaining the initial tension, and IV relaxing toward the tonic. Indeed, the ultimate projection of IV in mm. 9–12 compensates for the unusual absence of a cadential subdominant in any of the music from mm. 13–20 (compared with the strong IV–V–I cadences at 1–4, and 7–9, in C and G). Considered purely as a cadential model, the second half of the piece is a giant elaboration of the IV–V–I progression so conspicuously bracketed out of its foreground: four measures of subdominant (9–12), four of dominant (13–16), and four mostly of tonic (17–20). As an expanded F–G–C cadence, part two of the bagatelle is basically just a repetition, writ large, of the opening phrase, adjusted so as to start and end in C. There is no technical name for this weird amalgam of repetition, answer, and reprise. Whether one hears the piece as two interlocking arch progressions, descending by turns, from the two dissonant cruxes, F♯ and B♭, or as two IV–V–I cadences, the final impression of this bagatelle is, ironically, a conception which is extremely simple. The irony is that simplicity is reached through great complexity: the atomizing of material into its constituent parameters, so that it is able to adopt conflicting functions at the same time, while coming back together, at a higher level, at the end. Final simplicity is not quite the whole story, though, because we are left with *two* simplicities: a reified cadential model, and an arch gestalt; material, and its ghosts. At some point, the landscape's ghosts drift into the city of expanded forms.

5   Invisible Cities

THE FIRST MOVEMENTS OF OP. 101, OP. 106, OP. 109, OP. 110, OP. 111, OP. 127, AND OP. 130

Allegory—Ossified convention; dead nature; the inorganic; disharmony; dissociation; a splitting into unmediated extremes; historical materiality; the nonsubsumptive; expression of convention; nature recuperated.

Rising above the landscape of musical nature is the city of conventional large-scale forms: *sonata* forms. Without questioning the enormous range and intricacy of eighteenth-century materials, the real issue is why and how the sonata idea managed to colonize the musical landscape, to the extent that we can speak of practically any idiom, genre, or style as being "in" sonata form.[1] The triumph of sonata parallels the Enlightenment's rationalizing, or "pulverizing," of space into geographical units, such as the French *départements* (see Harvey 1990: 254). And, although a late arriver on the *galant* scene, sonata form came to resemble the European capital cities which made the style possible, cities which contain and regulate a Babel of languages and cultures. Daniel Heartz's magisterial *Music in European Capitals* (2003) paints an image of the *galant* style of 1720–80 as quintessentially *metropolitan*, facilitated by the cultural and economic bustle of cities and the institutions they supported. This bustle is borne out by the eclecticism of musical languages, a plurality which revisionist historians use to question the ostensible rigidity of the sonata-form concept (the plural title of Rosen's *Sonata Forms* speaks for itself). I would argue, by contrast, that the integrity of the sonata idea was the very condition of stylistic plurality, if only as a regulative concept and an agent of containment. The question is how, in the post-Napoleonic Vienna of Beethoven's last decade, this aging form could continue to rein in these centrifugal impulses.

To answer this question, the present chapter gives close readings of sonata-form movements from the last five piano sonatas and the first two "Galitzin" string quartets. Considering these pieces as wholes—as "invisible cities"—lets us examine how the raw materials of Beethoven's landscape (S3) interact with each other, subject to the interplay of two equal but opposite kinds of holism: the unifying compositional idea (S2) and the conventional sonata-form process (S1). One would imagine that Beethoven's Viennese sonatas crumbled, Bastille-like, under the onslaught of mimesis, in this case, what Adorno calls Beethoven's revolutionary *sansculottism* (Adorno 1998a: 45). Quite the contrary. Taking its allegorical turn, the negative dialectic also enshrines convention as an expressive ruin. Ruin and *Durchbruch* are expressed through the means of parametric noncongruence and lyrical parataxis.

Noncongruence: If convention forming requires the roping together of parameters into patterns where harmony, melody, and rhythm march in step, then the ruin of convention frees these parameters to go their separate ways. Beethoven manages noncongruence as a staggering or intercutting of formal cycles, typically with some parameters taking the argument forward, and others repeating or reprising. To a large extent, he merely activates tendencies already immanent within sonata form: for instance, the ternary scheme buried within its binary tonal plan; the Baroque ritornello procedure underlying thematic contrast, evoked in Haydn's "monothematic" expositions. A particularly important example is the late style's interest in the false (or "premature") reprise, a *galant* mannerism also beloved of Haydn. The false reprise harks back to the birth of sonata form from binary dance, when tonal, thematic, and structural returns were staggered across the second half of the piece at different points. It is the most salient example of noncongruence on an expanded scale in Classical music before Beethoven. In this way, noncongruence can have a historicizing outcome, reminding us that Beethoven evokes the recent past of the *galant* as much as the ancient past of Bach or Palestrina. Lyrical memory thaws out congealed material, disentangling the threads which have coalesced into conventions, and rendering ruins beautiful. Loosening the ligaments of the form releases lyricism in its guise as ancient parataxis.

Parataxis: Sonata form is a manifestation of systems thinking in music, where the parts are interdependent and conditioned by the whole. Adorno compares the musical system of the Classical style with the dynamics of a financial market: "The history of great bourgeois music at least since Haydn is the history of the interchangeable, or fungible: that no individual thing exists 'in itself', and everything only in relation to the whole" (1998a: 34). Wondering what to call his book, he muses that "*Beethoven and the State* would not be without sense as a title" (41), and he draws a direct analogy between the conflict of individual economic interests in society and the quasi-chemical interplay ("chemism") of Beethoven's language: "What [Beethoven] calls thematic work is the mutual abrasion of the antitheses, the individual interests" (43). Against this negative image of the musical economy, lyricism emerges as the token of everything against which "fungibility" militates: that individual thing which expressly *does* exist "in itself." Adorno valorizes a lyric syntax which is antithetical to sonata, a language of repetition rather than part/whole integration, of decorative variation instead of development. He associates it with the ancient grammatical category of *parataxis*.[2]

Parataxis, a concept Adorno elaborates most fully in his major essay on Hölderlin, describes the chainlike juxtaposition of independent clauses typical of epic recitation (see Scaglione 1981: 7). Because the individual clauses remain independent, one is not truly impelled from one clause to another, giving rise to a static impression strangely at odds with the telos of the narrative. By contrast, *hypotaxis*—an idiom Adorno regards as epitomizing more advanced discourse—binds clauses by means of a common noun or verb, thereby embedding them in a period.

The deferral of the link word to the end of the sentence—a device common to both the end-weighting of German sentences and the cadential closure of *musical periods*—performs a double service: endowing the chain of clauses with a conceptual unity, and heightening the sentence's teleological flow. This combination of unity and direction marks the essence of periodic construction; in the realm of music, it distinguishes the hypotaxis of Classical periodicity from the looser, paratactic, constructions of lyrical styles. To the extent that Baroque ritornello techniques, such as variation and fugue, are paratactic, they display a surprising affinity with Classical song forms. We often think of Baroque counterpoint as a stringent, abstract, idiom contrary to the subjectivism of song. Nevertheless, parataxis foregrounds lyricism's archaic character, which it shares with the Baroque, in contradistinction to the modernity of goal-driven Classical discourse. Thus Baroque and lyric tendencies make common cause against the ruling ethos of sonata and can be regarded as the "inner spaces" of the sonata city—or, even better, the personal *places* within sonata's abstract grid of *space* (see Harvey 1990: 254–55). The Baroque and the lyrical are also the city's historical memory bank.

Classical form is ruined, but still left standing, revealed in a newly aesthetic light. Imagining contemporary cities as ancient ruins was a common topos of early-Romantic painting and literature, as in Giambattista Piranesi's fantastic etchings of Roman architecture and Victor Hugo's poetic cycle *A l'arc de triomph*. In Benjamin's words, "The glorification of this architectural monument proceeds from the vision of a Paris Campagna, an '*immense campagne*' in which only three monuments of the vanished city have survived: the Sainte-Chapelle, the Vendôme column, and the Arc de Triomphe" (Benjamin 1989: 84). When Classical architecture decays, it blends with its setting, so that the historical seems to merge with the natural, creating allegory. History is naturalized into the timelessness of landscape, in a symmetrical countermove to the temporalization of lyric as shock or breakthrough. This gives us yet another window onto the "landscapes" of chapter 4. They are still there, in Beethoven's cities, but now viewed through brittle glass. In fact, the entire city has turned to glass, yet the kind of glass we look *at*, not *through*.

Late Sonata Forms

To say that the late style reflects on the principles of sonata form presumes that such a model existed as a compositional reality for Beethoven. The sketches prove that this was actually the case (Drabkin 1991b). Beethoven annotates his sonata-form drafts with the terms *prima parte* and *seconda parte*, or *erster Theil* and *zweiter Theil* (16), showing that he subscribed to the eighteenth-century conception of sonata form as *binary* (exposition plus development-cum-reprise) rather than the ternary model standard in the nineteenth century (exposition-development-reprise). At the same time, the frequency of "d.c." (da capo) markings in the sketches, to indicate the beginning of the recapitulation, attests to the coexistence of both binary and ternary schemes (15). The tendency of late Beethoven was to exacerbate the tensions implicit in this "counterpoint" of binary and ternary perspectives, tensions which naturally devolved onto the ambiguous role of the development. The development both extends the tonal tension raised in the second group and initiates the "journey home" to the reprise. It can look either *back* to the exposition, or *forward* to the recapitulation, by analogy with the function of a dominant in a I–V V–I cadential model (see Lerdahl and Jackendoff 1985: 245). As we saw with the bagatelle Op. 119, no. 8, but on a larger scale, Beethoven's developments display a "functional rubato" by floating on either side of the exposition and reprise.

The "floating development" is just one of the ways Beethoven attacks the sonata schema. The schema—a "punctuated form," according to Koch's theory (Spitzer 2004)—is normatively articulated as a series of "points," or "caesuras" (the fact that Koch speaks of caesuras will be critical to my theory of the late style in chapters 7 and 8).[3] The first point is a clear beginning, functionally distinguished from an optional slow introduction. The second is a modulation to the secondary key. The third, a cadence marking off the exposition. The fourth, the start of the development. The fifth, the head of the reprise. The recapitulation is undertheorized in compositional manuals, but two conventions stand out for Beethoven: Haydn's common practice of inflating the transition to the second-group reprise into a veritable secondary development, and the expansion of the coda into a virtual second development-cum-recapitulation. These tricks, together with Haydn's false reprise, the ternary/binary question, and the vestiges in the genre of Baroque ritornello, are growth points for lyrical parataxis in the late sonatas. On the other hand, while lyric helps Beethoven tinker with sonata's chief functional connectives, it also plays a full, if tangential, part in the dynamics of the form. Beethoven projects the theme onto the successive junctures of sonata, which behave like developing variations. These variations are staging posts along a narrative of disclosure, not decorating but unveiling. And the process is harmonized with the architecture of sonata form, so that its hidden spaces ("places") are also the sites for revealing the secrets and intimacies of the material. Measure 92 of Op. 132 is just such a place, and every work has "centers" like that. Such moments discharge all of lyric's various functions: syntactic rupture, instantaneous shock, breakthrough of the materially non-subsumptive, and archaic memory.

Elaine Sisman persuasively correlates parataxis with Haydn's variation procedure in sonata-allegro first movements, such as that of Symphony no. 88, "where there is a rhythmic similarity among the principal thematic areas" (Sisman 1993b: 101). Late Beethoven's sonata forms are *more* paratactic than Haydn's insofar as ritornello and variation come to the fore. This emergence is progressive: by gauging the degree to which parataxis afflicts the "punctuation schema," we can chart Beethoven's assault on sonata form as unfolding in two waves. The first wave, 1816–1822, breaks over the last five sonatas, Opp. 101, 106, 109, 110, and 111, whose many ambiguities never actually challenge the sonata model. The second wave, 1824–1825, encompasses the three "Galitzin" Quartets, Opp. 127, 130, and 132. Here, Beethoven radically attacks the articulation of the form's main junctures. Of course, there are profound continuities between these two cycles of works. In the sonatas, Beethoven rehearses many devices which will later be allowed to overflow their formal banks, such as recurring introductions, lyrical parenthesis, and false reprise. The clear difference between the two waves doesn't quite lend credence to Adorno's extreme view that the late style "proper" only begins with the quartets. But it does suggest that the late style proceeded in two main phases, the first exploratory, the second more radical. I would even venture that the C♯-Minor Quartet, Op. 131, begun in late 1825, launched a *third*, necessarily truncated, period of the late style. The sonata forms of the last two quartets are both, superficially at least, conventional (albeit, in Op. 131, shunted to the finale). In this group I would also include the Ninth Symphony, whose first movement is an outwardly conventional sonata form. Perhaps this heralded a newly Classicizing phase in Beethoven's career. Another pattern emerges when we include the two cello sonatas Op. 102, of 1815, an isolated pair to match the pair of Opp. 131 and 135. An approach which argues that Beethoven's late style was primarily a textural, rather than formal, affair would seize on these contrapuntal cello sonatas as the true beginning of the third period. Moreover, the piano sonatas Opp. 101 and 106 are in some ways creative reworkings of Op. 102, nos. 1 and 2. Both Opp. 102, no. 1, and 101 are lyrical works, with finales which return cyclically to the opening theme; and both the D-major sonata and the *Hammerklavier* are heroic showcases with long slow movements and fugal finales. If we do incorporate the cello sonatas, and we provisionally set aside the bagatelles and the *Diabelli* Variations, then the late period falls into a striking symmetry: two cycles (Opp. 101–11; Opp. 127, 130, 132), framed by two isolated pairs (Op. 102, nos.1 and 2; Opp. 131, 135), each cycle coordinating satellites around a huge work for orchestra and choir (the Mass and the Symphony, respectively).

Opus 101 in A

Strangely, Beethoven begins each cycle with the most lyrical of the group, first Op. 101, then Op. 127 (see Kerman 1967: 205). And, in each case, the lyrical work is blasted by a titanic follow-up in B♭ major, with a fugal finale. It is as if Beethoven intentionally stakes out the extremes of his late style, the capstone being song. There is more than meets the eye in Op. 101's pastoral movement (see Hatten 1994: 92–104). As Schleuning shows us, compound meters, such as $^{12}_8$ or $^6_8$, are prototypical of Baroque pastoral; although they persisted well into the Classical era, musical nature basically became *duple* (Schleuning 1998: 26–58). In other words, such dance patterns in Haydn and Mozart carried a whiff of the archaic; in the present sonata, Beethoven's pastoral is a veritable *Denkmal* mourning a dead style. This is both nature glimpsed through the window, and a monument sinking into the landscape. The operative word in Beethoven's expression marking is *Innigsten* ("Etwas lebhaft und mit der innigsten Empfindung"), suggesting a journey into the inner courtyard of the form, which is the development (ex. 5.1a–d). What we find at this center is a stock Baroque topos of mourning, when the first subject is recast in F♯ minor (mm. 41–43), underscored by the syncopated tonic-pedal figures which traditionally signaled lamentation (ex. 5.1c). Lament is the con-

Etwas lebhaft und mit der innigsten Empfindung
Allegretto, ma non troppo

Example 5.1. Four stages of Op. 101's journey
    a. Theme, mm. 1–2
    b. Reinterpreted in E major, mm. 35–36
    c. As a topos of mourning in F♯ minor, mm. 41–42
    d. Climax with the C♯–B♯–A–G♯ tetrachord, mm. 50–55

ventional shadow of pastoral in Baroque drama, and the major/minor variants echo those in many of Bach's works, such the opening chorus of the *Saint Matthew Passion*.

Beethoven's inward path unpacks the theme's contrapuntal complex. The original presentation is tonally unstable, on V of A major (ex. 5.1a). When Beethoven reinterprets the theme in *E major* at the start of the development (m. 35), it is the inner alto voice which he singles out (ex. 5.1b). In its E-major context, the theme is stabilized, since the line rises from the tonic (rather than from the leading note G♯ at m. 1). The theme is also straightened out into Beethoven's normative arch contour, with an apex on a C♯ $\hat{6}$. Schenker (1971–72: 16) and Hatten (1994: 98) draw attention to the anomaly of the original peak at m. 2, where the E♮ forms a consonant appoggiatura to the D chord tone of the V^7. Paradoxically, the anomalous apex is consonant, whereas the normative one at m. 36 is dissonant. Hatten sees the trajectory of the movement as "realizing the dissonant potential of the appoggiatura" (101). I would go further, and argue that the expressive weighting of the $\hat{6}$ appoggiatura is the gravitational center of the movement, drawing the music toward the F♯-minor ritornello which tonicizes the $\hat{6}$ into a key, and profiling the sixth degree, D, as a minor-ninth crux against the C♯. The journey continues to the movement's C♯-minor climax, mm. 50–53 (ex. 5.1d). Here, the theme's profile seems to be liquidated, but what emerges is another of Beethoven's archetypal melodic patterns: the chromatic tetrachord, C♯–B♯–A–G♯, actually an inner voice within the contrapuntal complex at m. 1. Thus the movement foregrounds the three voices of the complex in descending order: m. 1, soprano; mm. 35 and 41, alto; and m. 50, tenor. The music goes "down" as well as "inwards." The chromatic tetrachord which marks the nadir is of course the negative lodestar in all of Beethoven's late works. And yet Beethoven tells us that this negativity is intrinsic to pastoral; the snake is already in the garden. The transition into the recapitulation extrapolates the soprano theme's G♯–A incipit out of the $\hat{6}$ apex in C♯ minor through a simple trick of reversal. The reprise is actually buried within the "upward-resolving appoggiaturas over a contrapuntal 5–6–5–6" chain at m. 53 (Hatten, 102). In a flash, A is transformed from a $\hat{6}$ apex in C♯ to a tonic. And yet we are left with the lingering impression that the pastoral key of A major is really only a shining semblance, a *Schein*, with a tragic center in the minor keys of F♯ and C♯.

Formally, the movement epitomizes the leveling effect of lyricism in the late style, a flatness compounded by the unrelenting lilt of the pastoral meter. Resolutions are deferred, climaxes undercut, boundaries blurred. The exposition starts on the dominant, lacks a tonic cadence altogether, and defers any harmonic arrival to the end of the second group, m. 25. This leads to eccentric proportions, with the second-group-cum-codetta (mm. 12–34) more than twice the length of the tonic-group-cum-transition. Moreover, the sonata form is intercut with variational parataxis, hidden repetitions. The beginning does in fact attempt a tonic cadence, but it is embedded in the modulation to the dominant, creating a typically late bifocal twist: the pitches in m. 9 gesture toward a cadence in A, yet the context directs them toward E, with a signal example of a $\hat{3} = \hat{6}$ transformation around the pitch C♯.

(The transition in Op. 110 makes an even bigger meal out of this pun.) It is as if the music wants to go back and forwards at the same time. A more dramatic case of hidden return is the start of the development, which recasts the first subject in E major, as we have seen. Lack of a clear boundary between the exposition and development induces a further ambiguity, given that the coda is so cadentially understated, and the syncopations keep the music pulsing forward. Nevertheless, neither this nor any other of the junctures in the movement is seriously in question. "First-wave" late style ultimately honors the sonata schema. Comparing m. 35 with the parallel moment in Op. 127 captures the differences between these two sub-styles. We will see below how the return of the Maestoso introduction in G major creates the same three-fold ambiguity: simultaneously a da capo, an extension of the second group, and start of the development. But the effect in Op. 127 is to attack sonata form at its core. "Second-wave" late style raises lyrical parataxis to a much higher power, capable of arguing with sonata-form hypotaxis on equal terms.

Opus 106 in B♭

The *Hammerklavier* is a grand sonata on the scale of the "Waldstein" of 1804 and is as much a monument to a dead heroic style as Op. 101 commemorates the pastoral idyll. With its forceful grandiloquence, it is a more obvious watershed work then either Opp. 101 or 102. More frankly than Op. 101, the *Hammerklavier* knocks out the joints of the structure, in particular the modulation and retransition (ex. 5.2a–c). The transition (ex. 5.2a) leaps directly from the tonic to a chord of D, a *Rückung*. The end of the development slides from V^7 of B major into the tonic reprise, eliding the dominant (ex. 5.2b). Without proper grounding, the F♯ chord hangs like a cloud over the recapitulation, and eventually interrupts it with an explosive reprise of the theme in B minor (ex. 5.2c). The gambit seems to make nonsense out of sonata form, relegating the tonic reprise into a quasi false reprise within a plateau of B major/minor. Interestingly, the procedure pivots on reinterpretations of the pitch B♭, from a tonic to flat $\hat{3}$ in G, to the leading note A♯ in B. As shifting perspectives on a reiterated B♭, the movement suggests a paratactic monotonality.

Compared to Op. 101, the *Hammerklavier* attacks the junctures through a deficit, rather than excess, of continuity: it withdraws tonal mediation from the form. The direct model for a *cogent* modulation from B♭ to G major was the first movement of the "Archduke" Trio, Op. 97, of 1811. (Adorno's long essay on Op. 97 notes the similarity [p. 93].) Like the "Waldstein," which unfolds the modulation from C to E extremely smoothly, the "Archduke" spells out each step of the way: the bass B♭ drops to an A, supporting a $^6_4$–$^5_3$ progression on D, before resolving to G major for the second group. The passage's leisurely pacing (Adorno speaks of the music's "floating, suspended, character" [93]) contrasts markedly with the abruptness of the *Hammerklavier*'s *Rückung*. As in the "Archduke," Beethoven moves directly from a chord of B♭ to a chord of D. But here, the D major chord is in root position, since Beethoven withholds the expected dominant pedal. Rather than resolving to

Example 5.2. Three joints of the *Hammerklavier*'s structure
    a. Opening, transition, mm. 34–38
    b. Retransition, mm. 223–28
    c. Reprise of transition, mm. 266–68

its dominant, A, Beethoven cuts a corner, hangs on to D, and leads it directly to the new key of G. The *Rückung* between the B♭ and D triads is thus not mediated by the normative $^6_4$–$^5_3$ resolution. For the progression to work, we would need to infer a $^6_4$ chord somewhere in the passage, either within the octave D's or the subsequent D-major triad. In the first instance, we would fill in the octave with a G and B♭, deriving a $^6_4$–$^5_3$ resolution in G minor. Alternatively, the octave D's prolong the B♭ harmony, and we infer a bass A beneath the D triad. Since neither option transpires, the hinge of the modulation is broken, setting up a structural dissonance which the second group spends most of its time retrospectively trying to correct. From

m. 63, the music obsessively approaches G-major cadences through impeccably functional chains of thirds, yet ironically never beginning from, or taking in, the requisite B♭ triad. The nearest the second group gets to replaying, and healing, the originary breach is in the climactic $^6_4$ G-major chord at m. 96, leading to a coda melody inflected with C minor and G minor. The melodic arch of this theme, apexing on an E♭, and descending to B♭/B, recalls the pitches of the first group, effectively filtering the tonic through the new key. The B♭/B oscillations in the coda encapsulate this double perspective.

As always in late Beethoven, when considering the rationale for an anomaly, one is pulled back to earlier passages: paradoxically, even disunities are mediated (albeit not *resolved*) by context. Surprisingly, the origins of the *Rückung* lie in the point which seems most normal, the F-major arpeggiation of mm. 31–34. The F chord interrupts the E♭ bias of the transition of mm. 17–30, which itself composes out the E♭ preoccupations of the first subject (its 3̂–4̂–3̂ neighbor-note figures). Conventionally, subdominant-oriented transitions are more appropriate to a *recapitulation,* where they make the tonic reprise of the second group sound like a modulation. Hence the harmony at m. 31 should be not V, but *V of V*; not F but C. The interloping F is a wrench back to the tonic, a step away from modulation toward parataxis. This is an emerging constant in Beethoven's late transitions. Compare mm. 31–36 with the deceptive tonic cadence at m. 9 of Op. 101 and, to look forward, with m. 19 of Op. 110. In short, the tonic ritornello at m. 35 is a redundant da capo, which must be immediately brushed aside. It is *because* the piece has "missed the boat" that the modulation at m. 37 needs to be so drastic.

The centerpiece of the heroic Beethovenian sonata is the triumphant return of the first subject in the recapitulation. Adorno thinks that Beethoven's undercutting of this moment is the quintessential aspect of late-style critique of sonata form. By Adorno's lights, the deception practiced on us by the heroic sonatas is that the thematic return—a rule ordained by the conventions of the style—is presented as the inevitable outcome of a unique developmental process; that is, Beethoven conjures the unique out of the stereotypical. The attribute of late recapitulations, by contrast, is shock and surprise, discontinuous gestures which trigger flashes of new insight about the piece: *Apparitions.* The chief *Apparition* is of convention as something willed and forced, so that we recognize *structure* as *event.* This temporalization of structure also informs how we hear the theme of the *Hammerklavier,* not as a well-formed gestalt, but as a distillation of heroic swagger—a grandiloquent flourish. Adorno's notion of *Floskel* captures this blend of petrified cliché and dynamic flourish. In its narrative of disclosure, the *Hammerklavier Floskel* is revealed less and less as a melody, and increasingly as an agent of disruption. Accordingly, the "centers" where this happens are decentered to the margins of the form: respectively, the transition to the second group (as we have seen), the recapitulation of this juncture, and the first-subject reprise itself. Scandalously, the latter—ostensibly the center of the entire sonata—is set up as a marginal false reprise, albeit in the right key and at the right place. The trick turns on a dilemma of two pitches: is the A immediately before the B♭ at m. 226 an A♮ or an A♯?

Measures 216–26 unfold typically preparatory material signaling the imminent return of the first subject (compare with mm. 141–54 of the "Waldstein"), but on the dominant of the wrong key—B major instead of B♭. The integrity of the crucial accidental markings in the last measures (225–26) is deeply controversial (see Badura-Skoda 1980). The published text contains A's which are deemed sharp because of the key signature. According to the literature (Tovey 1944; Badura-Skoda 1980; Rosen 1972; Marston 1998), consideration of Beethoven's style and notational and compositional practice all points to the careless omission of a natural sign. Retaining the printed A♯ would break the pattern of rising semitones G♮–G♯–A♮–B♭ with the whole tone G♯–A♯ and would result in the curious progression from the seventh chord of B major directly into B♭ major through the rising semitone E♮—F, completely sidestepping the dominant. Nevertheless, I would counter that the retransition of the Fourth Symphony, also in B♭, supports retention of A♯. As in Op. 106, the symphony's development ends on the dominant of B major. The chord is enharmonically transformed into an augmented sixth in B♭ and shifts onto a second-inversion B♭ triad, without an intervening dominant (the drum rolls underline the transformation of B♭ [A♯] from the leading tone of B major into the tonic note). The $^6_4$ B♭ triad then refuses to make good the progression by resolving onto a $^5_3$ dominant. Instead, the dominant pedal in the bass is subsumed into a rising tonic arpeggiation around the real pedal, the B♭ trill. Against all expectation, the harmony here is not dominant but tonic. The dialogue between the basses' F's and the timpani's B♭ trills at the beginning of the reprise teases the $^6_4$ triad, but the B♭'s obstinately refuse to drop to A.

The Fourth Symphony is a Haydnesque work, and the affinity with the *Hammerklavier* points up the debt of late-style critique to Classical irony. And even if the A♯ *were* read as A♮, a single measure would still be much too slender a bridge to discharge the tension of twenty-four measures of B-major preparation (201–24). Haydn frequently destabilizes his reprise with inadequate tonal preparation, as a strategy for motivating an outbreak of secondary development leading to more solid resolution with the reprise of the second group. And often this secondary development returns to harmonic areas addressed just before the reprise. For example, the development of Symphony no. 46 in B major gravitates toward G♯ minor, the retransition inadequately prepares the tonic with a dominant in a weak $^6_4$ inversion, and after four measures the reprise is overtaken by a contrapuntal episode leading us back to G♯ minor. This is then cut short by a dominant pedal, discharging powerfully onto B major with the tonic reprise of the second group. Historically, Haydn's practice of deferring sonata-form resolution to the reprise of the *second group* is a vestige of the end-weighting of binary dances. This end-weighting becomes the norm again in early-nineteenth-century sonatas, such as Chopin's, by which perspective the centrality of the first-subject reprise—ostensibly the cornerstone of Classical form—is really a historical anomaly.

The *Hammerklavier* follows Haydn's practice even more radically. The recapitulation of the first group gradually slides into G♭, thus picking up from where the development left off, and the transition is transposed wholesale into this key. Rosen aptly calls the ritornello of the first subject at m. 267 "an explosion . . . the greatest example of a climax placed after, instead of just before, the beginning of the recapitulation" (1972: 414). But the B-minor entry is explosive not simply because it is loud and in an alien key, but because it is the nerve center for a complex web of effects, all packed into a vanishingly small singularity. These effects can be listed: B minor grounds the F♯/G♭ tensions of the primary and secondary developments, and thus overshadows the B♭ resolution of m. 227, which is consequently relegated—absurdly—into the position of a false reprise. To emphasize, the B♭ entry—in the right key and place—is rendered false relative to the B-minor entry—in the wrong key and place. Furthermore, the B-minor explosion gives vent to some long-distance rumblings. First, it resolves the subdominant tendency of the original transition: as we saw, mm. 23–30 want to move toward E♭, but are interrupted by the B♭ da capo of m. 35, with its dominant F. This subdominant bias is consummated at the second attempt, when G♭ shifts to B minor. Second, given that the B♭ da capo of m. 35 is *already* a subversive gesture, its transposition into B minor at m. 267 merely confirms a predisposition. Third, one can go further and argue that the explosion simply discloses the dynamic "event character" of the original theme, even at the sonata's opening. And with a gestalt switch, the grandiloquent opening triads become suddenly shaky when we consider them in the light of the movement's subdominant and submediant drift (the keys of VI [G], VI♭ [G♭/F♯] and II♭ [B] may be considered ever-more chromatic substitutions of IV). In other words, B♭ is made to sound like a dominant to an implicit key kept over the horizon. This is a common strategy in the late sonata forms, the most famous example being the finale of Op. 131, where C♯ is checkmated by F♯ minor, demoting I into an implicit V of IV (see Winter 1977: 121–24). In the *Hammerklavier*, undercutting the tonic groundedness of B♭ induces a "floating" quality, wildly opposed to the overt robustness of the music's rhetoric. Last, the B-minor explosion joins hands with the B♭ da capo of m. 35 and the false/correct reprise of m. 227 as a set of three articulation marks, which grip the building like a giant steel vice. These three junctures stand out not as themes, but as tonal ruptures. The trajectory of lyric, then, is opposite in Op. 106 than in Op. 101: toward shock rather than song; an emptying of material rather than a course toward plenitude.

Beethoven's invisible cities are all elaborations of the same city, and these first two masterworks of the late period already begin to stake out diverging pathways in a network of possibilities. The *Hammerklavier*'s contribution is a new concept of discontinuity, a rhetoric of the "instantaneous sublime." Sublimity is the inadequacy of finite reason to grasp the immensity of nature; with the "instantaneous sublime," it is too much musical information packed into too little time and space. The B-minor reprise is "explosive" because it exacts from the listener a kind of conceptual vertigo.

The Last Three Sonatas

Opp. 109, 110, and 111 belong together as a group, although Benjamin's notion of constellation best describes the peculiar nature of their interdependence. Each is a complete, self-sufficient sonata, and there can be no question of their constituting some monstrous, tripartite meta-sonata or musical narrative. On the other hand, the rising-third cycle outlined by their respective keys (E–A♭–C) is underscored by Beethoven's habit in the late style of stressing scale step 3̂ over 1̂, even at cadences. Thus Op. 109 ends with a strong G♯, which sets up the A♭ of Op. 110, whose climactic top C in the finale foreshadows the key of Op. 111. Moreover, the theme of Op. 109's variation finale gravitates toward G♯ minor, anticipating Op. 110's A♭ major; the latter returns the compliment with its digression into E major (F♭) in the reprise of its first movement, and Op. 111 follows suit with a second group in A♭. Over and above these tonal links, the three sonatas share common materials and procedures, as if each work were merely a snapshot of an ongoing problematic. These commonalities will be my principal interest. Although each is distinctive, the three sonatas introduce or bring out several features not evident in Opp. 101 or 106: (1) the role of the introduction, (2) lyrical parenthesis, (3) variation structure, (4) the abrogation of the development section, and (5) projection of arch contour onto form.

The Role of the Introduction

Rosen has famously demonstrated how the Maestoso introduction of Op. 111 presents three diminished-seventh chords which permeate the structure of the Allegro con brio (1972: 442–44). The Maestoso is integrated too tightly within the movement to be merely an introduction. In addition to its thematic and harmonic influences, its tempo is recalled at the "meno allegro" and "Adagio" moments of the second group, in a thread which eventually leads to the Adagio of the Arietta. It is comprehended within the conceptual dualisms of the entire sonata: slow/fast; minor/major; chromatic/diatonic; tragic/affirmative. The introductions of Opp. 109 and 110 dispense with the French Baroque dress of the Maestoso. The first four measures of Op. 110 recall the motto introduction of Op. 78 in F♯ major, which also ends with a turn and a fermata, although in Op. 110 the phrase is incorporated into the recapitulation. It might be eccentric to call the first seven measures of Op. 109, which Rosen reminds us occupy a mere seven seconds in performance (2002: 230), an introduction, since the tempo is Vivace, and the function is exposition of the tonic group. Yet the Vivace and Adagio together display what I have called "functional multitasking." The Vivace has the brevity and succinctness of an introductory motto; the Adagio tempo, typical of introductions, is relegated to the second group. Beethoven's strategy in these sonatas is to problematize the sense of beginning. Op. 101 had also done that, with its fluid, off-tonic opening. But Beethoven now formalizes this ambiguity through discontinuities of material, entailing sharper contrasts of texture, dynamics, or theme. He thereby lays the groundwork for the lyrical/dynamic antithesis which is such a marked feature of the "Galitzin" Quartets. In earlier Classical music, this antithesis is often played out in the dramatic opposition between first and second groups. Late Beethoven frontloads it to the beginning of his movements, suggesting that the compositional premise is not a unitary theme, but a conceptual dualism. The "idea" in all these works is the place of lyricism within sonata form.

Op. 109 opposes two kinds of temporality: a rushing *moto perpetuo,* and "cadenza time" (see ex. 4.3). The latter is a realm of freedom, expressed by an impromptu harmonic syntax of cadential evasions, *Rückung,* chromatic coloring, and prolongation. The Adagio espressivo is a static island in the stream, literally a cadenza parenthesis between the last note of the Vivace, the A♯ of m. 8, and the first note of the development, the B of m. 16. It is an expanded decoration of the dominant harmony—one could safely skip it, playing directly from mm. 8 to 16, and still make musical sense. A beautiful detail is Beethoven's decorated repeat of the F♯–E–D♯ bass line of mm. 9–11 in mm. 12–13, transforming the D♯ from a tonic $^6_3$ to the root of a D♯-major chord, then side-slipping (via *Rückung*) back to B$^6_3$ at the end of m. 13. D♯ major is presented as a vivid coloration of the dominant. In the motto theme of Op. 110, cadenza is signaled by its chief hallmarks of dominant harmony, fermata, and trill. Yet taking an opposite line to Op. 109, the cadenza is not partitioned from the frame of the music, but blended into the tail of the theme. Lyric in this sonata is not an enclave but a heightening: the material is in the process of *becoming* a cadenza. Compared with Op. 109, the transition to the impromptu second group is utterly seamless. How striking, then, that the structure of these two second groups is virtually identical. Both begin with $\hat{6}$–$\hat{5}$ neighbor-note procrastinations around Beethoven's favored VI–II–V–I cadential model: G♯–C♯–F♯–B in Op. 109, unfolding a G♯–F♯ apex; C–F–B♭–E♭ in Op. 110, with an apex on C–B♭. In each case, the model then undergoes a decorated repeat, in Op. 110 rather more extensive. Both groups conclude with a climactic descent from $\hat{8}$ (m. 14 in Op. 109; m. 32 in Op. 110), seeming to fill up tonal space, before rising scales which return the music to its starting point, the pitch at which the cadenza had first entered (B in Op. 109; C in Op. 110).

Opp. 109 and 110 could almost be variations on a single template. The brief lyrical interlude in Op. 111, mm. 50–55, is structured very differently, an elaboration of a I$^6_4$ chord above an E♭ pedal (ex. 5.3). Short as it is, the passage is nevertheless the most complex example of multiple embeddings in the sonatas. First, it stands out as an island of calm in a torrent of fugato. Second, its stability is compromised by its dominant pedal. Third, it sounds in the context not just of C minor or A♭ major, but of the Neapolitan "wrong turning" of mm. 45–49. The fugal transition, beginning m. 35, reaches the new key of A♭ with the entry of m. 43; the music will eventually reshape the fugue subject into a closing cadential theme in the coda of m. 58, suggesting a monothematic sonata form after Haydn. But at m. 45, the fugue overreaches itself, overshoots flatwards into D♭ major, and grinds to a halt with a crisis marked with astonishing five-octave leaps. It is the cadenza of m. 50 which rescues the music, diverting it back on the rails of A♭ major. Fourth, this "rescue" attempts to free the fugue from the control of the Maestoso, whose own lurch into D♭ from m. 5 determines the course of the Allegro. The rescue fails in the short term, since the lyrical interlude collapses into the Tempo I of m. 56, and the drop of A♭ to the G of the development, and back to C for the reprise, ends

Example 5.3. Lyrical interlude in Op. 111, first movement, mm. 47–56

up confirming the pattern of the Maestoso (mm. 11–16) after all. But it does set the scene for the Arietta, which completes the ascendancy of lyricism in the sonata, and which marks the sixth circle of embedding. Beethoven uses the lyrical mode as an escape hatch from the eternal recurrence of sonata repetition, as an antidote to the cyclicity of "fate." In the course of the work as a whole, lyric achieves this by moving from the margin to the center, so that "cadenza" and "frame" exchange places. But there are tensions to this strategy, not least the fact that lyric is an even more cyclical idiom than sonata, in the shape of *variation.*

Variation Structure

All three works graft variation form onto sonata, mixing the seemingly antithetical principles of repetition and modulation. Opp. 110 and 111 are built on the same three-part template of theme plus two variations, with tonic group comprising theme and variation 1, and variation 2 expanding to embrace the entirety of the transition, second group, and development. The sonata/variation fusion thus turns on this second variation.

That the consequent phrase in Op. 110, mm. 4–11, is an expanded variation on the motto, mm. 1–4, is evident from the bass line, which is identical apart from the G♭ of m. 9. Although Beethoven has stretched the duration of some of the notes, extending the phrase from four to seven measures and thus breaking a cardinal rule of strict variation procedure, it is still recognizable as a variation. The same holds for the florid transition, which evokes the theme unmistakably at mm. 17–18, especially with the contrary-motion neighbor-note turn around E♭ (after mm. 3–4). So far, the sonata mimics the cumulative diminution process typical of variation sets. But at this point, the sonata leaves conventional variation behind. The contrary-motion scales move well beyond the original apex, F, to reach the C apex of the new key. The music from m. 20 is a free elaboration of a neighbor-note oscillation around $\hat{5}$ of E♭; that is, $\hat{5}$–$\hat{6}$–$\hat{5}$ motions. A conventional Schenkerian reduction would reveal this, focusing on the registrally marked C of m. 31. We have crossed from the realm of foreground variation to *middleground* elaboration: at the level of deep structure, the content of mm. 20–38 corresponds to what originally occupied a single measure (mm. 4 and 11). Beethoven's hybrid sonata-variation thus entails both transposing and vastly expanding the apex of his arch progression. But there is more: just as the apex elides into a compressed descent at mm. 4 and 11, this falling scale forms the basis of the development section in mm. 40–55. This section unfolds a stepwise octave scale between two C's, the dominant of F minor, and the primary note of the reprise. The variation accordingly embraces transition, second group, and development into a single gestalt.

Op. 111 follows the same lines. The first subject is also an arch apexing on a $\hat{6}$, although with an unusually drawn-out $\hat{5}$–$\hat{4}$–$\hat{3}$–$\hat{2}$–$\hat{1}$ descent. The theme is stated three times, the third time highly elaborated. This entire three-fold scheme, mm. 19–28, is then varied in mm. 29–35, and is followed by a transition in the shape of a fugal exposition, taking the music to the secondary key of A♭. In some ways, the procedure here is more straightforward than in Op. 110, since the piece modulates to the flat submediant A♭, rather than the dominant: that is, it can modulate to the key of the melodic apex, A♭, without requiring a transposition. A♭ is prolonged throughout the second group, mm. 50–69, and slips down a semitone to G at the head of the development. Over the course of this short development, the G of G major is converted to the G of C minor at m. 91 for the reprise (paralleling the C–C development of Op. 110). Op. 111 pursues parataxis more single-mindedly than the other two sonatas. It is the only one which modulates to the submediant, thus chiming with the melodic apex. And the three-part variation scheme is embedded within the first subject itself, which divides into two plain statements followed by a highly figured elaboration. Most strikingly, there is the fact that the theme not only draws out the descent (in contrast to what I have termed the "sawn-off" nature of Beethoven's arches), *it progressively whittles away the head of the arch to concentrate on the descent.* By "decapitating" the arch, the sonata places undue emphasis on a closure as premature as it is overly insistent. Paradoxically, this obsessive closure is abetted by the variation cycle just as it is relieved by the lyrical enclave.

The Abrogated Development

The late developments rarely correspond to the Classical tripartite scheme described by William Caplin as "pre-core," "core," and "retransition" (1998: 139–55). Caplin's "core," after the introductory "pre-core," puts the conventionally developmental stamp on the section and "typically projects an emotional quality of instability, restlessness, and dramatic conflict" (142). It achieves this by submitting a "model" phrase, "normally four to eight measures," to processes of sequential transposition to distant keys, acceleration of harmonic rhythm, and motivic fragmentation (142). After a climax, the third part of the scheme—the retransition—takes the music back to the tonic, often via a circle of fifths.

The developments of Opp. 109–11 are "abrogated" in the sense that they do without a core and are, to varying extents, glorified retransitions. Beethoven drew his inspiration from aspects of both Haydn and Mozart's developments. According to Caplin, "Haydn, in general, constructs his development sections without a core," ostensibly because his sonata forms are so discursive that the development is used as relief (155). And the "developments" of many of Mozart's piano concertos are dominated by drawn-out sequences around the circle of fifths; rather than increasing tension, the development is in a process of relaxation into the reprise. The "development" of Op. 110, mm. 40–55, takes this Mozartian model to new extremes, being simply a sequential repetition of the theme's incipit. Unlike the sequence of a core, the phrase structure and harmonic rhythm is held absolutely steady, enhancing the Classical sequence's function as an agent of harmonic relaxation.[4] The development of Op. 111 is outwardly tripartite: a six-measure "pre-core" (mm. 70–75), introducing a core fugato (76–85), ending with a six-measure retransition (mm. 86–91). But appearances are deceptive (ex. 5.4).

The entries of the fugato—on G, C, and F—already constitute the fifth cycle of

Example 5.4. Op.111, first movement, mm. 72–87

a retransition; the phrasing is too regular for a real "core." And the ostensible re-transition, from m. 86, is actually a compressed recapitulation of the Maestoso introduction, with the successive diminished-seventh chords telescoped into the first subject (see Rosen 2002: 244). So the model has been shunted one place to the left, the reprise displacing the retransition, and the retransition occupying the core. The development in Op. 109 is the most complex and extensive, and ostensibly the best fit for the tripartite model. A seven-measure pre-core (mm. 16–21), which nods to the B major/C# minor alternation of the second group, launches the main business—a sequential rise to a climax on a high B at m. 42 (a near mirror to the sequential *descent* of Op. 110). This B is already a dominant of the tonic, hence a retransition. The problems with this scheme are the overlaps with both the second group and the recapitulation, harmonically as well as texturally. The B climax is the culmination of an ascent which begins in the first group and is cut short by the second. And the *motto perpetuo* texture flows without break into the reprise. Clearly, it makes no sense to hear the B of m. 42 as simultaneously the climax of the core, the arrival point of the second group, and the start of the retransition, but that is what the music suggests.

The displacement of the core by the retransition hollows out the psychological nerve center of the Beethovenian sonata. In heroic works such as the *Eroica,* the core (Caplin's translation of Erwin Ratz's *Kern* [141]) is the point where the issues of the sonata drama are finally worked through, earning the piece the right to proceed to the triumphant return. As much as this moment is unique and individual-izing, its substitution with a mechanical retransition seems to mark the triumph not of subjectivity, but of blank, mechanical convention. In Beethoven's invisible cities, lyricism is walled up by bricks and mortar. Nevertheless, petrification is just the first moment in a transfigurative gambit, by which convention undergoes a sea change into something rich and strange. The routine of retransition can create effects of stability and closure, and may even open up spaces for lyrical apotheosis. The development of each of the sonatas resolves anomalies in the first-subject arch. In Op. 109, there is an inconsistency between the G#–A#–B voice leading of the exposition and the music's unstintingly descending motion. The rising development corrects this imbalance and also stitches together the Vivace semiquavers with a quarter-note melodic line. This melody isn't in fact new: its rising-third kernel (F##–G#–A#–B) marries the quarter note E–F#–G# at the end of the Vivace's first phrase (mm. 3–4) with the left-hand inner voice of the Adagio espressivo. The lyrical apotheosis thus draws out, synthesizes, augments, and lifts up a previously suppressed detail. The development of Op. 110 is transfigured in a different way. The first subject is regularized into a four-measure antecedent/consequent pattern; its initial key of F minor marks the culmination of 6̂ as a tonal force; and the descending contour—otherwise fairly typical of retransitions—fulfills the repeatedly deferred falling half of the arch. Finally, aspects of the theme in Op. 111 are resolved in its own development, due to the addition of a new countersubject (the fugato is really a double fugue). The new cantus firmus converts the first note of the theme (e.g., the C of m. 78, against A♭) into a subdominant, thus correcting a cadential imbalance in the tonic group. Given the subdominant's role as an equal partner within the three diminished-seventh harmonies of the Maestoso (I: C–E♭–F♯–A; V: G–B♭–D♭–E; IV: F–A♭–B–D), its omission from the first subject (which oscillates between I and V) undercuts its gestures toward cadential closure. The exposition's codetta incorporates the subdominant as part of a descending sequence (mm. 58–61). The development goes one step further by reinterpreting the *head* of the subject as a subdominant. Moreover, the last entry of the fugato is in F minor, and the coda of the movement as a whole harnesses the relaxing function of subdominant inflection as a link into the Arietta. The development thus plays a central role within this narrative of stabilization.

Each of these developments is a transfigurative variation, a culmination of the variation cycle begun in the first group. Disclosing the "secret" of the work in such a place makes the recapitulation curiously *de trop*, superogatory, as if the return were not a triumph but a regrettable interruption, a breaking of the spell. Reversing the conventional order of things, Beethoven turns the development into a place of rest, and the reprise into a return to work. The spell, and the breaching, will be most powerful in the extraordinary developments of Opp. 130 and 132.

Form as Contour

I have shown how the "second variation" in the "three-part template" in each sonata consists of a middleground elaboration of the arch schema. Actually, once the contour penetrates to this deep level of structure, it extrapolates backwards to the very opening of the sonata, so as to absorb the entire exposition-cum-development into a single arch. In short, a middleground arch really begins in the first measure of the exposition. Schenkerian analysis can of course demonstrate that *any* tonal music unfolds a voice-leading contour. Nevertheless, Beethoven's sonatas project such contours more self-consciously and single-mindedly, by underscoring voice leading with particularly clear rhythmic, textural, and dynamic progressions. Their melodies accordingly "rhyme" with the modulation to the secondary key—the tonality seems to "rise" to an apex in phase with the contour. Moreover, the form becomes a gestural contour in itself, flexing and relaxing like a line. All this is an outcome of late Beethoven's holistic drive, by which every technical parameter (melody, harmony, rhythm, texture, dynamics) is recruited by a compositional gestalt. The gestalt is semantic as well as technical: the expressive corollary of a melodic or tonal apex is a literally *transcendental* or *elevated* idiom, typically the lyrical. In keeping with the holistic arch, the finale of each sonata "soars" into song.

One would think that the simplicity of the arch schema would constrain the variety possible in the three sonatas. The opposite is true, since the shared template serves to throw differences into sharper relief: as with all structuralist analysis, a common ground is the very condition of transformational change. On the basis of the arch, then, each sonata takes a unique course. The first movement of Op. 110 stands out for having a protracted descent (the development); Opp. 109 and 111 are more typically late in eliding ("sawing off") the fall from $\hat{6}$ to $\hat{3}$. Op. 109 stands out for placing its registral apex late in the development section, rather than in the second group, and in *moto perpetuo*, rather than lyrical, style (in Opp. 110 and 111, the apex leads to a more reflective, static, or expansive idiom). And Op. 111 is unique because it modulates to the submediant, the key of $\hat{6}$; the others move to the dominant, utilizing Beethoven's "$\hat{3} = \hat{6}$" gambit. The $\hat{3} = \hat{6}$ transformation entails a "counterpoint" between two arches, a tonic and a dominant version. The absence of such a dualism in Op. 111 is ironic, given that contrapuntal texture dominates its foreground. Absence of the deeper, "dialogic" kind of counterpoint helps foster Op. 111's sense of obsessive monotony, from which lyric will be a liberation. In the "Galitzin" Quartets, metaphorical counterpoint overtakes contour as Beethoven's regulative idea.

The "Galitzin" Quartets

What I have designated the "second phase" of the late style begins with the first of Beethoven's three "Galitzin" Quartets, Op. 127. These works are more radical than the late sonatas because they undermine the foundations of sonata form's "punctuation model": the articulation of the main structural junctures, and the central caesura between the exposition and development. Another crucial difference turns on a paradigm shift from contour to counterpoint, in natural keeping with the change of instrumental idiom. Homogeneous contour flows from the unitary space of a piano keyboard, with its low-to-high layout (i.e., left-to-right), and the fact that it is performed by an individual. By contrast, the chief fact of a string quartet is dialogue. Contour is of course assimilated into the quartet conversation, but its gamut is multiplied by four. The change is one of priority. Rather than being *subsumed* by contour, as in the sonatas, counterpoint now *regulates* contour, entailing a "counterpoint of contours." As with expressive contour, counterpoint is generalized into a symbol of multiplicity: parametric noncongruence at the micrological end of the spectrum; generic and stylistic plurality at the other extreme. Beethoven's holism thereby gains a new dimension, where details of textural layering encapsulate a polyphony of forms and languages. Looming over these works, as we will see in the next chapter, is the paradigm of the Ninth Symphony, which literally envoices counterpoint, in the shape of instrumental interplay yielding to choral song, as a metaphor of human discord and reconciliation.

Opus 127 in E♭

Each of the "Galitzin" first movements explores a stylistic dualism framed by the contrast between introduction and first group. Unlike those of Opp. 130 and 132, the introduction to Op. 127 does not peak on a dominant (or dominant-type) harmony, but a *subdominant* (ex. A.2, see appendix). This subdominant, inflected into a II^7, resolves at m. 8 on I^6, rather than V. Indeed, the weakness of chord V in the Allegro, capped by the substitution of the dominant key in the second group by the mediant G minor, helps compound the lyrical sensibility of the movement. The Maestoso introduction defines itself oppositionally against this lyrical world by beginning with forceful alternations of I and V. Inasmuch as the three-fold ritornello of the Maestoso, respectively in the keys of E♭, G, and C, parenthetically brackets the lyrical body of the movement, this IN-OUT scheme is associated with the contrast between chords IV and V. The Maestoso is an "external" world of dominants and functional tonality; the *teneramente* Allegro is an "inner" world ruled mostly by subdominants. The stylistic negotiation between Maestoso and Allegro, the frame and the center, is composed out by the gradual assimilation of dominant harmony into the fabric, so that the Maestoso can eventually be safely dispensed with. Although the Maestoso is never reprised in the tonic, its I–V–V–I harmonic scheme is absorbed into the second group, which accordingly marks a point of syntactic clarification. This process of interiorization nevertheless plays against a set of profound structural anomalies which radically breach the sonata form. Second groups in the mediant *major* are by no means unusual (see Op. 31, no. 1, and Op. 53), but the mediant *minor* makes the Maestoso ritornello in G *major* sound like a resolution: a climax of the exposition, rather than the start of the development. Beethoven thereby straddles the caesura between the two halves of the sonata and breaks the back of the form. Furthermore, by reinterpreting the first measure of the reprise in F minor (m. 167), Beethoven connects it to the G- and C-major Maestosos in a circle of fifths (ex. 5.5). Given that the tonality of G actually starts in the second group, the G–C–F cycle cuts across the symmetry of sonata form, leveling and decentering it. Is the movement, then, just one big retransition? The question is how this cycle is rooted in the framing tonics, and we can look to the way Beethoven inflects the main theme, mm. 7–10, with harmonies of G, C, and F minor. It is as if the keys of G, C, and F minor are extrapolations of harmonic color, and that the difference between color and function is simply one of degree. By this light, the secondary key of G minor is not a dominant substitute but, scandalously, *a substitute of the tonic*. Somewhere along the line, an inflection *of* the tonic flips into departure *from* the tonic. And F minor—the point of furthest remove—is disclosed at the climax of the development as really a point of return. In this way, Op. 127 interchanges the flatness of a lyrical state (colored by harmonic inflections) with the dynamic of a tonal journey (driven by a cycle of fifths). Metaphorically extending the notion of counterpoint, this "counterpoint" of static and dynamic perspectives is a projection from the iridescent interplay of lines at the opening. Raising the metaphor to a yet higher order, the quartet is also situated in a "counterpoint" of musical conventions, in that to make sense of its anomalies, the listener needs to navigate a network of stylistic codes gleaned from a knowledge of the Classical repertoire. Each of the movement's ostensible eccentricities actually has a precedent in Classical practice; the problem is that, through multitasking, the material references more than one practice at one time, with the result that its formal "coding" is as iridescent as its harmonic color. This universe of conventions can be mapped in detail.

First, the Maestoso ritornello scheme is a concerto device, and its dialogue with the Allegro evokes a concertante antiphony between orchestral tutti and solo in-

Example 5.5. Op. 127, first movement, mm. 161–69

strument. Op. 127 directly echoes the opening of Mozart's Piano Concerto no. 22, also in E♭, which similarly begins with a question-answer arching idea: a rhetorically powerful fanfare figure, moving from I to V, is answered by a lyrical descent from $\hat{5}$ to $\hat{1}$. Against this Mozartian template, we see how Beethoven apexes on $\hat{6}$ (C), rather than $\hat{5}$. Haydn's Symphony no. 46 in B also does this, although it is unclear whether Beethoven knew this piece. Second, Op. 127 is related to a family of Beethoven's own works in E♭. The piano sonata Op. 31, no. 3, begins with a harmonically veiled melody, whose subdominant ambiguities are clarified as the exposition proceeds. It is thus patently *introductory*, in which case we see that the harmonic transparency of Op. 127's Maestoso inverts the conventional role of introductions. Beethoven's "Harp" Quartet, Op. 74, is a halfway house in this matter, beginning with a harmonically obfuscatory Poco Adagio, which resolves with a kind of tonic-affirming triadic figure suited to a first group. This triadic flourish recurs at the head of the development in G major—a direct precedent for Op. 127, and it similarly proceeds from G to C. What is missing is the next swing of the cycle to F minor (Op. 74 proceeds, conventionally, to a dominant retransition); for this, we can turn back to Op. 31, no. 3, the F-minor *tinta* (chord II^7) of whose theme becomes a full-scale key in the development, leading to a reprise reinterpreted unambiguously in this key. Moreover, F minor is prepared by a plateau in C major, giving the development a simple C–F tonal structure. Nevertheless, C is not approached via G, as in the "Harp": Op. 127 synthesizes the two models (C–F and G–C) into a *three*-phase cycle (G–C–F). According to Caplin, the Classical development conventionally has only two main tonal resting points; giving it three, as Beethoven does in Op. 127, is one climax too many. For the device of a ritornello scheme in G and C major, we can look to yet another E♭ work, the finale of the Piano Trio Op. 70, no. 2, whose second group is in G major and is recapitulated in C. Even though its reprise unfolds in reverse order (second group before first), the trio's tonal scheme never challenges the break between exposition and development, as does Op. 127. The origins of this elision takes us to another group of conventions altogether.

The anomaly of the second group's minor key points in two opposite directions, each one validated by a Beethovenian convention. The first path leads to the composer's violin and cello sonatas, in which major/minor relationships are more prevalent than in the other chamber music (see Drabkin 2004). After its A-major introduction, the "Kreutzer" sonata, Op. 47, launches into a first group in A *minor,* modulating to a second group in E minor. This new theme, mm. 91 ff., actually enters more normatively in E *major,* so the subsequent return to, and conclusion in, the minor (after m. 107) is a direct and self-conscious flouting of convention. The late cello sonata Op. 102, no. 1, starts with a glowing C major, shifts to first group in A minor, which leads to a second group in E minor—as in Op. 127, the minor mediant of the opening key. Nevertheless, the other path takes us to the convention of the *transitional theme,* a practice especially common in Beethoven's earliest works. In many of the first-period sonatas, the second group is introduced as an unstable modulating theme, beginning in the minor and not finding its feet until it reaches the dominant. In Op. 2, nos. 2 and 3, it enters in the tonic minor of the dominant (respectively E minor and G minor). Schubert builds on this convention to create three-theme expositions and thereby influences Brahms (see Webster 1978).[5] For example, the middle theme in his "Great" C-major Symphony is in E minor, so that the three key areas of the exposition arpeggiate a C–E–G triad (the C-major Quintet arpeggiates C–E♭–G). Middle-period Beethoven turns away from the radical implications of his youthful invention—namely, a lyrical rounding out of the exposition's symmetry through a more gradual diffusion of tonal motion— and instead reaffirms the drama of the two-theme model. At the same time, he absorbs the "modulating theme" idea into the transition, so that the entry of the second group frequently pivots on a revelatory shift from minor to major. The most pertinent example is the "Waldstein," whose transition actually modulate from C major to E *minor,* creating a magical glow when the second subject corrects it to the major (a direct reversal of his major-to-*minor* gambit in the "Kreutzer," whose transition and second subject are clearly the model for the "Waldstein"). In this respect, then, the G-minor theme in Op. 127 isn't the second group after all, but a transition to an anticipated mediant *major*. The fact that what arrives is not a new theme, but a ritornello of the Maestoso, doesn't change this expectation at all: it just spins the paradoxes in new directions.

Whether the G-major Maestoso marks the arrival of the second group or the start of the development thus depends on whether we hear the G-minor material as a theme or a transition. Remarkably, Beethoven applies multitasking to reinforce *both* these options. On the one hand, the apparently new theme is really a hidden variation of the first group, a connection which comes rhythmically to light in the cello codetta figures at m. 57. Like the first subject, the second group is basically a contrapuntal elaboration of simple neighbor-note oscillations around B♭ and C (the second violin from m. 7 summarizes violin I's melody as a C–B♭–C–B♭ cantus firmus; a similar relationship binds the two violins at mm. 41–44). The main difference is that the second group shunts the pattern so as to begin on B♭, rather than C. The result is to stabilize the theme, so that it both begins on a tonic harmony and rearranges chords IV and V into a satisfyingly closed cadential pattern. If the chief flaw of the subdominant apex in mm. 6–7 is that it does not resolve to a dominant but to a I^6, then the kink is ironed out in mm. 45–47. There, an apex on $\hat{6}$ (E), supported by IV, leads to a strong V—a gesture compressed in the powerful V–I cadences of the codetta (mm. 64–75). But the variation is even more subtle than that, for the I–V V–I antecedent-consequent syntax of the beginning of the G-minor theme, mm. 41–44, also echoes the tonic-dominant alternations of the Maestoso introduction, thereby supplying an answer to its eccentric syncopations. Although the Maestoso is notated in a $\frac{2}{4}$ time signature, the rhythms suggests a clipped ternary meter: the sforzato quarter note at m. 2 is given the dynamic and durational emphasis of a *first beat* of a measure. We hear the music as a sort of "mensurational stretto," an implicit E♭ trochee in $\frac{3}{4}$ accelerating to a B♭ trochee in $\frac{3}{8}$, and then being brought back to speed at m. 3. The effect is not only a breathless rush to the Allegro, but also an anticipation of the movement's prevailing ternary meter. From this angle, the opening of the G-minor theme, which augments the I–V V–I figures into full measures, and recontextualizes them in $\frac{3}{4}$, is the place where the asthmatic Maestoso is first allowed to breathe, indeed to *sing*. Metrically as well as harmonically, therefore, the second group both reorganizes the relationship between the Maestoso and first subject, and resolves their constituent kinks.

On the other hand, astonishingly, the G-minor group is *also* a reworking of the transition of mm. 22–32, which had "botched" the modulation by failing to reinterpret $\hat{3}$ of E♭ as $\hat{6}$ of B♭. The cadential descent from G to B♭ is attempted at m. 25, but in the bizarre context of a variant of the Maestoso: mm. 22–31 elaborate the Maestoso's ascent to C, redirecting it toward a tonic cadence. Thereafter, the music makes a succession of attempts at a $\hat{6}$–$\hat{1}$ descent, the sequence ultimately leading to G minor. But the original problem was that the "correct" descent, from G to B♭, had been tucked into a V–I cadence in E♭ (mm. 25–26). Just as we saw in the piano sonatas (especially the *Hammerklavier*), the quartet's transition looks both backwards to the tonic, as a variation/ritornello of the opening, and forwards to the new key. In the present case, the normative dominant modulation fails utterly, and is mourned by the G-minor theme, whose B♭–B♭ octave descent obsessively rehearses that of mm. 24–25. Regardless of this thematic corrective, the section still sits in the "wrong" key, as a monstrously prolonged expansion of the eighth-note G♮ of m. 25; that is, the key of G is not so much the mediant of E♭ as the submediant of the displaced B♭. It consequently launches a neat symmetry: the second group converts 6̂ of B♭ into a tonic, just as the C-major Maestoso of m. 135 will tonicize 6̂ of E♭. The key of the second group is thus the first portent of the fate of the Maestoso, and the role reversal between base and apex which will be played out, climactically, in the retransition. What occurs between m. 133 and the reprise of m. 167 involves a complex sequence of gestalt shifts, not simply a case of 6̂ (C) becoming a tonic. Actually, this ritornello is the only one of the three Maestosos which is *not* a tonic, instead, a dominant: it is set up, via the cello D♭'s, as V of F minor, and the return of development at m. 147 resumes preparation for this key. The C-major Maestoso is entirely circumscribed by a voice-leading progression which rises from the E♮'s of mm. 133 and 147 to an apex a sixth above, which is of course the C of the reprise. In this brief context of F minor at m. 167, C is stabilized on a strangely skewed platform: no longer a submediant, it briefly becomes the fifth of a phantom tonic triad. In its evanescence, this moment is absolutely typical of the delicate pointillism of the late style. The moment is also a trace of an absence, for of course the expected reprise of the Maestoso in E♭—of which this C ought to have been the apex—has been canceled. And we retrospectively grasp the middle-ground ascent from the E♮ of m. 133 as its replacement: the Maestoso—the agent of the concertante outside world—has been digested by the lyrical stream. The business of the movement is effectively done when the frame has been assimilated to the lyrical enclosure. All that remains is for the G-minor group to be recapitulated as a positive *maggiore* in E♭, and for the Maestoso to ultimately be displaced by an unbuttoned elaboration of the tonic group in the coda. A telling gesture of liberation here is the affecting 6̂–7̂–8̂ ascents in the first violin in mm. 260–65: "soaring" technically gives the apex 6̂ a different way out—up, rather than down (the variations in the next movement will exploit this 6̂–7̂–8̂ reflex at every climax).

Clearly, an enormous amount of formal information, which will determine how we read the design of the whole movement, is packed into the G-minor section. For lyrical material, the music works extremely hard, being imbricated within a complex network of functional threads crisscrossing the entire piece. These threads ultimately lead to specific stylistic conventions, which is not to say that the music makes no sense without their precise knowledge, only that this sense is enriched by stylistic understanding. Furthermore, the tangential character of these conventions is odd, in that they engage not separate genres (i.e., *other* than sonata form) but the marginalia, riders, qualifications, and contractual loopholes *within* sonata form. Op. 127 has a retrospectively encyclopedic scope, and had Beethoven died after completing it, we would consider it a fittingly summatory valediction (indeed, just like many *other* late works, such as Op. 111, the *Diabelli* Variations, the Ninth Symphony, or the last quartet). Consider how Op. 127 gathers together gambits from each of the five last sonatas: Op. 101's lyrical flatness and the run-in between second group and development; Op. 106's faulty modulation and a retrospectively corrective second group in G major/minor; Op. 109's fast introduction in $\frac{2}{4}$ and its opposition to a $\frac{3}{4}$ lyrical parenthesis; Op. 110's archlike melody with its "thirds and fourths" pattern; and Op. 111's formally separate Maestoso. The nature of this syncretism is not static but dynamic, putting into play a heteroglossia of structural markers, each one pointing in a distinctive direction.[6] Face to face with the music, in an envelope of the ever shifting present-tense moment, the listener is confronted with choices: What happens next, Where do I go now? Importantly, experiencing this music is not a matter of making the "right" decision—there *isn't* one to be made; Beethoven has heaped up too many signposts, each of which is valid. Rather, the experience is one of being overcome, dazzled, by this lyrical cornucopia, while, miraculously, being guided by the composer's firm hand from A to B through a sonata form which ultimately proves to be perfectly satisfying. We *sleepwalk* though Beethoven's dreamscapes. We experience an alluring gap between our own cognitive paralysis and the music's sure-footedness, a gap which induces not deafness but yet another variant of *Schein*'s flicker.

Opus 130 in B♭

The genesis of Op. 130 and Op. 132 overlapped, with the B♭ quartet begun in June 1825, seven months *after* Beethoven started work on the A minor, in December 1824. And with Op. 132 already behind us, this chapter will end with Op. 130. Like its soul-mate Op. 101, the E♭ quartet was followed by a B♭ work with a grand sonata-form movement, one which superficially enunciates the junctures of the conventional form very clearly. It is as if each of the two main phases of the late style were signaled by a lyrical upbeat to a *rapel à l'ordre*. Nevertheless, Op. 130 foregoes the heroic pose of the *Hammerklavier* for the rather more dated idiom of the *galant* divertimento. The ultra-conventionalized and frankly shallow character of this *galant* material generates the problematic of the work—the hankering for affective and intellectual substance. The resurgence of counterpoint in the *Grosse Fuge*, Op. 130's original finale, supplies one kind of denouement; the first movement settles for an opposite kind, a remarkable development section which overwhelms the listener with a sudden access of lyrical intensity. It is as if the empty husks of convention were flooded with vital fluid; this momentary animation of the fossilized represents Op. 130's peculiar take on a gambit common to all three quartets. Beethoven was a dialectical thinker within works, but also *between* works, which often take a deliberately contrary line to their immediate precursor. The template of "arch to a $\hat{6}$, followed by descent" is a useful gauge of this dialectic. Casting our minds back to Op. 132, we remember that the arch was resolved by a cadenza-like sixteenth-note cascade, which signaled the turn from the slow introduction to the Allegro. With its lyrical time, the cadenza is the analogue for the *teneramente* answer to Op. 127's Maestoso. Compared to its sister works, the B♭ quartet seems to be the exception (ex. A.3, see appendix).

Its Adagio introduction does rise, admittedly, to $\hat{5}$ at m. 7, extended to $\hat{6}$ by the cello a measure later. But the cello's subsequent descent is covered, and obviated, by a violin rise which reinforces the modulation to F. In fact, the process is drawn out up to the fermata of m. 14, where a cadenza—closely paralleling that in Op. 132—breaks out in quite the wrong way. Rather than being auxiliary, like a conventionally introductory *Eingang* or "lead-in," the cadenza is rendered thematic. Not only does it start on the tonic, it even dominates the entire section group, so that the tonic group is swallowed up by a paradoxically stabilized cadenza. This anomaly motivates the search for a "normal" cadenza, which is achieved in the second group. There, the sixteenth-note figures find their place as upbeat runs to quarter notes. The course of the exposition, then, is to chop up and reconfigure a totalized, falsely stable, cadenza. Taking a step back, we need to reckon with the further paradox that by casting the Allegro in terms of the cadenza topic, Beethoven inverts the conventional relationship between exposition and slow introduction. If the Allegro behaves as a cadenza-like parenthesis, then the Adagio is the most substantial "introduction" of the "Galitzin" and lays robust claim to being the real beginning of the piece. Furthermore, the affinity with Op. 127 profiles another dramatic reversal. As with Op. 127, the second group of Op. 130 sorts out some problems with the tonic group, in this case by instituting a more stable and well-formed lyrical idea. But Op. 130's second group stabilizes the first group for opposite ends, since the regularizing of a cadenza naturally promotes motion rather than rest. Another difference is that Op. 127 wears its lyrical heart in its second group, whereas Op. 130 displaces it into the development, *by very virtue of the cadenza's newly auxiliary function.* By reaching its apotheosis in the development section, the process intersects with the central task of the movement, the transfiguration of convention into song. Op. 130's development section, the movement's emotional heart and intellectual soul, is thus implicated in a web of functional relations. To map out these relations, we must begin by outlining Beethoven's systematic deconstruction of each and every juncture of sonata form.

The deconstructions—the focus of much analytic scrutiny on the piece—can be quickly disposed of. The Adagio introduction recurs so early into the Allegro (five measures) as to challenge the very identity of the first group, the work's sense of beginning. Is the Adagio not an introduction after all, but the true beginning? The transition, especially from m. 37, goes through all the motions—excessively, one might feel—of a modulation to the dominant: sequential repetition, acceleration of phrase rhythm, cadential gestures. Exactly as with the *Hammerklavier*, it ends on F, rather than C, a bifocal close which might as easily tip back into B♭ as stay in F. Also, as in Op. 106, this is then dismissed by a subversive gesture: not a *Rückung*, but a tonally mystifying chromatic scale. Again, as with Op. 106, this leads to the submediant, albeit a flattened one. And again, similarly, the quartet's extensive second group spends most of its time correcting this rupture with fifth cycles. The development is more radical than the sonata's, however, because it is no "development" at all, but a static drift through the circle of fifths supporting a new melody. This fifth cycle is actually circumscribed by a fall of a major third D-B♭, itself continuing from the second group's G♭, symmetrically trisecting the tonal architecture as B♭–G♭–D–B♭. The *Hammerklavier*'s own triadic architecture was an asymmetrical B♭–G♯–E♭–C♭/B♭. The final kink (E♭–C♭/B♭), though generative in its own way, is less subversive than in Op. 130, because of the suggestion that the latter's regulative sonority is an *augmented triad,* a symmetrical structure inimical to functional tonality. Furthermore, the development's fifth cycle overflows its banks and diverts the recapitulation through B♭–E♭–A♭–D♭, neatly connecting with the key of the second-group reprise. This off-tonic reprise, closely corrected by a tonic version, is strange, though hardly unprecedented (see Op. 31, no. 1 [E major, then G], Op. 53 [A major, then C], Op. 110 [E major, then A♭], and the Op. 131 finale [D major, then C♯]). The difference lies in the smooth, even ineluctable, continuity between D♭ and the fifth cycle, effectively swallowing up the second group into the development. The systematicity of the two architectures—the augmented triadic (B♭–G♭–D–B♭) and the fifth cyclic (D–G–C–F–B♭–E♭–A♭–D♭)—amounts to a war between two conflicting perspectives on tonal space. This war is succinctly summarized in the counterpoint between the Allegro's dual themes: the first violin's sixteenth-note cascade in thirds, against the second's fifths, B♭–E♭ and C–F (mm. 14–18). The Adagio recurs three more times in the coda, broken up and mixed together with the Allegro.

All these deconstructions turn on the central "development" section of mm. 94–132, one of the most striking—and beautiful—passages in all late Beethoven (ex. A.4, see appendix). After the close of the second group in G♭, Beethoven brings back the Adagio introduction in this key. But after only two measures, it is interrupted by a snippet of Allegro, itself cut short by the same Adagio-Allegro pattern transposed down a third (or diminished fourth) to D major. There follows three more measures of Adagio, but now liquidated into its cadential appoggiatura figures. And then something extraordinary happens, a twenty-eight-measure plateau when the feverish *moto perpetuo* of the quartet comes to a halt in a dreamlike trance, featuring a haunting new melody, played mostly by the cello.[7] Although the effect is one of utter novelty, it is easy to see how this "development" draws on earlier material. In particular, the elements of the introductory alternations of mm. 93–103—the Adagio's throbbing appoggiatura figuration, and the Allegro's monotone repetitions and leap—are wired together into a delicate filigree. Moreover, the "new" melody is really derived from the somewhat ungainly second subject of m. 55, "an ugly duckling dream–transformed into a graceful arching element," in Kerman's happy phrase (312). And yet, for all its allure, this "development" is nothing but a glorified retransition; in Caplin's terms, the retransition has pushed out the "core" (a little like Op. 111), so this coreless development is actually quite hollow. Moreover, the retransition is embedded as a grotesque parenthesis within an elaborate game of false reprise. To appreciate this false reprise as Op. 130's quintessentially *galant* marker, a short historical parenthesis is in order.

In every third or fourth of Haydn's early baryton trios, the main theme returns in the tonic on the second phrase of the development, often after a preliminary statement in the dominant (e.g., in Trio no. 32 in G major, this reprise is false or premature with respect to the true reprise ten measures later). As Rosen says, "there is nothing inherently comic about its employment" (1988: 156). It is merely a formal convention, and Strunk calls it a "sterile mannerism" (1932: 126). In fact, it reflects the primitive state of the language before the stylistic revolutions of the 1770s when "the functions of the development and recapitulation are unmistakably clarified and distinguished as intensification and resolution respectively" (Rosen, 161). Only with the subsequent heightening of a sense of function did the false reprise emerge as a dramatic device: a new set of norms had to crystallize in order to be effectively frustrated, as in the first movement of Haydn's String Quartet Op. 17, no. 1. Later, the false reprise was not confined to the tonic, falling on the relative minor in Op. 33, no. 2, and the subdominant in Op. 50, no. 3. Such is the case in Beethoven's B♭ quartet, whose development is interrupted by a false reprise of the Allegro in F♯ (m. 96), and *another* in D major (m. 100). The retransition, mm. 104–31, is thus a parenthesis between the second false reprise and the correct reprise at m. 132.

The grotesquery, then, is that development has been squeezed out by its marginalia: all that is left is false reprise and retransition. That is one perspective; another is that mm. 104–31 comprise not an enclosure within a parenthesis, a footnote to a footnote, but a climax, a center, even a kind of recapitulation. Once again, as with the G-minor group of Op. 127, the music points in two directions. One pathway takes us to the piece's relentless alternation of Adagio and Allegro materials, by which each tries to frame the other as the center of an ABA da capo structure. But the da capos are constantly intercut, so that *the false reprise principle is wired into the material from the outset.* This "false reprise principle" is really an expression of a fine-grained parametric noncongruence; what appears to be a throwback to a *galant* cliché is in fact a late-style reconstruction. Namely, the very quintessence of *galant* convention turns out to be a projection of a unique compositional idea. The other pathway unravels the genealogy of Kerman's "beautiful swan" melody, and explains why it is an apotheosis.

The starting point for both interpretations is naturally the Adagio introduction, which begins perhaps the most dazzlingly dialectical argument in all of Beethoven's music. Appropriately, I will track this dialectic with the most sustained close-reading of this book. If at times the complexity of the argument seems wildly disproportionate to the modesty of the *galant* material, then the reader may simply savor this surely intentional irony on Beethoven's part. I call this disproportion "the dialectical sublime"—a density of argument in excess of audience comprehension. The twists and turns of the argument rotate too quickly, by analogy to the spinning sixteenth notes of the Allegro cascades. The reader should also keep in mind that this excess is opposite to that of Op. 127. There, it was a superfluity of conventional markers; here, it is an overabundance of an abstract, internal, patterning. Or rather, Op. 127 points outward, Op. 130 inward—a dichotomy which itself contradicts their respective outlooks. For Op. 127's lyricism is inward, while Op. 130 is in *galant* divertimento style, an entertainment genre traditionally played out of doors. Also, the effect of the dialectic on the place of the "development" is quite distinctive: it flashes its status repeatedly "in" and "out," like the flickerings of a cognitive traffic light.

The Adagio ma non troppo is the longest most autonomous introduction of the late quartets. It comprises a four-measure tonic statement, a modulation to the dominant (mm. 5–6), a central contrasting statement, and a move back to the home key (mm. 11–14). By the Adagio's own internal logic, this retransition points to a tonic reprise of mm. 1–4, instead of which the Allegro arrives. Since the Adagio returns five measures later, albeit in F, the Allegro so far behaves as a parenthesis within an Adagio. There *is* a precedent for this conceit, the finale of Haydn's String Quartet Op. 54, no. 2, in C major, where a compressed Presto sonata form is interpolated within a long and elaborate Adagio. Beethoven pushes the Adagio/Allegro dialectic much further than Haydn. Superficially, the Allegro appears to win out, yet in reality the Adagio recurs in the guise of the second group and development. Moreover, the Adagio constitutes a formal, tonal, and thematic template for the movement as a whole, yet with these dimensions fiercely at odds with each other. Simply put, it is a "negative image" of the exposition. Its tonic group, mm. 1–4, become the basis for the second subject, mm. 55–66, which reharmonize both its pitches and melodic contour in the new key of G♭. Conversely, the disjunct sixteenth-note third cycles of the Adagio's dominant phrase, mm. 7–8 (G–E♭–C), foreshadow the third cycles of the Allegro's *first* group, especially after m. 37. The Allegro phrase of mm. 14–20, despite developing the Adagio's middle phrase, reworks the modulation of its *first* phrase: a rise from B♭ to F. So the Adagio's thematic and tonal patterns are abstracted from each other and rearranged. Tonally, then, the Allegro phrase behaves like the Adagio da capo which it ostensibly displaces: multitasking, it blends the functions of the Adagio's "outer" and "inner" phrase.

The Adagio implies a regular da capo ABA structure, an archetype which is the formal analogue of Beethoven's arch contours. As well as matching Kinderman's "parenthetical enclosures," the ABA da capo, often called a *Bogenform* (or arch form) in nineteenth-century theory, also outlines the triplicity of Hegelian logic. On the simplest level, one may have expected a tripartite introduction to function as a stable template for a ternary movement. But the dialectic operates in a far more sophisticated manner than that, and for two reasons. First, *the ABA is never actually completed in the Adagio;* the retransition of mm. 11–14 might suggest it, but the Allegro enters instead. If the pattern is really a broken pattern, then which model does the movement follow: an authentic ABA, or a complex one? Second, Beethoven's dialectic consists in the systematic foreshortening or elision of interlocking *Bogenform*s, with ABA's turning into BAB's, which revert to ABA's, etc. A typical outcome is something like ABBAABBA, or, to better express the force of substitution, a cascade of

    AB(A)
     BA(B)
      AB(A)
       BA(B) etc.

A is not replaced by B so much as *transformed into* B, so that B institutes the new *Bogenform* in the shape of the old one. The pivot for these transformations is parametric noncongruence: A and B can share some of each other's thematic, tonal, or formal features, but never all of them. For convenience, in what follows I will short-hand both Adagio and "beginning" phrases "A," and both Allegro and "middle" phrases "B."

The "broken model" and the "intercut model" are part of the same process, whose outcome is essentially *parataxis,* a repetition of A or B which cuts across the da capo's. The movement jerks between clusters of AA's and BB's. The crucial point is that these "paratactic pairs" *are already present within the opening Adagio.* Despite appearing to be displaced by the Allegro, the Adagio's da capo is subtly woven into the modulation at m. 9 and the retransition at mm. 13–14, both of which incorporate references to the B♭ tonic within new tonal contexts (F and E♭). There is also a more overt *thematic* paratactic pair in mm. 8–13, by which the middle phrase is repeated down a fifth. The hidden da capo at mm. 8–9 is interesting, because it is a signal example of late-style bifocal counterpoint. While the cello attempts a retransition to the tonic at mm. 8–9, the second violin rehearses the modulation to the dominant of mm. 4–7, compressed from two measures to one. This counter-subject simultaneously suggests and disrupts the interpretation of the cello line at m. 9 in B♭. On the one hand, the dissonance treatment of m. 8, its sequence of off-beat passing notes, sets up the cello's first note in m. 9 as a harmony note, an elaboration of a tonic B♭ triad. On the other hand, the harmonic direction of the violin countersubject shunts the music into F major, so that we are forced to hear the cello's B♭ as an accented passing note to A. Given that the cello scale is a compressed version of the opening descent of mm. 1–2, this blend of modulation and return is perfectly in accord with the transitions of the late sonatas. The second disguised da capo, at mm. 13–14, is also notable for the way it sutures the breach between the Adagio and Allegro. See how the violin's E♭ of m. 14, after the fermata, resolves down the scale of the Allegro cascade, but in figurations probably too quick to hear, and is then picked up by the second violin's dotted half note E♭ of m. 15. Question: Does the Allegro resolve this E♭ (with the descending line of m. 15) or sustain it (violin II's countersubject)? Formal ambiguity beautifully shades into the counterpoint. The abstraction of Beethoven's thematic process is epitomized by m. 15, since the continuity of the line through the break of m. 14 is very difficult, if not impossible, to perceive.

The Adagio thus predisposes the movement toward irregularity, by setting up both a regular and an irregular paradigm. The Allegro's tonic group can thus be heard in two ways. Broadly speaking, it is a BAB structure, a central Adagio (m. 20) flanked by Allegro material. But then we notice that the Allegro da capo is attempted first in the wrong key, F major—that is, continuing the key of the Adagio—before being resolved at m. 31 in the tonic. From this angle, we have two interlocking paratactic pairs, depending on whether we focus on tonal repetition (the F major of the Adagio and the first Allegro statement) or thematic repetition (the two Allegro statements, on F and B♭). The patterns are thus either ABBA (tonal) or BABB (thematic). We therefore have three ways of hearing the tonic group's relationship to the introduction: (1) as inverted da capo (broadly, ABA becoming BAB); (2) as tonal parataxis (the bifocal return/modulation of mm. 8–9); (3) as thematic parataxis (the repeat of the middle phrase at mm. 11–14). Or rather, as with Op. 127, there is no right or wrong answer: all three perspectives are coextensive and induce a cognitive flicker by which the Adagio of mm. 20–25 flashes in and out of interpretational frames. The multiplicity of this Adagio sets the stage, in the next tier of *Bogenforms*, for the role of the G♭ group (ex. A.5, see appendix).

With the second group, Op. 130 accords with the sonatas' "three-part template of theme plus two variations." The arch to $\hat{5}$ and $\hat{6}$, presented at mm. 1–8 of the introduction, is elaborated by the Allegro's shift to F at m. 20, and completed by the modulation to G♭ at m. 55. The new theme at mm. 55–57 has many textural and thematic links with the Adagio, especially as mediated by the F-major ritornello of mm. 20–24 (such as the tonic pedal and the part writing in thirds and sixths). Also, in absolute-pitch terms, the two violins in mm. 55–57 reinterpret the pitches of the Adagio's original theme, modified to fit the new key: B♭–B♭♭–A♭– (G♭)–E♭–D(♭)–C(♭). This cuts across a simultaneous *melodic* reference to the original theme: eliding the opening chromatic slide, the first violin takes up the Adagio melody from the sixth leap and countervailing gap-fill motion, shunting it up so as to peak on a tonic G♭. The original leap at m. 1 is an awkward G–E♭, so the second subject can be heard to regularize it within a tonic triad. Hearing the second group as a further, off-tonic ritornello of the Adagio ostensibly confirms the shape of the exposition as a grand ABA: two Adagios framing a cadenza-like Allegro. But once again, the paratactic pairs come into play, and we can now address them in their more familiar clothing as a *false-reprise/correct-reprise sequence*. At this architectonic level, parataxis, noncongruence, and da capo elisions are revealed as having been the instruments by which this *galant* convention is inscribed within the texture of the music. Just as the F-major Allegro da capo of m. 25 is a "false reprise" relative to the tonic return of m. 31, the G♭ group is a false reprise of the Adagio, with respect to the B♭ da capo cued by the repeat marks at the end of the exposition: the G♭–B♭ pair is realized when we return to the beginning. And yet this reading disregards the creeping transformation of A into B, as the Adagio-type G♭ melody is progressively overtaken by Allegro-type cadenza figurations. The pivot for this transformation is the variation of mm. 64–70, where the second subject is elaborated in sixteenth-note figures which recall both the "B" phrase of the Adagio (mm. 8–12) and the Allegro cadenzas. The course of the music from then on is to realize a tendency implicit within this B material but so far repressed: the dynamic fifth cycle. The cello fifths at m. 8 (G–D; E♭–B) and the paired fifths of the first subject (e.g., violin 1's B♭–E♭; C–F at mm. 16–17) are melodically curtailed and harmonically contained. From m. 64 they are opened up and allowed to generate tonal cycles. Beethoven writes two fifth cycles, each ending on a perfect cadence. The first one, mm. 66–70, occupies five measures and outlines the cycle B♭–E♭–A♭–D♭– G♭. The third, mm. 76–90, is three times the length, at fifteen measures, and considerably elaborates the cycle. In between, mm. 71–75, comes a relatively static cadential group, so the three sections comprise an eccentric da capo structure—a stable midpoint framed by two sequential episodes, the latter much longer. The length and instability of this latter episode drives the music into the arms of the development section, mm. 104–32. At nearly thirty measures, the development is roughly twice the size of the fifteen-measure episode, confirming an elegantly cumulative design. Discounting the links of mm. 91–103, we have a pattern of: 5 + 5 + 15 + 29. Given that the development is modeled on the very same fifth cycle, transposed so as to cadence in B♭ (D–G–C–F–B♭), are there grounds for thinking of it, outrageously, as the recapitulation of the second group, as well as an outgrowth of its cumulative drive?

Three crucial tasks are achieved by the second group's cycles: they successively expand the tonal range of the Allegro, becoming the movement's de facto development section; they retrospectively correct the modulation to G♭, mediating it between fifth steps (B♭–E♭–A♭–D♭–G♭); and they anticipate the tonicized cycle of the "official" development section. The extraordinary implications of this double cycle should be stressed: *the second group becomes the "real" development, whose fifth cycle is reprised in the formal development so as to lead to the tonic B♭.* Remarkably, then, the relationship between the two sections becomes analogous to that between a false and a true reprise: the second group is a false reprise, corrected by the more sustained, stable, and tonic "development" of mm. 104–32. Looking back, and ahead, to Op. 132, we can reflect on the rigor of Beethoven's dialectic: if Op. 130 has three developments, then it builds on the idea of its immediate precursor, Op. 132, of having three expositions (or two recapitulations).

The genealogy of the swan: The transfiguration of the second subject into Kerman's "graceful arching element" compounds the "reprise quality" of mm. 104–32. The theme marks the concordance of two lines of evolution launched by the Adagio and Allegro. It resolves them individually and also brings them together. From the standpoint of the arch template, the Adagio theme at m. 1 is awkward because it *starts* on a descent, moreover, a descent from the tonic. And its sixth leap, G–E♭, is not only metrically and tonally weak, it is given too little space. The second subject, at m. 55, shunts this leap to prime position and stabilizes it on a tonic harmony. But its apex on 8̂ is still counterintuitive. A clue lies in the octave the violin G♭ sounds against the cello's tonic pedal; octaves surround this texture (e.g., the D♭'s between violin and cello at mm. 53 and 57) and point to the theme's final transformation. The mutation of the sixth to an octave at m. 106 thus has an air of inevitability, and casting it on the 5th, supported by a static tonic harmony, creates a fine balance of openness and closure. Beethoven's preparation for this moment is immensely calculating: follow the pitch A, from the first violin's note repetitions at m. 100, through the registral zigzag between the two violins at mm. 102–5, up to the cello's entry at m. 106. Beethoven derives the cello's octave leap both from the interval of entry and the Allegro theme's note repetitions. The cello simultaneously cross-refers both to the note repetitions and to the perfect fourth A–D, the first true *interval* of the Allegro theme. Referring back to mm. 15–16 of the Allegro, one is struck by how Beethoven dislocates the two parts of the theme through dynamic extremes: the B♭ repetitions are forte, the E♭ is a subito piano. By dynamically isolating the B♭'s, Beethoven almost suggests that the thematic kernel of the piece is a single note! The conceptual cross-relations here are vertiginous. The monotone, the fourth, the sixth, and the octave are different and diverging agents, yet the music of mm. 14–16 prefigures their climactic convergence in the "Swan" theme. Remember how the E♭ of m. 16 echoes and sustains the E♭ fermata of m. 14, thereby associating the Adagio's G–E♭ with the Allegro's fourth B♭–E♭. And notice how the first violin's cascade at m. 15 outlines a falling octave B♭–B♭, predicting the interchangeability between octaves and monotones. Nuclear fusion explodes with a brilliant flash of recognition at the very first measure of the reprise, m. 132, which reverses the cascade into a *rising* octave in violin 2. The "rising cascade" answers the final swing of the "swan" octave (the G–G of m. 130), clinches the affinity with the monotone repetitions, and propels the B♭ up a fourth to the E♭. Never has an *Apparition* been so blinding.

6   Ways of World Making

OP. 109, OP. 110, OP. 111, THE *DIABELLI*
VARIATIONS, OP. 131, OP. 135, THE NINTH
SYMPHONY

Apparition—Surface appearance; sudden illumination; work as firework; a coming
into appearance; disclosure of identity; perceptual shift; momentary epiphany;
grasping a work's mediated character; flash of conceptual understanding.

At the center, in the house of music, upon the musical landscape, sits Beethoven.
Beethoven's subjectivity embraces every aspect of a composition into a cycle, whose
circularity evokes the self-reflection of thought. Particular as they are, the late
works are also worlds, and in the dual sense of a world of convention and of natural
principles. The idea of a sonata can be a convention such as a trill, as well as the
oscillating contour enshrined in a trill. This "idea" need not be a thematic premise explicit at the opening; it can operate at background levels as a regulative concept. Mixing convention and nature, the idea (Style 2), is thus the outcome of the
interaction of convention (Style 1) and nature (Style 3). Because this interaction
is conflictual, the idea partakes of the qualities of resistance and overcoming which
we associate with the sublime. Beethoven does not passively present the world;
rather, by turning its principles upside down, he remakes it. He resensitizes us to
its particular aspects, countering the depletion of the Classical language by de-
familiarizing or estranging its axioms, and thereby disclosing the style's materiality.
His gambit is one of twentieth-century aesthetics' chief concerns, epitomized by
Heidegger's text on Van Gogh's famous peasant shoes:

> Truth happens in Van Gogh's painting. This does not mean that something is correctly
> portrayed, but rather that in the revelation of the equipmental being of the shoes, that
> which is as a whole—world and earth in their counterplay—attains to unconcealed-
> ness. (Heidegger 1975: 56)

Heidegger defends the concreteness and particularity of material against the concept, protecting content against function: "The material is all the better and more
suitable the less it resists perishing in the equipmental being of the equipment."
The axe "uses up" the stone, whereas "The temple-work, in setting up a world, does
not cause the material to disappear, but rather causes it to come forth for the very
first time" (46). Heidegger, as a critic of transcendental philosophy, makes common

purpose with other antisystematic thinkers such as Benjamin and Adorno. Truth, Heidegger believes, consists in freedom, and to be free is to apprehend the contingency of existing realities. For it is only thus that we attain the freedom to conceive of alternative languages and so to have a future. To think "ontologically" is to "let things be" by "disclosing" their historicity. Heidegger's disclosure parallels Adorno's negative critique, the process of freeing meaning from repressive systems. Adorno's long-standing polemic against Heidegger's ontology, with its "jargon of authenticity," clouds the commonality of their projects. Still, Heidegger's fatal flaw is absence of dialectic, in the guise of mobile categories such as *Schein, Apparition, Durchbruch,* and *Allegory.* Adorno's addendum to the ontology of material is a sense of processuality, driven by the aporias of self-reflection. Beethoven's homes are mobile. According to Ignaz von Seyfried: "No sooner had [Beethoven] taken possession of a new dwelling place than he would find something objectionable about it" (in Cooper 1991: 124). With his notorious "passion for changing his lodgings," Beethoven moved seventy times in forty-three years.

The present chapter lifts the focus from individual movements to entire multimovement cycles. I proceed in three steps. First, a step backward to the last three sonatas, which are the late style's freest and most holistic compositions. Second, a comparison of Beethoven's last two quartets, Opp. 131 and 135. Coming after the "Galitzin," they are ostensibly a Classicizing throwback. Yet I will argue that these final works, part of what I earlier identified as the "third phase" of the late style, are radical in their renewed confrontation with convention, through which they remake the world of the Classical style. Finally, the Ninth Symphony. Rejecting standard ideological interpretations of the Ode to Joy, I reaffirm the immanence of Beethoven's "ideas" in musical material. Altogether, I review three kinds of material: trills, tonality, and orchestration.

Three Trills: Op. 109, Op. 110, Op. 111

For Benjamin, "the eternal is in any case rather a frill on a dress than an idea" (in Hoeckner 2002: 235). Beethoven's most radical recuperation of the particular is his positioning of the trill—seemingly the most marginal and decorative of musical materials—at the center of his works. The trill is the epitome of Adorno's *Floskel:* the empty cliché or flourish. Beethoven's last three sonatas are each to some degree "about" the idea of trill and submit every aspect of their structure and narrative to this device. In focusing on the trill as a regulative idea, I partly follow in the wake of the great organicist analytical tradition of motivic unity. Theorists such as Schoenberg (1984), Réti (1967), and Epstein (1987) infer the broad tonal and structural aspects of a composition as inhering within a thematic gestalt, often presented at the opening. From one standpoint, the extreme part/whole relationships these theorists uncover are a profound validation of the context dependence, or mediation, which I argued to be foundational for Classical music, especially Beethoven's. On the other hand, the nature of part/whole unity in late Beethoven is not "symbolic" but "allegorical," turning on a distinction I explained in chapter 3. That is, the interrelationship has an abstract, forced quality, unmediated by the art of transition typical of middle-period Beethoven (the archetypal "symbolic" style). In practical terms, this means that the existence and operation of regulative ideas in late Beethoven are speculative, commensurate with the marginal nature of these ideas themselves. It is ironic, after all, to base a work on a trill—Benjamin's "frill"—since this reverses the priority of whole and part, originality and convention. But this reversal is just the first step to a further reversal, whereby the marginal detail is discovered to contain the universal and the personal. Allegorically, Beethoven takes the most conventional *Floskel* imaginable, and remakes it in his own image. Or rather, *three* images, in accordance with three distinct compositional strategies. Trills are important for Op. 109 insofar as they signal the end of a cadenza, followed by a da capo. Thus the work's structuring idea is that of parenthesis. Trills in Op. 110 are significant for their contour and so instantiate the idea of oscillation. And trills in Op. 111 signify upbeat impulses and diminution processes. In each case, the trill, as an interface between convention (S1) and natural contour (S3), is an allegorical index of an idea (S2). Furthermore, as a dynamic sign, the oscillating trill is a perfect vehicle for the mutability of Beethoven's cycles. For the cycles always end by reversing the terms of their opening. Susceptible to such diverse treatments, the trill idea's very mutability is itself an expression of Beethoven's compositional freedom.

* * *

The finale of Op. 109 is a suite of variations on an Andante theme and may give the misleading impression that this sonata, like Op. 111, ends with a slow movement. Actually, the variations in both works get faster and faster, and so discharge the traditional obligations of an Allegro finale. Like the diminution process, the cyclical return in both variation sets is cumulative, in that reference to the opening movement is at first only implicit and rises to the surface with growing force. A key difference is that the *Arietta* accomplishes this task comparatively early, in its climactic third variation, which boisterously reworks the diminished-seventh gestures of the opening *Maestoso*. Op. 109 strews echoes of its first movement throughout its finale (e.g., the "hocket" texture of variation 2 hints at the sonata's opening). Nevertheless, it positions its most *emphatic* return toward the end of the movement, from m. 168, where an outbreak of cadenza-like figurations recalls the second-group "parenthetical enclosure" in the first movement (ex. 6.1).

Cadenzas, especially in concertos, are associated with trills. Yet, whereas trills conventionally signal the *end* of the cadenza, and the advent of the closing orchestral ritornello, here they *precede* the cadenza, and continue underneath it, right up to the da capo of the unadorned theme at m. 188. Moreover, the trills are derived through the gradual diminution of the double dominant pedal which actually *begins* the sixth variation. The role of the trills thus mutates through four stages: part of the theme (mm. 153–64); harbinger of the cadenza (165–68); part of the cadenza (mm. 169–87); harbinger of the da capo (m. 187, in retrospect). The trills participate in both the theme and the cadenza, both "inside" and "outside" the structure, and thereby encapsulate, and frame, the convolutions of cyclicity in the work as a whole. How odd that Beethoven's cycle returns to the second group of

Example 6.1. Cyclic return in finale of Op. 109

the first movement, rather than the first—to material that had been marked as a cadenza-like parenthesis.

To emphasize, it is the *cadenza* which returns here, not the Vivace ritornello. By inverting the relationship between cadenza and ritornello, "outside" and "inside," Beethoven draws the parenthesis into the heart of the structure. This leads to conceptual aporia: the sonata as a whole occupies the space between two cadenzas. And the central Prestissimo, the movement which comes closest to a conventional sonata-allegro, is left out in the cold. Beethoven twists this Möbius strip with exquisite logic. Until its end at m. 184, the cadenza is really only an elaboration of the second half of the Andante theme, yet with the cyclicity disclosed, where it had first been hidden. The VI–II–V–I progression, which recalls the first-movement Adagios, is at first subtly disguised (ex. 6.2a–d).

There is no sense of interruption between mm. 8 and 9 of the Andante theme, nor is there yet much textural similarity with the first movement (ex. 6.2a). Beethoven pointedly leaves the first note of m. 9 unharmonized, so that the listener infers

Gesangvoll, mit innigster Empfindung
Andante molto cantabile ed espressivo

Example 6.2. Cyclic process in finale of Op. 109
    a. Theme, with unharmonized B at m. 9
    b. Variation 1, with B as V
    c. Variation 2, B displaced by D

Continues on the next page

Example 6.2. Cyclic process in finale of Op. 109
   d. Variation 4, D as V⁹ of F♯

a continuation of the preceding dominant, which is corroborated by the D♯ on the second beat. But the first bass note of m. 9 is implicitly a C♯, and the D♯ is actually a passing note linking C♯ to E♯. At the present moment, however, the measure unfolds not a chord of C♯ but of B. Whereas the theme promotes textural and harmonic continuity between its two phrases, the subsequent variations gradually widen the breach, until the second phrase interrupts with the force of a cadenza. Variation 2 provides the first intimation; the unisono D♯'s of m. 57 (implying the dominant ninth of F♯) rudely correct the impression that the dominant harmony is sustained across the divide (ex. 6.2c). The corresponding point of the fourth variation, m. 105, enhances the interruption (ex. 6.2d). Variation 6 clinches the textural reference to the Adagio's figurations (see ex. 6.1). The cadenza of m. 169 is thus fairly inevitable, but not without a struggle. It is striking that Beethoven realizes the interruption only in alternate variations: nos. 2, 4, and 6. The intervening variations, nos. 1 (see ex. 6.2b), 3, and 5, smooth over the caesura between the two phrases with more through-composed textures (such as two-part invention and a fugato) and reference the material of the Vivace, rather than the Adagio. The sequence of variations thereby reworks the ritornello/cadenza alternations of the first movement, but now giving the cadenza the upper hand and the last word.

The circle of Op. 109 is thus cumulative and inverted. The cyclical return is not announced at the finale's outset, but unfolded gradually, and in such a way as to reverse relationships proposed in the first movement. As on so many other occasions, Haydn gets there before Beethoven. His String Quartet Op. 33, no. 5, in G begins, inappropriately, with a cadence, featuring a strong rising fourth progression in the first violin. In the Allegretto variation set which forms Haydn's finale, the faulty cadence is at first only hinted at. But the cadence figure emerges explicitly in the last variation, where it comes into its own as a proper gesture of conclusion. Haydn's precedent nicely reminds us that there is even a convention for transforming convention. Or rather, following this infinite regress will never lead us to the mythical "normal" convention. As a work "about" the inside and outside of structure, Op. 109 lifts out and examines tensions already implicit within the Classical style.

The idea of Op. 110 is the oscillation of a dramatic arch, encapsulated by the trill's neighbor-note turn figures. Whereas trills figure in Op. 109 only as an index of a cadenza, Op. 110 engages more directly with the symbolic dimensions of the trill in itself. Its trills, therefore, are absorbed into the fabric of the sonata from the outset, rather than demarcating a late turn of events. There are no trills in the first movement of Op. 109, while Op. 110's opening melody apexes on one at each statement, and there are also passing trills in the second group (mm. 25–27) and one just before the reprise (m. 55). Moreover, the trill at m. 4 evolves organically from the zigzagging contour of the theme itself, as a compression of the thirds and fourths cycle, and is conversely widened into the oscillating arpeggiations of the transition, until these are telescoped, via broken octaves, into a single note, the C of m. 20. Beethoven's control over textural modulation is miraculous and creates the paradoxical interchange of the primary note of the melody with its cadenza. The continuity between structure and cadenza is taken by Op. 110 as a premise, whereas Op. 109 deduced it at its climax. This continuity informs how we hear the Adagio-Fuga alternations of the finale: not as discrete intercuttings of "inside" and "outside," but as fluid gradations of intensity across a dramatic spectrum. Namely, as an arch contour. By the same token, if the Op. 109 cycle requires discontinuities *between* its movements, Op. 110 fosters links such as common tones (C's between Moderato and scherzo; F's between scherzo and Adagio, etc.). Of all the thirty-two piano sonatas, the movements of Op. 110 hang together most tightly as a unified conception, anticipating Op. 131, Beethoven's most integrated quartet. To be sure, Beethoven had explored intermovement links in many earlier works (such as Op. 31, no. 2, Op. 53, Op. 57, and Op. 81a). Yet, with the partial exception of Op. 27, no.1 (an earlier "fantasy sonata"), Op. 110 is the only sonata to intercut its slow movement and finale as a double alternation (Adagio-Fugue-Adagio-Fugue).[1]

The idea of oscillation embraces practically every parameter available to Beethoven. Modulations in the first half of the sonata hover around E♭ and its neighbors D♭, F♭, and F minor. The Moderato slides into D♭ and F♭ in its recapitulation, and the scherzo and trio are in F minor and D♭, respectively. The second half—the Adagio/Fuga complex—focuses instead on tonic neighbors: B♭ minor neighboring A♭ minor in the first Adagio and after the first fugue in A♭ major, and the G minor-to-major of the second Adagio and Fuga. Globally, the sonata projects a tonal arch, flexing up to F, and then stooping down to a psychological nadir in G minor, before returning to A♭ major in the last pages. In this light, the tremolo figures at the climax of the finale, from m. 201, which elaborate an A♭ pedal, answer and ground the dominant-centered trills of the Moderato. In a nutshell, the cycle is framed by a call and response of a dominant and a tonic trill.

In addition to this tonal arch, the rigor of Beethoven's oppositional system is breathtaking. Fugue counters Adagio lament; second fugue inverts the first; fugal subjects alternate with answers. The latter is routine, but it is interesting that the interval between entries in the first fugue gets successively longer, increasing from four measures to fourteen, while the *Inversione* accelerates toward the stretto of mm. 168–70. Also, the registral compass of the first fugue gradually sinks to the bottom C of m. 107, whereas the *tempo primo* rises to the top C of m. 209. Accounting for the Adagio-Fuga alternation in itself takes us back to the opening eleven measures of the sonata. The opening phrase of the *Klagender Gesang* is a variation of the mm. 5–11, bringing out the lachrymose character of the left-hand accompaniment pattern and the melody's appoggiaturas. If the Adagio refers to the Moderato's consequent phrase, then the fugue subject is patently modeled on the antecedent phrase. Thus the Adagio-Fuga sequence recapitulates the two phrases of mm. 1–11 in reverse order. We could go on picking out detail after detail from this endlessly fascinating work. But one more example will suffice to indicate the intricacy of Beethoven's system. The Moderato's dominant group ends with rising neighbor-note figures followed by a drop of an octave (mm. 35–38); the trio section of the second-movement scherzo *begins* with a leap of an octave, leading to a sequence of *falling* figures (ex. 6.3a–b):

Example 6.3. Correspondences between first movement and trio of Op. 110
  a. First movement, mm. 35–38
  b. Trio, mm. 40–48

The rhythm of the octave leap is reversed from trochaic in the Moderato, to iambic in the Trio. The Moderato arranges its neighbor-note figures in seven groups; the Trio contains seven cascades. Taken by themselves, any of these patterns could be circumstantial. As a package, they bespeak compositional planning.

The system ultimately projects a contour of affective soul-states, which are self-explanatory. After a tender opening, the sonata suffers a downturn to the negative with a rebarbative scherzo, compounded by an Adagio lament. The narrative takes an upturn with the first fugue, which relapses to a second lament, before returning in triumph to close the sonata on a high point. Schenker's *Erläuterungsausgabe* interprets the double sequence as a narrative of sickness and recovery hovering in the balance: "a state of suspense" (*Schwebezustand*) between an "image of true exhaustion" and "a healthy impulse toward ever-more distantly projected goals" (Schenker 1971–72: 72; Spitzer 2004: 230–41). Schenker's "Schwebezustand" could be interpreted as a hermeneutic analogue of Beethoven's trill, whose conceptual oscillations have widened to embrace actual movements. Yet, by the rules of Beethoven's oppositional system, resolution is inevitable. The first-movement arches begin on the tonic and apex on a dissonant submediant or dominant. The finale reverses the cycle, rising from its G-minor nadir in the second lament to an apex which is consonant and triumphant—the top C of m. 209.

By reversing the cycle, Beethoven analyzes the staple gravitational metaphor of Western music. On the one hand, resolutions tend to fall, acceding, in Adorno's lovely phrase, to "the gravitational slope of musical language" (1992a: 48). On the other hand, triumphs rise. Bending music's natural gradient to his will, so that it *rises* in triumph, Beethoven is also triumphing over music's "nature." Reflection over nature is the Enlightenment's own song, but this is the first time that nature has been enshrined in such well-formed dynamic schemata. Beethoven thus gets to have it both ways: he objectifies nature as patterns and negates them through a cyclic reversal which, paradoxically, reconstitutes these same patterns more abstractly. For, of course, the reversal of oscillation is itself an oscillation, just as, in Op. 109, the reversal of cadenza is itself a cadenza-like interruption.

In Op. 111, Beethoven's iconic trills enter at m. 106 of the *Arietta,* just after the fourth variation, and famously figure in Wendell Kretzschmar's lecture in Thomas Mann's novel *Doktor Faustus:*

> "The chains of trills!" he yelled. "The embellishments and cadenzas [*die Fiorituren und Kadenzen*]! Do you hear how convention is left untouched [*die stehengelassene Konvention*]? Here—language—is no longer purified of cliché [*Floskel*], but cliché—of the appearance [*Schein*]—of its domination by subjectivity [*vom Schein—ihrer subjektiven—Beherrscheit*)—the appearance —of art is thrown off—at last—art always throws off the appearance of art. Dim-dada!" (Mann 1980: 76; translation emended from the 1948 Lowe-Porter trans.: 54)

Adorno, who helped draft these lines, and on whom the character of Kretzschmar was based, celebrates the trill as a *Floskel* (flourish), as a piece of petrified convention. Rosen is analytically more on the nail and puts this trill center stage in *The Classical Style*'s inspired *Abgesang*. He focuses, rightly, on temporality, and on the paradox that "a long trill creates an insistent tension while remaining static" (1972: 447). The *Arietta*'s trill, then, is the cardinal index of Beethoven's "power to suspend motion, seeming to stop the movement of time" (448). Rosen leaves it open whether this "hovering" (447) is ever resolved, which is where I think Kretzsch-mar's insight that the *Arietta*'s ending is strangely perfunctory has the advantage: "It breaks off," as he puts it (ex. 6.4).

"Quick, hard triplets hasten to a conclusion with which any other piece might have ended" (55). The great, overlapping, cadences at the end, based on a stretto of the *Arietta* incipit, are sententious and moving, but what remains in the memory is the trill on G. A little detail of harmony has escaped all the commentators: it is that the chords, at mm. 169–71, accompanying the D–G–G and C–C♯–D–G–G mo-tives should be dominant, not tonic, as at mm. 2 and 8 of the theme. The C-major chords sound like attenuated passing or neighbor harmonies, yearning for the dominant, rather than any global resolution, and Beethoven denies them that goal by suddenly taking the bottom away from the music at m. 172. This is a signal case of what I have called Beethoven's bifocal tonality: the left hand's C major at mm. 169–71 is delicately dissonant with respect to the right hand's G, and the dominant has been rendered the stable partner. Turning a root-position tonic triad into a dissonance is a technique which Rosen himself has called Beethoven's "most remarkable and characteristic effect" (387). Op. 111's closing V–I cadences are thus a mundane affair, superogatory to the starry skies of the G-major trill. As long as our attention remains fixed on these extra-temporal stars, which reminded even Schenker of "a Milky Way of tones" (1971–72: 61), the *Arietta* never really ends. The trills suspend time; they also escape the pull of tonal gravity.

Mann reports that Adorno performed the sonata for him on the evening of 4 September 1943: "Then Adorno sat down at the piano and, while I stood by and watched, played for me the entire Sonata Opus 111 in a highly instructive fashion" (1961: 42). To help the writer with his Kretzschmar episode, Adorno gave him not only his 1937 *Spätstil Beethovens* essay, but also a copy of the *Arietta* theme in his own hand, annotated with the remark that "the added, decisive note is C♯" (Hoeck-ner 2002: 227–37). This single note becomes the decisive point of Kretzschmar's lecture, where it marks the moment of the theme's transfiguration:

> After an introductory C, it puts a C sharp before the D, so that it no longer scans "heaven's blue," "mead-ow-land," but "O-thou heaven's blue," "Green-est mead-owland," "Fare-thee well for aye," and this added C sharp is the most moving, consolatory, patheti-cally reconciling thing in the world. It is like having one's hair or cheek stroked, lovingly, understandingly, like a deep and silent farewell look. . . . Then it breaks off . . . (55)

By investing so much importance in these undeniably affecting C♯'s, Adorno, along with legions of critics, is paying insufficient attention to the opening chord of the *Arietta* (ex. 6.5).

For, of course, the compulsion of C to rise to D is worked into the bass of m. 1. The C♯ in the parallel point in variation 1 (m. 17) merely heightens this tendency. C♯ realizes the tonic triad's placement as an accented neighbor to a second-inversion V⁷—and with all the tensions this reversal of function entails. The melody's echo of this C–D step across mm. 1–2 is crucial to Beethoven's transformation of the effect at the end of the work, mm. 168–71, where the C♯ is lifted up from the earth

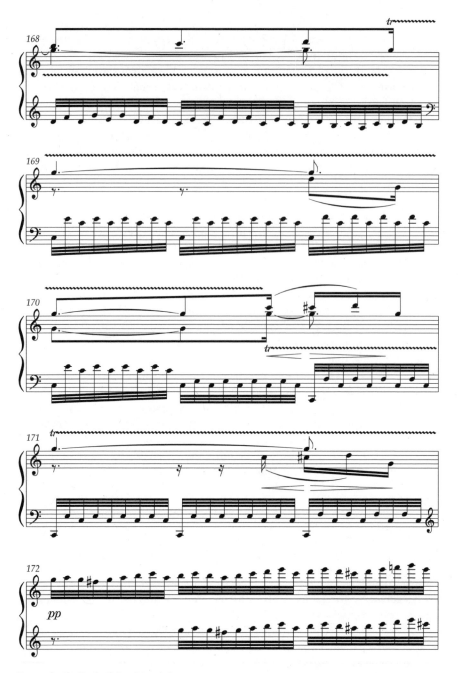

Example 6.4. End of Op. 111, *Arietta*
Continues on the next page

Example 6.4. End of Op. 111, *Arietta*

to the sky. We can now see that the refusal of the C triad to budge up a step to D across mm. 168–71 is a negation of the pattern at m. 1. The object of Kretzschmar's effusions, then, ought to have been the enigmatically stabilized C triads, not the C♯'s. If these triads *had* moved (necessarily down to B, since D's would have formed octaves with the melody), then he might have spoken, poetically, of the earth tilting, relative to the motionless trills. But the earth is fixed in the palm of Beethoven's hand, an act of Hegelian "positing," whereby reality is remade through sheer will. Suddenly beholding the fundamental triad as such a contingent, fragile thing ignites the brightest cognitive flash of this whole shimmering page. The trill is thus only an analogue for the "cognitive trill" of *Schein*, just as in Op. 130 the whirling cascades symbolized the over-fast dialectic.

It is extraordinary how this effect is already prepared by the very opening C-major chord of the *Arietta*, in the metrical ambiguity I examined in chapter 1. Whether the bass D of m. 1 is heard as a goal for the C, or as an anticipation of the B's dominant harmony, depends on how we hear Beethoven's anomalously grounded upbeat triad. Harmony has its own rhythm, which cuts across bar lines and notated rhythm. We can imagine a bar line in two places other than where it

Example 6.5. *Arietta*, mm. 1–16

is written: after the D, articulating a three-chord measure of I–I–V; or *before* the D, relegating the first two tonic chords to upbeats of a V–V–V measure. Such "functional rubato," as I called it, generates the immense metrical complexity of the *Arietta*. This complexity is borne out, overtly, by the archaic time signatures Beethoven uses—$\frac{9}{16}$, $\frac{6}{16}$, $\frac{12}{32}$—and the many occasions where the perceived meter conflicts with the notated one, producing trickles of additive, duple patterns (variation 1, mm. 16–19), or pools of hemiola (variation 2, mm. 33–35). A striking instance of Beethoven's play with notation is the extra double bar line between beats 1 and 2 of m. 26, which makes the downbeat sound like an upbeat (ex. 6.6):

Example 6.6. Ambiguous barring in *Arietta*, mm. 25–27

Historically, these complex compound mensurations had been phased out or rationalized by both the Classical style and enlightenment music theory (see Maurer Zenck 2001). Yet they permitted greater suppleness and gradation of accent than the periodic meters which superseded them. Beethoven exploits this richness to refine the grain of his material, compensating variation form for a lack of serious harmonic motion or modulation.

Nevertheless, it would be a serious mistake to read the metrical and rhythmic elements as the only source of motion in the piece, as a ripple on the surface of harmonic stasis. To stress: metrical play emerges from the harmonic "functional rubato" of m. 1 and composes out the "flicker" of the C's dual relations with the D. The issue couldn't be simpler: does the C aspire to the D, or does the D decorate a stable C? As with a trill, does the oscillation pivot on the lower or the upper note? There is a world of structural contour at stake here. The *Arietta* will climb toward its trill on the G, but will this trill resist the pull of gravity to descend back to the tonic? Remarkably, the upbeat is a growth point for this journey on three distinct levels: it is low (and will rise), it is slow (and will get faster), and it flickers (and will get brighter). At the climax of m. 169, when the cycle swallows its tail, these three growth points are folded into the real trill itself. This trill, then, is viewed in multiple dimensions: as a conventional *Floskel*, just a "trill"; as a cognitive flicker; and superimposed upon its cyclical origins.

The journey from m. 1 to m. 169 is of course mediated by form, and variation form is as undertheorized as fugue or fantasy. Diminution variations, such as the slow movement of the *Appassionata*, seem to proceed until they reach saturation or satiety; the convention for variation sets, like the *Eroica* Variations, Op. 35, or the *Diabelli*, Op. 120, is to incorporate a *minore* variation, a penultimate fugal variation, a da capo of the unadorned theme, and a free coda. Little can be predicted about the course of sui generis, single-movement variations, such as the finale of the "Harp" Quartet, Op. 74, apart from the likelihood that Beethoven will analyze the content of his theme (see Marston 1989). The *Arietta* hits saturation point with the third variation, after which it stops being a straight diminution variation, like the *Appassionata*, and becomes Beethoven's closest hybrid between variation and sonata before the finale of the Ninth Symphony (whose similarity is understated in the literature). Variations 1–3 are akin to a first group; variation 4 is a second group; there follows a short development, modulating through a chain of thirds,

E♭–C–A♭–F, reminding us of the *Arietta* melody's origins in the *Hammerklavier* Adagio (mm. 45–53); conversely, the da capo at m. 130, with its left-hand passage work, recalls the recapitulation of Op. 110; finally, after another, shorter, development, the second trill cues a reprise of the second group leading to a coda. This semblance of sonata is important for the *Arietta*'s oppositional relationship with Op. 111's first movement.

Still, we must focus just as much on how it is *not* a sonata—on the special things variation can do which sonata can't. Primarily, variation affords a microscopic level of concentration on the particularity of musical material, unavailable to the more dynamic genre. So how do we define this "material"? It cannot simply be the sixteen-measure theme as a whole, as an integral thematic-harmonic gestalt. The *Arietta* melody is not the passive object of variation, because *it is already embarked on a process of analyzing itself.* Moreover, its structure even prefigures the course of the movement's sonata form, and the ascent to the G trill. Remarkably, all three processes flow, once again, from the ambiguous upbeat.

Self-variation

The bass's C–D step, echoed by the right-hand sequence, launches the rise of the piece. By m. 4, the right-hand melody has climbed to E, and descended back to C. The second phrase, from m. 5, compresses the C–E rise into a single skip, as part of an arpeggio to G, the apex. This act of doubling back, and compressing the music into a single gesture, is the principal means by which the successive variations reflect on each other. It is also the cause of the music's acceleration—more than a simple matter of faster note values. For instance, the pairs of trochees of variation 1 accelerate the pace of sequence from the one-step-in-a-measure of mm. 1–2, to one per beat. And, if the *Arietta*'s opening phrase, mm. 1–8, is broadly an arpeggiation of a tonic triad, then this arpeggiation will presently become condensed *into a single beat*—the upbeat to variation 3 (ex. 6.7):

Example 6.7. *Arietta,* variation 3, mm. 48–49

It is this process of cumulative compression which gives variation 3 its intoxicating speed, not the thirty-second notes themselves. The *Arietta* takes compression in its stride, where the first movement had repeatedly become overwhelmed and short-circuited. Variation 4 lifts the process to a yet higher level, accelerating the arpeggio into a tremolo. By carrying the energy of the "transition" into the "second group," so that variation 4 seems simultaneously faster and more relaxed, Beethoven's variations emulate a paradox of sonata form, where a lyrical second subject is tonally more tense than the first.

Sonata Form

The theme comprises two repeated strains, the first wholly in the major, the second starting in the minor (hence a partial *minore*). This (initially) A-minor strain is like a diatonic version of the A♭-major second subject in the first movement. Whereas the latter's second group was "parenthetical," the *Arietta*'s second strain is by far the more stable, in terms of the metrical ambiguities which cloud the theme's opening. These are notably absent from m. 9, with its metrically on-the-beat accents, and the theme climaxes with the unadorned directness of the da capo, mm. 13–14.[2] The shining diatonic purity of this moment prefigures the movement's last pages; the theme's apotheosis is a miniature version of the sonata's. Typically for the late style, stabilization is introduced off-tonic (here, in A and on G), and then transmitted to the home key at the end. The goal for this process, though, is deferred: it will ultimately be the stabilization of the theme's final cadence. At m. 16, however, it is displaced, and every variation, including the recapitulation (at m. 146), will follow suit. Only the coda, at m. 169, will realign this cadence on the beat, and there, as we have seen, to complex effect.

A semblance of sonata form is achieved also through harmonic motion, not just metrical shift. How is this possible, given that Beethoven generally obeys the cardinal stricture of Classical variation, as practiced by Haydn and Mozart, of not tampering with the harmonic skeleton? Once again, it is the "functional rubato" of the chords which allows Beethoven to nudge the harmony in new directions. The second, A-minor phrase resolves to the tonic at mm. 13–14. The question is whether C major is regained at its dominant, the G chord of m. 13, or at its tonic, the C of m. 14. The ambiguity of both the beginning and da capo of the theme gives Beethoven leeway to grade its stability throughout the variations, especially in nos. 1–3. In variations 1–2, Beethoven uses textural and metrical contrast to direct the da capo to the dominant: hence the climaxes at mm. 29 and 45. Variation 3 breaks the mold by climaxing for the first time on the *tonic* chord, at m. 62—a *thematic* da capo, also, of the rising tonic arpeggios of m. 49 (ex. 6.8).

This long-range resolution rounds off the "tonic group" (theme + variations 1–3) as a satisfying tonal block. The finesse with which Beethoven engineers this gradation of harmonic weighting testifies to the micrological care of his sketching process, which often involves tiny alterations. An infinitesimal adjustment can tip the overall function of a time span in one or other direction. Consider the powerful dominant preparation for the tonic da capo at m. 61 of variation 3, which has swallowed up the third beat of m. 60 into its dominant orbit. The takeover of this up-

Example 6.8. *Arietta,* variation, mm. 60–63, with tonic climax

beat is incremental: the upbeat at m. 13 is a perfect A-minor triad; variation 1, at m. 28, eats into two-thirds of the triad; m. 44, variation 2 increases this to three-quarters (twelve sixteenths); finally, variation 3, m. 60, takes over the whole upbeat and marks it sforzato.

Similar shifts transform the beginnings of the variations. Returning to the striking case of variation 1's *minore* strain, we see how Beethoven's extra double bar line at m. 26, together with the hairpin dynamics on the second beats of mm. 26–

27, has reversed the harmonic pattern from I–V–I (mm. 9–10) to V–I–V. The A-minor strain had originally marked the theme's point of stability; reversing its character plays into Beethoven's game plan of displacing this arrival point, in the middle term, to the tonic-major climaxes of variation 3. Mediating between these two moments is variation 2, whose upbeat dissolves the tonic altogether into a $\frac{6}{4}$ chord around G. The tonic arpeggio which begins variation 3, together with its da capo at m. 62, brings this process to a conclusion.

The Ascent to G

The end is in the beginning. Like the second phrase of the bagatelle, Op. 119, no. 8, the *Arietta*'s opening phrase is a puzzle form, whose first and repeated statements are heard differently. Sketch no. 9 (Drabkin's numbering) in Artaria 201 conceives the melody as a series of suspended appoggiaturas at two-measure intervals, arpeggiating up from C through E to G (C–B E–D G–F) (ex. 6.9):

Example 6.9. *Arietta* sketch no. 9 (transcribed and numbered by Drabkin), mm. 1–6

Something of this model survives into the final version, which can also be heard as a rising sequence of appoggiaturas. The bass's C–D in m. 1 is answered in the right hand by a sequence of two suspensions, at two-measure intervals: the C–B of mm. 3–4, and the G–F of mm. 5–6. A third member of this sequence, D–C, is outlined in mm. 7–8, but heavily disguised: the D is transferred an octave down to an inner voice, and suspended for the full measure, so that *it only resolves with the da capo of m. 1, lowered a further octave to bottom C.* The third member of the sequence, which ought to have been D–C, is thereby converted into the *Arietta*'s upbeat, as C–D. End and beginning, up and down, falling and rising appoggiaturas: this Möbius strip of a phrase is a perfect symbol for the cycle as a whole.

The Path of the *Diabelli*

When Kretzschmar, Mann, and Adorno instruct us to "hear how convention is left untouched," they mean the trills which Beethoven objectifies as the "idea" of his *Arietta.* The convention is not left untouched. In the first movement, trills function, conventionally, as auxiliaries, upbeats to resolutions, such as the flourishes at mm. 1 and 3, and the great tremolo which rounds off the introduction (and which is incorporated into the sixteenth-note anacrusic figures of the fugal subject). Yet the third trill of the sequence, at m. 5, is arrested on the B♭ and points to what is to come. The *Arietta* will liberate trills as ends in themselves, as figures of *Schein*-ing beauty.

In each of the last three sonatas, the trill offers Beethoven an optimum fusion between convention and idea, the stylized and the natural. A trill is both a conventionalized style form, redolent of rococo aesthetics, and an idealized aspect of natural contour. It enables the cycles to be "about" both convention and nature. Insofar as the music is self-reflexive, and is about its own material, this material is both an aggregate of received techniques and a set of universal gestures. But these two aspects of material pull in quite opposite directions, and Beethoven's path after Op. 111 will mark a dramatic retreat from the landscapes of natural schemata even further into the brickwork of convention. As we have already seen with the "Galitzin," the last quartets engage much more directly with the artificial and historical character of material and are ostensibly a retrospective, Classicizing move for Beethoven. From this standpoint, the last sonatas are the tail end of the false Romantic dawn of the previous decade, begun with works such as the last violin sonata, Op. 96 (1813), and *An die ferne Geliebte* (1815), in which Beethoven appears to be marching in step with Schubert. A vital stepping stone between the "Romanticizing" sonatas and the "Classicizing" quartets is the *Diabelli* Variations, especially since Diabelli's theme has so many affinities with the *Arietta*'s.

For all its "clunkiness," this theme fits perfectly into Beethoven's new project, which is the transfiguration of conventions as received objects (Kinderman 1987). The theme's spiritualization from "an earthly waltz into a celestial minuet," as Solomon puts it (25), is very similar to the *Arietta*'s. It is a "metaphorical ascent from lower to higher" (189), with the rising path immanent to the theme's materials on many levels: for instance, the ascending sequence from C to D (mm. 4 and 17) to E (m. 21); the anomaly that the theme ends an octave above its start; and, most significantly, the ascending "cobbler's patch" itself. But there is a radical difference, in that the *Diabelli* Variations' purpose is ultimately to overcome an artificial convention which it associates with the symmetrical structure of the dance: two sixteen-measure phrases, articulating a sequential melodic rhyme (CD DE), divided by a caesura. Beethoven's target is elegantly simple. He will dissolve the caesura by removing the second D, thus converting the structure into a through-composed (in voice-leading terms) C–D–E progression. The process entails nudging the E ever closer toward the central double bar line, or even doing without the dominant modulation altogether. Beethoven's solutions are endlessly resourceful. Variation 5 modulates to E minor, rather than the expected G; the first phrase of variation 15 stays in the tonic, even though its melody thinks it's in the dominant (it descends, like the original theme, from D to G); the second half of variation 13 begins with a rude B♭, an ambassador of the tonic seventh (V^7 of F) four measures later; variation 23 dresses this B♭ in a diminished-seventh chord; variations 24 and 25 use V^7 of F and this diminished-seventh chord respectively. Both V^7 of F and the diminished-seventh E–G–B♭–C♯ represent alterations of the tonic harmony at mm. 21–24 of the theme. In effect, the variations edge it closer and closer to the dance's caesura, until the D step is dissolved away. The diminished seventh is the more extreme harmony, and its role in the *Diabelli* Variations is opposite to that in Op. 111. The *Arietta* exorcises the chord; here, the chord is an agent of reform, by which Diabelli's theme is increasingly appropriated by Beethoven's personal idiom. This moment takes a strikingly dialectical turn. On the one hand, the penultimate fugue represents a logical climax, since, as a through-composed genre, fugue is at the furthest remove from Diabelli's dance. And yet, after the great curtains of diminished sevenths at the climax, the harmonies are dissipated, continuity is rejected, and the dance returns. For Solomon, Beethoven's surprising eleventh-hour embrace of the ordinary represents an identification with the good-old fashioned, vernacular, quotidian virtues of Diabelli's *Deutsche* (German dance), which he compares to folk heroes such as Parsifal, Till Eulenspiegel, or Leporello. Beethoven celebrates the cobbler's patch, that handiwork of "the much-maligned shoemaker who manufactures those boots and shoes so vital to walkers on the road of life" (Solomon, 21). The material of cliché becomes an aesthetic object, like the bricks in De Hooch's courtyards, or the leather of Van Gogh's boots.[3] From this point, Beethoven's cycles will be "about" objects in the musical world. Technically, he will reflect more seriously on the cyclicity intrinsic to the Classical style itself—in other words, both the convention of cycle and the cycles of convention.

The Classical Cycle

Any consideration of the Classical cycle must begin with the seldom-asked question: Why these movements, in this order? Why did the Baroque dance suite, the historical progenitor of the cycle, coalesce into the normative succession of sonata allegro—slow movement—dance—finale?[4] The order of the two inner movements is interchangeable, but with a tendency in Haydn and Mozart to place the dance movement third, after the slow movement. A striking feature of Beethoven's late style is his preference for reversing this ordering, shifting the dance to second position, so that it directly follows the first movement as a kind of parody. This is the case *for every work with four or more movements, apart from Op. 127*: that is, Opp. 101, 106, 110, 130, 131, 132, 135, and the Ninth Symphony.[5] A plausible answer is that, by having lyric (dance and song) movements in the middle, the cycle mirrors the narrative of the first-movement sonata form, raising it to an architectonic level. The dance-song pair corresponds, roughly, to the form's inner sections, the lyrical second group and forensic development, with the finale analogous to a recapitulation.

Casting his eye over the entirety of the Ninth, Solomon argues that the symphony is "an extended metaphor of a quest for Elysium," a return to pastoral (1986: 11). But it is wrong to identify this narrative too closely with the Ninth, because it is actually embedded within the norms of the style. Classical cycles, like sonata form itself, initially journey "inwards." One could even say that they go back to source, to "nature," given that the song and dance are historically older than sonata form and become theorized as its conceptual models in composition manuals. Koch thought sonatas originate from an intermarriage and elaboration of miniature song and dance forms. Wagner goes further, arguing that "the symphony's formal germ survives till this day in its third movement, the Minuet or Scherzo, where it suddenly appears in its utmost naivety, as though to tell the secret of the Form of all movements" ("On Liszt's Symphonic Poems," vol. III, 1995: 244). As Baroque relics, song and dance actually enshrine opposite cultural values. A song expresses individual subjectivity and is static; dances encode patterns of bodily motion and social behavior, but are *objective* insofar as these patterns are conventionalized. One marker of the sonata dialectic, then, is its fusion of subjective song and objective dance. A negative perspective on this synthesis is that song and dance—venerable genres which represent an alternative, *alterior* voice in the Classical style—are coerced to fit within the sonata hegemony. Their emergence as movements in their own right in the middle of the cycle is thus a corrective, and an agent of balance. Late Beethoven raises the aesthetic status of these inner movements in a move which matches the ascendancy of lyrical parataxis in the sonata forms themselves.

The cycle journeys inward only from one angle; from another, it actually ventures out into the world, in that songs and dances retain closer links than sonata with music's utilitarian origins, albeit now as entertainment. The trio of Op. 132 reworks trivial dances Beethoven originally designed for the balls at the Redoutensaal; the scherzo of Op. 110 quotes the Viennese street song *Ich bin lüderlich*. The lyrical interlude, as a stepping back from the high seriousness of sonata, epitomizes that "nugatory" (*nichtig*) side of late Beethoven which critics such as Stephen Hinton have interpreted as a sign of the composer's stoic acceptance of death (Hinton 1996: 150). This gesture of "throwing away" is perfectly served by Beethoven's shifting of the scherzo to second position. For instance, the brusque opening gambit in the Ninth's Molto Vivace sounds like a travesty of the first movement's ethereal fifth progressions. Curiously, the notionally "serious" idiom of counterpoint can create a playful, even grotesque, effect in the context of Classical dances (see the canonic "Witches" minuet of Haydn's Op. 76, no. 2, in D minor). It is as if dances restore counterpoint's primevally ludic nature as a musical game of role taking. The critic of the *AMZ* thought of the Ninth's scherzo in this way: "The wildest mischief plays its wicked game . . . All the instruments compete in the banter" (in Cook 2000: 32). Chameleon-like, counterpoint fosters expressive intensification in the song movements. The textural stringency which gives the *Heiliger Dankgesang*'s last variation its visionary climax is wrought from the mutual abrasion of the voices. In particular, linear motion engenders the astonishing dissonances at mm. 189–93, perhaps the most lyrically extreme statement in all late Beethoven. In four-movement works, such as the *Hammerklavier,* the Ninth, and the last quartet, positioning the slow movement third highlights the symmetry of the cycle. After the scherzo's journey "outward," the slow movement's reflective tone marks the reversal of the cycle, a turning back into the seriousness of interiority and the closure of a frame—clinched by the finale's cyclical re-*turn*. This is why, in each of these three works, Opp. 106, 125, and 135 (one may also include the Cavatina of Op. 130), the slow movement flows naturally into the introduction to the finale. The effect is that of a pause for breath before an apocalyptic reckoning; this rhetoric is found, on a smaller scale, in the development sections of Opp. 106 and 125, which both end on a deceptively calm plateau, elaborating the lyrical second group.

After its zigzag "out and up" with the scherzo, and "in and down" with the slow movement, the cycle is drawn back to the ground where it started by the finale. One can picture the outer movements as complementary midpoints between excessive conventionalization (dance) and subjectivity (song). Or rather, it is here where the conflict between these two forces is most even. The finale, though, is as much a culmination as a return, which is why late Beethoven often displaces the cycle's center of gravity from the first to the last movement. Opp. 101 and 131, for instance, are extended upbeats to their finales, which supply the works' first strong structural downbeat in the home key. With the finale, the cycle regains the sonata dynamic, although mediated now through the looser episodic idioms of the rondo, which supports an effect of cadential repetition and closure. Another potential outcome of episodic form is sublime excess, an effect which can be heightened by counterpoint. Traditionally, since Haydn's Op. 20 quartets and Mozart's "Jupiter" Symphony, fugal textures have signified the sublimity of finale closure (see Sisman 1993a: 74–79). Finales are sublime because they pull things together, effecting all-embracing reconciliation through a process of liquidation and breaking down of distinctions. The wildest examples of such entropic, centrifugal energy are found in Beethoven's great fugal finales, those of Opp. 106 and 130. But these impulses are presented, in more formal terms, in the other finale types—the sonata, the sonata-rondo, and the variation—and they give cyclical closure a radically antinomic cast with respect to the sonata principle. On the one hand, the entry of the finale reconstitutes the sonata principle left behind with the first movement, now on a cyclical level. On the other hand, it indicates a sublation of this principle, an emancipatory leave taking from an idiom which is staged as a metaphor of "the law." Beethoven's cycles, then, are allegories of freedom, of breaking free and pushing on through a conceptual barrier. This barrier can be imagined, literally, as the double-bar sign at the end of the first-movement exposition. The main themes in the finales of Op. 132 and the Ninth are both closely related to the second subject of the first movement: ideas which originally marked a terminus or goal are taken up again as a starting point. This is much more than just a case of concluding unfinished business. It is a breakthrough (*Durchbruch*) into an unimagined new world.

Opus 131 in C♯ Minor: The *Schein* of Harmony

Beethoven's C♯-minor quartet is his most unified cyclic composition. It integrates seven movements in six keys (c♯–D–A–E–g♯–c♯) so tightly as to challenge the Classical distinction between the sections of a *movement* and the movements of a *piece*. Formally, the movements mostly all run into each other; thematically, the opening fugue subject permeates the cycle; tonally, the quartet is inflected by a subdominant axis, including the submediant (A major) and the Neapolitan (D major). And by starting with an Adagio fugue, and reserving the first sonata-allegro for the finale, Beethoven endows the succession of movements with a natural tele-ology. All the same, the much-touted "integration" of this work (see Tovey 1944; Kerman 1967) is only a means to the end of projecting a compositional idea. This idea engages the overarching style shift from Baroque fugue to Classical sonata, a change already implicit within the opening fugue subject's drift into the *Fortspin-nung* diminutions of its tail (ex. 6.10):

Example 6.10. String Quartet in C♯ minor, Op. 131, first movement, mm. 1–8

The *Fortspinnung* concept is a Baroque convention; Beethoven's move is to as-sociate it symbolically with the lyrical trajectory intrinsic to the Classical cycle. The subject's course from note-against-note counterpoint to a more florid lyrical style—a course also composed out across the fugue as a whole—is thus related to the quar-tet's homophonic dance and song movements. This leads to paradox: how can the *Fortspinnung* symbolize the cycle's inner lyrical movements on the one hand, and the sonata-form finale on the other? The reason is that the Classical cycle is a dy-namic one, where lyric is gradually repositioned from an auxiliary or interlude to a goal. The lyrical trajectory thus comprises not merely a change of idiom, but a process where the status of this idiom is transformed. The finale inverts the terms of the cycle's proposition, discovering, for example, that the fugue's head motive is already a cadential idea. And one should not be deceived by the ostensibly "homophonic" march which launches the finale; in some ways, it turns out to be more contrapuntal than the cyclic echoes of the fugue which answer it. The idioms of counterpoint and homophony, having been interchanged, are then "remade" on a more abstract level. This inversion of conventional markers is underscored by schematic transformations of the music's sense of "in and out" and "surface/depth."

We know from Winter (1977) that Beethoven worked out the details of the fugue subject long after sketching the tonal shape of the quartet. With the idea of the whole in mind, Beethoven constructs a miracle of compression, in which the trajectory toward lyric is pinpointed around a focal pitch—the A of m. 2, highlighted as the longest and loudest note of the subject (the dotted half note, the hairpins, and the sforzato).[6] Unlike the arches of the sonatas or the "Galitzin," Beethoven places this submediant as an *inner pitch,* not a melodic apex, thereby suggesting interiority. A is the key of the fugue's longest and most tonally stable episode, the lyrical plateau of mm. 63–82; it is the key of the fourth-movement variations, the still heart of the quartet. But A is in fact the agent of F♯, the subdominant. It anticipates the subject's anomalous subdominant answer, and the finale's tilt toward F♯ minor in its development and coda. The late style's affair with subdominant relaxation is all of a piece with its lyrical bent; the subject ingeniously combines both tendencies on several levels. A masterpiece of bifocality, the first two measures leave us in doubt whether the B♯ is a harmony note (i.e., an extension of the preceding G♯) or an accented passing note to the C♯. If the latter, then the harmonic rate of change halves from two to one in a measure, and the opening foreshadows the culmination of the fugue with the augmented entry of m. 100. This augmentation epitomizes the process of expansion unfolded across the movement, an outcome predicted in the head motive's very ambiguity. In fact, this head motive becomes harmonized with increasing clarity as a single chord, as in the stretto sequence of mm. 21–26 (see ex. 6.11b). Although the tonal orientation of mm. 1–2 is hardly in doubt (lack of harmony notwithstanding), it does carry the potential for being reinterpreted as a V–I cadence in the subdominant. That is, the first shift from C♯ to F♯ implicitly comes at m. 2, within the subject itself, rather than the subdominant answer. Measures 1–2 thus emerge as an augmented, subdominant version of the B♯–C♯ head motive, which is heard in double perspective—two keys, and two metrical levels at once. As well as coordinating impulses toward both tonic and subdominant ("bifocally"), the subject also sets the fugue on its path of tonal expansion and melodic diminution. This is because the *Fortspinnung* tail, mm. 3–4, outlines an expanded form of the appoggiatura head motive, F♯–G♯. Prolonged into a two-measure gestalt, it prefigures not just the augmented entry of m. 100, but the fugue's most radical pun, which is to reinterpret the fugal tail *as* the head motive in episodes after m. 37.

This journey unfolds with a consummate art of transition toward the A-major plateau of mm. 63–82 (ex. 6.11a–e):

Example 6.11. Expansion process in first movement of Op. 131
    a. Head motive, m. 1
Continues on the next page

Example 6.11. Expansion process in first movement of Op. 131
    b. Fifth cycle, mm. 20–22
    c. Chromatically altered *Fortspinnung*, mm. 37–38
    d. Head motive and *Fortspinnung* counterpointed, mm. 46–47
Continues on the next page

Example 6.11. Expansion process in first movement of Op. 131
    e. A-major plateau, mm. 62–69

First, the subject's B♯–C♯ head motive is subsumed into a higher-level fifth cycle from
m. 21 (C♯–F♯–B–E–A), whose course anticipates the general drift to A (ex. 6.11b).
At m. 37 (ex. 6.11c), Beethoven chromatically alters the neighbor-note pattern
of the *Fortspinnung*, activating its implicit affinity with the head motive (here as
A♯–B). Head motive and altered *Fortspinnung* are counterpointed at mm. 46–50,
until the latter takes over and the head motive is dissolved (ex. 6.11d). The abrogation of the head motive's cadential V–I character occurs at m. 63 (ex. 6.11e). Here
the music grinds to a halt on a four-measure pedal—the longest stretch of stability
in the movement—after which the fugal argument yields to canonic imitation between pairs of voices, and the fugue subject is temporally suspended in favor of a

new theme, based on a rhythmic displacement of the *Fortspinnung*. The music sinks down, via D major, back to the da capo of m. 83, but with only one measure of G♯ to prepare it—perhaps not enough to neutralize this block of radiant harmony. Both on account of its luminosity and tonal breadth, the A-major episode hangs over the end of the fugue, and dwarfs its own attempt at expansion, the augmentation of m. 100. If this fugue were a sonata form (which it is not), then the episode would conflate the functions of second group and development, recalling the similarly weightless development of Op. 130.

The salience of the episode leads to questions of disproportion: the fugue is "middle heavy." Local asymmetry admittedly fosters broader integration, since the A major helps motivate the shift to D in the Allegro. Even so, the disproportion and functional isolation of this A-major plateau is the first major inkling of lyric's impulse toward autonomy, at odds with its duties to the cycle. On a global level, the intoxicating freedom and joie de vivre of the fourth and fifth movements marks such a compelling highpoint that it requires the peremptory gesture of the G♯ octaves to wrench lyric back into line with its cadential obligations—the G♯–C♯ cadence staked out by the sixth-movement Adagio and Finale. This tragedy of lyric cut short is implicit in the drama of the IV/V conflict which preoccupies the late style. Beethoven discovers it in the tonal interstices I explored in chapter 4. Consider, once again, the A♮ crux of the fugue subject (Hatten 1994: 152, 158). Beethoven leans on this pitch as the most expressive feature of his theme and underplays the dominant note of resolution. (Is it the following G♯ quarter note, or the G♯ half note two measures later?) A paradox of tonal space is that the subdominant is much further away from the dominant than the semitone step $\hat{6}$–$\hat{5}$ implies; with this semitone, the music leaps from a point of furthest remove (a point of subdominant relaxation, a fifth below the tonic) to the stage of tonic return (the homeward impulse of the dominant, a fifth *above* the tonic). Elaborated into style change, the shift occasions the dramatic reversals of mood between the A-major plateau and the fugal da capo, between the E-major Presto and the G♯-minor Adagio. One role for the Presto is to keep apart the keys of the fourth and sixth movements, diffusing the cycle's overarching resolution from A major to the G♯, so prolonging its sojourn in lyric. The brutal G♯ octaves put an end to that, and redirect the interlude as an auxiliary to the G♯–C♯ structural cadence.

Lyric's dual face as auxiliary and goal is composed out through two intersecting key schemes (ex. 6.12):

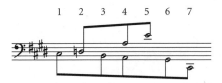

Example 6.12. Intersecting key schemes of Op. 131

A descending tetrachord of C♯ (mvt. 1), B (mvt. 3), A (mvt. 4), G♯ (mvt. 6) presses the quartet into an ineluctable I–V (8̂–7̂–6̂–5̂) preparation for the finale's structural tonic downbeat. Embedded within this scheme is a rising-fifths progression of D (mvt. 2), A (mvt. 4), E (mvt. 5), aspiring away from C♯ up to the ether. The A-major variations participate in both schemes, as befits both the scale step's functional ambiguity, and the movement's character as the quartet's point of equilibrium. The counterpoint between the two schemes gives rise to vivid effects of split-level tonality, where "background" keys shine (*Schein*) through the surface. Such tonal breakthroughs perforate each of the three rising-fifth movements at critical structural junctures. The D-major Allegro never manages to modulate to its dominant: the transition is beached on V of F♯ (mm. 44–47) and then deflected by a ritornello of the first theme in E (ex. 6.13a–b):

Example 6.13. Op. 131, second movement
    a. Deflection of F♯ by E-major ritornello, mm. 43–51
Continues on the next page

Example 6.13. Op. 131, second movement
   b. Momentary resolution to B, mm. 122–30

At the parallel moment of the reprise, which sets up V of B, this key is actually permitted to arrive, albeit extremely briefly. The dramatically exposed unison B's of m. 126 are, in their quiet way, one of the most impressive moments of the quartet. For an instant, the steel of the B-minor undergirding shows, anticipating movement 3, before an upsurge of fourth cycles blows the music back on (off) track to D. Technically, this flash of subterranean tonality follows in the footsteps of the *Hammerklavier* (the B-minor explosion at m. 267) and Op. 132 (the C-major sunburst of m. 92). The fourth-movement Andante builds in references to the fugue at the theme's apexes, and at each variation thereafter (ex. 6.14).

The music linking the melodic crux (m. 5) to the repeat (m. 9) is a compressed fifth cycle C♯–F♯–B–E–A: that is, approaching A major from C♯, and in a way which

Example 6.14. Op. 131, fourth movement, theme, mm. 1–9

stakes out a C♯–B–A descent. References to the fugue will grow in subsequent variations; for example, the canonic textures of variation 3, and the chromatic harmonies of variation 6 (mm. 203–16). Even more subtle is the way the variations progressively isolate the cusps of the theme's two phrases, so that the structure pivots on fugal flashbacks. The most powerful comes in the second strain of variation 6, which astonishingly reinterpret the theme's IV–V–I progression (mm. 21–22) in F♯ minor. The key, register, and tone of this climax, at m. 216, all remain suspended, as Beethoven, in order to avoid direct resolution to E, meticulously diverts the F♯ to D♯, then D♮ and C♯. The E-major Presto, for its part, is repeatedly deflected into C♯ minor by brusque G♯ chords, as if the quartet is stubbornly flying in the face of the imminent finale. Considered as a trio, these inner lyric movements use their local discontinuities for mutual support. The D-major Allegro fails to modulate to A and thus needs the A-major variations; these underplay E in favor of the F♯ apex, a debt which is explosively discharged by the E-major Presto.

And so to the finale. With grim irony, no sooner does the end come than Beethoven cuts the ground from under its feet and commutes C♯ into a dominant of F♯. Ostensibly a regular sonata form, the finale's proportions are warped by the brevity of its second group and the subdominant bias of its development. Lasting only twenty measures, the second group is an insufficient buffer between the C♯ exposition and the development's opening F♯ ritornello. The exposition is upended as a dominant upbeat to the development, throwing the movement's weight onto its center. This F♯ orientation becomes even stronger in the coda, where the *tierce de Picardie* ending almost suggests a half-close in F♯ minor, given the final chords' dual role, in Winter's words, as "both tonic and at the same time dominant of the subdominant" (120). This key remains just below the horizon, as if the entire work is a dominant introduction to an implicit quartet in F♯ minor.

The victory of homophony is similarly Pyrrhic. The march of death which strikes up at m. 5 is, in its own way, as lopsided as the march of Op. 132, afflicted not so much with lameness as rigor mortis. Stiffly going its own way, it obstinately resists lockstepping with the harmonic beat set up by the opening gestures—two measures of tonic, two measures of dominant (ex. A.6, see appendix). Against this beat, the instruments maintain a rigid tonic ostinato, and the A–G♯ apex pointedly rejects a dominant chord at m. 7. The belated V at m. 9 is a feint, immediately tucked back into the tonic, and when the phrase does decide to move, it surprisingly elects the Baroque protocol of a descending-octave sequence. The periodic, Classical pattern promised at mm. 1–4 is rejected in favor of the circular, sequential rhythms of Baroque tonality. Conversely, the Classically cadential tags which articulate the tonic group, at mm. 21–43, are carried by cyclical returns of the fugue's head motive. Homophony and counterpoint have exchanged functions. The irony is compounded by striking changes in the recapitulation and coda. With the reprise of the march at m. 168, Beethoven underlays another subject-answer fugal echo in canonic imitation. The march's A–G♯ step is echoed by the cello's cantus firmus two measures later, this time correcting the resolution to the dominant. The march resists the periodic beat; the cantus firmus imposes it. Altogether, the accretion discloses the counterpoint implicit in the march's noncongruence between harmony and rhythm. The second revelation comes in the coda. Molding the march's descending scales into the C♯–B–A–G♯ tetrachord figure, and transforming the fugal head motive into half-cadences in F♯ minor, Beethoven counterpoints both in a plethora of canonic imitations. Through the parataxis of canonic repetition, fugue slides into the world of lyric. The reversal is complete: homophony becomes counterpoint (the march's noncongruence), fugue turns into lyric (the canon's parataxis).

The cycle of Op. 131 turns two circles. It begins with the lyrical trajectory of the *Fortspinnung* principle. The variations put lyric first and consign references to fugue to apexes, middles, or endings. The finale at first appears to confirm this reversal—a sonata form with a fugal development (the conventional place for counterpoint). Yet it actually has it both ways: going back and reaffirming the original lyrical trajectory, but remaking it, at a more abstract level, as a progression from fraught noncongruence to dissipating parataxis. As with all the other conventions

Beethoven reifies, estranging counterpoint and homophony serves to profile their material character as objects in themselves.

So too with the quartet's persistent questions of "under" and "over." Does the rising-fifths architecture represents "cover keys," hovering above the C♯–B–A–G♯ descent? Or do these shining inner movements comprise the reality of Op. 131? The finale rages, but the abiding impression of this quartet "in C♯ minor" is actually one of abiding radiance. The paradox of *Schein* is that aesthetic beauty is a reality which is also a semblance, a surface appearance (*Apparition*). There *is* no underneath. Consider again the unison-B reprise at m. 126 of the second movement, an indescribably poignant moment: how can B light up D major, given that the Allegro is already a Neapolitan illumination of C♯ minor? But *Schein,* of course, is not a state but a dynamic flicker, a "quivering," as Benjamin calls it. *Schein's* flicker assumes a technical dimension in Op. 131 in the interplay between tonal schemes, between subdominant and dominant orientations. Winter demonstrates that this interplay originates in the vacillations of the compositional genesis itself, much of which turns on the mitigation of a subdominant bias which was originally much stronger. For example, earlier drafts included a fourth-movement scherzo in F♯ minor (outlining material which would become the finale), marked by Beethoven "4tes Stük in fis moll" (121). In the process of fine-tuning the tonal *Schein,* Beethoven absorbed the subdominant into the other movements. Winter's work on Op. 131, like Drabkin's on the *Arietta,* supports a powerful inference: that compositional vacillation carries through into the finished score, in the form of aesthetic *Schein.* Not in a way which challenges the identity of the work concept—Beethoven's pieces are "finished" like few others. Rather, in ways which can be tracked by technical concepts such as bifocal tonality, noncongruence, and functional rubato, and aesthetic ones such as *Schein* and *Apparition. Apparition,* or Appearance (*Erscheinung*), is particularly apt to describe the continuity between genesis and structure, *Schein's* "coming into appearance." It seems appropriate most of all for Beethoven's late style, which so often wears its compositional origins on its sleeve.

Opus 135 in F: The *Schein* of Creative Alternative

The thrust of Beethoven's allegories of freedom is to outline possibilities of alternative outcome; literally, to break the fateful cycle of the opening movement. Thus the watchword is alternative, and with alternative comes choice and compositional fiat. The most stunning example of compositional fiat in Op. 131 comes with Beethoven's late decision to cut the finale's projected D♭ postscript, a movement he later turned into the Lento of Op. 135. Such an ending would have utterly transformed the shape of the work. Crucially, it would have canceled the finale's subdominant ambiguity, since the shift neutralizes the altered scale degree E♯ into a notationally stable F, grounding the tonic. By omitting this postscript, and ending with the C♯-major chords, Beethoven resolves *Schein* neither one way nor the other, and leaves the quartet delicately poised on a knife edge.

The idea of alternative seems, at first blush, antithetical to the holism of cyclicity. Analysis of cyclic unity in Beethoven traditionally shows how every note is an inevitable consequence of the overall design. Only within such an overdetermined context can a vanishingly small detail, such as the eighth-note rest in Op. 135 which I belabored in chapter 4, generate such rich reverberations. Would the cycle really collapse if that rest were filled up, allowing the $\hat{3}$–$\hat{4}$–$\hat{5}$ cadential approach to unfold without interruption? The question assumes a much deeper dimension when we consider the intertwined genesis of the two last quartets. Op. 135's slow movement, originally the coda to Op. 131, plays beautifully with the $\hat{3}$–$\hat{4}$–$\hat{5}$ idea, consoling it with countervailing $\hat{3}$–$\hat{2}$–$\hat{1}$ descents (mm. 10–12). The figure is integrated within the F-major quartet's unique cyclic journey, and yet it must have first made some sense to Beethoven as a step in the earlier quartet's own cycle; for example, as an enharmonic variant of the C♯–B–A–G♯ tetrachord (see the Lento's D♭–C–B♭–A♭ opening). So can one speak of "alternative cyclicity"? Can a creative alternative, unfolded by different works, inform our attitude to a work in itself? In his powerful essay on late Beethoven's sense of an ending, Solomon reminds us that alternatives which made it into print—such as the two finales of Op. 130—are really manifestations of the "noninevitability" of Beethoven's compositional process itself, which similarly keeps in play a "plurality of potential, dormant alternatives" (147). Beethoven sketch scholarship has demonstrated that the genesis of these works is never a teleological unfolding of a conception determined at the outset. Beethoven not only constantly changes his mind, but he likes to keep at least two radically different genetic branches in growth throughout the process, choosing one or the other at a very late stage. But are the choices really so final? I have suggested that compositional vacillation can indeed survive into the "finished" score. A higher order of vacillation obtains between finished works themselves. Just as the last three sonatas are three variations on a trill, his final two quartets are alternative cycles.

Op. 135 is outwardly as different from the C♯ minor as it is possible to be. With its four movements, beginning with a Haydnesque sonata form, it seems to be a conventional throwback. It is surprising, therefore, that it reworks Op. 131's descending-tetrachord scheme, albeit with minimal key change. All but the D♭ Lento assai are in the tonic F major. Within this F–E♭–D♭–C pattern, the E♭ and C are given neither a key nor a movement to themselves, but are instead absorbed into movements 1, 2, and 4 as salient pitches or harmonies. The E♭ is *so* salient as to suggest that the finale's famous "Muss es sein" conundrum is a pun on the German word for E♭ (Reynolds 1988: 190). Beethoven asks us "Must it be E♭?" Like an irritant, E♭ deflects the first-movement development into a false reprise in B♭ (m. 82), echoed in the coda (mm. 182–87), and is the source of farcical interruptions in the Vivace (mm. 16–22). It is this E♭ which forces the music down to the D♭ of the Lento. C, the last step of the descent, is integrated as the goal of the finale's Grave introduction, which harps on the D♭–C resolution. The development brings the entire F–E♭–D♭–C progression to the light of day in its climax (mm. 138–60), ushering back the Grave, this time fortissimo and with the C projected over grating dissonances. This D♭–C idea is of course also where the quartet started, with the cello motive of mm. 1–2.

Op. 135 has no need of Op. 131's drive for homophony, since it is Classical from the start. Of the two lyrical alternatives available to the cycle, it picks not song but dance. It is dominated by the spirit of the dance, and its driving impulse is toward paratactic repetition. The D♭ Lento is touching, but it is eclipsed by the extraordinary scherzo, in particular the overwhelming fifty-one-measure ostinato in the trio. Amazingly, the passage of most sustained violence in the entire late style is found not in Op. 131, nor in the *Grosse Fuge*, but here, in this ostensibly mild-mannered pastoral work. Riezler advisedly chose it to end his book. This "storm" (to give it its pastoral topic) is never really contained in the quartet, which makes it a far less unified piece than Op. 131. The scherzo is to the first movement what the A-major variations are to the fugue in the earlier quartet. It confirms an impulse enshrined in the opening gambit; indeed, it is the repeated A–B♭–C figure of mm. 5–9. The "idea" here is repetition, rather than tonal expansion. In particular, it is repetition interrupted by its cadential obligations. Coincidentally, the two problem points in the quartets both turn on the pitch A. In Op. 131, it is A's questionable resolution down to G♯; here it is A's problematic *rise* to B♭. Accordingly, the subdominant plays opposite roles: in Op. 131 it is associated with A; in Op. 135 it is the function which *interrupts* A. The subdominant, represented by E♭ and D♭, troubles Op. 135 all the way through. The seed of repetition, planted at m. 5, blossoms in the development section at m. 86. The A–B♭–C motive is reiterated, generalized into a dance around C major (mm. 97–100), and then dismissed by the noisy reprise at m. 101, with its grating D♭ (ex. 6.15).

Repetition is taken further in the Vivace, in the twin guise of canonic imitation and ostinato moto perpetuo. Parataxis becomes variation in the Lento. The finale is a succinct sonata form, but one riddled with canons. Indeed, the first subject's consequent phrase (mm. 17–31) is practically lifted from the canons in the C♯-minor fugue's A-major plateau. Canons mark the endpoint of the C♯ quartet's finale; here they are present from the opening of the Allegro. The tonic subject, based on Beethoven's favorite "thirds and fourths" melodic pattern, is varied twice, first in the reprise, and again in the coda. The three ritornellos negotiate canon variously (ex. 6.16a–c).

First (ex. 6.16a), canon is associated with the Op. 131 figures (actually, an ingenious variant of the "thirds and fourths" pattern), and the subdominant turn which derails the tonic group after only four measures. At the reprise, mm. 174–88 (ex. 6.16b), the Op. 131 figures disappear; the "thirds and fourths" melody itself becomes canonic and is allowed to flow more continuously. Nevertheless, the music is pushed into B♭, as before. Finally, at mm. 267–74 (ex. 6.16c), the subdominant problem is eradicated; the "thirds and fourths" pattern is permitted a regular descent to the tonic, and it is counterpointed by a new idea—a falling scale from F to A. The two scales imitate at the fourth; the canon has been resolved and compressed into a potentially infinite round. Canons traditionally symbolize the eternal circling of the stars. Beethoven's last quartet *could* go on for ever, and the final cadential gesture, though exhilarating in its white-note unison purity, is felt as an intervention from without—literally, from outside the canonic circle and the quartet's cycle.

Example 6.15. String Quartet in F, Op. 135, first movement, mm. 99–103

Beethoven amused himself by composing many short canons during this "third phase" of the late style, including one on *Muss es sein?* Counterpoint, as parataxis, can be ludic, as well as fateful, and the creative alternatives of his last quartets ultimately offer us this choice of perception. Like Op. 131, we can rage, or we can dance into the night with Op. 135.

Conceptualizing the Ninth

Diesen Kuss der ganzen Welt! Beethoven's setting of Schiller's ode *An die Freude* in the finale of his Ninth Symphony kisses the whole world of styles (*Volkslied*, religious hymn, march *alla turca*, military music, archaic a capella, Handelian double counterpoint), genres (concerto, recitative, sonata, four-movement form, variations, rondo, fugue, cantata, operatic finale), and often contradictory aesthetic

Example 6.16. Op. 135, finale, three ritornellos of the tonic subject
    a. Opening of Allegro, mm. 12–20
Continues on the next page

values (French-revolutionary rhetoric vs. the Romantic ideal of monarchy, bourgeois *Bildung* vs. the metaphysics of music, nationalism vs. internationalism). The
listener is compelled equally by the centrifugal energy of this superabundance and
the firmness of Beethoven's cyclical embrace. There is lack of space, here or anywhere, to do justice to any of these strands, such that the work may be said to defeat
analysis—even to resist any overarching theory of style. Adjusting Schleiermacher,
one may simply conclude that "there can be no concept of the Ninth Symphony."
Nevertheless, I will hazard two observations. First, that this very tension between
the compulsion of cyclicity and resistance to cyclicity is central to our experience.
And second, that this tension is a deliberate strategy of the music, rather than a
mark of our own hermeneutic impotence. Or, as Derrida says of Hegel: "Teleology
is here not a product of the critic's projection, but is the author's own theme" (1981:

Example 6.16. Op. 135, finale, three ritornellos of the tonic subject
    b. Reprise, mm. 174–84
Continues on the next page

22). The Ode to Joy frames itself locally, because, as a variations movement, the template of the theme is periodically reimposed; globally, because this theme references the fifth progressions which are seminal for the entire symphony; and stylistically, because it extrapolates a paradox of the Classical cycle itself, by which the finale's job is to retreat from cyclicity. That is, with its looser, paratactic, often rondo-like, structure, the finale typically breaks the circle of sonata form. It completes the work by freeing it. The Ode to Joy thus neither invents musical freedom nor transcends Classicism, with its gambit of "Nicht diese Töne." What is new, however, is the cataclysmic force of this collision between the irresistible and the immovable, a clash which is loudest in the closing pages. Toward the very end of the Prestissimo coda, Beethoven drives the Ode to an intoxicating fever pitch of

Example 6.16. Op. 135, finale, three ritornellos of the tonic subject
   c. Coda, mm. 267–78

Bacchic hysteria, the climax compounded, as much as it is nailed down, by a series of stamping downbeats, accelerating to the five quarter notes of the last cadence (ex. 6.17).

Classical meter, with its periodicity and articulation, is both the engine of this climax and the grid through which we view it. Everything telescopes into this final measure: the sublimity we feel arises not in the Dionysian frenzy itself, but from an act of withstanding—by Adorno's lights, the "mimetic" standing firm, on the part of this four-beat "measuring," against an equal but opposite force. Schenker (1992) heard the A–D falling fifth of this cadence as a reworking of the opening gesture of the symphony; one might also imagine these last beats as condensing, through the logic of stretto acceleration, the entire symphony as a hyper-measure of four movements. The whole world is in this last measure, recalling Borges's par-

Example 6.17. Ninth Symphony, finale, ending

able of the Aleph, the mystical point where one can see all the time and space of the universe, or Hölderlin's letter where he claims "that all sacred places of the earth are together in one place" (in Henrich 1997: 229).

The pattern of beats which holds this rhetoric together functions like a mental *concept,* an analogy common in late-eighteenth-century music theory. In his article on "uniformity" (1771–1774, *Einformigkeit*), Johann Sulzer writes that meter turns time into spatial concepts. A series of beats (or indeed, a series of *any* objects) can, through a uniform pattern, be "united with a concept" (*mit einem Begriff zusammen gefasst*). Through uniformity, an infinite succession of events can be surveyed at a glance and held in the mind. The four-movement symphonic cycle is the ultimate expression of this quadratic logic; periodicity is the mechanism by which listeners and composers map from metrical pattern to large-scale form. Although Beethoven's Ninth draws from the same rhetorical image bank as the *Missa Solemnis* and, indeed, the three underrated precursors of the previous decade (the *Fantasie für Klavier, Chor und Orchester, Wellingtons Sieg,* and *Der glorreiche Augenblick*), it is the first work which attempts to regulate this image bank with Classical form: to *conceptualize* it. This mediation of expression through form is responsible for both its aesthetic integrity and its sublime power. It is crucial, nonetheless, to grasp this dialectic as inhering within form itself—we are not dealing with a clean-cut opposition between form and expression. The paradox of Classicism's metrical paradigm is that rhythmic beats are a measure of order *as well as* a mimetic gesture. This duality is epitomized in the rhythmic excitement of Beethoven's climax; it is also implicit in the makeup of the Ode to Joy melody. The tune's semblance of *volkstümlich* simplicity is belied by the marathon of sketching which went into creating it; the theme is quite as complex as the *Arietta* melody. For a start, as a populist hymn in the style of Haydn's *Emperor* anthem (*Gott erhalte Franz den Kaiser*), the *Marseillaise,* or the British *God Save the King* (see Buch 2003), it shares with these models the paradox that formal squareness (periodically articulated phrase endings), which is the chief agent of their expressive transparency, is also a marker of the rational in Classical music. In this light, it is difficult to rule that the entry of the Ode melody in the double basses signifies the advent of the "vocal" in the symphony, or to appraise its course as a single-track journey toward ever-more-direct expressiveness. The finale is "twin-tracked" at all times. This dialectic is intrinsic to the theme as *type;* as an anthem. It is compounded by its particular details, and the Chinese-box intricacy of its staging.

The melody's arrival is dramatized as the climax of a series of conceptual dialogues: between the *Schrekensfanfare* and the bass recitative; between this recitative, as a sign of present-tense urgency, and past-tense quotations of the previous movements; between the recitative's free idiom and the Ode melody's periodic form. The transitions are wrought by two especially subtle details. Beethoven marks the bass's declamations "Selon le caractère d'un recitative, mais in tempo," leveling the conventional opposition between free and measured styles. And the last ghost at the feast—the fourth quotation, mm. 77–80—has no name (ex. A.7, see appendix). It is introduced like a quotation, yet, following on from the recall of the third movement (mm. 63–65), it throws the present, fourth movement into quotation marks as well. Actually, it casts the loop back to the first movement again, referencing the contour and wind sonorities of the second subject, gene-spliced with the rhythms of the coming Ode melody. Beethoven's strange "neither-here-nor-there" quotation compounds his self-reflexive mise-en-scène and thereby throws the tune into maximum relief, very different to Haydn and Mozart's practice of *blending* the popular style. And finally, as the melody percolates up the orchestral ranks to the tutti of m. 164, it becomes the "musical symbol for a political community" (Buch, 107), on the basis of the venerable analogy between the orchestra and humanity (see Dahlhaus 1991: 178).

And yet the melody's naive simplicity is deceptive. Taking its cue from the instruments, it is less "vocal" than the recitative on the one side, and the much more frankly declamatory style of "Seid umschlungen" on the other. Also, the alignment of melody and harmony is subtly problematic, reminiscent of the pseudo-homophony of Op. 131's own finale. The descent from A to D in mm. 2–3 is either cadential—in which case, it ought to go at the end, not the beginning—or it predicates a tonic pedal, which paradoxically *does* obtain at the end of the symphony discussed above (where, strangely, the very final A–D figure *abstains* from a V–I progression). In fact, the melody participates in the symphony's general problematizing of fifth progressions; that is, the intercutting of melodic and harmonic fifths, as we shall see. A second tension concerns the interaction of the F♯–E cue which punctuates the antecedent phrase at m. 4, and the melody's penchant to descend in thirds. Measure 3 begins as a sequential repetition of mm. 1–2 a third below, suggesting that the melody will outline a F♯–D–B–[G] third sequence. But the F♯–E denies this sequence by refusing to continue down to D. This tendency will actually be realized in the G-major "Seid umschlungen" episode, which reinforces the association between the third sequence, the subdominant, the declamatory, and the nonperiodic fugal (paratactic) style. In all these respects, "Seid umschlungen"—the bugbear of many formalist analyses of the Ode—discloses the "Other" lurking beneath the melody's surface. But the melody also has "An-Other": the mutation at m. 20 of the last Allegro ma non tanto. This joyfully canonic round of interlocking perfect cadences (an echo of Pamina and Papageno's "marriage duet" from the *Magic Flute*) marks the opposite triumph of the tonic-dominant axis. The two axes, the functional I–V and the lyrical I–IV, are then juxtaposed, twice, across mm. 20–70, a blast of canonic cadencing ("Deiner Zauber") countered by cataracts of plagal thirds ("Alle Menschen"), as if Beethoven, having extracted the Ode's two primary colors, begins throwing them around like titanic blocks (ex. 6.18a–b):

Example 6.18. The Ode's two "primary colors"
    a. Canonic cadences
Continues on the next page

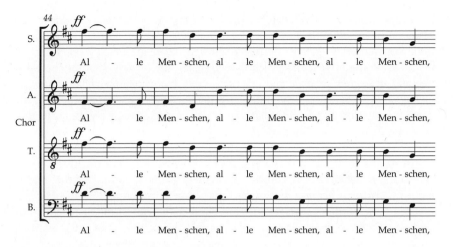

Example 6.18. The Ode's two "primary colors"
  b. Descending thirds

At issue, simply, is conflicting dominant and subdominant perspectives on the same source set; in this light, the famous Ode melody is just another refraction of the Kyrie "germinal motif" identified by Riezler and discussed in chapter 4. Here, in the symphony, these poles become attractors for a different set of principles altogether. The question of what the symphony is "about" takes us beyond the genre shocks, the leap to language, and the philosophemes of freedom to the axioms of Beethoven's analytical project: once again, the fundamentals of musical nature and convention, of S3 and S1.

The image schemata are as salient as they are in the mass, with striking similarities. The UP-DOWN coelum/terra juxtaposition, with its paradigm of the Gloria's opening text ("Gloria in excelsis, et in terra pax"), is elaborated into contrasts between "high" and "low" social registers, most spectacularly in the plummet to the Turkish *Alla Marcia*. Following the top A of "vor Gott," the bottom B♭ of the double bassoon creates a delicious pun, since it is the very depth of the note, together with its timbre, which elicits the grotesque bathos. The Credo's IN-OUT schemata of parenthetical enclosure are reproduced by the containment of the Turkish march and "Seid umschlungen" episodes by overarching voice-leading connections (also akin to those in Op. 109): that is, the top A is registrally picked up by the top G of "über Sternen muss er wohnen," to resolve to the F♯ of the Allegro energico "finale." SUFRACE-DEPTH and PART-WHOLE schemata are germane also to the Ode's project of integrating levels of discourse and material, constantly redefining the priorities of instrumental and melodic styles. While these schemata are explicit in the Ode's global contrasts, they are already encapsulated within its melody. The UP-DOWN contour is the most obvious, particularly with the rise from

F♯ to A and subsequent descent (prefiguring "vor Gott"). But the periodic articulation of the melodic stream with cadential markers predicates differences of level (SURFACE-DEPTH) and structure (PART-WHOLE). These are much more salient in the series of cognitive shifts which have prepared the melody, shunting between free and measured, internal and external, vocal and instrumental. Although the melody appears seamless, it vibrates with the conceptual dialogue which engendered it. In terms of salience, then, the schemata telescope in and out, pivoting around the unisono rendition of the Ode melody.

The second branch of Beethoven's analytic is the musical conventions of Style 1. It is in this respect that the Ode sends its roots furthest into the instrumental core of the symphony, namely, the first movement. Demonstrating that the "meaning" of the work inheres in musical material, rather than in political ideology associated with Schiller's text, is crucial to counter the pattern of so much Ninth reception. The symphony has come to bear an enormous load of interpretation. Buch, who sees it as "a narrative 'on' the concept of hymn," singles out its synthetically utopian aspects (2003: 107). Rumph's more jaded reading casts Beethoven's "synthesis of *vox populi* and *vox dei*" as a "historical regression," a crawling "backward into the womb of pre-individualistic, feudal Christendom" (2004: 221). Against such directly historicist readings, I would cite Umberto Eco's caveat, also quoted by Solomon: "to decode a symbol is to render it mute" (Solomon 1986: 10). The music assuredly does have a political dimension, yet one whose dialectical mediations always exhaust one-to-one correlations with cultural units. The meaning of the Ninth lies in the "politics" immanent within its technical material; insofar as it taps the metaphor of "orchestra as humanity," it is really "about" orchestration itself. Or rather, *timbre* approximates to the stuff, or material, of that "sense drive" which Schiller opposes to his "formal drive."

Timbre, taken for granted when it is congruent with the more structural parameters, leaps into view if it plays against their grain. Timbral noncongruence in the Ninth has a formal and textural dimension, when orchestral dialogue cuts across voice leading, or when the layering of parts doesn't chime with the harmonic bass. In the first case, the resolution of a dissonance in a contrasting tone color can be as destabilizing as registral displacement within a single part. For instance, the cadential interruption at m. 95 of the first movement is a timbral as well as harmonic affair, since the leading note A of the first violins is resolved by the B♭ of the clarinets; that is, it is not resolved properly at all, arguably, until the closing tutti of the exposition. In the second case, texturally, the question of whether the heterogeneity of the orchestra is truly assimilated by harmony is epitomized by the paradox of the pedal. Pedal points lie "outside" the fundamental-bass progressions which they underscore; they don't participate directly with the inner progressions of the harmony, except as its frame. It is with the pedal, then, that disjunctions between acoustic and fundamental bass lines (between the lowest note and the functional one) can become most jarring. A striking example of such divergence comes with the first main cadence of the Allegro first movement. The tonic arrival at m. 34 and the resumption of the string tremolo which opened the symphony conclude the first paragraph of the exposition (ex. 6.19):

Example 6.19. Ninth Symphony, first movement, mm. 28–35
Continues on the next page

Example 6.19. Ninth Symphony, first movement, mm. 28–35

Yet the cadence oddly avoids the dominant chord, moving directly from a preparatory ♯IV to I$^6_4$ in m. 33. The tonic $^6_4$, instead of resolving to V, slips into root position at m. 35 when the double bass and the timpani shift from A to D. At issue is the interaction of the V–I cadential model with not one but *two* pedals: a dominant pedal stretching back to m. 27, and a tonic pedal suggested at m. 32 and explicit at m. 35 with the da capo of the opening tremolos. The great climaxes at the development and recapitulation are founded on such tonal disjunctions. Measures 245–46 of the development polarizes the battle into a thrilling bifocal clash of tonic and dominant. And at mm. 319–22 the cellos and basses ignore the V–I cadence of the upper strings and trumpets and go their own way, tipping the music into G minor (implicit in the shocking tonic major triad of the reprise).

These "formal" and "timbral" noncongruences are the real ground for the much noted, yet often disputed, cyclical links between the second group and the Ode melody. Tovey dismisses the correspondence as "superficial and entirely accidental" (1989: 96), even though the wind theme in mm. 74–75 is a patent fore-echo of the Ode's rising and falling thirds. His reasons are sound, if understated: the affinity goes beyond facile thematic motive spotting. I suggest the connection concerns the evolution of "vocality," and that the second group prepares the outbreak of the Ode melody—with all its nested stagings after the *Schrenkensfanfare*—as a formal propaedeutic.

The finale's leap to language—in many ways the defining, epoch-making gesture of the symphony—is already outlined by syntactic category leaps rendered in the terms of dialogue and pedal. These shifts are kindred with the kinds of transformation we have seen in the sonatas and quartets: allegorical *Apparitions* of the lyrical within the conventional; reversals of frame and parenthesis; and the breakthrough of underlying forces. The process is framed by the beginning and end of the B♭ group. The group starts on an F dominant pedal (m. 74) which answers, but does not properly resolve, the A pedal on which the tonic group ended (mm. 63–71). Across mm. 71–75, in a passage of structural collapse, the dominant of D is derailed, and the rising-and-falling cadential figures (G–F–E–D–C♯–D–E–F–G) are hammered into the second subject (ex. 6.20):

Beethoven's category leap is from neutral convention (strikingly reminiscent of similar gestures in Mozart's D-minor Piano Concerto K. 466) to thematic particularity. The birth of "vocality" is already encapsulated here, in the *Durchbruch* of expression out of cadence. The "modulation" takes an opposite course to the genesis of the square Ode melody out of recitative. Still, this moment is as yet only part of a relay of transformations which will come to a head, at the end of the section, with a countervailing shift from melody back into cadence. The drive to this cadence is one of the symphony's densest and most provocative passages.

The music at mm. 138–50 is so extraordinarily complex that an uncomprehending Richard Wagner retouched the orchestration in his own edition of the work (see Cook 2000: 53–56). "Who," asks Wagner, "can declare that he has ever heard this passage, with distinct perception of its melodic content, at any of our orchestral performances?" (in Cook, 53). The fascination flows from a rupture at m. 146, where dialogue and pedal collide, sparking off the brightest *Apparition* in the move-

Example 6.20. Ninth Symphony, first movement, mm. 69–77

ment (ex. A.8, see appendix). From m. 138, fortissimo string octaves and piano wind cadenzas alternate in rising scales above a brass pedal, reaching G at m. 144. Yet the next step of the pattern, the dominant, is strikingly withheld at m. 146, when Beethoven knocks out the expected string octave and lets the wind and brass sound alone. Suddenly, the horns' B♭ pedal is transformed from an outsider to the harmonic sequence into an active member—the *bass*. This shift from being outside the harmony to within is too sudden for the horns to sound convincing as the tonic of a I$^6_4$–V$^5_3$ progression, and the doubt is aggravated by the uncertain tonal context: does B♭ want to resolve down to A♮ (a $^6_4$ cadence in B♭) or up to E♭ (a perfect cadence in E♭)? The previous string entry casts its subdominant shadow over the wind figurations. The wind semiquavers in mm. 138–144 had elaborated the harmony between the string steps, and the E♭ step of m. 144 is still active at m. 146. The E♭–D flute figure (eighth notes) at m. 146 is a subtle metrical displacement of the same figure (sixteenth notes) at the end of m. 143, thus maintaining the subdominant feel. The descent of the flute line through mm. 146–47 seems to continue the sixteenth-note descent of m. 145 in augmentation; the two-measure wind parenthesis is not interrupted at m. 146 but extended. That the appoggiaturas of mm. 146–47 are truly intended to be heard as augmentations of the sixteenth-note figures is confirmed by mm. 148–50. Once the appoggiaturas are transferred to the strings, the winds answer them with diminutions of the major seventh and octave figures played by the strings in mm. 138–144. So the expansion of the parenthesis in mm. 144–47 can now be understood in its proper role: it revises the terms of the strings-wind dialogue of mm. 138–44. The strings now answer the wind sixteenth

194 *Music as Philosophy*

notes in augmentation, while the winds answer the string percussive figures in diminution.

The premature E♭ cadence at m. 146, based on a dramatically internalized horn pedal, is a wonderful echo of the horn's false-correct reprise in the *Eroica*—and *in the same key*. And, as in the *Eroica*, the entry is brusquely swatted aside by the tutti statement. Together, the successive entries create a dauntingly compressed *Schein* of two *Apparitions*, flickering in and out, up and through the two frames of pedal/harmony and parenthesis/structure. And they forecast the interchanges of the finale, where the reconciliation of strife essentially concerns dialogue and blend: how to combine voices and orchestra both formally and texturally. Pun intended, Beethoven "orchestrates" "Alle Menschen werden Brüder." If the signs of freedom lie in the shift from a conflictual orchestral idiom to a harmonious one, then the meaning of the Ninth is a practical fact of orchestration. When accompanying voices, the orchestra necessarily plays more simply. Tovey wisely reminds us, in his essay on the *Leonora* overtures, that effective instrumental writing in opera is always "sketchy and bald" when lifted out of its dramatic context (1989: 129). Of course, the Ode's simplicity is a semblance. The Ode melody's ostensibly innocent V–I accompaniments can be heard as objectified referents of the fifth progressions thematic to the symphony (again, echoing Op. 131). For instance, the finale's cyclical debt to the opening fifths of the first movement (quoted, of course, just after the *Schrekensfanfare*) becomes explicit at its very end. The last thirteen measures of the coda stick steadfastly to a tonic pedal, with the strings resisting the winds' up-rush to the final V–I gesture. Why, in the event, this bifocal, short-circuited, cadence sounds affirmative and *not* conflictual has much to do with the vicissitudes turned by the finale's form.

The conceptual leaps inscribed within the first movement are opened up and filled out by the finale, and in ways which *confirm* their grounding in Classical convention: in particular, the conventions of concerto and rondo. The leap from music to language is implicit in the routine of following an orchestral introduction with a solo ritornello; the "second time," Beethoven gives the bass recitative actual words ("nicht diese Töne"). And the leaps of consciousness, by which we conceptualize the evolving finale at rising levels, is intrinsic to rondo. Each ritornello of a rondo retrospectively reassesses and regroups the preceding material. In both, the stakes are high, questioning the boundaries of music and its contexts, and the very integrity of form. Despite the leap to language, the singers sing like instruments, the language is musicalized, and the text dissolves. Conversely, the Ode's overlapping, multitasking instrumental forms cross over into the antithetical world of dramatic music, where laxer rules apply. Even the most tonally integrated of Mozart's operatic finales (such as that to the second act of *The Marriage of Figaro*) are basically chain forms comprised of self-enclosed units. In Beethoven's Ode, the onset of the dramatic style in the G-major "Seid umschlungen" creates the biggest genre shock. It sounds like the beginning of a new movement, rather than a section within an instrumental genre. From its standpoint, the variations "movement" has been satisfyingly rounded off by the tutti ritornello of "Freude, schöner Götterfunken." There is no compulsion to return to the Ode theme, just as operatic finales or cantatas do not require a thematic da capo. Thus the contrapuntal fusion of the "Seid umschlungen" melody with the Ode theme in the subsequent Allegro energico is a deliberative act of return to the formalist protocol, inflected with the fugal markers of recapitulation. And from this second, higher, perspective, "Seid umschlungen" is reintegrated into an instrumental aesthetic, where it joins the B♭ Turkish march as two tonally deviant episodes in a rondo-like variations movement. In fact, it precisely follows the precedent of the variations movement in Op. 127, of two complementary episodes in the submediant and subdominant, prior to a da capo (A♭–E–A♭–D♭–A♭ in Op. 127; D–B♭–D–G–D in the symphony). The listener is lead outside the world of cyclicity itself, and then back in. The paratactic coda moves back out again, abrogating cyclicity like every good Classical cycle should.

According to Terry Eagleton, Schiller defines "the aesthetic as exactly the hinge or transitional stage between the brutally sensual and the sublimely rational" (Eagleton 1990: 103). Schiller's notion of the aesthetic as hinge will eventually become Hegel and Adorno's concept of mediation, whereby ideas are immanent in musical material, not bolted on from above, or from the outside. Schiller believes that the sensuous must already be predisposed toward liberty for the leap into reason to be possible. If Matter contains reason *in potentia*, then the role of the aesthetic in realizing its possibilities is essentially propaedeutic. The aesthetic permits man to "play the war against Matter into the very territory of Matter itself" (Schiller, in Simpson 1988: 169). Insofar as Matter corresponds to the sonic material and reason corresponds to the articulate language of the poem, then textuality is not so much imposed on the symphony as an alien addendum as it is drawn out of its very essence, inscribing it "formally from the inside as a kind of fifth columnist in the enemy camp" (Eagleton, 105). This is the way mediation operates in the Ninth Symphony. The formal processes in the first movement are propaedeutic for the category shifts, conceptual leaps, and genre shocks of the Ode to Joy. Even so, it would not do to identify Beethoven and Schiller too closely. The tensively sublime relationship between Beethoven's categories (S1 and S3) is not harmoniously "playful" in Schiller's sense. It has much more in common with Schiller's friend Hölderlin's dynamic model of "modulation" (*Wechsel*), and his view of the *Grund* as an originary source of conflictual opposition, rather than as a harmonizing principle.

Something similar can be inferred by the "ground" of the symphony in its opening *Klang*, the fifths. These are so often taken for granted. Against the precedent of the introduction of Op. 132, however, it is striking that the E/A alternations are *not* matched by a tonic/dominant sequence in the harmony. The music invokes the protocol of the fugal exposition, like Op. 132, only to resist it. The entries of the oboe and flute at mm. 9–11, respectively on E and A, are consequently static not in a passive way. Rather, the tonic pedal is a willful gridlock. The arrival of the tonic D minor is thus a paradox, as much a resolution of these tensions as a failure to confront them directly, that is, in A minor. Perfect fifths, seemingly the fount and origin of musical harmoniousness, are actually a source of conflict in the symphony. With the finale's curiously gridlocked last cadence, this conflict is transformed into an act of affirmation.

Following the symphony's propaedeutic arc from first movement to last leads inexorably outside the work to our own world. There is a compulsion to interpret the music, or else to live by its example. The final leap must presumably be into praxis: practicing the ideology Beethoven preaches in political action. That would be a mistake, in view of the innumerable, and often reprehensible, political causes that have hijacked Beethoven's Ninth Symphony over the centuries (see Buch 2003). To think that music's political meaning can be as overt as that is to betray music straight into the hands of ideology, whereas one of the Ninth's true political messages is that music must be protected against neutralization by the world of contexts, *while passing through this world unscathed, with "mud on its shoulders."*[7] Its symbols, as Langer would put it, can never be consummated by hermeneutics. Rather, keeping faith with the intrinsic musicality of Beethoven's message, it would be truer to say that the symphony teaches us to think musically about the world. The Ninth's various leaps instruct us to reimagine both the boundaries of music and the complexity of concepts. As a multiplicity of styles held together by a whole subjectivity, the piece is also an object lesson in regulating globalization in the modern world. Its mediation of the radical through the conventional counsels a responsibility toward tradition, and a continuing respect for the Enlightenment. I will return to these issues in the book's coda. Toward that end, we need to go back to the beginning again and pursue a historical turn via three narratives of origin. The notion of stylistic multiplicity will be elaborated in a chapter on *Kunstvereinigung*. A chapter on the Classical style will explore Beethoven's responsibility toward music's Enlightenment tradition. The practice of "thinking musically," perhaps the crux of Adorno's lesson to both music and philosophy, will be addressed in the closing chapter on critical theory.

7 Kunstvereinigung

HISTORICAL THEORIES OF STYLISTIC MIXTURE

Parataxis—Additive, repetitive, chainlike structure; grammatical loosening; anti-development; suspension of telos; lyrical stasis; natural or archaic discourse; epic; heterogeneity; stylistic mixture; summatory embrace of history.

In a beguiling footnote which Beethoven appended to his letter to Archduke Rudolph, dated 29 July 1819 (interpolated here into the main text), the composer speaks of a projected *Kunstvereinigung*—a fusion or unification of the arts:

> I was in Vienna in order to collect in Your Imperial Highness's library what was most useful to me. The chief purpose is rapid execution (together with artistic unification [*mit der bessern Kunstvereinigung*], wherein practical considerations, however, may necessarily admit certain exceptions); in which connection the older composers render us double service, since there is generally real artistic value in their works (among them, of course, only the German Händel and Sebastian Bach possessed genius). But in the world of art, as in the whole of our great creation, *freedom and progress* are the main objectives. And although we moderns are not quite as far advanced in *solidity* as our *ancestors,* yet the refinement of our customs has enlarged many of our conceptions as well. (Anderson 1986: 822)

The picture of Beethoven, a musician not famed for his academicism, wandering through the stacks of the imperial library (which contained 430 music-theoretical works) in search of archaic compositional sources for his new style, is an unfamiliar one. Hans-Werner Küthen, who has analyzed this letter at length in various places, puts forward the novel image of Beethoven "der gelehrte Komponist" (Küthen 2003: 2). As Küthen points out, the letter is densely packed with clues about Beethoven's artistic belief.[1] Beethoven clearly had a defined historical sense as an heir to Bach and Handel in an evolving German tradition. He aimed at an artistic synthesis, a *Kunstvereinigung,* of old and new—of Baroque "solidity" and "modern" (i.e., Classical) "freedom." The neatest musical embodiment of this philosophy is the *Diabelli* Variations (Kinderman 1995: 211–18), Beethoven's most polyglot conception. The last three variations in particular seem to compose out the 1819 manifesto as successive pastiches of a Bach-Handel-Beethoven holy trinity: an affectionate parody of a Goldberg variation, a Handelian fugue, and a self-quotation from the composer's own *Arietta* from Op. 111 (portentously, the last movement of his last sonata). There is also the *Hammerklavier* sonata, finished shortly before the letter to Rudolph, with its fugal finale whose performance direction ("con alcuna licenze") hints at the same union of Baroque *Festigkeit* and modern *Freiheit*. Compared with the Ninth Symphony, whose finale summons up the ghosts of its previous movements, the three Baroque snippets which punctuate the *Hammerklavier*'s introduction are false memories of music which never actually happened (ex. 7.1).

In fact, the interludes are really flash-forwards to the fugue, and comprise the germs of its subject's three successive modules: a descending-third cycle between tonic and dominant (B♭–G–E♭–C–A–F in the subject; G♭–E♭–C♭–A♭–F–D♭ in mm. 1–2); rising and falling scales alternating tonic and dominant; and neighbor-note figures around the dominant (around D♯ at m. 3–4; around F at mm. 23–25). Introductions *conventionally* face forward, of course, and Haydn and Mozart's are often archaic, thereby referencing a standard Baroque-to-Enlightenment narrative sequence. Beethoven's gambit is striking because it dramatizes the paradox that the future can be Baroque, that an archaic style can be stylistically regenerative. Such was also the way with Beethoven's first stylistic quantum leap, the so-called "New Path" of the *Eroica*, in 1802–3. This earlier breakthrough was equally a product of Beethoven's renegotiation with Baroque idioms, in particular, variation technique—the two great variation sets Opp. 34 and 35, the *Eroica*'s tour de force variation finale, and the inception of a general "developing variation" idiom in the three piano sonatas Op. 31.

Beethoven's letter fits easily into the discourse of old-new reconciliation rife in German critical writings, a historical context which is a vital corrective to the perceived abstraction of the late style. The three following chapters tell the story of this history in three different ways. In the present chapter, I shall tease apart the "old/new" model into four strands. The first strand considers the resurgence of the Baroque, and its reconciliation with the Classical, as a new event. The second stresses not novelty but continuity, recognizing that the Classical style was *already* a *galant*-Baroque hybrid. Indeed, Beethoven's "New Path" was directly modeled on Haydn's "New and special way" of 1782. Moreover, hybridity and style mixture are already implicit in Baroque *obbligato* textures, an idiom which Beethoven knew well, and which Adler extrapolates back to the Middle Ages. The third strand throws the weight back onto discontinuous style shift as an agent (and product) of historical consciousness, specifically, an awareness of "Das Neue." The kind of music created in the *Eroica* had never been heard before and was appreciated as such by contemporary listeners. Following the historiographical theories of Reinhart Koselleck, Martin Zenck argues that the historical rupture of the *Eroica* creates the very critical distance which enables Beethoven to constitute a historical self-consciousness.[2] Beethoven is self-reflective because, in a phrase of Jean Paul's, he writes "music about music" (Zenck 1995: 739). Far from being an antipode to the late style, then, the *Eroica* is a paradigm for its historically distanced character. As we saw in chapter 2, the late style is essentially a *meta-style*, a regulative or combinatorial position toward other styles. Given that conventions are always preexistent,

Example 7.1. Piano Sonata in B♭, Op. 106 (*Hammerklavier*), finale, mm. 1–8
Continues on the next page

Example 7.1. Piano Sonata in B♭, Op. 106 (*Hammerklavier*), finale, mm. 1–8

Beethoven's self-reflection is mediated through reception of the past: in Zenck's words, "a putting-into-relation of oneself with a pre-given music" (*ein Sich-in-ein-Verhältnis-setzen zu einer bereits gesetzten Musik* [2002:7]). A subtle upshot of the *Kunstvereinigung* letter is that all three of the main styles available to Beethoven in 1819 were equally dated: not just the Baroque of Bach and Handel, but also the two constituents of "modernity," the Classical style of Haydn and Mozart, and Beethoven's own heroic style, which had already degenerated into pastiche with populist potboilers such as *Wellingtons Sieg* (1813) and *Der glorreiche Augenblick* (1815). Beethoven's vantage point in 1819 was thus "beyond" history, beyond both old and new.

The fourth strand relates to the peculiar mobility of *Kunstvereinigung*. The three styles—Baroque, Classical, and heroic—dance around each other like stars in a constellation. *Durchbruch* is a floating signifier, since all three break through each other: counterpoint can be a *Durchbruch* of objectivity, emancipating subjectivity from petrified Classical convention; or we can strip dense contrapuntal textures to reveal Classical purity; alternately, the Classical carapace is shattered by the heroic gesture; heroic ideology is in turn debunked by the objectivity of counterpoint; and so on through the circle of style. Astonishingly, a contemporary of Beethoven theorized a similarly hydraulic stylistic system, based on the circular interdependency of lyric, epic, and tragic-dramatic literary genres: the poet and philosopher Friedrich Hölderlin. That Hölderlin's dialectical system of *Wechsel der Töne* has touch points with Beethoven's late style was hinted at by Adorno, but it was never developed. Hölderlin offers two other parallels with Beethoven: as a poet with his own celebrated late style, and as a philosopher who critiqued Hegelian idealism. If the unique phenomenon of Beethoven's late style benefits from historical contextualization, then this three-fold comparison with Hölderlin may afford the most focused perspective.

Ancient and Modern

The ancient versus modern dichotomy invoked in Beethoven's 1819 letter to Rudolph links into a family of oppositions underpinning early-nineteenth-century aesthetics, such as beautiful versus sublime (Kant), naive versus sentimental (Schiller), mechanical versus organic (August Schlegel), and on a nationalist level, Greek-Classical versus "Hesperian"—the name Hölderlin gave to renascent German culture. Aligning these oppositions with old and new reflects a broad tendency to map a philosophy of historical progress onto poetic or aesthetic categories. Antiquity was a moveable feast, a relative rather than absolute concept, encompassing Classical Greece, European Gothic, the German reformation, and the musical Baroque. Moreover, the relationship between ancient and modern was imagined as a spiral, insofar as nobody actually advocated going back to any of these periods. Rather, historical knowledge of the past would become a force for cultural renewal. A famous example of such rediscovery was Goethe's amazed reevaluation of Gothic architecture, on visiting Strasbourg Cathedral in 1772 (Goethe 1986). Goethe had previously rejected the Gothic as "indefinite, disorganized, unnatural, patched-together, tacked-on, overladen," a prejudice typical of most educated Europeans (5). After Strasbourg, he changed his mind, and these identical qualities were now appreciated for their sublimity. Precisely the same turnaround raised the fortunes of Baroque counterpoint, an idiom which by midcentury had fallen into such disfavor that the theorist F. W. Marpurg could lament that, should one speak to a fashionable modern composer of learned contrapuntal idioms such as canon, "He will be seized by an icy shudder, considering barbaric that century in which this element of the art of composition was particularly practiced" (Marpurg 1753: ii). By the end of the century, however, praise for the "sublimity" of counterpoint had become a critical commonplace, in line with renewed appreciation for the great Baroque composers. The Bach and Handel revival was a real stimulant to compositional advance for Haydn and Mozart. Beethoven's own situation is illuminated by two other documents from 1819, the year of his letter to Rudolph. One is by Rochlitz, the other by the prolific writer on music Christian Friedrich Michaelis.

Rochlitz's piece (Vienna *Allegemeine Musikalische Zeitung*, 3 March 1819, 133-40) is a review of Bach's Mass in A major, which had been brought out by Simrock the previous year. The mass's publication marked a crucial step in extending Bach reception from keyboard to vocal music, and in associating Bach with the Kantian concept of the sublime—then the preserve of Handel's oratorios. The edition of the Mass in B minor was announced that same year, and an interesting letter survives from Beethoven to the Swiss writer and publisher Nägeli (9 September 1824), requesting a copy.[3] In the event, the work would not appear until 1833, but the A-major Mass is likely to have been one of the items Beethoven consulted in the Archduke's library (for its strong influence on the *Missa Solemnis*, see Zenck 1986: 254–63). The significance of Rochlitz's review is that it hails the reawakening of old-German music (*die wiedererweckte altdeutsche Musik*, 133) as a cure for the trivialization of contemporary musical taste, corrupted most of all perhaps by the

Rossini craze sweeping through Vienna. Rochlitz saw Bach as an agent of cultural regeneration, a process already underway with the rediscovery of old-German poetry and art (especially Dürer). As in the late eighteenth century, the key quality noted by Bach and Handel's nineteenth-century listeners was *sublimity*, arguably the most influential aesthetic category of the time. In a letter addressed to the publisher Franz Anton Hoffmeister (15 January 1801), concerning plans to publish the works of Bach, Beethoven speaks of "the *sublime* and magnificent art of that first father of harmony" (*Urvater der Harmonie*). The interest of Michaelis's 1819 essay *Über die Kritik musikalischer Werke* (published in the Leipzig edition of the *AMZ*) is that it explicates the links between the musical sublime and the ideas of Kant and Schiller.

By "sublime" (*Erhaben*) Kant means our feeling of intellectual and physical limitation when confronted by the "absolutely great" (1989: 94) immensities of nature, such as the "shapeless mountain masses towering one above the other in wild disorder" or "the dark tempestuous ocean" (104). Beethoven's heroic style seems to have been the most obvious analogue of the sublime in music, on the basis of E. T. A. Hoffmann's celebrated review of the Fifth Symphony, as when he writes how "Beethoven's instrumental music unveils before us the realm of the mighty and the immeasurable" (in Charlton 1989: 238). Nevertheless, sublimity was actually ascribed to the mature Classical style as a whole, and then increasingly to the Baroque as well. Despite its fame and influence, Hoffmann's review is indebted to Michaelis, who was the first major exponent of Kant's ideas in music, beginning with his 1795 book *Ueber den Geist der Tonkunst. Mit Rücksicht auf Kants Kritik der ästhetischen Urteilskraft*, and continuing through a number of essays for the *AMZ* (see Zenck 1986: 70–76). Throughout these writings, Michaelis's musical interpretation of the sublime is constantly evolving, in line with both the Baroque revival and the ascendancy of Beethoven. In 1795 he ascribes sublimity to the emotional, variegated, and contrast-driven "odelike" Classical style of C. P. E. Bach, Haydn, Mozart, and Clementi (123–24), opposing it to the "lyrical" *galant* music of the recent past. (It is crucial to note, given our constructions of a "Classical style," that these composers were thought of not as "Classical" but as *modern*. The "we moderns" of Beethoven's letter includes Haydn and Mozart). Michaelis's articles of 1801 and 1803 make two changes: they incorporate Beethoven's name into the sublime pantheon of the "modern" age (circa 1800; i.e., *before* the Fifth Symphony), and they extend the notion of sublime to the "antique" style of Bach and Handel (74). At this point the noble simplicity of the Baroque becomes the very paradigm for modernity; the two periods are *both* sublime, albeit distinguished, respectively, as "*Pathetisch-Erhabenen*" (modern) and "*Einfach-Erhabenen*" (ancient). The most important result of these shifting alignments is that the noble simplicity characteristic of sublime epic poetry became identified with the strict style of counterpoint. The reevaluation of counterpoint as an idiom of Romantic imagination is explicit in Hoffmann's influential 1814 essay, "Old and New Church Music" (in Charlton, 351–76), and it is even possible, in the words of a recent critic, that the *Missa Solemnis* was "a response to Hoffmann's request that a new style should be created out of the old" (McGrann 2003: 135).

With the simultaneous consolidation of both Classical and Baroque traditions, discourses of reconciliation proliferated. For Beethoven scholarship, Michaelis's 1819 essay is the most pertinent of these, especially since it clarifies the links between the musical sublime and the work of a poet-philosopher who would become increasingly significant to Beethoven in the 1820s: Friedrich Schiller. Building on Schiller's treatise *On Naive and Sentimental Poetry,* Michaelis argues that a "naive melody" obtains in the "antique style" of church music, wherein "harmony" governs "melody" (it is striking that Michaelis designates Baroque textures as "harmonic," rather than melodically linear). Conversely, he proposes that "sentimental melody" governs the secular Classical style (Zenck 1986: 75). Michaelis emphasizes that the future of Classical music depends on the reconciliation of this opposition between the style of Haydn and Mozart and that of Bach and Handel. Hence the discourse of ancient and modern is ultimately predicated on the dualism's resolution, on what Beethoven himself calls *Kunstvereinigung.*

The *Obbligato Akkompagnement*

Yet perhaps this resolution lay not in the present or future, but in the past. Or rather, stylistic synthesis is actually a fact of *all* musical material in *every* period of history. *Kunstvereinigung* is thus not a leap but an ongoing strategy. Both music historiography and compositional practice seem to bear this out. Although *Kunstvereinigung* came to critical attention in the early nineteenth century, it was already in place at the dawn of the Classical style, as seen in the writings of music theorists such as Heinrich Koch. Regarding the composers themselves, Haydn assimilated counterpoint into his Classical textures at every stage of his career; Mozart began doing so in earnest under the guidance of Van Swieten in the early 1780s; and Beethoven absorbed Bach's "48 preludes and fugues" as a teenage piano student. Earliest testimony to Beethoven's lifelong reckoning with the Baroque is a report in C. F. Cramer's *Magazin der Musik* of 1783 (387), which records that the thirteen-year-old "played mostly Sebastian Bach's *Well-tempered Clavier,* which Herr Neefe [Beethoven's teacher] put into his hands."

Twentieth-century style analysis has heightened our sense of the Classical style's interdependence on the Baroque, characterizing this relationship typically as a discourse of reconciliation, embracing four moments. First, the opposition is identified, and enshrined in a set of stylistic categories or aesthetic paradigms, such as Wilhelm Fischer's dichotomy of Baroque *Fortspinnungstypus* (figurative elaboration within a context of directed tonal motion) versus Classical *Liedtypus* (formal periodicity), and August Halm's *Von zwei Kulturen der Musik* ("cultures," respectively, of fugue and sonata). Such oppositions have driven German musicology from the time of Adler, Blume, and Schmitz through to Ludwig Finscher and Carl Dahlhaus. Second, the Baroque is recuperated as an agent of stylistic enrichment, leading to, third, mixture and reconciliation. As Webster points out, Haydn's extraordinarily long career was the prototype of this narrative, which was invented by Adolf Sandberger in 1900 (Webster 1991: 431–47). "Sandberger's tale" runs as follows: The superficial *galant* style represents a drop in quality from the High

Baroque, and Haydn's Op. 20 quartets of 1772 attempt to recuperate this lost richness by infusing counterpoint into the quartet texture. But Haydn fails to properly blend counterpoint and homophony; the two idioms are juxtaposed in a state of contradiction. After ten years of further experiment, the Op. 33 quartets of 1781 finally produce "the marriage of freedom and counterpoint," with their child being Sandberger's seminal concept of *thematische Arbeit*. "Thematic development," the modern idiom of a linear discourse integrated with harmonic accompaniment, comprises a grand synthesis of Classical and Baroque procedures. Along with most current Classical scholarship, Webster (1991) is extremely wary of such narratives, which seem to support an evolutionary model of style history oriented toward the perfection of the Classical style. Not only does the model enshrine a narrow view of "Classicism" (typically excluding the wealth of music composed *earlier* than 1781, and in cultural centers *other* than Austria; see Heartz 2003), it also predicates a formalist aesthetics of unity. Webster's broadside is basically directed at the organicist style history of Adler, but I would contend that Adler's "organicism" cannot be dismissed so easily. It is often overlooked that Adler's paradigm of stylistic reconciliation is not static unity but, on the contrary, playful mixture (*Stilmischung*) and contrast. The name for this more deconstructive kind of mixture is the *obbligato* style, and it forms the fourth and most pregnant moment of the discourse of reconciliation. It is a style which Beethoven knew well.

In a letter to Franz Anton Hoffmeister, dated 15 December 1800, Beethoven wrote: "I cannot compose anything that is not *obbligato*, seeing that I came into the world with an *obbligato* accompaniment." Beethoven here refers to his having been born "accompanied" by a caul, the inner membrane enclosing a fetus, part of which is occasionally attached to a child's head at birth (Anderson 1986: vol. 1, 42, n.5). The pun accompanies Beethoven's claim to Hoffmeister that his Septet Op. 20, one of his most popular works at the time, is written "tutti obbligati." Beethoven means that all seven instruments play *concertante;* the septet is a dialogue of equals, with none of the voices being consigned to mere accompaniment. As a synthesis of counterpoint and homophony, *obbligato* style is the essential exemplar of *Kunstvereinigung* in early Beethoven. Although it is evinced in all the genres Beethoven commends to Hoffmeister (the Septet, the First Symphony, the Second Piano Concerto, the Piano Sonata in B♭, Op. 22, the String Quartets Op. 18), *obbligato* style is epitomized in the genre of the string quartet. It also fits the refined textural hybrids of his last quartets, suggesting that a profound continuity undercuts the "early," "middle," and "late" junctures. In a comment reported by his friend Karl Holz, the late Beethoven called this *obbligato* hybrid "a new kind of voice leading [*Stimmführung*] . . . meaning the instrumentation, the division of roles."[4]

The ambiguity of Beethoven's *ésprit* acknowledges his inheritance: Beethoven is both a born *obbligato* composer, and hence its inventor, and *born into* an *obbligato* culture which predates him. The *obbligato* composer par excellence is Bach, given his historical role as reconciling the great polyphonic tradition with the harmonic perspective of *basso continuo*. The image of Bach as a rigorous contrapuntist is actually anachronistic: as we saw with Michaelis, his posthumous fame was largely as a *harmonist* (see Wolff 2001: 471), hence Beethoven's reference to Bach, in the above-cited 1801 letter to Hoffmeister, as the "Urvater der Harmonie." The open-ing of the B-minor Mass, the so-called "Kyrie-*Anruf*" (an example which became celebrated among eighteenth-century critics like Nichelmann), is thus *obbligato* in its flexible synthesis of melodic part writing and harmonic intensity. Zenck re-fers us to 1819 *AMZ* reviews of Bach's *Magnificat* (BWV 243a) and A-major Mass (BWV 234)—music Beethoven may have studied in Rudolph's library—in which the *obbligato* term is used (e.g., "Alle Chöre sind durchaus *obligat* 5 stimme durch-geführt").[5]

The continuity of the *obbligato* tradition, stretching backwards from Beethoven through Haydn to Bach and even beyond, undercuts the historical oppositions which are held to divide Beethoven from his past. From one angle, Beethoven dis-tances the Baroque; from another, he is a Baroque composer *malgré soi*. Or rather, the Baroque constitutes a background horizon, against which the Classical style stands as something of an aberration, a figure against a ground. Certainly, the com-plexity of the *obbligato* concept rewards further scrutiny. Adler was the first major theorist to entertain the idea, and it emerges toward the end of his *Der Stil in der Musik,* where he considers music history as a grand dialectic between the two *Satzarten* of counterpoint and homophony:

> From the beginning, two streams came forward, which, although actually organically connected, in the course of theory became understood as oppositions, confronting each other in specific artistic forms: homophony (harmony) and polyphony. (240)

The two oppositions interpenetrate, drift apart, come together again, throwing up a variety of hybrid idioms, one of which is the "obbligato accompagnato." For Adler, this is not a single device so much as a constellation, a family of terms in-cluding thematic working (*thematischer Arbeit*), the art of variation, and concer-tante texture. Adler's concept entails four main technical aspects: broken textures, part-writing crisscrossing between different voices, heterogeneous material, and stylistic synthesis. These entailments are compounded by a further concept, of which *obbligato* turns out to be only a subcategory: what Adler calls *durchbrochene Arbeit.* This is a nuanced and richly loaded notion in German music theory. Its literal meaning is "open work," a category of design denoting a lattice-like pattern in lace, leather, or metal (266–68). It also carries the sense of "broken style," akin to the *stile brisé* of French Baroque harpsichord music. It was one of Adorno's most felicitous neologisms to adapt *durchbrochene Arbeit* into his concept of *Durch-bruch,* by way of describing the eruption of latent, yet repressed, stylistic forces. Adorno dynamically informs his notion of structural breach with the force doing the breaching, thus blending structure with history.

What is most striking about Adler's treatment of *durchbrochene Arbeit* is its his-torical extension to cover broken textures and stylistic mixture across the entire spectrum of Western art music, from the Middle Ages through the Baroque, the Viennese Classical style, right up to Brahms. He discovers it in the punctuated tex-tures of thirteenth-century hocket, whose singers take turns picking up the line (266), as well as in the concertato style of Gabrieli, Banchieri, and Monteverdi (261–62). Here the voices are "neither entirely polyphonic, nor entirely homophonic, but in a hybrid fusion [*Mittelverhältnis*] of both styles" (261). Adler associates the maturity of *durchbrochene Arbeit* as a fully fledged stylistic principle with the rise of *basso continuo* in the early seventeenth century. Arguing, contra Riemann, that the concertato's basis was harmonic, not polyphonic, Adler contended that it was the continuo which first released voice leading to cross between different parts. If *durchbrochene Arbeit* becomes a style proper circa 1600, then it reaches its highpoint in the Viennese School of Haydn and Mozart, and its climax with late Beethoven (although Adler concedes that Brahms develops it even further [270]). Regarding the richly variegated textures of the Andante from the String Quartet in B♭, Op. 130 (mm. 1–6), Adler observes that the voices of the *accompagnato* unfold with varying shades of "concertante" independence: "Sometimes they move contrapuntally, contenting themselves with ostensibly contrapuntal devices filled out with complementary rhythmic figures, or they sink back into harmonic padding [*harmonischen Füllstimmen*]." Adler stands in awe of the suppleness and resourcefulness of *obbligato*, an "almost infinitely variable way of using voices" (*fast unendlich variablen Stimmbehandlung*) (268) which permits musical material to be optimally responsive to a compositional idea. This is why Adler places his discussion of *obbligato* in the culminating chapter of his book on style history. In the Hegelian spirit of the times, *obbligato* style is the ideal means to resolve the war between form and content.

For Adler, the supremacy of the Classical style in general, and late Beethoven in particular, is thus due not to its unity, but to its *obbligato* variety. Adorno's conflict model is surprisingly close to Adler's historical vision, albeit with some crucial twists. Where Adler sees a harmonious play of contrasts, Adorno finds contradictions which drive successive stylistic breakthroughs. Adler foregrounds the continuity of style history, whereas Adorno emphasizes sudden change, as in the striking final line of the 1934 *Spätstil* essay: "In the history of art, late works are the catastrophes" (1998a: 126). Finally, while Adler interprets style history as ongoing stylistic mixture (*Stilmischung*), with neither of his two poles, harmony or polyphony, having the upper hand, Adorno is very clear that the fate of music is a "Zwang zur Durchkonstruktion" (1998b: vol. 16, 156), a drive toward the total organization of the artwork on the basis of equal-voiced counterpoint. Polyphony, in Adorno's dialectic of enlightenment, is the realm of human freedom, "the means best suited for the organization of emancipated music" (1987: 58), liberating "the vertical from the blind force of harmonic convention" (90). The ideal of well-constituted melodic voices, generalized into a perfectly linear counterpoint, which Adorno found in the music of late Schoenberg, thus becomes the horizon against which *obbligato* mixture is gauged and found wanting. This ideal asserts itself in outbreaks of linearity, which breach the continuities both of music history and musical works in themselves. In this regard, Adorno uses the textural, and catastrophic, sides of *Durchbruch* against each other. On facing pages of his 1957 essay on counterpoint ("Die Funktion des Kontrapunkts in der neuen Musik" [1998b: vol. 16]) he states, on the one hand, that Viennese Classicism creates "*durchbrochene Arbeit* through leaps of the main motive from one instrument to another, without any real impulse to fully realize the individual voices" (156). On the other hand, he speaks of the "resurgent subjectivity" (*durchbrechende Subjektivität*) of the Romantics, which dispenses with the "modesty" of this compromised *Scheinpolyphonie* (157).

Much is to be gained by considering *obbligato*, or *durchbrochene Arbeit*, as a broad historical continuum. It helps us place Beethoven in fuller context; it also undermines the intractable arguments on periodization *within* Beethoven's oeuvre. Thus Klaus Kropfinger (2001) regards the 1802–1803 and 1818–1819 watersheds as surface distractions from the underlying continuity of Beethoven's development. After reviewing and rejecting the various narratives of periodization, Kropfinger interprets Beethoven's career as a "process of permanent renewal" (194) based on an increasingly refined and concentrated treatment of "the variation principle mediated through *durchbrochener Arbeit*" (196). Even so, a series of lines need to be drawn through this continuum, to register the violence of real historical change. *Durchbruch* as revolution entails the birth of historical consciousness.

"Das Neue"

The new heroic style was in every sense a future-oriented style, with musical time rushing on toward an imagined victory, apotheosis, or utopia. It is important to grasp the technical basis of this "experiential temporality" in the composer's new approach to formal integration. After 1802, Beethoven's themes are often dissolved into developing variation and may have no status outside the formal process which unfolds them across the work as a whole. In this respect, the past/future dialectic, which becomes so pronounced in the late style, is only the corollary of the interaction between goal-oriented development and the retrospective pull of variation technique. For all its forward drive, the *Eroica* symphony climaxes with a set of variations. Equally, the first-movement development section, which jacks up the gears of the exposition still further, comes to a head with a fugato and an archaic theme in E minor (ex. 7.2):

Example 7.2. Third Symphony, first movement, mm. 284–87

The "newness" of this theme is the fulfillment of the movement's future orientation. Technically, its stability and formal closure have been singularly lacking in the exposition, particularly in its second group. The theme thus provides the movement with a goal and a breathing space. Yet to repeat, its most important aspect is its novelty, which seems to flash forward to the future. The 1807 review in the *AMZ* seizes on this moment as the arrival of *das Neue:* "The first subject, which had been only lightly touched upon in the exposition, is elaborated by Beethoven in the development section brilliantly, and with care and thoroughness . . . It is a total surprise when, in a novel and beautiful way, just as the development of this earlier material becomes almost excessive, an entirely new, as yet unheard melody [*ein ganz neuer, noch nicht gehörter Gesang*] suddenly enters in the wind . . . " (in Zenck 2002: 16). Although the derivation of this ostensibly "new" melody from the first subject is fairly easy to analyze (see Rosen 1972: 393), Burnham does well to point to a critical tradition which foregrounds its quintessential *strangeness* (Burnham 1995: 9–13). Writers including A. B. Marx, Wilhelm von Lenz, Aléxandre Oulibicheff, and Arnold Schering all "emphasize the otherness of the new theme, the effect of supreme disjunction that it brings to the musical discourse" (10). And yet what Burnham misses is the archaic tone detected by Peter Schleuning (1989). The E-minor theme reminds Schleuning of both the old German hymn *Christ ist erstanden* and Luther's chorale *Christ lag in Todesbanden* (in the same key, as used by Bach's E-minor Cantata no. 4). Its sacred air suggests to Schleuning a sense of divine intervention from without, in accord both with Beethoven's "Christ worship" (as in the contemporaneous *Christus am Oelberge,* Op. 85) and with his "self-image as a martyr" (119). The "new," then, is presented by the *Eroica* as the very old—a dramatization of the old/new dialectic of developing variation. Moreover, this is not an "old" seamlessly blended into the Classical style, as was Haydn, Mozart, and Beethoven's practice before, but rather one celebrated for its alien distance. Indeed, August Halm's (1929: 483) description of the E-minor theme as a "foreign body" (*Fremdkörper*) in the frame of the symphony can be extended to the "otherness" of the Baroque as a whole. With the *Eroica,* Beethoven's relationship to the past becomes self-conscious, predicated on a newly perceived epistemological gap.

By many accounts, this gap registers the seismic shock of the French Revolution. Although published in 1927, Arnold Schmitz's *Das romantische Beethovenbild* has still to be bettered as a guide to how Beethoven's heroic style was influenced by the sound world of French revolutionary composers such as Grétry, Méhul, Cherubini, Berton, Catel, Dallayrac, Gossec, R. Kreutzer, Lesueur, and Spontini. The exact similarities Schmitz identifies between, say, Kreutzer's "Ouverture de la journée de Marathon" and Beethoven's First Symphony, and between the rhythm of Cherubini's "Hymne du Panthéon" (to a text by M. J. Chénier) and the opening of the Fifth, are extremely compelling. Most persuasive is the notion that Beethoven's biggest debt to the French sound was a new kind of time consciousness, encapsulated in a paraphernalia of military topics, such as fanfares, signals, and march rhythms. These are materials imbued with revolutionary hope for the future, a sort of utopian semiosis. The horn fanfares which overwhelm the close of the "Eroica" first movement are semiotic indexes of this future, albeit paradoxically blended with past-consciousness, given the horn's topical associations with farewell and nostalgia. When we turn to the source for many of Schmitz's ideas, Ernst Bücken's *Der heroische Stil in der Oper* (1924), it even becomes possible that the enigmatic E-minor theme from the development section is nothing less than a perfectly normative convention from revolutionary opera, what Grétry calls a "manière indirecte d'imiter," that is, an indirect "reminiscence motive." Reminiscence motives—ancestors of the Wagnerian leitmotiv—jut out from Grétry's drama with all the discontinuity noted of the *Eroica* theme. Whereas a "direct imitation" recalls an event earlier in the opera, a "manière indirecte d'imiter" is oriented to the future: "It doesn't musically portray any phase of the action itself, but rather symbolically points to its future appearance [*Folgerscheinung*]. Instead of having to paint a true-to-life musical picture of battle, one can allude to the future start of the battle through its corresponding fanfares" (in Bücken, 79). We don't need to construe the E-minor theme as a premonition of the finale variations (which it possibly *is*) in order to hear its rhetoric as future-oriented.

In a particularly grand claim, Adorno discovers in the *Eroica*'s E-minor theme the very origins of the late style: "In Beethoven's compulsion to introduce the new theme lies the secret of the decomposition of his late style" (1998a: 66). Adorno hears the theme as the prototype of the Hölderlinian caesura, the rupture which marks the intervention of the subject and the turning point of the drama (see chapter 3). Caesuras have a dark and light face. If the *Eroica* theme is a "dark caesura," then the "light caesura" is epitomized by the dramatic trumpet signal halfway through the third *Leonora* Overture (65). Adorno follows Ernst Bloch's *Geist der Utopie* in hearing this signal as the archetypal symbol of peripeteia and hope, a *Hoffnungssignal*. Bloch is a key figure in the historical interpretation of musical material, notwithstanding his absence from Zenck's discussion. Bloch makes great play with the signal's infolding of past and future timeframes: it is a "memory of the future" (*Erinnerung an die Zukunft*). Although rooted in the contemporary sound world of the *Marseillaise*, it also carries a biblical as well as an eschatological meaning, an echo of that trumpet which shattered the walls of Jericho, and a foretaste of the Second Coming's *tuba mirum*. This is why Bloch calls the *Leonora* Overture "a utopian memory, a legend of fulfilled hope in the Now and Here" (Bloch 1986: 1102). "Utopian memory" turns distopic in the "dark caesura" of the *Eroica*'s E-minor theme, and the dialectic of past and future is given a critical slant. Crucial, in this regard, are the E-minor theme's following aspects: its echo of the first subject, the first subject's suggestion of *horn* rather than *trumpet* fanfares (realized by the horn scoring of the reprise), and the above-mentioned associations of horns with nostalgia and farewell. The E-minor theme could thereby be designated an involuted trumpet signal. Perhaps this is why Adorno heard it as a fore-echo of the twisted caesuras of the late style. No longer signs of a hopeful future, or of the interventions of a subject, the signal instead marks the contours of the subject's flight, footprints in the sand, moments of "breaking free," when "the work falls silent as it is deserted, turning its hollowness outwards" (126).

The twists and turns of Beethoven's historical consciousness might usefully be grounded within the political situation of Napoleonic (and post-Napoleonic) Europe (see Rumph 2004). More pertinent to the phenomenology of musical experience is the approach Zenck suggests in linking the *Eroica*'s E-minor theme to Koselleck's work on historical temporality. Zenck seizes on Koselleck's key notion of "futures past" (*vergangene Zukunft*) to describe the reversed relationship between past and future in the early nineteenth century, where history constantly corrects its projected utopias (Koselleck 1985). In a powerful sense, Beethoven's late style is a style written *after the future*, postdating and correcting the utopian futures imagined in the heroic period. To make good this claim, we need to pursue and reinforce Zenck's rather sketchy references to Koselleck. We also need to make the link between Koselleck's *vergangene Zukunft* and Bloch's notion of *Erinnerung an die Zukunft*, to which it is surely indebted.

To some extent, the partial conservatism of Beethoven's late style is characteristic of many Europeans after the Congress of Vienna. Or rather, Beethoven's idiosyncratic games with history—his use of the past to renovate the present—defines the composer as a radical reactionary, and thus a typical creature of the post-revolutionary restoration. Koselleck's concept of *vergangenes Zukunft* elaborates this dialectic of past and future. Of course, a mode of revisionism is intrinsic to the phenomenology of time perception in everyday lives, in the interplay of prospection and retrospection. We constantly make plans, and adjust them in the light of experience. But the process assumed a world-historical status in the defining *Durchbruch* of the French Revolution. Koselleck argues (1985; 2002) that the period around 1789 created a revolution essentially in how we relate to time, hence his concept of Modernity as *Neuzeit*, "new time." With *Neuzeit*, time ceases to be merely the frame in which history unfolds, and enters the historical consciousness as a perceptual reality—most obviously, Zenck infers, in music, and most effectively in Beethoven's heroic style (see Brinkmann 2000: 7–10). Evidence for Koselleck's claim includes the fact that, within the epochal period 1770–1830, Grimm's dictionary contains over one hundred neologisms involving the word *Zeit* (the most famous being *Zeitgeist* [1985: 257]). Looking back on the previous twenty years, the historian E. M. Arndt writes in 1807:

> Time is in flight; those who are clever have known this for a long time. Monstrous things have happened: the world has suffered great transformations silently and noisily, in the quiet pace of the day and in the storms and eruptions of revolution; monstrosities will occur, greater things will be transformed. (in Koselleck, 252)

Modernity entails "the dynamization and temporalization of the experiential world" (168), and to do it justice required a new kind of history. The neologism *Geschichte*, whose strange collective singular form crystallized in the 1780s, conceives of history as a general, universal, force, divorced from subject or object (246). Faced with "monstrosities" such as the French Revolution, the old-fashioned story-based annalistic history collapsed, since it was simply impossible to register the history of one's own time according to personal experience. The enormity of events around 1789 demanded a higher degree of abstraction from historians, "to compensate for the disappearance of direct experience" (255). This compensation took two forms: time (rather than events) impinged upon human consciousness as an object in itself; second, since events can no longer be grasped in the present, history becomes "temporalized" into a future-oriented process. Koselleck conceptualizes this process in four "historical criteria," each of which illuminates an aspect of Beethoven's own historical consciousness, beginning with "temporalization" itself:

1. *Temporalization.* In 1828 the historian F. Ancillon wrote: "Everything has begun to move, or has been set in motion . . . The love of movement in itself, without purpose and without specific end, has emerged and developed out of the movement of the time" (in Koselleck, 251). Time cuts into sensuous human experience as a phenomenon in itself, so that history "no longer occurs in, but through time" (246). Koselleck does not treat aesthetic texts, still less music. Yet Zenck makes the connection between the objectification of time in the nineteenth century and the temporal experience peculiar to music, particularly of Beethoven's heroic style. Works such as the *Eroica* are our most vivid guide to the historical consciousness which made them possible (see also Brinkmann 2000).

2. *Acceleration.* As Gervinus wrote in 1853, the movements of the nineteenth century "succeed each other in almost geometric progression." Periodization accelerates, and *Neuzeit* defines, brings to a climax, and is swallowed up in this process of acceleration. The fact that we worry about Classical periodization at all is as a symptom of this phenomenon. After the broad epochs of early, Renaissance, and Baroque, the stretto tightens with a shift, within a vanishingly short interval of historical time, from *galant* to High Classical, and then through Beethoven's early, middle, and late styles. The *fact* of periodization in Beethoven's career is itself a function of temporalization.

3. *The doctrine of subjective historical perspective.* Consciousness of forward movement was linked to the specificity of historical judgment relative to the observer's cultural and temporal position. Thus the specificity of the present was marked off against the "otherness" of both the past and the future. This is why Beethoven's modernity needs to measure itself against both a "Classicized" Classical and an alienated Baroque style.

4. *The noncontemporaneity of the contemporary (and the contemporaneity of the noncontemporaneous).* The specificity of past, present, and future enabled cultural and historical difference to be judged by the tribunal of an overarching agency, such as the notion of "world-historical progress." Judged according to their progressive tendencies, contemporary cultures could be ordered diachronically as relatively "civilized" or "primitive." Conversely, different historical epochs could be comprehended by a single unifying perspective. Beethoven's late style, with its plurality of coexisting styles, each one marked by a different historical context, is a concrete analogue of such a unifying intelligence. In Beethoven's late style, historical materials are both relativized and brought together from the perspective of his present-day subject position.

Zenck makes a persuasive case for considering late Beethoven's historical consciousness as a corollary, rather than a contrary, of the instauration of his radical "new path" of 1802–1803. The same revolutionary move which had created a breach in music history, by analogy to 1789 in political history, simultaneously opened up a conceptual space by which the past could be objectified as "other."

Reflection requires distance from the object reflected upon; the call of the new and consciousness of the old are thus inextricably bound up together as aspects of the same stylistic advance. Nevertheless, Zenck understates the extent to which this consciousness changed with the general reaction to French Revolutionary values after 1815, and the collapse of the associated philosophy of historical progress. What is exceptional about Beethoven is the acuity of his historical analysis, enabling him to discover in the Baroque and Classical styles unlikely sources of revolutionary energy. The past is not enshrined, museum-like, as an object of historicist nostalgia. Rather, it is coopted into a radical compositional project very different from the developmental *telos* of the middle period. On the other hand, Beethoven's solution was not altogether unique, as Adorno claims, in the light of the late style Hölderlin forged some two decades earlier. The poet steals a march on the composer, and yet, twisting the historical loop still further, Adorno will argue that the paradigm for Hölderlin's abstraction was music.

Beethoven–Hölderlin

Grounding composers in their cultural and historical *milieu,* we often seek their literary or philosophical equivalents. The holy grail of a perfect match for Beethoven is of course unattainable. Perhaps intrigued by their contemporaneity, Adorno nevertheless consistently links the composer with two other Germans born in 1770: Hegel and Hölderlin. Beethoven's association with Hegel is much better known, while comparisons with Hölderlin are scattered and brief, as in this line from the Beethoven monograph: "The language of music or the material of music speaks by itself in [Beethoven's] late works . . . in a way perhaps not quite dissimilar to what took place with poetic language in the late style of Hölderlin" (1998a: 189). At one stage of *Parataxis,* Adorno's essay on Hölderlin (1992c: 109–49; 1998b: vol. 2, 447–91), the 1770 trinity is brought into conjunction. Referring to Hölderlin's poem *Hälfte des Lebens,* in which the positive and negative halves of life are juxtaposed in two antithetical strophes without any explanation, Adorno argues that:

> In a manner reminiscent of Hegel, mediation of the vulgar kind, a middle element standing outside the moments it is to connect, is eliminated as being external and inessential, something that occurs frequently in Beethoven's late style; this not least of all gives Hölderlin's late poetry its anticlassical quality, its rebellion against harmony. (1992c: 132–33)

Hölderlin's own "late style" describes the period between 1801 and his descent into madness after 1807, the so-called *Umnachtung*. Strictly speaking, the analogy is flawed; the phase is roughly contemporaneous with Beethoven's *middle* style, and we may balk at designating the work of a poet in his thirties (and who wrote into his seventies) as "late." We may agree with Szondi (1986: 25–26), nevertheless, that lateness is an aesthetic, rather than chronological category, in which case the affinities are manifold. Two decades sooner than Beethoven, Hölderlin steps back from an idealist initial phase to a more abstract style. The late hymns and odes—poems such as *Patmos, Brod und Wein, Friedensfeier,* and *Andenken*—are as enigmatic and syntactically gnarled as any late-Beethoven quartet. They also share with Beethoven a fragmentary construction, a resort to archaisms and stylistic mixture, a mobility of perspective, a concern with historical memory, and a self-referencing of the materials of language. Where Beethoven recuperates Baroque counterpoint, Hölderlin adopts the highly elaborate rhyme and metrical schemes of the fifth-century Greek poet Pindar, or studs his poems with arcane allegories of the Hellenistic gods. Parataxis afflicts every level of the poetry. Serial transitions replace logical connectives, lines held together with conjunctions and coordinating particles such as *aber* or *nämlich* rather than argument. The stream of language tends toward the "reine Sprach" (1998b: 470) of epic prose, throwing together imagery from every sphere of life: present and past, human and divine, Christian and pagan, German and Greek, in a cosmological parataxis aptly described by Benjamin as "men, heavenly ones, and princes—crashing down from their old order [and] linked to one another" (2002: 25). This heterogeneity prefigures Beethoven's own stylistic and topical mixture. On account of its syntactic/semantic parataxis, Hölderlin's poetry loosens the integrative hold of subjective intention (while resisting the reader's own urge to supply an even more powerful one). According to Adorno, the poetry's abstraction thereby emulates the peculiar "aconceptual synthesis" (unity without concepts) of music itself, which is the "*Urbild* of Hölderlin's late poetry" (1998b: 470). Adorno means "music" in the broad, as a nonrepresentational medium which is nonetheless unified by form. With a musical style which is not just aconceptual but also formally dissociative, the affinity is raised to a higher power. Just as Beethoven's aconceptual synthesis releases tonality as an object in its own right, Hölderlin's retreat from subjectivity lets language speak: "Sprache selbst zum Sprechen zu bringen" (478).

The crisis which motivates Hölderlin's late turn occurs a couple of years earlier than Beethoven's own spiritual watershed, the "Heiligenstadt Testament" of 1802. Szondi (1986) pinpoints the threshold to the late style in the final, incomplete, stanzas of the great poem *Wie wenn am Feiertage* (1799–1800), the first of the hymns inspired by Pindar. The poem both recounts and enacts a cautionary tale warning of the hubris of unmediated congress with "die Himmlischen," following the myth of Semele, who "desired to see the god in person" and was consumed by Jupiter's fire. The seven completed stanzas elaborate metaphors of successful human-divine mediation. From Semele's ashes was sprung the baby Bacchus, "the thunderstorm's fruit," allowing "the sons of Earth to drink heavenly fire" without danger; and wine becomes a symbol for the intercession of poets, who "stand bareheaded beneath God's thunderstorms [and] grasp the Father's ray, no less, with their own two hands."[6] And yet, recoiling from this sacrilegious image of the poet as priest, the eighth verse breaks off with the cry "Weh mir!" and Hölderlin abandons the poem with a fragmentary prose sketch depicting "den falschen Priester" cast down into the dark in punishment for his hubris. Hölderlin's theory of tragedy, worked out in the contemporary notes to Sophocles' *Oedipus Rex*, argues that Oedipus's crime is also that of false prophet, "interpreting the words of the oracle *too infinitely,*" as a religious command. By assuming the mantle of priest, Oedipus presumes "the monstrous and terrible coupling of God and man . . . the total fusion of Nature's power with man's innermost depth." Blindness is the reward for looking upon the light. Hölderlin's subsequent poems are dominated by metaphors of abnegation, separation, and mourning for an irrevocable past. And yet, rather than darkening his palette, the late odes and hymns are his most radiant creations. Miraculously, he renders absence luminous. Their light trembles between a holding fast to the memory of "the Gods," and an enraptured expectancy of a chiliastic return.

Hölderlin's style change, like Beethoven's, was motivated by a complex of biographical and medical factors—in this case, a renunciation of his own immortal beloved (Susette Gontard, Diotima to his Hyperion), and the affliction of mental illness. Unlike Beethoven, however, the conceptually articulate Hölderlin actually philosophized his turn as a rejection of metaphysics, and by creating an elaborate theory of style itself. This theory of style will be my main object of interest here, but we must approach it through Hölderlin's privileged position as a founder, with Hegel and Schelling, of the Jena philosophical school. His influence on Hegel cannot be overestimated; in Dieter Henrich's words, "Hegel is completely dependent on Hölderlin" (1997: 139), on his ideas on oppositional thinking and dialectic which survive in Hölderlin's fragmentary philosophical writings. Hölderlin's double-insider status, as a world-class thinker and poet, is unique. This is why his work has attracted the attention of philosophers such as Adorno, Heidegger (2000), Szondi (1986), Henrich (1997), Paul De Man (1984), Haverkamp (1996), Lacoue-Labarthe (1998), and many others. Although Hölderlin abandoned a career in philosophy, his late poems are philosophical discourses all but in name. Hölderlin did not *reject* philosophy, therefore; it was a question, rather, of choosing poetry as a medium in which to philosophize. If Beethoven composes "*music* as philosophy," then Hölderlin writes "*poetry* as philosophy."

Hegel began as a conservative acolyte of Kant. But he was a different philosopher after Hölderlin introduced him to Fichte's dynamic notion of consciousness as a conflict of oppositional drives. On his part, Hölderlin rejected Hegel's emphasis on synthesis, and his demotion of poetry to a mere stepping stone toward philosophical knowledge. As much as any of his colleagues, Hölderlin was preoccupied with discovering the grounding unities which resolved opposition. Yet part of his reason for renouncing his philosophical career was his conviction that such a *Grund* was only thinkable in poetry (Heidegger would reach the same conclusion in his own "turn"). A letter to Schiller explains: "I am attempting to prove that what must be continually demanded of any system, the union of the subject and object in an absolute I . . . is undoubtedly possible on the aesthetic level . . . but not on the theoretical level" (in Lacoue-Labarthe, 132). Subject/object unity occurs via intense intuition of finite objects; that is, the sensorium of lyrical experience—Hölderlin's poetry itself. Even when he departs from Hegel, however, he maintains a dialectical relation between finitude and wholeness. Indeed, Hölderlin reasons that we can only perceive the harmony of the world as a dynamic system through its disintegration into warring oppositions: "The perceptibility [*Fühlbarkeit*] of the whole arises in accordance with, and to the same extent as, the division into parts" (Hölderlin 1992–1994: vol. 2, 556). The quote comes from an essay on poetic genres, *Über den Unterschied der Dichtarten,* a fragment in which Hölderlin outlines his extraordinary theory of the modulation, or *Wechsel,* of tones. By "tone," Hölderlin means a formula of experience distilled into a poetic genre. Thus the three classic genres of lyric, epic, and tragic are conceived not as dry schemata, but in dynamic and existential terms as projections of diverse worldviews. Crucially, their distinct qualities are defined interactively, relative to the entire system: that is, through the flow of "modulation," whereby the genres turn (modulate) into each other in an eternal circle. Harmonious modulation releases each of life's particular tendencies momentarily, in a Schilleresque "play" which expressly avoids static closure. Where Schiller's play is binary (the sense drive versus the formal drive), Hölderlin proposes a triad: First, a striving to overcome finitude in order to achieve perfection; second, a limitation to the sensorium of finite experience; third, "aware of the ungraspable origin, [we] must soar idealistically beyond everything and oscillate freely between [our] own drives" (Henrich 1997: 134). The first drive is associated with the heroic genre of epic striving; the second with lyrical sensation; the third with the idealized forms of drama. This is how Hölderlin can integrate the generic triad of epic-lyric-dramatic as a dialectical system.

Before we confront that system, the *Lehre vom Wechsel der Töne,* it is important to tease out the hermeneutic and historical dimensions of Hölderlin's resistance to Hegelian synthesis. For Hegel, the circle of thought is closed when the subject returns to itself in an act of recollection. Such a return is not possible with the play of modulation. Rather, with each intercutting of the three drives, a new perspective opens up, giving rise to a succession of momentary insights. These can never be gathered together into a synoptic view or memory. The thrust of this perspectival parataxis is that recollection is not an act of interiorization or appropriation (Hegel's *Er-Innerung*), but of "preserving, subject to the demand of faithfulness, which therefore seeks and embraces the past in itself" (Henrich 1997: 136). Hölderlin's attitude toward the past takes on the exteriority of mourning, which is commemorated, as Freud and Benjamin have argued, in the external and physically reified "krypt" of allegory (Haverkamp 1996: 16). Modulation is thus Hölderlin's devious path to allegory. Allegory, an aesthetic which Benjamin associated with the Baroque, is reconstituted via modern dialectic. This mirrors late Beethoven's mediation of contrapuntal textures and *galant* schemata through the heroic style. Like Beethoven, Hölderlin "mourns" the past by displaying its ossified remains. Hence Haverkamp applies a deconstructive jolt to Hölderlin's best-known, yet most misunderstood, maxim, the epitaph to his *Andenken:* "But what remains, establish the poets" (*Was bleibt aber, stiften die Dichter*). This is often taken to celebrate the priority of lyrical immediacy, which poets record. What *really* remains, argues Haverkamp, is semiosis, the artificial play of poetic signifiers, "stiffened" into allegorical materiality: "The 'institution' accomplished by the poet (*Stiften*) lies in the—etymologically motivated 'stiffening' of signs (*Stifen/Versteifen*)" (72). The poems become, in De Man's terms, allegories of the impossibility of reading, or even remembering. Hölderlin's last completed poem, before he succumbed to his *Umnachtung,* tells of a scandalous, unheard-of event: the death of memory

herself, the muse Mnemosyne. "A sign we are," the poem begins, "without interpretation" (*Ein Zeichen sind wir, deutungslos*).

The Modulation of Tones

Theories of stylistic and generic mixture at the turn of the eighteenth century were divided as to whether syncretism was associated with the rise of the
novel or the lyric poem (see Lacoue-Labarthe and Nancy 1988: 81–100). Friedrich
Schlegel thought the novel, albeit with the proviso that the novel was not so much
a distinct literary form in itself as a super-genre encompassing all the others, akin
to what he famously terms "progressive, universal poetry" (fragment no. 116 from
the *Athenäums Fragmente*, in Simpson 1988: 192). Hölderlin discovers this *Mischung* in *actual* epic poetry—his own. Both thinkers relativize genres as differences
within a combinatorial system, and both historicize literary style as a recuperation
of ancient epic. This return of the epic is called *Episierung* by Szondi (1970: 147),
parataxis by Adorno. Of the two systems, only Schlegel's has garnered any attention
by Beethoven scholars; for example, John Daverio persuasively compares the late
style to Schlegel's notion of "tendency" (*Tendenz*), meaning "the replacement of
the self-sufficient, rounded forms of Classicism with the intentionally fragmented
structures of modernity" (Daverio 2000: 152). Nevertheless, Hölderlin's ideas far
surpass Schlegel in their intricacy and dialectical rigor. The *Wechsel der Töne*, the
name of Hölderlin's system as well as the title of a fragmentary essay, is a stylistic
calculus which schematizes the gradations of *Mischung* in graphs and tables. Only
Lacoue-Labarthe has followed "Adorno's suggestions in his *Mahler*, that this entire
dialectic of tones (and, in a certain way, dialectic in general) is undoubtedly not so
alien to the mode of composition of the great symphony after Mozart," and that
this *combinattoire* climaxes with Beethoven's late style: "And it is in this way that
we can also understand why Adorno was quite justified elsewhere in comparing the
'parataxis' characteristic of Hölderlin's late style with the writing of Beethoven's
last quartets" (Lacoue-Labarthe 1989: 226).

Hölderlin's (fragmentary) essay, *Über den Unterschied der Dichtarten* begins
with a gnomic definition:

> The lyrical poem, with the appearance [*Schein*] of the ideal, is in its significance
> [*Bedeutung*] naive. It is an ongoing metaphor of a feeling.
> The epic, with the appearance of naive poetry, is in its significance heroic. It is the
> metaphor of great strivings [*Bestrebungen*].
> The tragic, with the appearance of heroic poetry, is in its significance idealist. It is
> the metaphor of intellectual perception [*Anschauung*]. (Hölderlin 1992–1994: 553)

Reception of Hölderlin's elliptical sketch is necessarily a matter of interpretation;
the best is Szondi's study *Gattungspoetik und Geschichtsphilosophie* (in Szondi 1970);
the most extensive is a full-scale book by an Australian scholar who wrote in German, Lawrence J. Ryan (1960). Ryan's schematic of the *Wechsel der Töne* is a compelling summary of its complexity and elegance (see fig. 1). My own interpretation
is indebted to these two authors.

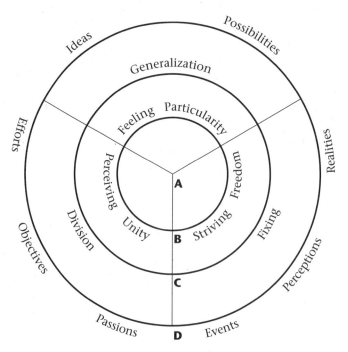

Figure 1. Hölderlin's *Wechsel der Töne* (after Ryan)
A = *Geist*
B = *Stimmung*
C = *Kunstcharakter*
D = *Stoff*

Hölderlin departs from tradition by defining the three literary *Dichtarten*—lyric, epic, and tragic—not in themselves, side by side, but systematically, so that each completes a lack in the other. Together, the interaction bears out Hölderlin's vision of an endless striving to regain wholeness, and his thesis that the whole comes into its own only through separation. Each *Dichtart* is a "tone," expressing a particular formula of experience: with lyric, the individual rules the infinite; with epic, the infinite rules the individual; and tragic reconciles the two. Hölderlin conceives the tones as a negotiation between the spirit of the poet (*Geist*; point A of Ryan's circle) and his materials (*Stoff*; the outer ring, D), and each genre deals with a different set of materials: a series of events or perceptions (lyric); a series of efforts or objectives (epic); a series of imaginative ideas, or *Phantasien* (tragic). The struggle between *Geist* and *Stoff*, by which the spirit of the poet confronts the poetic material, corresponds to the subject/object dialectic I have called S2 versus S1. A striking aspect of Ryan's diagram is that the character of the three genres changes as we move from the center (A) to the periphery (D) and back again. For instance, the arc of D on the bottom right, which indicates the lyric materials of events, perceptions, and realities (*Begebenheiten, Anschauuen, Wirklichkeiten*), is dialectically opposed to the epic-heroic impulse of "striving" at the center of this segment. And when we locate the *Stoff* of "striving" (*Bestrebungen*) on the left segment, we see that it, in turn, opposes an inner arc of intellectual ideas, etc. This is because Hölderlin thinks of the tones not as discrete genres, but as transitions, *Wechseln*, within the circle of style. Each *Wechsel* is propelled by an impulse reflecting an imbalance within the tone; the finitude of its specific character strives for the infinity and perfection of wholeness. Thus a particular feeling strives to be generalized; an objective to be realized; an abstraction to be concretized. So lyric particularity aspires to the generality of tragic; epic motion to the fixity of lyric; tragic abstraction to be incarnated in the action of epic. The tones are unstable because they each contain conflicting tendencies, in line with the subject/object dialectic. Returning to the opening definition, above, we may ask what Hölderlin means when he states that lyric has an ideal appearance but a naive significance (*Das lyrische dem Schein nach idealische Gedicht ist in seiner Bedeutung naiv*)? Simply that a lyric poet ought to convey ideas in concrete (= naive) imagery. Hölderlin's late poems may be elaborate philosophical discourses, but he takes care to ground them in plastic observations of nature, as in the landscape painting which opens *Wie wenn am Feiertage* . . . ("The grapevine drips, and gleaming in tranquil sunlight stand the trees of the grove . . . " [Hamburger 1980: 373]). The vine's distillation of "das himmlische Feuer" is a symbol of the ideas' "transmission via the medium of the naive" (Szondi 1970: 151). Likewise, the naive worldview of epic is rendered in terms of heroic actions; and the characters who people a heroic tragedy are nobly idealized. *Bedeutung* (plastic imagery, heroic actions, tragic ideas) determines the specific *Grundstimmung* of each tone, Ryan's circle B. Conversely, *Schein* is given the name *Kunstcharakter*. *Metapher,* the "third term" which mediates the contradiction between *Bedeutung* and *Schein,* describes the transformation from one pole to another. Ryan's circle C indicates the three metaphorical processes of "generalization" (*Verallgemeinerung*), "fixing" (*Festsetzung*), and "division" (*Trennung*). Lyric moves, metaphorically, from the particular to the general; epic from the free to the constrained; tragedy from unity to division. Adding a further layer of complexity, Hölderlin then discovers another, more dubious, kind of "third term," called *Geist* (confusingly, distinct from the *Geist* at Ryan's center). With each tone keeping two of the three *Dichtarten* in play, they are united by the third, which they lack. Hölderlin infers the gravitational pull of this third term by a logic of complementarity. Szondi's table (140) neatly demonstrates this complementarity, based on a permutation of three tones (*naiv, idealisch, heroisch*), three genres (*Epos, Tragödie, lyrisches Gedicht*), and three formal categories (*Grundstimmung, Kunstcharakter, Geist*):

	NAIV	IDEALISCH	HEROISCH
EPOS	Kunstcharakter	Geist	Grundstimmung
TRAGÖDIE	Geist	Grundstimmung	Kunstcharakter
LYRISCHES GEDICHT	Grundstimmung	Kunstcharakter	Geist

According to Hölderlin's dialectic, the three genres complete each other in an endless circle. The lyric poem, entailing a conflict between a naive ground and idealized expression, is unified by its epic-heroic *Geist,* which is in turn the *Kunstcharakter* of tragedy, whose *Geist* is lyric, and so on.

An elegant machine, a perfectly closed system, Hölderlin's *Lehre vom Wechsel der Töne* is nonetheless fraught with difficulties which he never resolved. As with Hegel's own attempt to historicize genre classification, the system comes unstuck with the tensions between its linear and cyclical tendencies (Szondi 1970: 144–46). According to Szondi, the rationale for Hölderlin's project was to construct a historical teleology for the genres; in particular, to explain why the destiny of lyric poetry was the heroic epic, its *Geist:* that is, Hölderlin is legitimating the epic turn his own poetry takes in his late style, its *Episierung* and parataxis. Analyzing the poetry is thus not a matter of labeling and tracking the *Töne* (as Ryan tried to do), but of appreciating the modulation of three broad principles. Epic means the syntactic parataxis, the chainlike unfolding of the longer poems like *Patmos,* and their distanced attitude to the heroic sagas of myth and history. Lyric means Hölderlin's commitment to plastic natural imagery, a disciplined Classicism which Benjamin calls *Nüchternheit,* sobriety (Benjamin 2002: 35). And tragic means the philosophical, idealist discourse driving the poetry, and the free oscillation of modulation itself. We recall that each of these tones also corresponds to the three "drives" of Hölderlin's system—striving after the infinite, the sensorium of the finite, and an ideal soaring, with its interplay between the three drives. As an oscillation of drives, modulation is kindred with Hegel, Benjamin, and Adorno's notion of *Schein*'s flicker. Yet Hölderlin's theory makes it clear that *Schein* engages a flicker of three kinds of *Durchbruch,* as history, nature, and reason break through each other in a relay of shifting and mutually interrupting perspectives. The thrust of this interplay has been called by Adorno Hölderlin's "Anamnesis der unterdrückten Natur," or a philosophical memory of a historically suppressed nature (1998b: 482). A product of modulation, this "nature"—Hölderlin's "Style 3"—can only be a dialectical concept. The epitome of this dialectic is Hölderlin's conflictual notion of *Grund,* which is simultaneously a natural source, a historical trace, and a philosophical foundation (literally, the ground of an argument or theory). Preoccupied with recuperating the unifying ground for the world's oppositions, Hölderlin is all-too aware of the impossibility of an actual return—to nature, to the past, to first principles. *Grund* is the lynchpin of Hölderlin's system, yet paradoxically as a token of all-pervading contradiction. The base of modulation is "the totally self-opposing character of the ground" (*der sich selber überall entgegengesezte Charakter des Grundes*) (in Ryan 1960: 39). Hölderlin's late lyric *Der Winkel von Hahrdt* is an allegory on *Grund*'s fraught nature. This epic miniature is also an astonishingly condensed example of the *Schein* of modulation and is deservedly the first poem which Adorno discusses in *Parataxis.*

> *Der Winkel von Hahrdt*
> Hinunter sinket der Wald,
> Und Knospen ähnlich, hängen
> Einwärts die Blätter, denen
> Blüht unten auf ein Grund,

Nicht gar unmündig.
Da nähmlich ist Ulrich
Gegangen; oft sinnt, über den Fusstritt,
Ein gross Schicksal
Bereit, an übrigem Orte. (321)

The Shelter at Hahrdt
Down sinks the forest,
And like buds, hang
Inward the leaves,
Against which blooms a valley floor,
Far from mute.
For there had Ulrich
Come; often there broods, over the footprint,
A great destiny,
Ready, at this humble place.

The poem moves simply through the three tones: lyrical nature, epic history, and tragic idea. But the tones break through each other in a series of nested eruptions. A deceptively calm observation of an autumnal woodland scene, the leaves falling onto the valley floor, is interrupted at the beginning of the second sentence (line 6) by what Adorno calls "the shock of the unexpected name Ulrich" (111). The idyll is shattered by the storm of history, for the name refers to Duke Ulrich of Württemberg, a Swabian national hero, who legend has it hid from his pursuers in a nook, formed of two interlocking sandstone plates, in a forest near Hahrdt, Hölderlin's birthplace. The so-called "Ulrichstein," together with the nearby "Fusstritt"—a flat stone appearing to bear his footprint—have become national monuments. The poem's allegory now clicks into position: "The event that took place there is supposed to speak with the voice of nature, which is therefore called '*nicht gar unmündig*,' 'far from mute.' Surviving, nature becomes an allegory for the destiny that once manifested itself on that spot" (111).

The syntax, unusually gnarled with inversions and embeddings, is fissured by three particularly ambiguous words: *Grund, unmündig,* and *übrigem*. The *Grund* is the valley floor, but Hölderlin elsewhere tends to prefer the more common *Thal*. A couplet in his poem *Heidelberg* juxtaposes these two words: "Aber schwer in das *Thal* hieng die gigantische, Schiksaalskundige Burg nieder bis auf den *Grund*" ("Heavily though, looming into the valley, the gigantic Fate-acquainted castle, to its very foundations" [Hamburger 1980: 133]). In this case, *Grund* means foundation, as of a building or monument, but it can also be the *ground* of an argument, as in Kant's famous metaphorical reading of the word as a "symbol for reflection" (Kant 1989: 223). The "brooding" of line 7 (*sinnt*) is accordingly grounded here. The word *unmündig* is normally used to describe an underage child; this connotation compounds the anthropomorphizing of the valley and hangs into the infantile *Da* of the next line, which introduces "Ulrich," on first-name terms, as if he were a boy. Indeed, there is the sense that retreating into his womblike shelter, Ulrich attains a second gestation, before springing out ("blossoming") to reclaim his destiny. Hölderlin was born near here; he identifies with Ulrich. His "footprints" are the words of the poem on the page. The poem's penultimate word, *übrigem*, is particularly elusive, since, as Jochen Schmidt shows, in addition to its standard usage as "left over," it has a meaning in Swabian dialect of *überflüssig* or *unscheinbar*, a place too humble to be even worthy of notice (Hölderlin 1992–1994: 842). The point is not, as Adorno remarks in *Aesthetic Theory*, that "a stand of trees becomes perceived as beautiful . . . because it bears, however vaguely, the mark of a past event" (Adorno 1999: 71). It is more radical than that: poetry, harnessed to the democratic arbitrariness of allegory, can make us notice the particular beauty of absolutely anything in the world.

These ambiguities admit us into the circular rhythms of the poem, which unfold the backward-and-forward modulation of reflective memory. Time seems to reverse itself; trees fall ("sink") in autumn, yet here to a ground which is "blooming," as if in spring. The leaves, retreating inward to become buds again, echo Ulrich's withdrawal into his nook, which is "blooming" because pregnant with history. Ulrich will break out of his *Grund* to found the city of Württemberg and fulfill his "great destiny," which "broods over the footprint," now merged into the landscape as an object of nature. With a chiastic reversal, nature is articulate, while history falls as silent and calm as its stone monuments. Brooding begins not in line 7 but at the very outset; the forest, imitating the course of poetic reflection itself, moves back in time to the source—*Grund*—of history, nature, and thought, into an aporia concretized by the stone nook, which in turn symbolizes both a womb and an empty crypt ("krypt"). What had once been there (*Da; ist*) is now gone (*gegangen*), leaving nothing but the two indexical signs, the *Urlichstein* and the *Fusstritt*. This presence/absence is beautifully crafted by the splitting of *ist gegangen* across two lines.

In one respect, *Der Winkel von Hahrdt* is a straightforward example of a defined poetic genre, that of trees in a churchyard. According to Haverkamp, "the formal pattern of branches hanging over blossoming ground" is a common motif in Hölderlin's late poetry, for example, his *Der Kirchof*, and is identified with "the image of the empty place" (Haverkamp 1996: 99). Theologically, it is the image of Christ's empty tomb. More generally, this lacuna is the hole left behind by departing subjectivity; not just the footprint and shelter at Hahrdt, but the nooks and crannies of Hölderlin's very language—his caesuras.

The Modulation of Notes

Hölderlin's *Wechsel der Töne* forbids as much as it suggests direct analogies with late Beethoven's stylistic system.[7] To start with the similarities, Hölderlin's many ternary divisions (epic, lyric, tragic; heroic, naive, ideal; *Schein, Bedeutung, Metapher; Kunstcharakter, Geist, Grundstimmung*) parallel Beethoven's three styles (Baroque, Classical, heroic) and the three "styles" of my theoretical model (S1, S2, S3), although it is not clear *how*. Like a Hölderlin poem, a late-Beethoven sonata is generically mixed, formally dissociated, and allegorical in foregrounding the materiality of its language. The music is mixed insofar as it mediates Baroque counterpoint and Classical forms through the idealism of the heroic style. As with the

Wechsel der Töne, Beethoven defines his styles interdependently in a circle of mutually interrupting breakthroughs: Baroque through Classical, Classical through
idealist, idealist through Baroque, and back again, within a closed system. So too
with the forms and idioms associated with these styles: sonata, fugue, variation,
and character piece. In Dahlhaus's words: "the meaning of one form seems to
emerge precisely from its transformation into another" (1989: 86). A fugue can end
as a sonata, a sonata can turn into variations, variations can constitute character
pieces which, in turn, can unfold a sonata, etc. But Dahlhaus strikes a path to the
wrong door: "Friedrich Schlegel's notion of a 'progressive universal poetry' comes
immediately to mind," he reckons, whereas the real analogue is Hölderlin (86).

Difficulties arise when we sharpen our focus. A genre for Hölderlin is not a formal schema but a formula of experience, perhaps close to what Wittgenstein calls
a "form of life" (Wittgenstein 1984: 11). A sonata is not a genre in quite the same
way, although Beethoven wrote epic, lyric, and tragic sonatas (see Hatten 1994: 84).
Further, no direct correlation is possible between epic, lyric, and tragic on the poetic side, and Baroque, Classical, and heroic on the musical. Epic and Baroque
are admittedly kindred in being the more ancient categories, yet epic poetry for
Hölderlin is the domain of heroic striving, a notion we associate with Beethoven's
heroic style. Conversely, the idealism with which Beethoven works out his heroic
style connects it, by Hölderlin's lights, to the *tragic* genre. The Classical style is particularly problematic. The well-formedness of its structural conventions suggests
the concretely naive experience of lyric, whereas lyric music is actually epitomized
by the non-sonata genres of song and dance. Nevertheless, given that Adorno has
taught us to think of stylistic categories as a force field of tensions, this noncongruence between Beethoven and Hölderlin's ternary systems does not necessarily
lead to an impasse. On the contrary, Hölderlin's nuanced concept of "tones" as conflicting impulses within the *same* genre makes the correspondences more discernible. For instance, just as the lyrical poem has an ideal appearance (*Schein*) and a
naive significance (*Bedeutung*), so the Classical sonata is ideal in its formal abstraction, and naive on account of its accessible conventionality. Likewise, in the same
way that the epic has a naive *Schein* and a heroic *Bedeutung,* counterpoint combines
a lyric idiom based on diminution with the discursive telos associated with heroic
striving. Finally, if the tragic poem is heroic in its *Schein,* but idealist in its *Bedeutung,* then Beethoven's heroic style is a music where the heroism of counterpoint
is permitted to break through the formal abstraction of sonata form. It is a style in
which heroism switches from *Bedeutung* to *Schein:* the heroic comes literally into
"Appearance." We can also construe analogies for the three impulses which drive
Hölderlin's modulations. A particular feeling strives to be generalized, and lyric
particularity aspires to the generality of tragic. In a similar way, Beethoven, in
the footsteps of Haydn and Mozart, expands (= generalizes) the miniature lyrical
forms of the *galant* into large-scale sonatas. Epic motion strives toward an objective; Beethoven's lines surge toward their goal. Tragic abstraction strives to be concretized in the human actions of epic. Beethoven personalizes sonata form around
subjective themes. Like the poetry, the music is driven by an interplay between
generalizing, objectifying, and concretizing tendencies.

The interpretive latitude of the analogy between the two stylistic systems eases somewhat when we raise our sights to the broader historical horizon. Classical theorists such as Koch thought of sonata form as a fusion of the three genres of song, dance, and fantasy, mixing processes of formal expansion, logical unification, and the heightening of affect (Koch 1782–1794). Moreover, what Szondi terms *Episierung*—the historical drift toward the epic style of the ode—is paralleled also by the triumph of the symphony. Sulzer compares the symphony to the Pindaric ode, and the Classical symphonies of Haydn are as much all-encompassing meta-genres as the odes conceived by Hölderlin (see Bonds 1997; Gerhard 2002: 174–75).[8] Crucially, however, Haydn gets there a lot earlier than Hölderlin. This is another, although much more specific, example of how music is a paradigm for Hölderlin. It helps explains why Hölderlin's ostensible twenty-year "head start" on late Beethoven is not as anachronistic as it first seems.

Two other problems, nevertheless, raise themselves at this point. First, it becomes apparent that the real and insuperable tension between Hölderlin's and Beethoven's systems is ultimately a function of the differences between music and language. Music may mime language metaphorically, but always from a position of critical distance (Adorno 1992b). To read Beethoven's late style through Hölderlin's language model, in opposition to Hegel's philosophical model, is to foreground its allegorical element. "The real problem," to repeat Adorno's conclusion, "is to resolve this allegorical element" (1998a: 136). Through allegory, music becomes *like* language, but always in a musical way, mediated through the technical properties specific to its material. To address this problem, we need to consider the allegorical element intrinsic to musical style; in particular, the *Classical* style. This is why the next chapter shifts the focus to Beethoven's position within the drama of musical Classicism, from Haydn through Beethoven's heroic style to the late style.

The second problem concerns the different natures of style history in literature and music. Poetry does not have an eighteenth-century "golden age" to match music's Classical style. German letters admittedly centers on its *Goethezeit* (see Blackall 1959), but Hölderlin is tangential to that tradition, notwithstanding his debt to Klopstock, who is portrayed as a founder of modern German poetry perhaps to the same degree that Haydn is seen as the "father" of music's Classical style (see Beissner 1942). Nevertheless, the telos and well-formedness of musical structure imparts similar qualities to musical history, in a way which is simply alien to how literature unfolds. Some music critics (particularly Webster 1991) reject this phenomenon as a metaphorical conflation; a vice of organicist/evolutionary historiography. Yet I would strongly contend that a continuity between music's structure and history is rather an irreducible aspect of music's ontology. As a result, the stylistic constituents of late Beethoven's *Kunstvereinigung* have both a precise identity and a historical specificity not possible for Hölderlin. That is, while both Beethoven and Hölderlin are "post-historical" artists who "mourn" their pasts, there is a sense that Beethoven's past comprises a self-enclosed block, beginning with Bach and Handel (with Palestrina in the far background), in which the strata have their names and places. Of course, it goes entirely without saying that this is a history constructed through the experience of Beethoven's music. To critique this perspective, in the name of a history "as it really is," begs the question of whether a non-musical history of music is even possible, or has any value.

But we are not finished with Hölderlin yet. With another dialectical twist, his language model provides a surprising interface with the technical analysis of music's Classical style. The link is his concept of *caesura*, explored earlier in this chapter and in chapter 3. Caesura, as Adorno interprets it, has a local "micrological" dimension in the cracks which fissure Beethoven's structures as well as a global aspect in the music's dramatic turning points. Adorno, however, misses caesura's *normative* dimension as punctuation or articulation, and hence its "analogy" with "the traditional theory of form [which] employs such terms as sentence, phrase, segment, ways of punctuating" (1992b: 1). Caesura, or *Einschnitt* in German, is the prototypical category of Koch's formal theory; my "punctuation schema" of Beethoven's sonata forms (see chapter 5) engages caesuras. The "analogy" Adorno observes originates in the classic Enlightenment trope of construing the rhythmic gesture as the source of both poetic and musical expression. Hölderlin and Beethoven come together, then, in the vanishing point of a rhythmic singularity. Nor should we miss caesura's *historical* function for Hölderlin as a philosophical critique; a rejection-cum-sublation of a prior epoch or paradigm. Hence Hölderlin's language model is a "caesura" of Hegelian metaphysics, just as Beethoven's late style is a caesura of Classicism, including its heroic variant. The grammatical and historical combine as a dialectic of articulation. Each phase in the Classical style's drama is characterized by a different mode of articulation, or caesura. The critique of one phase by the next is a historical articulation. Mixing the two dimensions, Beethoven's caesura of the Classical style unfolds as a caesura of caesuras.

8 Caesura of the Classical Style

THE FIRST MOVEMENTS OF HAYDN'S SYMPHONY NO. 45, HAYDN'S OP. 74, NO. 1, AND BEETHOVEN'S OP. 53; THE SCHERZO AND TRIO OF OP. 135

Caesura—Punctuation; articulation; *Einschnitt;* metrical pulse; rhythmic inter-ruption; dramatic turning point; structural juncture; breach; fissure; crack; trace; moment of breaking free; moment of expressionless violence; thunderbolt; inter-vention of subjectivity; defiance; endurance; assertion; negation; critical turn; sublime condensation; synthesis; instant; star; black hole; singularity.

Hölderlin and Beethoven never met, and didn't influence each other. Yet they touched once in Hölderlin's late poem, *Das fröhliche Leben* (*The Happy Life*), which parodies the rhyme scheme and the imagery of Schiller's *Ode to Joy,* and which Haverkamp reckons was "composed so that it could be sung to Beethoven's melody" (Haverkamp 1996: 82):

> O vor diesem sanften Bilde
> Wo die grünen Bäume stehen,
> Wie vor einer Schenke Schilde
> Kann ich kaum vorübergehn.

> Oh before this pleasant picture
> Where the green trees grow
> As before a tavern's shield
> I can't resist to go.

The "sanfter Flügel" of Schiller's brotherhood of man ("alle Menschen werden Brüder wo dein sanfter Flügel weilt") turns into the pub sign's "sanften Bilde." Where Schiller and Beethoven reaffirm transcendental borders, Hölderlin "can hardly resist a pint" (83). Hölderlin wrote *Das fröhliche Leben* well into the period of his madness, and strictly speaking it is the work of a "post-late" style. Until recently, the poetry after his *Umnachtung* of 1807 was generally written off as an artistic failure, with none of the complexity or fervor of the earlier hymns and odes. This oeuvre is now being reassessed by revisionist critics such as Haverkamp, who sees it as representing an even more radical step in the poet's career; a whole-sale stepping outside of the idealist tradition into a more modest, pragmatist worldview. Insofar as late styles are critical, and are thus still implicated in the same ideas which they critique, Hölderlin is probably unique among artists in having a post-late style which breaks the cycle of self-reflection, to push on into a truly unknown (and unknowable) terrain. Because of his madness, this terrain has proved better suited to Lacanian psychoanalysis than philosophical hermeneutics. From a Lacanian standpoint, the trees which figure in poems such as *Der Winkel von Hahrdt* and *Der Kirchof* (considered in chapter 7) are elders, symbolizing Hölderlin's patronym (*Holder* = elder). And so the rejection of the late style's symbolic order is literally the expulsion of the "Name of the Father" which underwrites all law, including the rules of language (95). Hölderlin's post-late style is predicated, therefore, on the failure of a whole symbolic system. Beethoven never went this far; given that Hölderlin did, his example constitutes something of a limiting case in our understanding of late style.

Where Hölderlin *can* offer a technical touch point with Beethoven, on the other hand, is in his theoretical category of caesura. The present chapter contextualizes Beethoven within the Classical style, and does so by considering the Classical style as a generalizing of caesura. We should start with the philosophical definition of caesura Hölderlin gives in his *Anmerkungen zum Ödipus,* an interpretation which moves well beyond caesura's conventional poetic function as a break between words in a metrical foot, or a pause near the middle of a line. The passage reads:

> For the tragic transport is actually empty, and the least restrained.—Thereby, in the rhythmic sequence of the representations wherein the transport presents itself, there becomes necessary what in poetic meter is called caesura, the pure word, the counter-rhythmic rupture—namely, in order to meet the onrushing change of representations at its highest point, in such a manner that not the change of representation but the representation itself very soon appears. (in Benjamin 2002, vol. 1: 340–41)

Benjamin provides the most famous reading of this passage, embedded in his great essay on Goethe's *Elective Affinities* (2002: 297–362). For Benjamin, Hölderlin's caesura is the expressionless (*das Ausdrucklose*) moment of sublime violence which interrupts a tragedy, as in Tiresias's intervention in Sophocles' *Oedipus Rex.* It is an expressly *rhythmic* device (Hölderlin's "counter-rhythmic rupture"), albeit at several orders of abstraction: thinking of drama as a kind of "rhythm," and of the interruption of a rhythmic sequence (the "onrushing change of representations") as itself "rhythmic." Adorno, confusingly, translates Hölderlin's caesura to Beethoven in two opposite senses. On the one hand, he identifies the caesura as a particular moment in Beethoven's sonata forms, located in the turning point between what he calls the "descending" and "ascending" curves of his two-part model of the development section, according to Hölderlin's "calculable law of tragedy" (64). This is "the moment where subjectivity intervenes in the formal structure" (64), and it is epitomized, as we have seen in chapters 3 and 7, by the new E-minor theme in the *Eroica.* In this regard, Adorno keeps faith with Hölderlin's prescription of a *single* caesura within a dramatic work (the E-minor theme, then, is Beethoven's "Tiresias moment"). On the other hand, caesuras in the early *Spätstil* essay are multiple and pervasive, a network of cracks and fissures across the entire late landscape. Between them, Adorno's unitary and generalized models suggest that musical caesura is actually a spectrum of devices, ranging from the local level to the architectonic. This is entirely in the spirit of the recursive, periodic nature of Classical phrase structure, by which language-like articulation ("punctuation") operates at all levels of the piece. Caesura happens to be the normative category of late-eighteenth-century compositional theory, in its German form *Einschnitt*. Koch's notion of *Einschnitt* derives from the verb *schneiden*, to cut, just as caesura comes from the Latin *caedere*. In Koch's *Versuch*, *Einschnitte* are the quasi-linguistic punctuation marks which articulate, or cut into, Classical discourse, with phrase endings and cadences.[1] On the lowest level, punctuation is intrinsic to the stream of metrical pulses, the *Schlagreihe*, which constitutes the metaphorical model for Classical syntax in the writings of Sulzer and Koch. On the highest level, the articulation of a sonata-form movement into thematic groups and sections is a metaphorical mapping from this *Schlagreihe*. In short, Classical musical form, at all levels, is "rhythmic," predicated on caesuras.

Caesura is thus foundational and normative for Classical syntax in such a way as to profile a basic difference between music and language. To be sure, the Classical style has a profound "language character," on account of its punctuation, periodicity, and conventionality. And yet music's permeability of level, whereby caesura functions as punctuation, form, and content at the same time, is alien to propositional language (if not to poetry), with its separation of phonology, syntax, and semantics. Classical music is *fractal* in this respect. Precisely because of its fractal character, music becomes a model for the sort of philosophical leaps outlined by Hölderlin. Hölderlin raises caesura from a poetic to a dramatic and ultimately to a philosophical category; this kind of recursiveness is already immanent within the material of music. Conversely, giving philosophy its own due, Hölderlin's perspective on caesura helps take us out of an empirically landlocked perspective on interruption fostered by contemporary style theorists such as Meyer and Narmour. Meyer believes that musical meaning emerges from the subversion of pattern (the inhibition of a "tendency to respond"). The setting up and frustration of pattern constitutes a modern-day theory of musical caesura. Admittedly, the glory of this approach is the infinitesimal calculus of Narmour, whose intervallic scales measure the precise implicative property of each parameter. The method's limitation, however, is a certain rigidity, and an inability to reflect on its own foundations, which are reified as natural ("cognitive") absolutes. For example, the Meyer-Narmour "implication-realization model" is powerless to entertain a historical concept of one style interrupting—being a caesura of—another; or the philosophical idea that caesura blocks a style's totalizing impulse. It is in this respect that Lacoue-Labarthe calls Hölderlin's critique of Hegelian dialectic "a caesura of the speculative" (Lacoue-Labarthe 1989), and Benjamin defines the "expressionless" instant of the caesura as that "which survives the legacy of chaos in all beautiful semblance [*Schein*]: the false, errant totality—the absolute totality" (2002: 340).

In short, to treat caesura dialectically, rather than schematically, is to incorporate it within the constellation of terms we have considered in earlier chapters—

specifically, to triangulate it with the twin stars of *Durchbruch* and *Apparition*. Implicit in Hölderlin and Benjamin's definition is the notion that caesura simultaneously elicits both a resurgence of a natural, chthonic power (Hölderlin's "anamnesis of repressed nature") and a cognitive jolt of awareness ("the representation itself very soon appears"). In very practical terms, a rhythmic pulse achieves three things: it can interrupt (a caesura); it can be a mimetic gesture, expressing the "natural" (*Durchbruch*); and it can institute a metrical pattern, at rising levels, that helps listeners grasp the music's form, allowing them to "see" it (*Apparition*). This dialectic of interruption, expression, and cognition is not obviously captured by empirical style analysis. But it is fundamental to the Classical style's rhythmic paradigm, and the fount and origin of certain effects we attribute to Beethoven's late style. To get the full measure of Beethoven's originality, it is absolutely imperative to ground his achievements in the technical possibilities of the Classical material. Without needing to invoke historical teleology, we can certainly see how his techniques are immanent within this material. Three particular techniques spring to mind: the allegorical objectification of convention or tonality, so that we "see" it; the eruption of archaic, or Baroque idioms; and the modality of the instantaneous, packing an enormous amount of information into a single point, a caesura. All these are bread and butter for Haydn and Mozart. The difference in late Beethoven is many orders of reflexivity, so that caesura's dialectical axes of rotation are multiplied vertiginously. Benjamin's most evocative metaphor—the star—here becomes especially telling. Referring to the embrace of the tragic lovers in Goethe's novel, Benjamin writes:

> That sentence, which to speak with Hölderlin contains the caesura of the work and in which, while the embracing lovers seal their fate, everything pauses, reads: "Hope shot across the sky above their heads like a falling star." (354–55)

As noted by Hoeckner (2002: 18–20), Benjamin seizes on the falling star as the perfect image of a fleeting hope emerging "from the semblance [*Schein*] of reconciliation" (355), supporting his gnomic thesis that "only for the sake of the hopeless ones have we been given hope" (356).[2] The metaphor can be turned at various angles to illuminate Beethoven. To Hoeckner's symbols of wishful radiance, as in Leonora's "Come hope, do not dim the last star of the weary" (25), may be added their shadow image of star as black hole. Dead stars implode into astral singularities, and Beethoven allows us to voyage, miraculously, in and out through these exit holes of the music, his caesuras. These are some of the meanings compacted into his stars:

> *The Normative:* Caesuras are foundational to Classical articulation, on the level of meter, phrase structure, and expanded form, and thus have a normative dimension.
> *Tropes:* As interruptions, musical caesuras subvert regular syntax by analogy to the grammatical inversions theorized in Enlightenment linguistics.
> *Metaphor:* Rhythmic gestures restore a mimetic naturalness bracketed by linguistic abstraction, corresponding to the function of poetic metaphor in Enlightenment semiotics.
> *Allegory:* A caesura is a rhythmic pulse, but unlike lower-order interruptions, it resists

subsumption into any overarching pattern ("troping"). By denying formal closure, it is allegorical.

History: Inducing a breakthrough of nature, it also recuperates historically repressed styles.

Kunstvereinigung: The many styles—old and new—interrupt each other in a two-way street. Classical freezes Baroque, just as Baroque shatters Classical.

Aesthetic plurality: Different historical periods (Baroque, Classical, heroic) entail different styles of caesura, and these themselves interact along the interface of caesura, which forms a junctional degree zero of articulation.

Apparition: Caesuras make the music "visible" in two opposite ways. The flash of insight lets us grasp the form; it also reveals the materiality subsumed within that form.

Schein: The caesura momentarily petrifies *Schein's* flicker, spellbinding the undulations of life into a standstill. It also perpetuates motion, by interrupting *Schein's* semblance of static reconciliation (see Benjamin, 340).

Late-style rhythm: Beethoven's restitution of a rhythmic style based on caesuras in his late period, rejecting the "melodic" style of the heroic, is itself a rhythmic gesture of heroic endurance. It is what Benjamin calls "the rhythm of the hymn as objection" (341). Beethoven's late linguistic turn affirms Hölderlin's language model contra Hegel's philosophical model. Self-reflexively, Beethoven's recuperation of caesura is itself a caesura of the Hegelian absolute.

In what follows, I track the growth of the Classical style from 1770 to 1827 in terms of a variety of caesuras—simply put, through changes in techniques of articulation, backed up by aesthetic paradigms and kindred analytical orientations (Kantian, idealist, allegorical). Although wary of Hegelian teleology, I contend that "development" is not the same as goal-driven evolution. I thus represent the story as three critical "turns," each turn being a caesura on the grandest scale. Mozart's enormous influence notwithstanding, I happen to believe that Haydn was Beethoven's major precursor, a "Rubens" to the musical "Rembrandt" (see Schama 1999). Haydn's "first turn" opposes the incipient rhythmic paradigm of the Classical style to Baroque contrapuntal caesura. Beethoven's "second turn" sublates articulation into Hegelian negation. And his "third turn," the late style, restores rhythmic articulation, but now as an act of sublime defiance, Hölderlin's "rhythm as objection." The stress, therefore, is always on the immanence of Beethoven's ideas in the properties of Classical material. My historical model is thus somewhat perpendicular to that proposed by James Webster (see note 5 to chapter 2). And my Classical perspective thus differs markedly from the modernist position so eloquently described by Hoeckner (2002) as the "hermeneutics of the moment." The moment—a word which in German means both instant of time (*Augenblick*) and formal part (*Bestandteil*)—is a central category in early-Romantic and modernist aesthetics of the fragment. Indeed, the Romantics saw the fragment as a model for all structures, with the accent on formal separation, the fleetingness of lyrical experience, and the listener being drawn to what Adorno calls *schöne Stellen,* particular passages. Hoeckner maintains that, both formally and temporally, moments are dialectical, in that the part is mediated by the whole and may symbolically be taken to stand for the whole. Nevertheless, this is difficult to show, unless we ground details—be they "caesuras" or "moments"—in a dynamic stylistic context. Otherwise, one slips back, willy-nilly, into "atomistic" listening: the culinary savoring of isolated impressions. To call my standpoint backward-facing Classical, instead of forward-facing modernist, would be inaccurate, since Classicism is already modernist. The heart of the matter, rather, is to grasp caesura's dialectical tensions, to flow with the dialogue between the normative and the tropological.

The First Turn: Caesura as Concept Formation, Interruption, and Vision

Music analysis of the Classical style doesn't *seem* to have a Kantian tradition to match the Hegelian-Beethovenian line which I will review below. Actually, one could be reconstructed, since Sulzer, the spiritual godfather to the most influential compositional tract of the late eighteenth century, Koch's *Versuch,* was a pre-Kantian philosopher (whom Kant admired). Sulzer's essay on *Rhythmus* from his *Allgemeine Theorie* was the first attempt to psychologize rhythm as a process inhering in the mind rather than in the objects of perception (Spitzer 2004: 236–39). Sulzer held that listeners actively organize a stream of undifferentiated pulses (the *Schlagreihe,* or *Schlagfolge*) into metrical groups at rising levels. Beats organize into measures, measures into the "compound rhythms" (*zusammengesetze Rhythmen*) of periods, thematic periods into the two or three structural periods of sonata form, etc. The process by which we leap from beats to measures to phrases to large-scale form is metaphorical, as suggested by Sulzer's important essay on language, "Observations on the Reciprocal Influence of Reason on Language and of Language on Reason." The nuts and bolts of this metaphorical progression are worked out in the sequential compositional regime of Koch's treatise, which takes the novice composer, step by step, from small to expanded forms. And Sulzer's essay on *Einformigkeit* (Uniformity) makes the all-important link between metrical-formal patterns and concepts. Meter turns time into spatial concepts; a series of beats (or, indeed, a series of *any* objects) can, through a uniform pattern, be "united with a concept" (*mit einem Begriff zusammen gefasst*). Through uniformity, an infinite succession of events can be surveyed at a glance and held in the mind. As with meter, so with form: *Einformigkeit* captures the predictability of the Classical style, which is its most revolutionary innovation. On listening to a sonata form, we know exactly where we are from moment to moment, in a way which is not possible in less conventionalized Baroque genres such as fugue. We literally hold the music in the mind, subsuming it under a *concept* of sonata form.

As well as concept formation, beats—that is, caesuras—also interrupt patterns and create poetic expression. In order to trigger the formation of a higher-order pattern in the listener's mind, a beat must first interrupt a lower-order grouping. Rhythm is thus an instrument of *troping.* Sulzer describes this process using the pre-Kantian aesthetic terminology of Christian Wolff, a Leibnizian philosopher. Absolute uniformity (*Einformigkeit*) works only upon the attention (*Aufmerksamkeit*) and affords merely a limited kind of pleasure. Meter binds "obscure" (*dunkel*) sensory perception, allowing the clear (*klar*) spirit to freely unfold. The mind un-consciously counts the units of the primitive *Schlagfolge*, but is awoken only when something unexpected happens, such as a sudden change of tempo or interruption. Whereas the obscure faculties react to disturbance as a shock, the clearer faculties seek to understand deviations from the norm as speechlike aesthetic statements. This brings us to the third outcome of caesura—vision. Sulzer is in line with En-lightenment semiotics in arguing that the goal of artistic discourse is to recuperate an expressive immediacy provisionally bracketed by the institution of the arbitrary signs of language. Sulzer, together with a wide spectrum of thinkers, including Wolff, Meier, Lessing, Herder, and Moses Mendelssohn, identify this effect with *metaphor*. Mendelssohn held that metaphoric use of language helps transform symbolic cognition into intuitive cognition, making us feel that that "objects are presented to our senses as if without mediation" (in Wellbery 1984: 79). Unmedi-ated perception, of course, is impossible, as Kant proved. Yet, *contra* Kant, Men-delssohn suggests that, with metaphoric intuition, "the lower faculties of the soul experience an illusion in that they often forget the signs and believe that they are viewing *the object itself*" (79). Outbreaks of "natural," metaphoric expression were linked by these writers to Enlightenment speculation on the origin of language in mimetic gestures, enshrined in onomatopoeic *Machtwörter* such as "thunder" (Greek *brontae*, Latin *tonitru*, German *Donner*, French *tonnerre*, etc.). Metaphor also has a syntactic dimension, in that a more "natural" word order can be con-trived through grammatical inversion. Placing strong nouns at the front of sen-tences is akin to indexically gesturing to the material object of one's attention. The cognitive flash elicited by metaphor thus has both a formal and material compo-nent. On the formal side, the caesura is a moment of intellectual grasping, when we comprehend the structure of the piece beneath and above the surface disrup-tions. On the material side, we "see" the sensuous particularity hitherto subsumed within this structure. By Adorno's lights, this is the moment when we recuperate the nonsubsumptive, aesthetic character of the art object.

These two sides of metaphoric "seeing"—that is, of Classical *Apparition*—cor-respond to the two poles of the dialectic of Enlightenment, by which rational free-dom from nature simultaneously commutes nature to an aesthetic ideal. It also par-allels the aesthetic interplay of concepts and sense impressions in Kant's *Critique of Judgment:* or rather, the faculties which *produce* them, the understanding (*Ver-stand*) and the imagination (*Einbildungskraft*). According to Kant, the imagination is responsible for constructing the manifold of perception, while these represen-tations are united by the understanding. It is the free and harmonious interplay of the two faculties which produces aesthetic beauty. Leonard Meyer's theory of style is "Kantian" insofar as it also splits cognition into two levels: a data-driven faculty for perceiving psychologically hard-wired and culturally/historically invariant ge-stalt gap-fill principles, and a top-down, concept-driven faculty for processing data through learned stylistic schemata. In Meyer's model, schematic and gestalt per-ceptions interact harmoniously, just like Kant's *Verstand* and *Einbildungskraft*. One factor which Meyer has never chosen to foreground is the relative weighting of these two faculties, although his last major book, *Style and Music* (1989), suggested a historical gradient from the schematic to the gestalt. In "changing-note melodies" (such as the $\hat{1}$–$\hat{7}$ . . . $\hat{4}$–$\hat{3}$ schema discussed in chapter 2), Meyer proposes that "nurture (syntactic convention) dominates nature, while in axial [and gap-fill] melodies nature dominates nurture" (1989: 245).

Meyer never took the logical next step of exploring this shifting priority synchronically, in musical structure itself. Gestalt principles rise up to dominate schemata in moments of lyrical parataxis and parametric noncongruence, often toward the end of utterances, or second groups. Meyer theorizes these changes in terms of "realization" of "implications" set up in openings, typically countervailing gap-fill motions. Yet Meyer's theory can be tilted another way, not toward realization, but rather *recuperation of particularity:* "seeing" material. Returning to the case of Mozart's $\hat{1}$–$\hat{7}$ . . . $\hat{4}$–$\hat{3}$ melody from his G-major piano sonata (see ex. 2.2), it is clear that the gap-fill descent which answers the schematic first half also liberates style features which were initially subsumed through congruence and conformance (ex. 8.1):

Example 8.1. Mozart, Piano Sonata in G, K. 283, first movement, mm. 1–11

That is, the first four measures line up features such as appoggiaturas, arpeggiations, and scale steps harmoniously, so that they are attended to not "in themselves," but functionally, instantiating a type. By contrast, in mm. 5–10 the music's phrase structure is scrambled, creating all manner of asymmetries, so that these features are appreciated in their own right. For instance, the suspensions at mm. 5–6 (F♯–E;

E–D) promote the appoggiatura from a neutral phrase ending or semiotic marker (G–F♯ and C–B at mm. 1–4), to expressive sighing gestures. Parametric noncongruence discloses the particularity of the material, what Kant calls "the sensuous manifold." Such moments of material *Apparition* tend to cluster around lyric junctures, in middles or endings. Their distribution conforms to the dialectic of Classical communication, and the need to say things twice: first, schematically, to make grammatical sense, and then materially, because conventions perforce suppress detail. Implicit in Meyer's Mozart analysis is the notion that the ear performs a cognitive "flip" from concept-driven to data-driven perception, in that required order; and that this flip may even be entrained by—affordant from—the Classical style itself.

Stepping back from this debate, one can now adduce a fourth, historical dimension of caesura. Namely, the Classical style's rhythmic paradigm had a defined lifecycle, reaching maturity, by Rosen and Webster's reckoning, in the early 1780s, when Haydn discovered the "new and special way" of his Op. 33 string quartets, and Mozart moved to Vienna. By the same token, there was an earlier time when this paradigm interacted with an alien style of handling caesuras. Classical phrasing is articulated by pattern, by a grid of phrase endings and cadential formulae. Baroque articulation works quite differently, impinging immediately on the contrapuntal line or harmonic sequence. Interruption is the engine of Baroque discourse and is a syntactic axiom, since the cycle of fifths requires constant cadential evasions to forestall premature closure. The difference, then, is between articulation mediated by pattern, and interruption directed at the "stream of rhetoric." Because both principles engage pulses or caesuras, they may interface within the same material, despite being fundamentally noncommensurable. Hence the ambiguous casing of the "caesura of the Classical style," both genitive and accusative. Classical caesuras function within the economy of the style as an autonomous system. But one may also imagine a caesura *of* that system, interrupting the functioning of the whole. Caesura's dual intra- and interstylistic axis is especially apparent in the transitional *galant* period, when Baroque and Classical idioms interact on a level playing field. The maturation of the rhythmic paradigm circa 1780 can be counted as music's "critical turn," by analogy to philosophy's Kantian turn. Here, an abstract, systemic caesura, oriented to pattern, displaces the rhetorical immediacies of Baroque interruptions (i.e., Baroque articulation as deflection of the "stream of rhetoric"; see Spitzer 2004: 214). Crucially, however, this "first turn" (which will be followed by Beethoven's second and third turns) is itself subdivided into two moments. In the first moment, epitomized by Haydn's *Sturm und Drang* music of the early 1770s, the incipient rhythmic paradigm defines itself in historical opposition to the Baroque and cannot stand alone. The rhythmic paradigm comes of age in the second moment, after Haydn's "new and special way," and achieves autonomy, while Baroque caesuras drop out or become accessory. The internalization of caesura in works such as Haydn's Op. 74 quartets marks a point of mature subjectification, when music becomes as free-standing as the model of mind predicated in Kant's critiques. Caesura's *Apparitions* now turn self-reflexive, turning back to reveal the workings of music's underpinnings: tonality.

Moment 1: Haydn's Symphony No. 45 in F♯ Minor

The fact that the Classical style becomes fully autonomous by the 1780s in no way depreciates the *Sturm und Drang* masterpieces of the early 1770s.[3] On the contrary, these works confront the Baroque with an energy and directness which is arguably diminished once the older style becomes fully absorbed. Elements of the rhythmic paradigm are already embedded within the *galant* style, in particular, the functional distribution of Baroque traits such as counterpoint and harmonic sequences in structurally "marked," that is, unstable, junctures, such as introductions, transitions, and development sections. The difference is partially one of degree, in that "*inter*-stylistic" play—the conflict between Baroque and Classical—is stronger in the 1770s than the "*intra*-stylistic" play of the later style. The Baroque has a real presence in these *galant* works, whereas the music of the 1780s *re*-presents it entirely from the viewpoint of Classicism. (The persistence of Baroque elements into the *galant* period was strongest in the Habsburg lands, as Webster has observed [2004: 52]). Haydn's "Farewell" Symphony, no. 45 in F♯ minor (1772), epitomizes the high-water mark of this early phase of Classicism, when Baroque elements are still so much in contention (ex. A.9, see appendix).

These elements include motoric ostinato bass lines, contrapuntal textures, and harmonic sequences often involving interlocking suspensions. The dynamism of these processes contends with an incipient Classical style predicated on periodic repetition and balance, as in the symphony's opening sixteen measures. These display a perfect periodicity of 4×4-measure phrases, which correspond like questions and answers. Measures 9–16 "answer" mm. 1–8 as an almost literal da capo, although they cadence differently. At the next level down, the phrases "rhyme" through their end notes, with the D of m. 4 connecting with the C♯ of m. 8, which then relates to the next D of m. 12. The punctuation marks of these head and end notes form a grid which cages in the music's forward drive. Hence the conflict between Baroque and Classical is expressed as a contradiction between two types of musical logic: a linear logic based on note-to-note continuity, and a "metrical" logic formed of discontinuous correspondences, or "rhymes." A Baroque compulsion to argue is punctuated by Classical obligations to repeat.

To critique the Baroque in this context means to actively suppress immediate linear connections in the interests of longer-range continuities. The violins' initial thematic gambit affords a precise example of this, by halting on the D♮ of m. 4 and frustrating the expected resolution to a C♯ by leaping up to the high B of m. 5 for the antecedent phrase. By contrast, the themes of Bach's prelude and fugue in F♯ minor (book 2), which also fall through the tonic triad, resolve normatively, filling in the arpeggiation with linear descending scales to the tonic (the fugue subject even falls by step from its melodic crux on the D). The German concept of *Fortspinnung*, meaning figurative elaboration within a context of directed tonal motion, captures the way Baroque themes are "spun out" like this toward their cadence. In the Haydn, however, the D is interrupted by mm. 5–7 to connect with the C♯ of m. 8 and is reactivated by the second D of m. 12, which is then left hanging when the wind drops out and the texture suddenly thins. Technically, the D is picked up by the violins' C♯ at m. 14, but the resolution is relatively weak, since it is on the unmarked measure of the phrase, and is overshadowed by the suspended oboe D's of mm. 11–13. Most importantly, the cadence at mm. 14–16 is denied the descending scale which is de rigueur for satisfying resolutions in music of the common-practice period. The cadential C♯ of m. 14 remains registrally unresolved—a tension sustained until the very final measures of the last movement, which is saturated with descents from the dominant to the tonic (or Schenkerian $\hat{5}$–$\hat{4}$–$\hat{3}$–$\hat{2}$–$\hat{1}$'s). Such overarching long-range connections are absolutely fundamental to the Classical style, with its "comic" rhetoric of "disconfirmation followed by a consonance" (Bonds 1991: 190).

Strikingly, the resolution D–C♯, followed by a descent toward a tonic harmony, is actually *given* in the wind accompaniment of mm. 1–8. The violin D of m. 4 is shadowed by the second oboe; whereas the violin leaps to a B, the oboe proceeds to resolve the D to the C♯ in m. 5, which is then transferred to the first oboe's B in m. 6 and resolved by step to an A. The linear counterpoint of the oboes' part writing stands, as it were, "in counterpoint" to the interrupted logic of the strings' periodicity. And when the wind is removed in the final phrase of the section, mm. 13–16, this contrapuntal logic is conspicuously suppressed. The caesuras at m. 13 are thus not merely a textural affair; they mark the interruption of one style by another. In short, the architectural design of the symphony is motivated by a critique of the shorter-term logic of Baroque progressions. The abstraction of Haydn's "critical turn" consists in a bracketing of Baroque immediacy.

Moment 2: Haydn's String Quartet Op. 74, No. 1 in C

Baroque idioms disappear from the surface of this quartet, which is dominated by the *intra*-stylistic play of the Classical *combinattoire* (fig. 2).

The watchword of the new style was normativity, regulating textural and structural categories into a well-formed and predictable "syntax" by analogy both with spoken language and with danced metrical patterns. Texture is polarized through division of labor between melody and bass, with harmonic "filler" in the middle (Ratner 1980: 108–9). Form becomes conventionalized into a regular schema of beginning-middle-end (Agawu 1991: 51–79), recursively from small-scale through expanded structures. These "vertical" (textural) and "horizontal" (formal) axes combine into a *combinattoire,* insofar as it is this very normativity which permits

The classical combinattoire

Form:		beginning	middle	end
Texture:	melody			
	filler			
	bass			

Figure 2. The classical *combinattoire*

combinatorial play without danger to the underlying coherence. The whole point of a conventionalized syntax is to permit the elaborations and inversions which are the stuff of expression. In this respect, musical play which keeps within the coordinates of the Classical *combinattoire* (such as wittily starting with a cadence, or evading closure) tallies with eighteenth-century theories of grammatical "inversion," as associated with poetic metaphor.

Haydn's quartet plays the *combinattoire* in order to ring fresh changes out of tonality, so that it literally resonates. The *combinattoire's* infinitesimally precise articulation enables him to stage these tonal *Apparitions* against an intricate context. This is why the cadential false opening—the locus classicus of Haydn's wit—can reverberate at every level and juncture of the movement (ex. A.10, see appendix). But it is not in itself an *Apparition;* the most striking *Apparition* comes in the cello line of m. 39, which is the exact analogue of (and perhaps the model for) the cello interruption at m. 9 of Beethoven's Op. 135. Like Beethoven, Haydn interrupts an approach to a cadence, stalling on the IV. Here, the cello drops out for three measures, and its C is picked up by the viola. Although the viola technically completes the progression, the timbral disjunction serves both to undermine the cadence and to profile the cello's dislocated B–C step as a motivic event. Haydn induces a cognitive flash which lets us see several things at once. The line's motivic particularity is rescued from the schematic dimension of this standard cadential approach. Second, it cross-references the B–C melodic step of the opening cadence, mm. 1–2, its absolute-pitch relation cutting across the modulation. Third, it opens up a rich seam in tonality, exploiting the fact that scale steps $\hat{7}$–$\hat{8}$ in the tonic are the same as $\hat{3}$–$\hat{4}$ in the dominant. This "tonal fact" helps Haydn draw the music's seemingly disparate events into a tight nexus. For instance, it is related to his monothematic gambit of bringing back the first subject in the dominant group. The viola accompaniment in mm. 31–32 transposes its original line, E–F–D–E, from mm. 3–4, reinforcing the previously only implicit link between the cadence's B–C, and the viola "filler." The awakening of this dormant relationship is the burden of the first group. Thus, the connection becomes much clearer with the cello augmentation of the viola's E–F figure at mm. 7–8, since its longer note values now recall mm. 1–2.

At the deepest level, Haydn's quarry is the biggest prize of all: the identity of chords I and V^7, which constitute the polar opposites of the Classical tonal system. These are of course the chords of the opening cadential gesture, and they will be analyzed, reassembled, and ultimately interchanged. Haydn's analysis moves in two directions, yielding *Apparitions* of this cadence alternately more abstract and more concrete as the piece unfolds. On the one hand, he abstracts the V^7–I progression from its cadential shape into higher-level pitch progressions which flow across metrical groupings, and ultimately drift across to trespass, monotonally, on the second group. Thus, violin I's B–C motive at m. 4 is really part of a broad unfolding of a V^7, from the B through to the F of m. 6. To be sure, the status of this V^7 unfolding is presently abstract, held in check by the tonic pedal. But its striking eighth-note diminution in mm. 9–10, now unambiguously on the dominant, retrospectively confirms the opening's tensions. One could even extrapolate this unfolding back to the piece's introductory V^7, in which case the tonics of mm. 2–4 are dissolved away. And we have already seen how the B–C motive transfixes the dominant group as absolute pitch relations. On the other hand, Haydn lets us hear the V^7–I cadence as a metrical gesture more fundamental than tonality; that is, the gesture could be represented by *any* chord sequence, including, paradoxically, I–V^7, the reverse of the cadence. At this gross material level, m. 3's C–D motive is clearly an echo of mm. 1–2's B–C, despite the reverse harmony.

These two impulses, the abstract and the material, of course work hand in hand, toward the pastoral *Apparitions* of the coda. The journey is beautifully paced. Hearing C–D as an echo of B–C is confirmed by the progressive destabilizing of the tonic, displacing C and E as suspensions (E against F at m. 8), as $^6_4$ chords (m. 9), and as a complex prolongation against the bass's F♯ and G at mm. 14–17. All this serves to make us hear the C metaphorically *as* an F, as a seventh. Haydn is preparing us to hear the C in the dominant group as part of a V^7 (m. 30), or as a passing note to D (mm. 34, 40, 48). This metaphorical interchange of I and V^7 is abetted by the successive augmentation of C from a half note (m. 3) to a full measure (m. 7) to four measures (mm. 14–17). The climax of this process is, once again, the enigmatic three-measure "hole" which interrupts the cello at mm. 39–41. This caesura is the major *Apparition* of C in the movement, yet paradoxically in absentia: as a gap. Thereafter, the B–C gesture is integrated into the bucolic flourishes of the coda. Like many of Mozart's expositions (see his String Quintet, K. 515), Haydn ends with a pastoral topic. Yet by filtering this topic through a cage of common-tone relations, including the rhyme with the B–C cadential opening, he is subscribing to the Enlightenment semiotics of metaphor, where nature is always qualified by cultural representations. The peasant stamping is circumscribed by the *combinattoire,* so that the *Apparition* of nature is abstractly contrived. Much of Beethoven's late style is already present in this quartet: the paratactic overlap of the tonic group onto the dominant, the illumination of tonality as a material object, the condensation of these effects in instantaneous flashes of insight—*Apparitions.*

The Second Turn:
Caesura as Negation, Synthesis, and *Erscheinung*

Count Waldstein's 1792 prophecy to Beethoven that "with the help of assiduous labor you shall receive Mozart's spirit from Haydn's hands" (Thayer 1964: 115) charmingly suggests the dialectical course of the Classical style, with Beethoven as synthesis of two extremes. Tia DeNora's debunking of Waldstein's trope as a "narrative construction" which belies the *social* construction of Beethoven's genius (DeNora 1995: 83–114) is nevertheless irrelevant to the music's *compositional* construction, which actually confirms Count Waldstein's prognosis surprisingly well, as Rosen has shown (1972). To what extent, then, *pace* our wholesale rejection of Hegelian teleology, can we speak of a dialectic of the Classical style? First, the relationship of Beethoven to Haydn and Mozart, and Haydn and Mozart with each other, is of course far more complex than that. Haydn and Mozart, although highly individual compositional personalities, constantly learned from each other, and

Haydn outlived the younger man by almost two decades. But a basic difference is that Mozart was born further along the historical timeline toward the conventionalization of the style in the 1780s. Where Haydn's sonata forms tend to be through-composed (his expositions monothematic, his recapitulations extended codas), Mozart's are more schematic, since he works with broader conventional blocks (defined second subjects, literal recapitulations). It is Mozart, according to Rosen, who taught Beethoven to handle large-scale tonal contrast. On the other hand, Beethoven learned his motivic logic from Haydn, a composer who was eighteen at the death of J. S. Bach, and who never shook off the Baroque art of thematic *Fortspinnung*. On chronological grounds alone, then, the two composers slant caesuras in diametrically opposite directions. Mozart, the more Classicized figure, inherits caesura as a force of pattern formation and deploys it as a gestural agent of disclosure, revealing the lyrical materiality subsumed within these patterns. His instrumental technique is of a piece with the operas' rhetoric of comic unmasking. Haydn, who found his creative voice before the historical conventionalization of musical material, scatters caesuras in a general play, in a witty rhetoric of fleeting connections and sudden flashes. When Haydn catches up with conventionalization after the 1780s, in works such as Op. 74, these coalesce into an idiom of tonal illumination, where the tonal system displays itself in instantaneous *Apparitions*.

It goes without saying that Haydn and Mozart were far from the only compositional influences on Beethoven. His Viennese style received nudges from the Paris of Cherubini, the Berlin of C. P. E. Bach, the Mannheim/Swedish style of Joseph Kraus, and the "London Pianoforte School" of Clementi, Cramer, and Dusík.[4] The influence of Muzio Clementi is particularly underestimated and extends to Beethoven's mature thematic practice and architectural thinking, rather than just to the brilliant passagework of the early piano sonatas as Rosen thinks (1972: 22–23, 380). *Pace* Rosen, Anselm Gerhard convincingly argues that late Beethoven's Baroque turn was actually mediated through "late" Clementi's own *Bach-Rezeption,* as evinced in the contrapuntal *Exercises* of his *Gradus ad parnassum,* first published in March 1817 (2002: 235).[5] Moreover, the strong presence of Domenico Scarlatti in Clementi's style recruits Beethoven, at least as a keyboard composer, into an Italian-Spanish-English tradition markedly perpendicular to the Haydn-Mozart axis. Clementi, in short, has the capacity to submit our traditional Viennese-Classical image of Beethoven to a cognitive jolt. All this notwithstanding, Rosen's concentration on Haydn and Mozart as ideal types is persuasive, as is his thesis that their lesser contemporaries "must be seen in the framework of the principles inherent in Haydn's and Mozart's music" (Rosen 1972: 22). There is a long German tradition of evaluating Haydn's and Mozart's stylistic principles as logical oppositions, for example, Haydn's *Entwicklung* and "parataxis," versus Mozart's *Fortspinnung* and "hypotaxis."[6] While bearing in mind the richness of their historical horizon, we continue to conceptualize Haydn and Mozart as exemplary of their epoch, whether as "ideal types" in Max Weber's sociological sense (Gossett 1989; Webster 2004: 49), or as "prototypes" in the current cognitivist discourse (Spitzer 2004: 20). But can Haydn and Mozart's opposition, with its putative resolution in Beethoven, also be considered "dialectical" from an idealist standpoint?

The "Waldstein" Sonata beautifully confirms the synthesis prophesied by its aristocratic namesake, blending Mozart's symmetrical planning and tonal breadth with a through-composed melodic development drawn from Haydn. I touched upon this work in chapter 3, when we considered Adorno's frankly inadequate "Hegelian" analysis. It is now time, finally, to cash in Adorno's so-far unwarranted claim that the sonata instantiates Hegelian logic in tones. The tools are already provided by the established Hegelian tradition of Beethoven analysis. But I want to approach this task via the mutation of caesura in accordance with a shift from Haydn and Mozart's rhythmic paradigm to the melodic, dynamic paradigm discussed in chapter 7. Just as the rationale for musical form changed from articulation to developmental process, so caesura becomes a matter not of interruption but of *negation*. And with negation comes a different order of *Apparition,* taking us back to the origins of this concept in Hegel's notion of *Erscheinung* (Appearance), as explained in the glossary in chapter 2. The Hegelian flash of insight illuminates not structure or material, but origins and goals. Actually, the situation is predictably more complex than that. Looking at the first page of the "Waldstein," Haydn and Mozart's grid of articulation is still there in its Classicizing skeleton. The new order of caesura supervenes upon and coexists with the old, rather than displacing it, just as Hegelian philosophy assimilates and sublates Kant. Once again, we are dealing with a counterpoint of paradigms: the Classical caesura handed down to Beethoven, versus Beethoven's caesura *of* the Classical.

Whereas Adorno's *Apparition* is directed toward the visionary quality of artistic aura, and Hegel uses *Erscheinung* mostly as a category of logic, the gap between these kindred concepts narrows when we consider dialectical logic *within* artworks. This is why, in my analysis of Beethoven's Hegelian style, I subsume *Erscheinung* within *Apparition.* What "appears" in Hegelian logic is the reality of the world in all its vivid and circumstantial detail. By positing the "manifest-ness" of nature, and its continuity with surface phenomena, Hegel is reversing Kant's notion of an essentially hidden, transcendental realm of the "thing in itself." There is no reality underlying semblance—or at least none which can be differentiated from it. *Schein* is both surface and depth. This continuity is borne out in musical terms by the all-embracing dynamic paradigm by which middle Beethoven collapses the form/content distinction on which Classical articulation depends. Musical *Apparition* (*Erscheinung*) in the age of Beethoven and Hegel entails two orders of "seeing": the flash which reveals, first, the part "as" motivated by the whole, and, second, the artificial convention "as" emergent from—*appearing* out of—the expressive substance ("Essence") of the piece. In his *Science of Logic,* Hegel refers to these two orders as, respectively, "The Relation of Whole and Parts" and "The Relation of Outer and Inner," and they very roughly correspond to our understanding that a musical work is organically unified and socially mediated. Such understanding tends to happen both gradually and in qualitative leaps, and there is a famous passage in Hegel's *Phenomenology of Spirit*—actually referenced in Adorno's Beethoven monograph—where Hegel interweaves a variety of breakthrough metaphors: "The bud vanishes as the bloom bursts forth"; the "child's first breath [which] interrupts the gradual, merely cumulative process"; "the evolving mind slowly and quietly ripens toward the new form"; and "this gradual crumbling . . . is interrupted by the sudden flash which reveals the image of the new world" (208). When Adorno reworks Hegel's categories, he exploits *Erscheinung*'s multiple meanings. The surface appearance of a work (*Schein*) is an active appearing (*Erscheinung*), a process which originates in a previous state and is on the way to becoming another state. Third, *Erscheinung* is the dawning recognition, in the mind of the beholder, of the (interlinked) whole/part and outer/inner mediations. And fourth, it is the fact that this metaphoric "seeing as" effect is itself an illusion (*Schein*), and thus open to a further *Durchbruch* of a reality principle which shatters this mirage. Seen in this light, the breakthrough of the late style is implicated ineluctably within the heroic style's Hegelian character.

Musical *Apparition* must be studied in the context of what Janet Schmalfeldt (1995) has aptly called the "Beethoven-Hegelian" tradition of music theory. This tradition perhaps originates with Friedrich Schlegel's trenchant formulation of the "music as philosophy" model: "There is a tendency of all pure instrumental music toward philosophy . . . Is the theme in it not as developed, confirmed, varied and contrasted as the object of meditation in a sequence of philosophical ideas?" (in Bowie 1990: 201). Beethoven's critics, assuming a yet more holistic position, have perennially heard the form, content, and process of his works to be unified in the expression of an "underlying idea" (Dahlhaus 1991: 143). Louis Schlösser alleged in 1885 that sixty-two years earlier Beethoven personally told him that he composed by allowing a "zugrunde liegende Idee" to germinate and grow in his imagination, "so that it rises, grows tall, [so that] I hear and see the image in my mind in its entire extent, as if cast in a single mold" (quoted ibid.) That Schlösser's claim was probably fabricated does not in the least stop it from sounding the keynote of a "Beethoven-Hegelian" tradition which extends from Hoffmann, A. B. Marx, and Halm through Schoenberg and Schenker, Adorno, Ratz, and Dahlhaus, up to present-day theorists such as Schmalfeldt and William Caplin. All are united in seeing the music as a logical and self-reflective unfolding of an argument. Nevertheless, two distinct lines are discernible within this tradition, just as there are not one but two Hegels—a "left" and a "right"—which take their cue from the two moments of the dialectic, negation and synthesis. For a musical passage to be grasped contextually, its immediate (i.e., nonmediated) aspect needs to be canceled: the positive is negated. Synthesis is the moment when the negated impression is incorporated into a broader context. The emphasis can duly fall on either one of these moments. We can hear the music "from left to right" as an endless process of self-negation, as one repeatedly reinterprets the piece in the light of its unfolding. Or we can proceed, "right to left," from the endpoint of the present situation, whereby Beethoven ends up confirming handed-down Classical conventions. So too the "left Hegel" of the early *Phenomenology of Spirit* foregrounds the infinite striving of self-consciousness, while the "right Hegel" of the later texts is politically reactionary, insofar as he rationalizes the Prussian status quo as historically necessary. Although *The Science of Logic* is not a political text, Hegel's endeavor in this work to codify philosophy into a set of well-defined logical categories presumes that philosophy has reaches a high summit, from which the thinker can survey the terrain. A comparably static viewpoint informs the "right Hegelian" tradition of Schoenberg, Ratz, and Caplin, which systematizes phrase structure according to the logical patterns of identity and contrast, enshrined in normative categories such as sentence and period. "Left Hegelians" such as Dahlhaus and Schmalfeldt prefer to see formal functions not as stable entities ("positivities"), but as expressions of a thematic process undergoing developing variation. Actually, both "left" and "right" orientations, the developmental and the normative, are implicit within Schoenberg's theory of the *Grundgestalt*, the inheritor of A. B. Marx's Hegelian *Idee* (see Burnham 1990; 1997). And, going back to the eighteenth century, the duality ultimately flows from the antinomy of musical form as both "conformational" and "generative" (see Bonds 1991). So, after comparing Schmalfeldt's "leftist" orientation with Caplin's "rightist," I will pull them back together by looking at the "Waldstein" as arguably Beethoven's most satisfying synthesis.

Developing variation, the technique which Beethoven worked out at the time of the three Op. 31 sonatas and the *Eroica* Variations Op. 35, embodies the spiral-like character of Hegelian dialectic as a mixture of departure (negation) and modified return (synthesis). Building on Dahlhaus's work on the "Tempest" Sonata, Op. 31, no. 2, in D minor, Schmalfeldt (1995) argues that the dialectic emerges from the problematic relationship of the two-measure Largo introduction to the four-measure Allegro consequent phrase (ex. 8.2). Again and again as the work proceeds, the listener is forced to reassess the function of this Allegro theme, each revision engendering a new flash of insight. First, the Allegro sounds like an answer, complementing the Largo's rise to A with a fall to D. Second, the Allegro ends up reinforcing the Largo, dressing up the progression to A as a compressed sentence phrase (two-measure statement, a one-measure continuation, and a cadence). Third, since the sentence ends unconventionally on the dominant (instead of a close or half-close on the tonic), the phrase becomes an antecedent phrase of a period when the Largo-and-Allegro pair recur after m. 7 (Schmalfeldt sees mm. 13–20 as a cadentially extended consequent phrase). Fourth, the entire material, mm. 1–20, is revealed as introductory to the "real" theme of m. 21, which synthesizes the arpeggios, scales, and turn figures of both Largo and Allegro into a single gestalt. Fifth, this passage starts with the tonal solidity and thematic profile of a proper beginning, but its identity is undercut as soon as we realize that it is actually the transition to the second group. The cycle of reinterpretation continues throughout the rest of the movement, confirming Dahlhaus's thesis that form in Beethoven's is a process of Becoming. Form only makes sense retrospectively, and ultimately from the movement's endpoint. On the way to this endpoint, each juncture (caesura) opens up a new perspective, a fresh *Apparition*. Beethoven's *Apparitions* triangulate the part/whole and inner/outer orders. From one perspective, the moment in time is defined by its context. From another, the "inner" game of the dialectic miraculously squares with the "outer" set of conventions Beethoven has inherited from the Classical style. For all its sui generis negativity, the sonata finds its way to confirm the normative sonata schema, so that the music's conventional surface is heard

Example 8.2. Beethoven, Piano Sonata in D Minor, Op. 31, no. 2 ("Tempest"), first movement, mm. 1–24

Continues on the next page

Example 8.2. Beethoven, Piano Sonata in D Minor, Op. 31, no. 2 ("Tempest"), first movement, mm. 1–24

to *appear* from within its expressive depths. The listener colludes in Beethoven's illusion that Classical conventions are freely invented. What the listener "sees" (the *Apparition*) is the coming into being (*Apparition*) of the surface (*Apparition*). That this illusion (*Apparition*) is ripe for deconstruction will bring the late-style critique in its train.

Coming from the "right," Caplin (1998) idealizes convention in an opposite way: not deriving it from a dialectic of developing variation, but from a normative set of logical categories.[7] The opening sentence-phrase of Beethoven's first sonata, Op. 2, no. 1, in F minor, as much a locus classicus as the "Tempest," introduces Caplin's adaptation of Schoenberg and Ratz's *Formenlehre* (ex. 8.3):

Example 8.3. Piano Sonata in F minor, Op. 2, no. 1, first movement, mm. 1–8

"Presentation," the first of the three quasi-Hegelian functions which make up the sentence, consists of a statement and repetition of a two-measure "basic idea." Its "continuation" fragments this basic idea so as to detach and repeat the turn figure in its second half ("motive b"). The third function, which concludes the sentence, is a half cadence. The most interesting point about Caplin's interpretation is his claim that, at the end of the phrase, the continuation and cadential functions, the developmental and the conventional, *fuse*. In fact, the phrase can be seen, dialectically, as a move from the normative to the particular, followed by a synthesis. Beethoven's presentation phrase (mm. 1–4) is an instantiation of a Classical convention called a "Mannheim Rocket" (as in Mozart's C-major String Quintet, K. 515; see Agawu 1991: 88). The continuation phrase (mm. 5–6) focuses on the characteristic turn motive at its end. We may say that the function of the turn motive has changed. From being an abstract syntactic marker, functionally inflecting the phrase, it becomes the starting point for a motivic sequence which focuses on its particular identity. So far, then, the music has moved "inwards," in Hegelian terms, from the socially conventional to the aesthetically particular. The third function, cadence, marks a synthetic stage in this process, which both carries the motivic stretto forward to a climax and harks back, in a circular manner, to the grammaticality of the opening. To a certain extent, the end of the theme bears out Schoenberg's classic notion of "liquidation," which is "to strip the basic idea of its characteristic features, thus leaving the merely conventionalized ones for the cadence" (Caplin 1998: 11). Nevertheless, Caplin adds that the thematic stretto *continues into* the cadential descent, that the falling scale in mm. 7–8 takes the accelerating phrase rhythm of the A♭–B♭–C rising scale to its climax and reverses it. While descending scales of this type are extremely typical (as in the Schenkerian *Urlinie*), the thematic discourse creates an illusion that they are *motivated,* in both a causal and thematic sense, by Beethoven's characteristic material. Once again, as with the "Tempest," the characteristic is *identified* with the conventional or, as Caplin puts it: "the two functions of continuation and cadential normally *fuse* into a single 'continuation phrase' in the eight-measure sentence" (11). The phrase thus unfolds a "three-stage rhythm" of convention, expression, and a convention/expression hybrid. A similar three-stage rhythm is staked out across the level of the exposition as a whole, which Caplin defines as a succession of three "interthematic functions," respectively, "main theme," "transition," and "subordinate theme" (17).[8] Main themes are accordingly presentation; transitions, like continuation phrases, are developmental; and subordinate themes are hybrid, performing both a thematic and broadly cadential function. From a Hegelian perspective, the confluence of the developmental with the cadential at the end of Beethoven's utterances, at rising levels from the phrase to the entire movement, reveals an *Apparition* of the individual "as" the social; or the spiritual "as" the corporeal. The thematic *subject* gradually comes into its own as a formally embodied, socially contextualized, *subjectivity.* This course of animation builds on Mozart and Haydn's trajectory toward the recuperated particular. But the heroic style changes the paradigm of the caesura from the poetic to the anthropomorphic: in Hegel's words, "the child's first breath." What appears, then, is the *heroic subject.*

The "Waldstein" as Synthesis

The opening phrase of Beethoven's "Waldstein" Sonata elegantly blends left-and-right Hegelian orientations into a sentence in developing variation (ex. A.11, see appendix). From the right, the sentence comprises a repeated four-measure presentation (mm. 1–8), followed by a four-measure consequent which fuses continuation and cadence (mm. 9–12). The figurations in mm. 9–11 are hybrid, being both cadential and a development of the sixteenth-note motive of m. 3. This cadenza-like passage thus "appears" in a double perspective as expressively free and conventionally articulative. From the left, Beethoven fills the sentence with a narrative of evolving consciousness, which will be seized by Adorno as the optimum example of Hegelian phenomenology in the musical literature. The music may begin on a C-major triad, but the F♯ of m. 2 suggests a IV–I progression in G. The B♭ of m. 5, a true *Durchbruch,* shatters that impression, and when it resolves down to A in the next measure, the listener grasps mm. 1–8 as a sequential repetition of IV–I, respectively, on G and F. It is only when the bass A moves through A♭ to G for the V^7 chord of m. 9 that the full C-major perspective is revealed. A sense of C as tonal center properly arrives with this V^7, and the preceding G and F regions are retrospectively reinterpreted within that centered perspective. As a consequence, the C-major triad at m. 14 is perceived quite differently from the one at the beginning (over and above the changed texture). The music's phenomenal "center" thus shifts dialectically, but perfectly in line with the overarching sentence form. And both left and right *Apparitions* meld at the climax of mm. 9–11, when we "see" the cadence as thematic, and the opening as part of a whole.

This process is staked out on a grander scale across the transition and subordinate theme. The second subject at m. 35, exactly as the cadence from m. 9, is the focus for two converging *Apparitions;* indeed, the conformity between these two moments bespeaks an extraordinary unity between the local and global dimensions of Beethoven's sonata. The first *Apparition* is that of the new theme itself, which emerges gradually out of the cloud of sixteenth-note figures in the transition (mm. 23–30). The subject is a *Durchbruch* of the thematic out of the blankly conventional. The cadential figures in the transition are conventional enough to fit within *any* piece; indeed, it comprises a virtually note-for-note transposition of the equivalent passage in Beethoven's Second Symphony (mm. 61–70). On the other hand, it is easy to see that the theme's falling and rising lines clearly derive from the cadential figures' zigzagging (diminished) fifth progressions in mm. 23–26, which in turn stem from the cadence of mm. 9–11, which itself flows from the opening. Step by step, then, Beethoven leads us from the first subject, through the sixteenth notes of the cadence at m. 9 and the tremolo da capo of the theme at m. 14, to the transition and then to the second subject. He makes us "see" each step of the journey as connected, the parts determined by the whole, the conventional identical with the thematic, and the first subject related to the second.

By "rhyming" the cadence of m. 9 with the second subject, Beethoven merely dramatizes an axiom of sonata form: the function of the dominant group as a higher-level cadence. Of course, the "Waldstein" is famous for substituting the dominant with a mediant. E major is not merely a coloristic key; rather, it is functionally prepared by a transition, and properly balanced in the reprise by a complementary move to the submediant A. By metaphorically identifying the mediant "as" a dominant, Beethoven opens up a fresh set of tonal interconnections. The music's opening gambit, the bass resolution C–B, becomes reinterpreted from V^7–I in G to an augmented sixth preparation for V of E at m. 22. At a gestural level too, it is possible to hear the relationship between the first and second subjects as encapsulated in the "up-beat" quality of the opening eighth-note repetitions of mm. 1–2, which resolve to the structural downbeat of the G at m. 3. Compared to the prevailing anapaestic (short-short-long) patterns of the first group, the dactylic second subject (long-short-short) sounds like a long-term resolution. The G♯ of m. 35 is thus a complex metaphor for the G♮ at m. 3: a "return" as well as a point of maximum remove, a functional analogue as much as a metrical/formal completion. Beethoven seems to marry Mozart's sensibility for thematic and tonal contrast with Haydn's predilection for the monothematic and monotonal. Even so, while being the locus for a fantastically elaborate set of unities, the G/G♯ identity is also a dissonance, which reminds us of the *force* underpinning Beethoven's system. The third "essential relation" of Hegel's *Apparition* (Appearance), which I have yet to mention, is "The Relation of Force and Its Expression." *Apparitions* erupt with force, and they are forcefully motivated. Our object thus becomes the force with which Beethoven contrives his various identities, and the force which is explosively released when these unravel.

A moment of unraveling comes in the awkward lurch from A major to C major in the recapitulation of the second subject (ex. 8.4):

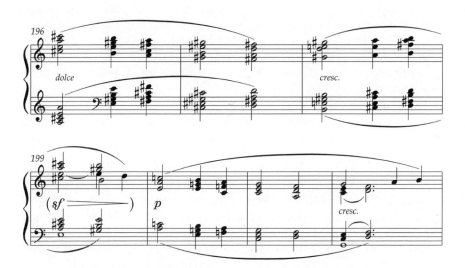

Example 8.4. Reprise of second subject

The consequent phrase ought to represent the work's rhetorical goal—its ultimate point of release. This is the case with Op. 110, Op. 130, or Op. 131/vii, all of which recapitulate the opening phrase of the second group twice, first in the distant key, then in the tonic (see Spitzer 1996). In Op. 110, for example, Beethoven brings back the second subject initially in E, or F♭, major (mm. 76–77), before sliding back into A♭ via the characteristic *Rückung* progression at the end of m. 77. Rather than functionally mediating the E major and tonic phrases, the chromatic slide sets the two tonalities apart so that they shine (*Schein*). Such abruptness would have been out of place in a middle-period work like the "Waldstein." Its consequent phrase fulfills two roles. On the one hand, it brings back the tonic step by step, with a mobility of function which recalls, *in nuce,* the protean tonality of the work's opening. Beethoven introduces the note C♯ in the context of an A-minor triad (m. 200); then a C-major chord as a local dominant of F (m. 201); then as a weak $^6_4$ C chord hinting at C major (m. 202); finally, C major as a confirmed tonic key (m. 203). On the other hand, the striking "white-key" music of this transitional phrase projects a contrast of modal genus in relation to the chromatically bright A-major antecedent. The sanctimonious modal harmonies of mm. 200–202 anticipate the more rarified idiom of the *Heiliger Dankgesang.* Resolution, then, comes both *within* the transitional phrase, as idiomatically contrasting, and *through* it, with the arrival of the figured variation at m. 204. The "Waldstein"'s ultimate point of tonic release is thus spread across two junctures, whereas Opp. 110, 130, and 131 are arguably clearer in reserving it for the second group's tonic repetition. If the "Waldstein"'s reprise is a "fudge," then it flows from Beethoven's compositional dilemma in seeking to reconcile the conflicting entailments of his experiment with dominant substitutes. From one standpoint, goal-directed heroic works accentuate their moment of recapitulation, which is their center of gravity. And yet extended tonality undermines this climax by deferring true resolution to the reprise of the second subject. Beethoven compromises by displacing resolution to the middle of this reprise. Approaching the heroic style as part of a lifelong compositional problematic rather than as an achieved perfection leaves open the possibility that some problems were solved in the late style. This is to give the late style a positive, as well as negative, aspect.

Several deconstructive turns are deducible from this conundrum. Reversing the received view, we may conclude that late works are sometimes more coherent than middle ones. Listening to an ostensibly unified work like the "Waldstein" with deconstructive ears suggests that lateness can be an ontological as well as historical quality, inhering in music of all times. That is, syntactic breaches—figures of "lateness"—may be immanent within Beethoven's music prior to the late style. Such conjectures elicit a different kind of *Apparition* altogether: the *Apparition* of disunity. An ear cocked for the cracks and fissures in the landscape moves the caesura one step along, to a third critical turn. Beethoven's third style, his late style, is a caesura of his caesura of the Classical style. On the one hand, this lateness inheres in the corpus of works composed in Beethoven's last decade. On the other hand, the late works educate us to grasp "lateness" as a function of the analytical enterprise itself—a shadow of its illumination. The *Apparition* of lateness, from this perspective, is universal, and not confined to the music of 1817–1827. Perhaps the most sober way to express this paradox is to say, after Adorno, that the late works are "extreme cases" of general tendencies. Lateness, as a modality of perception epitomized in Beethoven's late style, will be my closing topic in this chapter. Extending chapter 3's discussion of allegory into Kantian territory, I will call this modality the "allegorical sublime."

The Third Turn

The Death of Beethoven: Caesura as Sublime Resistance

Beethoven died during a thunderstorm, shaking his fist at nature:

> After Beethoven had lain unconscious, the death-rattle in his throat from 3 o'clock in the afternoon till after 5, there came a flash of lightning accompanied by a violent clap of thunder, which garishly illuminated the death-chamber. After this unexpected phenomenon of nature, which startled me greatly, Beethoven opened his eyes, lifted his right hand and looked up for several seconds with his fist clenched and a very serious, threatening expression as if he wanted to say: "Inimical powers, I defy you! Away with you! God is with me!" . . . When he let the raised hand sink to the bed, his eyes closed half-way. (Thayer 1964: 1050–51)

Or at least according to Anselm Hüttenbrenner, who along with Therese van Beethoven, the composer's sister-in-law, was one of the two witnesses at the death. Hüttenbrenner's ventriloquism of Beethoven's gesture ("as if he wanted to say . . . ") may strike us today as absurdly melodramatic, but it does conform to how his contemporaries viewed him, and to a central topos of Beethoven reception in the last two centuries. The composer's resistance to nature epitomizes the human freedom at the root of Enlightenment models of subjectivity. Yet an opposite strand of this same tradition seizes on Beethoven's much-chronicled *rapport* with nature, as in his alleged remarks to the London harp manufacturer Stumpf in 1824: "I must refresh myself in unspoilt nature, and wash my mind pure again . . . Here, surrounded by the products of nature, I often sit for hours at a time, and my senses feast in the contemplation of nature's children" (Schleuning 1998: 207). Nature, as echoed in these two quotations, shows us two faces: as an expressive force, and as a principle of contemplation. Riezler, for whom Beethoven was, quoting Kant's definition of genius, "die gestaltende Kraft der Natur selber" (1936: 261), ends his book marveling how the composer sublimely reconciles the force with the contemplation:

> Even when Beethoven seems to have lost all self-control, and to have worked himself up into the wildest frenzy, he sees the world with eyes that are as clear as ever. But he is not afraid to draw aside the curtain that veils the abyss. He knows no fear of chaos, out of which matter is made form, because he is aware of his power to give form to all that his eyes have seen. (261)

Beethoven's "frenzy" is one of articulation; the "shaken fist" is the rhythmic paradigm of the Classical style, imposed with willful defiance. Beethoven's late style, seen in the broadest terms as a Classicizing style, is an act of sublime withstanding against the death of the Classical style itself. We get to the heart of what Hölderlin calls "the rhythm of the hymn as objection" (341). The rhythms of the late style are an objection against death. It is appropriate, therefore, that Riezler is referring to the trio of the last quartet, Op. 135, the middle of which features a storm in the pastoral tradition of the Sixth Symphony, exploding (*hineinbrechen*), as Riezler eloquently noted, "like a bolt from the blue into the calm and unconstrained ease of the movement" (261). This is Beethoven's most violent music, yet it is compounded almost entirely of a madly reiterated cadence—the locus classicus of the Classical style. Each iteration is a gesture of "objection" (ex. 8.5):

Example 8.5. String Quartet in F, Op. 135, second movement, mm. 144–50

In the face of such controlled violence, one can perhaps only marvel, else fumble for an analysis. How can any analysis ever be adequate to the experience of the late style? Or to any style at all? To return to Schleiermacher's dictum, which serves as the watchword for this entire book: "there can be no concept of a style." But analysis can also be "sublime," as an enterprise of defiant withstanding subject to what Andrew Bowie aptly terms "the hermeneutic imperative," the ethical drive to grapple with the world, despite the lack of any apparent rules:

> Given the impossibility of complete self-transparency and the fact of one's ability both to grasp the world cognitively and to re-articulate the world in an individual manner, the hermeneutic imperative becomes perhaps the most vital imperative in the Romantic conception of a modernity which can no longer appeal to absolute foundations. (Bowie 1997: 89)

The imperative to grasp the style is the counter-side to the "deconstructive hearing" elicited by the "Waldstein": together they comprise the two sides of the late style considered as a modality of listening. Moreover, *pace* Bowie's farewell to "absolute foundations," analytical listening *does* in fact have a guide: in the shape of the sublimity of the music itself, of which it partakes. As I argued with the Ninth, music may be said to conceptualize and analyze itself, given the tradition (started by Sulzer) of thinking of musical form (epitomized by a pattern of beats, or *caesuras*) as a concept. The hammer blows of the Ninth's final cadence conceptualize and "embrace" the whole symphony into its cycle. In framing itself, under enormous pressure, music such as the Ode to Joy and the trio of Op. 135 mimics, and surpasses, what theory is unable to do. Or rather, music does it *better,* and thereby functions as an ideal for theory. Our being aware of the contingency and force of interpretation is thus not a self-destructive insight, or the beginning of a deconstructive infinite regress, but the very condition of a true aesthetic understanding. Certainly, "there can be no concept of a style." Yet, on account of its form, *a style may have concepts.*

My analytical engagement with Beethoven's late style begins its closing cadences here, the endgame proceeding in three moves. First, I do want to attempt an analysis of the trio of Op. 135, because I think the way the music frames itself is paradigmatic for understanding the late style as a whole. Given the parenthetical nature of this, and perhaps all, analysis, it seems appropriate to interpolate it under erasure (*sous rature*) between lemata, to follow two common conceits of Derrida's.[9] With that, my treatment of Beethoven's notes comes to an end. Second, I will conclude this chapter by sketching an "ethic" of the allegorical sublime, which places Beethoven's gestures of "opposition" in their aesthetic context. Third, this context finds its broadest horizon in the final chapter, where I suggest a rapprochement between critical theory and the current "communication model."

The piece is not quite so "calm" as Riezler thinks, since the rebarbative E♭'s which famously interrupt the two strains of the scherzo can perhaps be heard as rumbles of the thunder to come. That is, if the E♭'s are caesuras on the local level, then the trio is very much the global caesura of the entire quartet, according to Hölderlin's unitary definition. The trio's 135 measures are almost exactly twice the size of the scherzo's sixty-seven. The lower strings drive their minimalist ostinato for an incredible fifty-one measures, above which the first violin "screams a wild triumphant leaping dance" (Kerman 1967: 360). Such passages were radical enough in the *Grosse Fuge,* but here the shock is all the greater because it emerges from the clear blue sky of a pastoral F major. In the Sixth Symphony, Beethoven had to invent a fifth movement (between movements three and four) in order to fit in the requisite storm. In the quartet, he simply folds the storm into the trio, so that the proportions are literally bursting. Beethoven widens the breach implicit within convention in general, but which is distilled in the dance's schism between formal perfection and lyrical immediacy. The genre of scherzo and trio, which Beethoven inherits from Haydn, focuses this tension most acutely. Its mechanical dance patterns give the storm a surreal clockwork quality. And the genre's concentric construction encloses the storm in multiple circles, as if in a Chinese box.

The violence of the storm seems inversely proportional to the movement's concentric design, which seeks to cage its centrifugal energies with interlocking frames. First, the storm actually breaks only in the middle of the trio, after nearly eighty measures of preamble (note that the outbreak and the modulation are also staggered: A major arrives at m. 123, twenty measures before the storm). Second, the trio is a miniature dance tucked within a minuet or scherzo, which is, third, itself a miniature embedded within a sonata, symphony, or quartet. This is conventionally the nearest Classical form gets to portray the pastoral. Classical trios are typically peasant dances, their bagpipe drones referring as much to the social nature of rural life as the acoustic nature of a fundamental bass (see the inverted C pedals at mm. 8 ff. and 67 ff.). With their static diatonic harmony, they represent nature in a state of rest and purity. Yet, at the same time, no genre was more conventionalized, and hence more artificial, than the dance. Despite its simplicities, the trio is an infinitely malleable sign. The natural can easily become the heroic, the shepherd the revolutionary *sans-coulotte,* as in the astonishing trumpet pedal point which breaks through the trio of the Seventh Symphony. Not only does Beethoven invert the pedal, quite literally: he turns nature 180 degrees from idyllic past to utopian future, so that the *Dudelsack* becomes a Blochian trumpet signal of freedom. Like Benjamin's famous storm of history, which blows *backwards* from Paradise, revolution points us to the futures implicit in Beethoven's first quartet.[10] The reason concerns the unusual key of Op. 135's storm, A major. The key is uncharacteristic of Beethoven, since he prefers to keep his trios in the same key as the main dance. Haydn, by contrast, likes to nest his late trios in a chromatically distant key, emphasizing their interiority (those of his last two quartets are both on the submediant: Op. 77, no. 1, in G has a trio in E♭; Op. 77, no. 2, in F moves to D♭). Beethoven begins as a Beethoven, but veers toward Haydn's practice halfway through the trio, albeit on the mediant. Curiously, in doing so he circles back to Op. 18, no. 1, also in F. The trio of Op. 18 achieves this trick much more succinctly, its first period starting and ending in F, but interpolating a plateau on D♭. With its D♭ parenthesis, the Op. 18 quartet instaurates Beethoven's subgenre of a scherzo with "double trio." The movement is full of many other clever touches, such as reprising the parenthesis at the tritone, on G minor/major, a gambit prepared by the chromatic sequences of the scherzo. But the underlying issue of this "double parenthesis" is one of containment. Here and in the last quartet, the question is whether any such disruptions can *really* be absorbed.

There are moments even in the early music where Beethoven throws the focus on the act of assimilation itself, as in his first Bagatelle, Op. 33. A moment of sheer caprice at m. 21—a miniature "storm"—is gradually converted into an elaboration of the upbeat lead-in (ex. 8.6). Beethoven's conjuring trick, rather than explaining the disruption away, really works to labor the very process of assimilation. Toward the close of his storm in Op. 135, Beethoven seems to challenge us to comprehend it, leading us by the hand, step after step, as one would spell something out to a difficult child. The ostinato is slowed down, ironed out and naturalized, finally merging with the da capo (ex. 8.7).

Like Benjamin Franklin's famous kite, his lightning conductor of 1752, this motivic "red thread" seeks to conduct the trio safely back into the scherzo's firm earth. But all that this achieves is to profile the hermeneutic wire itself, and its pitiful incapacity to truly "explain" anything at all. Actually, analysis can easily construct a narrative to rationalize this trio, starting with the E♭ caesuras of mm. 16–22— rumbles of distant thunder. The jarring "wrong note" which augurs an eventual

Example 8.6. Bagatelle Op. 33, no. 1, mm. 20–26

outbreak is one of Beethoven's favorite gambits (compare with the finale of the Eighth Symphony: the fortissimo C♯ at m. 17 is discharged at m. 379, where it derails the movement into F♯ minor, and a secondary development section which works through the remaining tensions). In Op. 135, the tritone distance between the local and global caesuras (the E♭ interruption and the A-major storm) adds spice to the relationship. Technically, the E♭–E natural resolution of m. 23 is made good when reinterpreted as a D♯–E preparation for A, at m. 111. But this is not quite enough to bridge the E♭–A tritone. It is more helpful to think of the successive modulations of the trio—F to G, and G to A—as filling a gap left by the scherzo's tonal stasis, in particular, the failure of the first strain either to cadence properly (chord IV is frustrated) or to modulate (to V), and its severely truncated development section. E♭ and E natural, the two pitches of mm. 16–24, are traces, or substitutions, of a displaced tonal action. One might have expected a simple sequential progression, a rising or falling "cobbler's patch," as indeed occurs, belatedly, in the scherzo's reprise. The E♭–E♮ step is fleshed out in two distinct progressions: the cadential (I⁷–IV [V⁷]–I, mm. 41–44) and the sequential (VI–II V–I, mm. 44–47), that is, alternately around the subdominant and the supertonic. Both are compensations, respectively for the faulty cadence at mm. 15–16 (the elided subdominant) and the missing tonal action at mm. 17–24 (the missing sequence). The music's logic, then, is retrospective, discharging functional obligations too late. Thus the logic of this discharge is cumulative: two notes (mm. 15–24), then two progres-

Example 8.7. Op.135, second movement, da capo
Continues on the next page

Example 8.7. Op.135, second movement, da capo

sions (mm. 41–47); finally, two modulations (mm. 66–123). The cello's rising scale at mm. 45–46, from D to G, is a crucial link, spawning both the trio's motivic material (rising scales) and the successive rising modulations to G and A. Doing things back to front, if the first half of the trio compensates for the missing development, then the A-major "storm" substitutes for the dominant modulation suspended in the Vivace (as in the "Waldstein," the mediant is literally a dominant substitute). Thinking of the trio as a displaced "dominant" modulation is particularly radical, since Classical trios conventionally *lower* the tension on the flat, subdominant side (a more routine key would have been D♭ major, a flat submediant, as in Haydn's Op. 77, no. 2, in F). Nevertheless, Beethoven motivates this hearing by withholding a dominant modulation from the scherzo. The crucial question, then, is whether we hear A major as a substitution of a dominant, or of a *subdominant* function—by no means, *pace* Rosen (1996: 237–57), a settled matter for nineteenth-century, or neo-Riemannian, harmonic theory.[11] Rosen may be correct in claiming that "the complementary function of dominant and subdominant was almost forgotten by 1830" (257). The point is, however, that in 1826 Op. 135's A major is a locus for a sharply articulated functional ambiguity: a *Schein*-like trembling between IV and V. As we saw in chapter 6, the A is also the focal pitch for the first movement's tensions, and it is pertinent, to look ahead to the finale, that its second group is in A major.

Adding yet a further layer to the storm's ambiguous station, we should note that its ostinato is compounded entirely of cadences, affirmatory V–I (E–F♯–G♯–A) figures. Cadence is another of the scherzo's "lacks" to be filled, in addition to modulation. Of course, these two solutions—the modulation and the cadence—cut across each other: modulation signals departure, cadence expresses return. Although it is the climax of the piece's cumulative logic, the storm discharges the music's energies in conflicting directions, simultaneously affirming and denying. The contradiction ultimately plays out the absurdity of a nature which is clockwork, a storm built from cadences. This is a paradox intrinsic to caesuras: rhythmic gestures both affirm, by creating patterns, and deny, by interrupting them. The paradox is also intrinsic to the artificiality of musical material—especially that which seems the most "natural." To repeat, for all its furious iterations, what this storm of nature hammers out is a conventional formula. Beethoven's greatest caesura of nature is a storm in a rococo teacup.

The Death of Nature, and the Allegorical Sublime

To give them their proper names, the two natures Beethoven wrestled with until the end, the contemplative and the stormy, are indices, respectively, of the beautiful and the sublime—Kant's two major aesthetic categories. Nevertheless, the peculiar compact Beethoven forges between them goes far beyond the aesthetic norms envisaged by Kant or his immediate followers in the early nineteenth century. Sublimity in its classic, Kantian, form describes that intoxicating sense of freedom human subjects feel when they confront, and rationally transcend, overwhelming natural forces. But what happens when the subject's rational autonomy from nature is denied? When nature, in the shape of death, is discerned in the workings of reason itself? In this case, the object being withstood changes from a hostile nature to the meaninglessness of the universe. The category of the sublime mutates under the aegis of modernity. Wellmer captures this distinction between the Kantian and modern sublime, discovering the latter at the core of Adorno's theory of aesthetic beauty:

> The point of entry for the sublime in modern art is not an absolute that cannot be represented (i.e., an absolute in the Kantian sense), but the disappearance of the absolute, the death of God . . . The horrific, the unintelligible, the abyss—these words no longer signify an overpowering, threatening, and infinite nature, which the gaze of the intelligible subject is capable of reducing in stature; rather they signify a natural world that encompasses even the intelligible subject and its historical world. The abyss is an abyss of meaninglessness *in the midst* of a world of linguistic meaning. This abyss signifies a negative absolute, nothingness, the empty place, as it were, which was left by the absolute of metaphysics. For Adorno the name of this negative absolute is death. (Wellmer 1998: 170–71)

Late Beethoven's heroic affirmation of Classical convention, in the very course of denying the Classical principles of formal unity which his own middle-period works had taken to their extreme, fits Wellmer's concept of the modern sublime very well. In particular, the discovery of "meaninglessness," that is, nature, "*in the midst* of a world of linguistic meaning," corresponds to Adorno's account of the late style as *allegorical*. In works such as the trio of Op. 135, nature is discerned in the cracks of the convention, the "storm in the teacup." For this reason, Beethoven's late style could be said to invent the category of the "allegorical sublime," a music written in the face of death.

To end this chapter, I will detail the steps which take us from the Kantian sublime to late Beethoven's "allegorical sublime": (1) the beautiful and sublime as opposing perspectives on nature; (2) the importation of the sublime from nature into artworks, including music (Michaelis); (3) the commuting of the beautiful and sublime into moments of the dialectic of artistic form (Schiller); (4) the affinity of this dialectic with Hegelian idealism; (5) the beautiful and sublime's transformation, in Benjamin's hands, into opposing categories of symbol and allegory; (6) allegory in Adorno as the "nonidentical" which "suspends" the (symbolic/dialectical) unity of artworks and thereby recuperates a nature repressed by society. Finally, (7) I will suggest that by rescuing a fallen nature, Beethoven's allegorical sublime has things to say about the role of the aesthetic in modern life.

Nature is "beautiful" on account of its ordered system of laws. Pre-Kantians had understood this, from the ancient tradition of Universal Harmony, to post-Leibnizian eighteenth-century philosophers such as Wolff. But whereas harmonious part/whole relationships induce a purely *logical* kind of "perfection," pertaining to qualities inhering in the object, Kant psychologizes beauty by commuting it to a cognitive process. Kant's greatest achievement in his aesthetics is to reconcile nature with freedom, two principles which are opposed, given that human dignity consists in rising above nature, and subjectivity defines itself through its critical detachment from the world. Disinterested contemplation of the art object, in its autonomy from interests, purposes, or concepts, becomes an arena for such freedom; it is even freer than the moral sphere, because ethical freedom denies our sensuous side, whereas artistic experience engages the senses. This reconciliation takes the form of a harmonious "play" between the mental faculties of imagination and understanding. Since play occurs not between defined data or concepts themselves, but the faculties which create them, Kant is able to show that art is freely creative and not bound by rigid or even explicable rules: in his famous phrase, it evinces "purposefulness without purpose." Whereas concepts subsume sense impressions in nonaesthetic experience, artistic imagination may be subsumed by the *Verstand* and still remain free. This is how Kant can argue that art may be both pleasurable and rational. We find art pleasurable not so much for itself, but because it stimulates aspects of our mind to function harmoniously.

In its sublimity, by contrast, nature inspires aesthetics not on account of its perceived order but by its seemingly infinite wildness, and Kant cites stock images of "Bold, overhanging, . . . threatening rocks, thunder-clouds piled up the vault of heaven, borne along with flashes and peals, volcanoes in all their violence of destruction," and such like (110). Longinus and Edmund Burke had known of these effects before, but once again Kant's contribution is to internalize the sublime as an aspect of mind. The infinity of sublime nature, since it exceeds our conceptual grasp, appeals instead to our reason, and thereby forces our mind to soar above the natural world and revel in its freedom. Magnitudes which defy experience can often be understood as rational abstractions (such as the *idea* of infinity), and so Kant aptly calls this transcendental category the "mathematical sublime," in contrast to the "dynamic sublime," which is a source of fear. Although nature may be terrifying in its potential danger to the subject, the dynamic sublime affords us a pleasurable sensation of freedom in the resistance of our reason to such a threat. Both of Kant's aesthetic categories are mediated by the mind, but there is a key difference of emphasis: where beauty leads to restful contemplation of the object, the sublime is directed firmly to our power of reason itself. And this leads to an asymmetry in the weighting of the beautiful and sublime. For Kant, they are more or less equal, but for the nineteenth century, the sublime became the prototype of an aesthetic freedom epitomized in Beethovenian *overcoming*.

Kant's distinction between the mathematical and the dynamic is less than clear. In one respect, the latter enshrines the pre-Kantian, Burkean, concept of the sublime as a quality inhering in nature, rather than the *effect* of nature as a stimulus to reason. Confusingly, however, Kant also co-opts the dynamic type as a moment in the course of sublime experience, which sets the mind in motion:

> The mind feels itself set in motion in the representation of the sublime in nature . . . This movement . . . may be compared with a vibration, i.e., with a rapidly alternating repulsion and attraction produced by one and the same Object. (107)

Everything turns on the "finality" of the process, that is, the point at which our quest to grasp nature—and by extension sublime art—reaches cognitive closure: what Kant terms "comprehension in *one* intuition" (102) or "*under* a concept" (103). Presumably, the dynamic sublime is merely a staging post on this path, ascending to the overview commanded by the mathematical. Conversely, it would not be an exaggeration to say that the entirety of post-Kantian aesthetics is an argument as to whether the dynamic sublime is really the end, rather than the means. That is to say, perhaps closure is a dream, and the reality is incessant "vibration," *Schein*'s flicker.

Kant never applied his aesthetics to music, and he was even skeptical about the role of the sublime in the fine arts, which he held ought to be consonant rather than discordant with nature. Yet it is easy to see how the notion of the beautiful is reflected in the formalist compositional theories of Matthesohn and Koch, as well as the pastoral tradition in music. Similarly, when Michaelis, Kant's major musical disciple, attempts to interpret sublime effects as technical procedures, he draws on conventional topics of nature in motion (Webster 1997). Michaelis persuasively polarizes the musical sublime between excessive uniformity and diversity. On the one hand, "Uniformity so great that it almost excludes variety [such as] the constant repetition of the same note or chord." On the other,

> When innumerable impressions succeed each other too rapidly and the mind is too abruptly hurled into the thundering torrent of sounds, or when (as in many polyphonic compositions involving many voices) the themes are developed together in so complex a manner that the imagination cannot easily and calmly integrate the diverse ideas into a coherent whole without strain. (Webster 1997: 62–63)

The closing proviso of the above quotation makes the sublime into an ultimately cognitive impression of incommensurability. Later, Michaelis describes the process in terms which are, as Webster notes, unmistakably Kantian: "Such emotions are aroused as . . . prevent the integration of one's impressions into a coherent whole" (62). All the same, this cognitive orientation sits awkwardly with the attempt to essentialize sublime effects in specific materials. Does the sublime inhere in the object or the subject, in compositional poetics or the hermeneutics of listening? That is, one could well imagine that even "beautiful" materials can be turned to "sublime" account by a Beethoven, as of course happens in Op. 135. The formal definition of the scherzo-and-trio genre is essentially beautiful, but Beethoven folds a storm into the idyll. Conversely, not all musical storms are sublime in the Kantian sense. There is a venerable Baroque theological tradition of associating disturbances in nature with the judgment of a wrathful God, yielding apt musical settings in many of J. S. Bach's cantatas and passions (Schleuning 1998: 59–85). With its explosive broken chords and rushing sixteenth-note figures, the double chorus "Sind Blitze, sind Donner" from the St. Matthew Passion certainly partakes of the *Erhabene* topic (Schleuning, 60–64). But the topic must undergo the cognitive turn of the Classical style to become authentically sublime as an aspect of mind. At this point, paradoxically, the topical correlatives (Michaelis's "torrent of sounds") need no longer be present at all, since sublimity shifts from the textural object to the subjective form.[12]

Much of German aesthetics after Kant was preoccupied with resolving the instability of this object/subject dialectic. The path which led from Kant to Adorno, via such thinkers as Schiller, Hegel, Schlegel, Schleiermacher, Schopenhauer, and Nietzsche, is much too circuitous to be dealt with here. But the thrust of this story is that the beautiful and sublime were conflated in the course of being projected onto aspects of formal structure, so that "sublimity" arose from the resistance of a work's expression to its material; second, this resistance engendered a hermeneutics of unity and, ultimately, *disunity* in the work of Adorno. Schiller, Kant's most gifted pupil, was seminal in applying the sublime to aesthetics, writing widely on the subject (e.g., *Vom Erhabenen*, 1793, and *Über das Erhabene*, 1793–1800). But Schiller's boldest move, in his *Briefe über die ästhetische Erziehung des Menschen* of 1793–94, was to locate sublime resistance in the domain of the beautiful itself, as in his highly influential notion of a conflictual relationship between a "sense drive" (*Stofftrieb*) and a "formal drive" (*Formtrieb*), mediated by a "play impulse" (*Spieltrieb*) (Kinderman 1995: 7–10). In his *Kallias* of 1793, Schiller argues that aesthetic beauty proclaims its freedom by actively resisting and triumphing over its technical form: "For it is precisely when it overcomes the logical nature of its object that beauty shows itself in its greater splendor, and how can it overcome if there is no resistance?" (Miller 1970: 93). Kant's hostile forces of nature now become "heteronymous" forms and techniques inimical to subjectivity, yet essential for artistic expression. Freedom needs rules to kick against. In Hegel's aesthetics, these rules become the butt of a process of artistic "negation," when the artwork internalizes its materials into the expression of an individual "idea." With the dialectic, nature and reason become inseparable components of a journey toward idealist enlightenment.

Once again, a central question for modernist aesthetics is whether this process of resistance, rooted in the Kantian sublime, and interpreted differently by Schiller and Hegel, can ever reach closure in the mind of the reader or listener: whether the artwork is amenable to comprehension, as Kant would say, "in one intuition" and "under a concept," or in Hegel's terms, "synthesized" in the Idea. Adorno's quarrel with Hegel turns on whether one might posit a synthesis at the end of the dialectic. Adorno's "negative dialectic" retains negativity as the engine of thought but dispenses with any resolution, which is why it has been called an "atonal philosophy" (Buck-Morss, 15). Crucial for this development is Benjamin's transformation of the beautiful and sublime—aesthetic categories—into modes of interpretation, alternatively closed or open-ended: the symbolic and the allegorical.

Benjamin's essential insight is that nature and history, far from being abstractly opposed, cross over into each other on the common axis of temporality. With time, history blends into its natural environment through decomposition: "In the process of decay, and in it alone, the events of history shrivel up and become absorbed in the setting" (Benjamin 1998: 179). At the same time, nature, perceived "in the over-ripeness and decay of her creations," rather than "in bud and bloom," is an order of "eternal transience" (179). Allegorical nature-history, conveyed into the domain of language, interprets the arbitrary character of linguistic conventions as a similar intimation of history decaying into nature. Allegory thus rescues a fallen nature by taking artificiality to excess, when language begins to break up and reveals its natural materiality. Adorno, in the *Aesthetic Theory,* detects moments of natural beauty in conventions which have joined their setting: "everything made by man that has congealed into nature is able to become beautiful, luminous from within" (Adorno 1999: 70).

With Adorno comes an extraordinary return of nature into aesthetics, neither as a harmonizing principle nor as an inimical threat, but as a casualty of reason requiring rescue. Recalling Husserl's phenomenological reduction as much as Hölderlin's "anamnesis of repressed nature," Adorno associates "nature" with a sensuous reality which is occluded or repressed by concepts in the world, and conceptual closure in artworks. The natural is an index of particularity, of the nonidentical, the momentary, and the transient, a "standstill" of the dialectic which is both allegorical and sublime:

> Natural beauty is suspended history, a moment of becoming at a standstill. Artworks that resonate with this moment of suspension are those that are justly said to have a feeling for nature. Yet this feeling is—in spite of every affinity to allegorical interpretation—fleeting to the point of déjà vu and is no doubt all the more compelling for its ephemeralness. (71)

When "suspended history" happens within artworks, we sense the allegorical sublime. In Zuidervaart's words, "sublime art suspends itself," and "Beethoven's final string quartets . . . carry the suspension of the artistic totality into artistic form" (1994: 201). Nevertheless, "allegorical sublime" is perhaps too gnomic a name for a tendency which is actually rather pervasive in the current cultural situation. In my next and final chapter, I will argue that this category symbolizes no less than the persistence of critical theory, with the Enlightenment model of subjectivity it predicates, against the perceived death of that model. I will also assert that Beethoven's sublime allegories prefigure the possibility of a rapprochement between this subjectivity model and the intersubjective "communication model" which is often deemed to have replaced it. That we can continue to believe in nature at all in our postmodern age depends on slender rafts of the Medusa such as the trio of Op. 135. No one believes any more that Beethoven's lifeboats safeguard a vision of idealist social utopias. A more sober reading is that they achieve, in musical terms, what has still evaded current Western thought: a harmony of conceptual paradigms.

9   The Persistence of Critical Theory

Critique—Reflection; analysis; genealogy; taking apart; revealing contexts; inter-relating; unmasking; disenchantment; reenchantment; emancipation; foregrounding, resolving, and projecting contradictions; to set ideas in motion; to think.

Critical Theory versus Postmodern Knowledge

Theodor Adorno (1903–1969), philosopher, sociologist, cultural theorist, musicologist, pianist, and composer, was a founding member of the Institut für Sozialforschung and the Frankfurt School. Adorno's affiliation to the Frankfurt School of Critical Theory brought him into contact with a group of radical left-wing thinkers which included Max Horkheimer, Herbert Marcuse, Leo Lowenthal, and Walter Benjamin. His additional association with the Second Viennese School, as a compositional student of Alban Berg, gave his position as critic of aesthetic modernism a unique double-insider status. Although the unusual scope of his interests can be roughly divided between music and philosophy, Adorno felt that his work in both fields reflected essentially a single activity.[1] One could even argue that, rather than applying philosophical concepts to music, the influence actually flowed the other way. According to Susan Buck-Morss, with regard to Adorno's early philosophical writings on the phenomenologist Edmund Husserl,

> Schoenberg's revolution in music provided the inspiration for Adorno's own efforts in philosophy, the model for his major work on Husserl during the thirties. For just as Schoenberg had overthrown tonality, the decaying form of bourgeois music, so Adorno's Husserl study attempted to overthrow idealism, the decaying form of bourgeois philosophy. (Buck-Morss 1977: 15)

By "overthrow idealism" is meant Critical Theory's project of questioning the widely held assumption (epitomized by the Logical Positivists) that "reason" and "science" float calmly above human and social concerns. The perversion, or "reification," of reason in the twentieth century into the alienated world of late capitalism, with its ever-more repressive technologies of control and administration, gave the lie to the central myth of the Enlightenment. Critical theory claims that theory only *becomes* rational when it "critiques," reflects upon, its hidden contexts. That being said, if the model for Adorno's "atonal philosophy" was music, it would be a distortion to explain his critical theory of music as simply the application of "critical theory" *to* music. His approach, rather, was to a large extent also immanent within, and emergent from, the specific materials of the musical discourse. This is why it is useful to look to a musicologically oriented study such as Paddison's essay "Critical Theory and Music" (1996: 1–44) in conjunction with classic overviews such as Raymond Geuss's *The Idea of a Critical Theory* (1999).

Critical theories and scientific theories differ in both aim and method. The goal of scientific theories is "successful manipulation of the external world" via "instrumental reason" (Geuss 1999: 55). Critical theories, by contrast, "aim at emancipation and enlightenment, at making agents aware of hidden coercion, thereby freeing them from that coercion and putting them in a position to determine where their true interests lie" (55). Scientific theories are "objectifying," in that they presume a gap between data and their observer. Critical theories are "reflective," insofar as they are part of the object domain they describe. They are reflective upon the beliefs of society, and critical theorists are themselves members of that society. This presupposes that processes of self-reflection in society and in the individual human subject are *continuous with each other*. Both aspire toward emancipation from repressive practices which foster "false consciousness." By relating notions of "repression" and "false consciousness" in this way, critical theory brings together key ideas of Freud and Marx.

Paddison centers the critical theory *of music* around the debate on musical autonomy. Standard music theory is "objectifying" in that it represses the "social content of music" (Paddison 1996: 23). Paddison quotes Adorno's claim that analytical approaches that "see the thing itself in the actual notes alone" are suffering from a "neutralized consciousness" (in 11). Musical "false consciousness" comes in two chief varieties, the immanent and the contextualist. On the one side, it is a mistake to imagine music as purely immediate; on the other, it is equally wrong to consider it as merely a social or cultural document. The latter also has an epistemological dimension, in that no model can ever be adequate to musical experience, whether this model be formal (analytical) or cultural (musicological). In other words, a musical-critical theory attends both to its implicitly social character *and* to its adequacy to the irreducibly *musical* part of musical experience. It is sensitive, therefore, to the object and subject sides of the equation—the quintessential "dual-character of music: as self-contained, self-referential structure and as social fact" (23). Finally, Paddison situates this argument within the historical origin of autonomous music in the early-to-mid-eighteenth century. Here, the "dual-character" of autonomous music is evinced in the irony that instrumental music became a pure object of contemplation, free from social function and responsibility to textual expression, *at the same time* that it became an object of economic exchange in the musical market: a simultaneous withdrawal from, and assimilation into, the social context. This is expressed in the autonomous musical work's "dual-character" as both aesthetic particular and general type; this, in turn, is reflected in the paradox that even the most authentic works of Haydn, Mozart, and Beethoven are comprised of conventional materials. The nature of musical reality is therefore contradictory, and if it is to do it justice, a critical theory of music must "embrace contradiction methodologically" (15). Unlike "objectifying" music theory, then, a critical music theory is methodologically dialectical and open-ended.[2]

Critical theory springs from the German idealist tradition and has had less impact on Anglo-American musicology than the predominantly French tradition of postmodern theory, associated with writers such as Derrida, Foucault, and Lacan. Critical theory and postmodern theory are divergent responses to modernism, and hence have similarities and differences. Both dismiss the modernist resort of rationalizing the perceived fragmentation and transitoriness of experience in unified representational pictures or "meta-theories" (see Harvey 1990: 44–45). Both embed human subjectivity in objective contexts such as "language," "power," and the "body," thereby rejecting the Enlightenment belief that reason is self-grounding, that a subject can be "self-present." And both question the ability of contemporary art to afford a critical distance on the status quo, since even the artwork has become totally infected by the commodity culture of late capitalism.

The main differences stem from issues of periodization: critical theory is continuous, albeit critically so, with the Enlightenment, and this means that the priority of the subject, although problematic in practice, is sustained in principle as an *idea*. By contrast, postmodernism, especially in the many forms of poststructuralist thought, breaks cleanly with the past by predicating subjectivity on philosophies of language (Derrida's deconstructionism is the prime example). Fragmentation for critical theory is sustained by the Utopian hope of an unspecified future reconciliation; postmodernism is relaxed about the existence of multiple worlds, plural ontologies, competing "interpretive communities." It gives up on the ideal of global social or rational consensus in favor of local and relativistic pragmatics. There are many other shades of difference, which have been surveyed with particular energy by Jameson (1991). For example, postmodernism outgrows "four depth models" (9–10) which characterize modernist thought (essence/appearance, latent/manifest, authenticity/inauthenticity, signifier/signified), in favor of the depthless imagery of "the logic of the simulacrum" (from TV pictures to Andy Warhol). The most *important* difference, however, is political: one can either resist the postmodern condition, as critical theory tries to do, or embrace it enthusiastically:

> Every position on postmodernism in culture—whether apologia or stigmatization— is also at one and the same time, and *necessarily*, an implicitly or explicitly political stance on the nature of multinational capitalism today. (3)

Characteristic of this dispute is that postmodern and critical theories each try to depict the other as reactionary. Jameson thus points out that critical theory still clings to the old model of capitalism based on industrial production, in the face of the new "world space of multinational Capital" (54). In view of this change, the high-modernist notion of a frontier between "high culture" and so-called mass or commercial culture is no longer tenable. Instead, this "new space" of postmodernism cannot be resisted and must rather form a "framework and precondition" (50) even for politically engaged artworks.

From the perspective of critical theory, however, it is *postmodernism* which is reactionary, in that it entails a historically retrograde step which undoes all the essential achievements of the European Enlightenment. Despite its profound skepticism, critical theory never abandons its commitment to the critical and Utopian power of Enlightenment thought, nor to its faith in the autonomy of the human subject. This commitment is upheld especially in those "second-generation" critical theorists who came after Adorno, such as Jürgen Habermas, Karl-Otto Apel, and Albrecht Wellmer. In Habermas's shrewd phrase, theorists who appeal to "post-modernity" are really "cloaking their complicity with the venerable tradition of counter-Enlightenment in the garb of post-Enlightenment" (1987: 5). This is critical theory's double bind: a faith in the *idea* of reason married to skepticism toward its reality or even possibility.

The battle lines between critical theory and postmodernism are drawn around two key positions: first, the notion that the "postmodern condition," *pace* sympathetic commentators such as Lyotard, Jameson, and Harvey, can be actively resisted; second, that the key to such resistance is precisely the pivot within the Adornian "double bind": the idea of the work of art. Art functions within Adorno's system as the paradigm for an emancipated rationality, a noncoercive form of truth toward which conceptual reason ought to aspire. In essence, the debate between Adorno and postmodernity turns on the relationship between art and truth. Postmodern theory, for which "philosophy" is just another mode of "literature" or "writing," relativizes and aestheticizes truth. It demonstrates that reason is characterized by the same sort of tropological tricks present in art. By contrast, critical theory argues for a clear separation between aesthetics and philosophy, as different spheres of thought. The details of this separation form the arena for much debate in contemporary theory, proceeding from Kant's originary demarcation of human interests into the three spheres of reason, morality, and aesthetics (the three Critiques of pure reason, applied reason, and judgment). It is notable in this regard that second-generation critical theorists tend to enforce this separation somewhat hermetically, in what is surely a postwar reaction to the Nazis' aestheticization of politics. By contrast, Adorno held that the opposition between art and philosophy is not schematic but dialectical: each "completes" the other in the course of negating it. Philosophy articulates truths intuited in art, while art captures a kind of truth beyond philosophy's grasp. This view is by definition self-contradictory, or, to use Adorno's favored Kantian parlance, "antinomic." Adorno develops it into an "antinomy of modern aesthetics."

It must be said, before we enter into these issues more deeply, that the complexity of Adorno's dialectical method is consistently misrepresented by postmodernism's most eloquent defender in musicology, Lawrence Kramer (1995: see especially 1, 14–15). The rigid oppositions (between subject and object, fact and value, mediation and immediacy, music and language) which Kramer imputes to the "hard epistemology" (3) of critical theory are actually of his own making. Adorno's categories are every bit—and more—"historically relativized" as those Kramer requires of the New Musicology. Ironically, this accusation of schematism rebounds squarely on "postmodern knowledge" itself, with its overly simplistic portrayal of musical autonomy.

The Antinomy of Modern Aesthetics

Adorno's dialectical model of how art and truth relate to each other blends two distinct streams of traditional aesthetics which Christoph Menke (1999: vii–

xiii) identifies, respectively, as "autonomy" and "sovereignty." "Autonomy" follows Kant's irreducibility thesis, presented in his *Critique of Judgment*. According to Kant, art is "autonomous" insofar as it follows its own inner logic. Although it works side by side with other spheres of human experience, art is essentially *irreducible* to these spheres, on pain of losing its identity and freedom as art. Kant's notion of artistic autonomy assisted at the birth of music aesthetics as a distinct area of study, fully worthy of "disinterested" attention. In music, Kant's ideas gave rise to a theory of musical formalism, articulated most clearly in the nineteenth century by Hanslick in his *Vom Musikalisch-Schönen* (1854). Kant's most recent serious exponent is Roger Scruton, whose ambitious *The Aesthetics of Music* (1999) is conversant with the huge advances in music-analytical thinking that have been achieved since Hanslick's day.

To talk of "sovereignty," by contrast, is to claim not only that artistic expression trespasses on social and philosophical domains, but that it deals with these matters *better*. This is an argument associated with the Romantic philosophy of Schelling, Novalis, and Friedrich Schlegel, and to some extent also with Hegelian idealism. Art is *sovereign* to philosophy since it can express a form of truth unavailable to abstract modes of thought. Art also has a politically Utopian dimension when it points to an ideal of social reconciliation, as it does so powerfully in much of Beethoven's music. This notion that music has a content in excess of Hanslick's "forms moved in sounding" has been characterized by Lydia Goehr as "enhanced formalism" (1998). "Enhanced formalism" is evinced in the hermeneutic interpretations of A. B. Marx and Wagner, and it is the ancestor of our recent tendency, following Lawrence Kramer, to analyze musical structure in terms of "cultural tropes."

The paradox, or "antinomy," at the heart of Adorno's aesthetics is his attempt to bolt autonomy and sovereignty together. It is precisely due to its *autonomy* that art can criticize reason, can exercise *sovereignty* over it. Menke calls this irresolvable tension, a tension which keeps artistic cognition mobile, "aesthetic negativity." Problematic though it may be, the antinomy of modern aesthetics cannot be resolved in favor of either of its extremes. Each pole taken by itself leads to a nostalgic yearning for varieties of aesthetic engagement which have become outmoded: a desiccated objectivism on the one side, an ideological subjectivism on the other. Aesthetics becomes objectivist when art is cut loose from human concerns and reified. It turns ideological when we overburden art with truth claims which are alien to its nature, moreover, with a *type* of truth which is suspiciously metaphysical.

Interestingly, Schenkerism—the canonic music-theoretical approach of the late twentieth century—has been attacked from both positions, and sometimes, as in Joseph Kerman's case, by the same author. Kerman's *Contemplating Music* (1985) finds no contradiction between, on the one hand, advocating a contextualist, humane "criticism" over the "abstraction" of Schenkerian analysis (hence: sovereignty), and, on the other, criticizing the "ideology of organicism" intrinsic to Schenker's theories (see also Kerman 1980). Schenker's organicist ideology is just as often attacked, however, by proponents of autonomy, especially in its recent manifestation as cognitive or psychologically oriented music theory (see Narmour 1992; Lerdahl 1996). A recent example of this debate is Pieter Van den Toorn's polemic against Leo Treitler's *Music and the Historical Imagination* (1989). Treitler's book sought to nudge critical scrutiny away from positivist analysis toward its historical and sociopolitical dimensions. Van den Toorn (1995) objects that this endeavor conflicts with the immediacy of aural experience, thereby removing music's capacity to suggest alternative worlds. In one respect, Van den Toorn's position is impeccably Adornian, in that it attacks the depredations that "tax relief measures and a severe recession" have inflicted on "'technical' knowledge in music education" in California (2). This dissolution of technical literacy is hardly helped by "the strategy of the New Musicologists, that of promoting appreciation by encouraging more and more interdisciplinary study." "Increasingly," claims Van den Toorn, "Western art music will be transformed into something artificial, be experienced secondhand as an artifact apart from itself, as a way of understanding, if not those other disciplines, then larger cultural issues" (2). Van den Toorn's defense of music's "immediacy," however welcome, is nevertheless in breach of music's antinomic (or "dual," in Paddison's phrase) character. Alastair Williams, in his incisive review of the Treitler/Van den Toorn debate, rightly observes that *both* critics in fact fall foul of an overly rigid distinction "between immanent and contextual approaches to music" (1998: 285), whereas the strength of Adorno's theory is to interrelate these positions dialectically.

New Musicology, the music-theoretical analogue of postmodern philosophy, tries to outwit this antinomy by rejecting its premises. It escapes formalism by embedding music analysis in the full spectrum of cultural practice, appealing to a range of postmodern discourses (see Kramer 1995: 1–25). It refutes idealism by denying that there is anything especially transcendent about music ("Immediacy becomes a performative effect"; Kramer, 17), and, by an opposite token, by leveling off the difference between "art" and supposedly nonaesthetic modes of language or experience ("[Immediacy's] truth says nothing special about music. Language cannot capture musical experience because it cannot capture any experience whatsoever, including the experience of language itself"; Kramer, 18). Yet the result is that the aesthetic and nonaesthetic are assimilated to each other, to the detriment of both. Aesthetic experience is reduced to social or cultural discourses; social or cultural discourses are aestheticized. The casualties are, respectively, a notion of art's particularity, and a notion of "truth" which would provide the postmodern condition with an external perspective on itself.

Adorno's philosophical aesthetics gets round this problem by keeping immanent and contextual approaches, or autonomy and sovereignty, constantly in play in a "mediated immediacy." Many of Adorno's critics see his notion of "mediated immediacy" as arising from a rebarbative fusion of Kant's transcendentalism with a historical materialism stemming from Hegel and Marx. According to Geuss, "One way of putting Adorno's final position is that autonomy and formalism are not a priori properties of all art and of all artistic experience, as Kant thought, but historical features that have developed in contingent ways" (1998: 311). In other words, the privilege of experiencing autonomous art is socially conditioned and hard-won—and worth fighting for if current social conditions militate against it. Adorno's signal insight for musicology is that this battle is carried through into the musical material—in short, that music's relationship with "the world" is implicated with the *inter*-relationships of musical form: the internal dynamics of musical material. Adorno was basically the only first-rank philosopher who took an interest in the *form* of music, rather than just the general *trope* of "Music" with a capital letter. This interest led him ineluctably to the forms of Beethoven.

The Autonomy and Sovereignty of Beethoven

Music is the most autonomous art. In the late eighteenth century, musical material finally shook free from the dictates of text and ritual and began to follow its own immanent laws of organization (see Goehr 1992). Yet the more it retreated into itself, the more music chimed with the patterns that govern thought, language, economic exchange, and social dynamics. A conventionalized musical structure, since the content it subsumes can be exchanged without loss of meaning, resembles (a) the abstraction of a concept, (b) the normativity of syntax, (c) the fungibility of a commodity, and (d) the order of a bureaucratically administered society. Music, then, is also the sovereign art. This, in a nutshell, is the antinomy of enlightened music. Adorno believed that Beethoven embodied this antinomy at its most extreme. Historically, this is borne out by the fact that Beethoven is claimed by both the formalism of Hanslick and the expressionism of Wagner; he is not only the "God" of motivic unity but also the "hero" of the countless Utopian plots of musical Romanticism.

Virtually the entirety of Adorno's critique of Beethoven—a critique which Adorno reckons is implicit within the late style's own reflection on the Classical style—flows from the fact of this four-fold congruence between the music and its contexts (rational, linguistic, economic, and social) and the problematic nature of this apparent synthesis. The "Beethoven synthesis," as it were, looks virtually unique from our vantage point a century after the end of the common-practice period; it goes a long way to explain Beethoven's preeminence in the canon (see Burnham 1995). Adorno's purpose in problematizing this synthesis is neither obscurantist nor debunking. Rather, by focusing on the tensions in the harmony, he aims to celebrate Beethoven's achievement as a product of effort, of human labor, instead of as something "natural" or inevitable. This is a vital point: removing Beethoven from our "imaginary museum of musical works" has nothing to do with the voguish canard that "genius" is merely a figment of reception history, by which case Beethoven is simply the lucky recipient of political investment, and is in principle no better than Cherubini or Spohr (see DeNora 1995). On the contrary, it is to shift the weight back onto the shoulders of the "artist as laborer," to switch our critical focus from the discourse of reception to the realities of production. And this brings us to the much-misunderstood question of Adorno's Marxist credentials (for an instance of this misunderstanding, see Klumpenhouwer 2001). Classical Marxism views art as part of the cultural "superstructure," far removed from the economic base of society. Adorno's unusual preoccupation with musical form and technique nicely recuperates the original Latin meaning of opus as *work*. The artwork is no static configuration; it is humanly situated in space and time. According to Lambert Zuidervaart, technique is Adorno's "tertium comparationis," containing the "primary code for deciphering links among musical production, the economic base, and the social formation" (1994: 105). Adorno's Marxist perspective foregrounds the processive and material aspects of music. Crucially, music's "materiality" is theorized in *aesthetic* terms, rather than through any vulgar appeal to social realism, as in the (late) Lukácsian party line of Eastern Block aesthetics in the 1950s. Hence Adorno's concern with allegory as the central aesthetic category of Beethoven's late style. Allegory is historical, arbitrary, artificial, and opaque. Its contrary, symbol, is synchronic, motivated, natural, and transparent. Adorno's dispute with traditional aesthetics is very much a quarrel between allegory and symbol.

Adorno's affiliation with Hegelian dialectic, albeit in its "negative" form, is equally misunderstood. Dialectic—a generally discredited term today—has a wider purview than is suggested by its frequent caricature as a rigid ternary formula of "thesis-antithesis-synthesis." More broadly than that, it signifies the essentially fluid character of Adorno's mode of argument, in which concepts and categories are set in motion to the point where it is impossible to pin them down according to fixed definitions. Every received notion, upon closer inspection, flips over into its opposite, and this engenders a retrospective reinterpretation of the premise, ad infinitum. As an example of dialectic in action, consider the four main aspects of the Beethoven synthesis in terms of an order of derivation. Pursuing the circle of Adorno's thought will widen our exposition of his theory; it will also put some distance between his dialectical method and more "objectifying" (in Geuss's phrase) or scientific approaches (such as much semiotic and music theory) in which categories and oppositions are neatly carved up.

The rise of musical autonomy is commonly portrayed as a retreat from language (see Neubauer 1986). A Classical sonata hangs together through a play of forms and has no need for a text to validate its integrity. Yet far from confirming music's withdrawal from the world, such autonomy is only possible through economic factors: developments in capitalism which produced a bourgeois class capable of contemplating or "consuming" music *in itself*. Musical material betrays its economic underpinnings in the way the circulation of its ideas mimics the exchange value of commodities. On the other hand, in music this exchange value is reconciled with the "use value" of aesthetic particularity: an artwork is valuable precisely because it cannot be exchanged; it is unique. Aesthetic particularity has cognitive implications, since the "meaning" of an artwork can never be exhausted by interpretation, or adequately modeled by a theory. It is in this respect that art critiques society. "Critique" is a misleading word, because it suggests the anthropomorphizing of art into a political agent. Art is *critical*, rather, because it is a sphere of value or truth which provides observers with an external perspective on society. Here, art's cognitive negativity (its resistance to interpretation) enables it to resist being neutralized by the "culture industry"; unlike "mere" entertainment, authentic art doesn't "sell out." Nevertheless, art effects this critique not by cutting off all links. If art had nothing in common with us, how then could we understand it? Hence its critique is *immanent*—assimilating aspects of the world so as to negate them from within. Art's material is accordingly split (again, dialectically) into contextual and immanent levels. On the contextual side, music imitates language. Yes, autonomous music has been emancipated from text proper. Yet it internalizes the *character* of language (see Adorno 1992b) in the form of syntax, lexicon, and periodicity (see Ratner 1980). On the immanent side, this same "language character" can look like a *concept* character. Musical patterns are analogous to concepts, since form subsumes content just as mental concepts subsume sensory experience. Moreover, music can argue, pursue a logical chain, develop a motivic "idea." Or an "idea" in a broader sense can encompass an entire piece and make sense of its parts. This "idea," more generally, suggests the wholeness of a human subject who reflects upon her own thinking. Reflection itself has both a rational (immanent) and a social (contextual) dimension. Rational "reflection" in music is repetition or recapitulation—a temporally advanced statement "reflects" upon a previous statement. But reflection also has a worldly side, and Adorno (following Hegel) subscribes to the modern view that consciousness is constituted through the subject's interaction with objective reality, that is, other people. In musical terms, "social reality" is the sedimentation of compositional practices in musical conventions, conceived by Adorno as objectifications of human consciousness rather than as abstract schemata. A composer's thought is thus *mediated* through his dialogue with (musical) society, and this in turn is mediated in his dialogue with inherited musical techniques. Beethoven comes on the scene after Haydn and Mozart have already developed these conventions. Yet he makes it seem as if they can arise naturally from his unique musical thought processes. We are back, then, at our starting point of musical autonomy, but viewed now through several orders of reflection. We have seen, further, how the individual terms of Adorno's constellation of "culture, polity, and economy" (Zuidervaart 1994: 19) are mediated through each other within his rich concept of the artwork and can hardly be considered as separable categories.

As a process, a dialectic is subject to time, and this means that it is ultimately grounded in the temporal unfolding of history. Any circle of thought takes place against the broader background of the history of human consciousness in its overall progression toward freedom. Whether or not we accept this Hegelian elision of logic and history, it is at least obvious that there is something historically contingent about Beethoven's music; for example, it would be difficult to accept a piece written in Beethoven's style today as anything other than pastiche. But Adorno gives this historicism a philosophical gloss with his claim that aesthetic sovereignty, epitomized in Beethoven's music, was only *possible* in the early nineteenth century. Adorno reads this otherwise contentious diagnosis from the state of musical material, and it is indeed remarkable how Beethoven strikes a seemingly unique balance between the claims of musical logic and the requirements of conventionally ordained communication. Beethoven is aesthetically authentic, yet widely accessible. After Beethoven, logic and communication drift apart, climaxing in Schoen-bergian serialism with a style which is both maximally organized and totally alien-ated from the public. In Schoenberg, the antinomies which had such positive issue in Beethoven become frankly dissonant. "The Antinomy of Modern Music," a chapter from Adorno's *Philosophy of Modern Music*, pairs Schoenberg's alienation and Beethoven's idealism as philosophical and historical antipodes:

> The material transformation of those elements responsible for expression in music, which—according to Schoenberg—has taken place uninterruptedly throughout the entire history of music, has today become so radical that the possibility of expression itself comes into question . . . The mere idea of humanity, or of a better world, no longer has any sway over mankind—though it is precisely this which lies at the heart of Beethoven's opera. (19)

Adorno's baleful narrative is told from the standpoint of aesthetic modernism. The modern artwork (Schoenberg's atonality, Picasso's cubism, Kafka's elliptical prose) evinces the historical character of artistic material at its most extreme. By Adorno's lights, it is thus valid to illuminate the general tendency from its extreme cases. The problem with this approach—if it is indeed a problem—is that it collapses the his-torical narrative into a synchronic model of aesthetic authenticity (see Subotnik 1978). Adorno extrapolates musical modernism backwards to Mahler, to Liszt, to Beethoven, to Bach, each of whom is judged to be "modernist" *avant la lettre*. So the aesthetic stringency which characterizes "modernist," or authentic, art, is ulti-mately an *aesthetic* rather than historical quality, and it is epitomized by the notion of allegory. Adorno is as likely to speak of the allegorical in Beethoven as he is in Wagner or Kafka.

The historical and aesthetic poles of Adorno's thought remain in tension. A symptom of this is his tendency to elide the processual character of aesthetic unity into disunity *tout court*. From one angle, the synthesis of an *Eroica* can look com-pelling. With a flick of the modernist light switch, it seems questionable. Adorno tries to have it both ways. On the one hand, he needs the synthesis of Beethoven's middle-period style as a "positive" counterpole to the "negative" Schoenberg. On the other, he suspects the miraculous "fit" of art, language, logic, and mass appeal in Beethoven of being illusory, rhetoric without substance, effected through force. Such force is heard most nakedly at the extremes of Beethoven's achievement: in moments of supreme authority, as at the point of recapitulation of the great sym-phonies, but also in works of empty showmanship, like the populist *Wellington's Victory. Wellingtons Sieg oder die Schlacht bei Vittoria* (1813), an anti-modernist extreme case which distills the *Eroica*'s ideals into ideology, draws in its wake the authentically modernist *Hammerklavier* just five years later. The temptation to in-fer that Beethoven's late style critiques his heroic style is irresistible. But by what tortuous dialectic do we get from Beethoven's Enlightenment to the endgame of Mann's novel, where the Schoenbergian Adrian Leverkühn "takes back" the Ninth Symphony? To answer this question, we must examine more carefully what Haber-mas memorably terms "the philosophical discourse of modernity."

Dialectic of Enlightenment

Critical theory basically deals with how objects go into concepts; specifically, the tragedy that "objects do not go into their concepts without leaving a remainder" (Adorno 1990: 5). Percepts are shoehorned into concepts only under duress, since there is always something left over—hence the complicity between reason and power (or reason and force). This complicity was manifest to Adorno most dramatically by the way science and technology are so often co-opted by forces of political oppression. There can be no such thing as a politically neutral theory. At one level, to "critique" reason for Adorno is to expose the secret interests and power claims lurking beneath theories which purport to be objective or even "natural." At a far more radical level, however, the possibility of critique is itself denied, since reason is coercive through and through. In these (but not all) respects, Adornian critique parallels Derridean deconstruction. As with postmodern and poststructuralist theory, Adorno wonders from what perspective one could ever reflect on the limits of rationality, given that the mechanics of such a reflection are part of the problem? Jürgen Habermas, the foremost member of the "second-generation" critical theorists, names this aporia the Enlightenment's "second-order reflectiveness": "The drama of enlightenment first arrives at its climax when ideology critique *itself* comes under suspicion of not producing (any more) truths—and the enlightenment attains second-order reflectiveness" (1987: 116). But how did this "drama" begin?

Habermas defines "modernity" as a critical attitude toward models (1987: 8). It is also a crisis of grounding. With the fading authority of the religious and feudal world, the late eighteenth century needed to generate fresh normative standards of judgment on the basis of human reason alone. We call this crisis the Enlightenment. Adorno's critical theory is a rejection of the Enlightenment, or, paradoxically, an attempt to safeguard the "Enlightenment Project" by critiquing its operative assumption: the efficacy of reason. This endeavor may sound circular, or self-defeating. It is best understood by realizing that modernity is actually comprised of not one but two narratives, a rational and a social, which more and more pulled apart from each other. The first is a conceptual horizon—a way of theorizing the workings of mind—which originated in the epochal writings of Kant and Hegel. The second is the increasing rationalization of society, registered in growing bureaucratic administration and the rise of science and technology. It would seem, initially, that these two streams shared the common interest of the "demythologization" of an enchanted world, to use the terms of the sociologist Max Weber. We are emancipated from magic and myth by controlling nature through "instrumental reason" (purposive rationality). Adorno and Horkheimer (1989) locate a tragic irony at the heart of the Enlightenment: that domination of external nature is achieved at the cost of a repression of internal nature. This is registered in the fact that the "administered" world can coerce or alienate people, and that science and technology can be turned to barbaric ends. Hence the mythical, or natural, forces which the Enlightenment was supposed to free us from return with a vengeance in the shape of modern technology and bureaucracy. In musical terms, this paradox is evinced in the modern-day split between the rationalization of musical material in "high" art, and the commodification of artworks into exchangeable (fungible) products in the culture industry (entertainment). The autonomy which began by liberating music ends up alienating it; the public is as "alienated" from serialism as it is from state bureaucracy.

Although the philosophical and sociological streams are fairly distinct, Adorno takes the radical step of conflating them. The disaster of "stream 2" (the sociological) is extrapolated into "stream 1" (the philosophical) in order to critique reason itself. Much of Adorno's thought is rooted in a critique of Hegel and Kant—or more precisely, in a critique of Hegel's critique of Kant. It might not be immediately obvious what relevance these two eighteenth-century philosophers can have for us today. Nevertheless, Kant—arguably the foremost Western thinker since Aristotle—has never really gone away, and Hegel, after a long eclipse in the Anglo-American tradition, has leapt back to life in the work of contemporary philosophers such as Charles Taylor and Robert Brandom.[3] From an Adornian perspective, the ongoing importance of German idealism is connected to the persistence of Beethoven's appeal. In some ways, Beethoven could be said to contain the *truth* of Kant and Hegel. For Adorno's Beethoven critique to make clearer sense, we need a short digest of the idealist debate.

Kant had grounded reason in a subject's capacity for judgment and reflection. Kant's "Copernican revolution" entails a leap of freedom, since human certainty no longer depends on the "positivities" of dogma for validation. Hegel, in the dialectical spirit, both rejects and completes Kant's project. In brief, he swallows it whole, but puts it on a social and historical footing. Hegel grasps that the achievement of reflective freedom must be understood in the historical context of a need to regenerate the sort of integrative function previously fulfilled by myth and religion. At issue is the reconciliation of human reason and nature, or subjectivity and the objects of experience. Kant had argued for a separation between cognition and reality—that we can have no knowledge of things "in themselves," only as they appear to us. Indeed, such separation is even *constitutive* of our freedom. This separation is denied by Hegel; by the very fact that the subject/object opposition is conceived by consciousness, it can be overcome by consciousness. What makes this possible is the natural dynamic of self-reflection: the mind's ability to take itself as object. Objectifying oneself in the course of thinking ("I know that I know that I know . . . ") is no different from reflecting on the objects in the world. Hence the enlightenment we achieve through self-reflection is played out within and dependent upon a narrative of social emancipation: the historical and intellectual (or "phenomenological," as Hegel puts it) are two feet on the same march toward freedom.

A crucial result of Hegel's critique of Kant is that reason's aspect changes from the formal to the developmental. Kant had analyzed mind into its formal components: categories, concepts, ideas, and intuitions; analytical and synthetic judgment; apperception, schematism, productive imagination, and pure reason itself. With Hegel, these divisions are reconciled—are literally comprehended—as part of an ongoing process of reflection. The unifying concept is *negativity*. Everything that is the case is merely a point on a developmental curve between coming into being and passing away, with each successive "moment" *negating* the previous. To philosophize, then, is to expose ostensible "positive" dogmas or institutions as contingent, thus converting the positive into the negative.

Music theory is comfortable with the holism of this approach; the notion that material is heard processively, either as part of a motivic discourse, or the unfolding of voice leading, is basic to the discipline. But there is a signal difference: whereas synthesis is valid aesthetically—we are dealing with whole artworks—it is problematic in philosophy. Where or when, exactly, does philosophical synthesis arrive? Hegel is careful never to stipulate a goal; the endpoint of reason is transcendental, not historical. Nevertheless, it is difficult to avoid the conclusion that the goal is identified politically with the Prussian state as Hegel found it in the 1820s, a nondemocratic monarchy (for a more charitable interpretation, see Singer 2001: 54–59). Thus for Hegel, "the real is the true." This is the major sticking point for Adorno who, in the second of this *Three Hegel Studies,* writes: "More than any other of his teachings, that of the rationality of the real seems to contradict the experience of reality" (1993b: 85). Accordingly, Hegel's mantra is reversed by Adorno into "The whole is the untrue" (87). What began as a radical philosophy of negativity with the *Phenomenology of Spirit* (written against the backdrop of the French Revolution) congeals, with later works such as *The Philosophy of Right,* into a reactionary justification of the status quo.

If a final synthesis cannot be stipulated, then it can hardly explain, or resolve, a previous contradiction. And this can be extrapolated back to each of the preceding steps of the dialectic as well. This is the heart of Adorno's contention against Hegel. Accordingly, Adorno's "negative dialectics" seeks to preserve the negativity of Hegel's procedure but *without* synthesis. On a logical, as well as historical, level, synthesis (as defined by Hegel) makes no sense, since it seeks to subsume the particularity of experience within a general concept. We now see why Adorno feeds the social critique he lodges against "strand 2"—the social side of modernization—into the operations of reason itself. We also see why Habermas calls Adorno's critical theory a "second-order reflectiveness," by which "doubt reaches out to include reason" (1987: 116). The Kant-Hegel-Adorno dialectic unfolds in three steps: (1) Kant critiques dogmatism, (2) Hegel critiques the dogmatism inherent in the rigidity of Kant's own presuppositions, (3) Adorno critiques the totalizing impulse inherent in Hegel's drive to make every particular accountable to an overarching context. This same "three-step shuffle," as it were, is mirrored also in the unfolding of the Classical style. The formalism of Haydn and Mozart is "Kantian"; the developmental style of middle Beethoven is "Hegelian"; late Beethoven critiques Hegelian logic just like Adorno. Notice the subtlety of Adorno's argument. He is not *comparing* Beethoven to Hegel. The similarity is not a comparison but a reality— "not an analogy but the thing itself" (1998a: 11), or even, according to the third Hegel study, "an analogue which transcends mere analogy" (1993b: 136).

Adorno's split notion of "analogy," blending difference and identity, is yet another aspect of his critical theory of mimesis. Music (Beethoven) imitates philosophy (Hegel)—as it mimics language, subjectivity, and nature—only so as to critique it. Yet this dialectic is potentially short-circuited when we critically reflect on the validity of Adorno's position itself. We do well to remember that Adorno was always controversial, and has become even more so with the onset of new philosophical orientations since his death. Indeed, Habermas talks of Adorno very much in the past tense, as a philosopher downstream from the Dialectic of Enlightenment's present course. It would be dangerous, therefore, to identity Beethoven's fortunes too strongly with the philosopher, unless, twisting the latter's *bon mot* about Hegel, we simply conclude that "Beethoven is really more Adornian than Adorno" (1998a: 160). Beethoven could be said, perhaps, to contain the truth of Adorno.

Beethoven and the Intersubjectivity Paradigm

This study has drawn nourishment from Adorno's ideas. But to do them greater justice, we need to understand, first, why they have been attacked by recent proponents of critical theory, and second, why these attacks are not as serious as they first seem. Second-generation critical theorists such as Habermas, Apel, and Wellmer propose an "intersubjectivity paradigm," rejecting Adorno's "subjectivity paradigm." Late Beethoven, through the lens of Adorno's model, suggests the persistence of the older paradigm in alliance with the new.

Adorno's vision of a critical theory endlessly reflecting on reason's situated and contingent character can seem pessimistic at best, and at worst self-defeating or incoherent. Totalized self-critique appears to trap us in an endgame from which there is no escape, other than the "micrological" freeze-frame analysis of "metaphysics at the time of its fall" announced at the end of *Negative Dialectics* (1990: 408). It is a position scabrously parodied by Georg Lukács as "Grand Hotel Abyss": Adorno has "taken up residence . . . in a beautiful hotel, equipped with every comfort, on the edge of an abyss," daily contemplated "between excellent meals" (Lukács 1988: 22). A lighter analogy is Douglas Adams's 1980 science-fiction novel *The Restaurant at the End of the Universe*, where diners overlook an indefinitely suspended Cosmic Crunch. Adorno, from Lukács's grimmer standpoint in communist East Germany, denies the efficacy of free and rational communication, while enjoying the luxuries afforded by Western liberal democracy. In Apel's terms, he is committing a "performative self-contradiction" (1998: 21), along with all the other "end of philosophy" philosophers (Wittgenstein, Derrida, et al.). The way out of this endgame is offered by the second-generation critical theorists, with their new intersubjectivity paradigm.

That language and society are a medium for reason can be a positive as well as negative fact. The difference turns on how reason is defined. While Adorno's paradigm for reason is that of subjective self-reflection, the generation of critical theorists who followed him espoused what Habermas calls "intersubjective communicative action," paralleling developments in pragmatic and analytic philosophy across the Atlantic (Habermas 1987: 297–327). Reason is here no longer conceived in terms of a subject's relationship to an object, a situation which Adorno (and Derrida) demonstrated leads either to a coerced remainder, or to an infinite regress. Rather, reason can occur performatively, in the way people recognize, respect, and understand each other in an uncoerced speech situation. The pronomial "I-Thou" intersubjective speech situation is for Habermas the paradigm for language; by contrast, language for Adorno is primarily the fit of concepts to precepts experienced by a single subject. Similarly, Habermas can recuperate the normative content of modernity without needing to appeal either to received tradition or to idealist abstractions such as *Geist*. The ideal which underwrites social practice is ultimately that of free communicative action, a situation which may not obtain in the present state of affairs, but one which can be striven for. Extending Habermas's emancipatory model to the foundations of "truth" itself, Apel calls this ideal "the transcendental-semiotic" (Apel 1998: 60). Following Peirce, Apel proposes that the language game of argumentative discourse is also built on a pragmatic foundation: certain presuppositions shared by the community of scientists and all truth-seekers, such as a respect for "phenomenal evidence, logical consistency and theoretical coherence" (57). The same protocols apply within the community of musical scholars, legitimating the dignity of music theory as a professional discipline, and putting its search for musical truth content on an intersubjective footing within that discipline. From a transcendental-semiotic standpoint, the frequently voiced charge that music theory has left the lay listener behind because it is too abstract, that it renounces "a viable public discourse about classical music" (Kramer 1995: 4), simply has no substance.[4]

I think a focus on Beethoven's late style has the power to cushion the force of these objections to Adorno's thought. Adorno's emphasis on the music's *allegorical* character foregrounds the role of convention, and convention is social and therefore intersubjective. Of course, one could criticize Adorno for adulterating convention's intersubjective aspects with the subjectivity model intrinsic to the Austro-German musical tradition: that is, Adorno considers late-style allegory against the horizon of personal experience, in terms of an individual subject's relationship to time and history. He is interested in the *subject's* experience of intersubjectivity. A more positive interpretation, however, identifies not compromise but reconciliation, insofar as Adorno suggests ways in which the two paradigms might be brought together. A failing of second-generation critical theory is its insufficient attention to aesthetics, particularly to art's productive role in society. It is so concerned to differentiate and circumscribe the separate spheres of science, society, and art, with their distinct rules and validity claims, that their interactions can be underexplored. To be sure, problems can often arise when spheres are confused, distortions caused by "the aestheticizing, or the scientizing, or the moralizing of particular domains of life" (Habermas 1987: 340). On the other hand, the differentiation thesis is flatly contradicted by the mimetic quality of Beethoven's music. The thrust of this book has been to show how Beethoven's late style imitates convention, subjectivity, and nature, crossing and recrossing these domains in dialectical spirals. Taking this argument one final step further, I want to suggest three ways in which this dialectic can also encompass the intersubjectivity paradigm. Externally, the music affords an ideal for the institutional interactions Habermas desires of a well-regulated society. Internally, it predicates style as the exercise of a performative skill on the part of the listener, continuous with the skills she uses in social negotiations. Finally, the dialectic between these two axes themselves creates a sublime tension, where the sublimity of the music can be socially regenerative. I here continue my discussion of the "allegorical sublime" in chapter 8, and develop Wellmer's important thesis that the sublime gives art and society an opening into each other.

In the first case, the dynamic relationship between the three styles I have explored—Style 1, Style 2, Style 3—corresponds also to the free and open dialectic between the three Kantian spheres (cognitive, moral, aesthetic) as embodied in social domains and institutions. It evokes Habermas's vision of a liberal democratic society as a coordination of functionally specialized subsystems (the market economy, the administrative state, the private life world), each pulling their separate ways, yet held together by what he beguilingly calls a "virtual center of self-understanding" (Habermas 1987: 359). What is this "center"? Habermas's account is intriguing, since it puts us in mind of the aesthetic sphere he notoriously neglects, and most of all, perhaps, of the virtual centers we have explored in works such as Beethoven's Op. 132:

> This center is, of course, a projection, but it is an effective one. The polycentric projections of the totality—which anticipate, outdo, and incorporate one another—generate competing centers. Even collective identities dance back and forth in the flux of interpretations, and are actually more suited to the image of a fragile network than to that of a stable center of self-reflection. (359)

Beethoven's late style helps us imagine "centers of self-reflection" in the flux of the world. It also constitutes a center by its very existence: a social enclave, sheltered from that world, where we can reflect.

In the second respect, social experience can be intrinsic to the aesthetic contemplation of music, notwithstanding its private dimension. Listening to complex music is a skill which has to be learnt. It requires an ability to handle conventions in harmony with our sensual and intellectual faculties, mirroring our negotiations with the various worldly spheres. In its holistic engagement with our entire person, the most challenging music involves us in the creation of its meaning, partaking of the performative and interactive aspects of the intersubjectivity paradigm. An intersubjective "I-Thou" relationship obtains not only between the players of a string quartet, its role taking of "listening" and "speaking," or in the trace of conversation inscribed within its materials (Wheelock 1992: 90), but also in the quartet's dialogue with its listener. And yet, crucially, music affords listeners an opportunity to practice these performative and interactive skills more harmoniously than is currently possible in the world. Paradoxically, it is *music* which prefigures Habermas's "ideal speech situation," an insight which updates Adorno's thesis that music is a sounding symbol for an absent absolute, social harmony, and the reconciliation of the subject with nature.[5]

In fact, performativity is already implicit within the processual character of Adorno's "aesthetic negativity," in Menke's reading. It is also present in Nicholsen's interpretation of Adorno's concept of "exact imagination" (*exakte Phantasie*), which is arguably the crux of his theory of aesthetic experience. According to Nicholsen, exact imagination describes a kind of attention which is faithful to aesthetic objects in all their particular detail (Nicholsen 1997: 4–5). Such attention is both sensuous and intellectual, thereby critiquing the separation of these two modes of experience. It is both passive and dynamic, requiring immersion in the object, but also an act of effort, concentration and memory, even love. Exact imagination is processual: we literally *follow* a work, tracking its tensions and motions (Adorno uses words such as *mitvollziehen, nachvollziehen, nachfahren*). Thus it is a kind of miming, or imitation, through which we even make ourselves similar to our object. This bodily yielding, this tendency to lose ourselves in our environment which is characteristic of mimesis, is hereby enacted in the listening process—what Taussig, after Freud, calls "ideational mimetics."[6] Hence the mimetic activity of exact imagination lets us hear music as an inner performance, recomposed by the ear. In Adorno's words, the experience of music "finds its ideal form in a mute internal experience" (17). This is a much more nuanced form of mimesis than music's various analogies with the world. "Aesthetic experience is *mimetic*," according to Menke, "because in it we internally reenact—within the play of forces of understanding— the process by which the dimensions of this aesthetic understanding are related to one another" (Menke 1999: 98).

In the third and last respect, a relation obtains between these "external" and "internal" forms of mimesis (of intersubjectivity). The classical Adornian position already deconstructs the neat art/society division staked out by Habermas. Adorno's point is that, though exact imagination is oriented toward the object of attention, the space and leisure to exercise such attention can only be sanctioned by a culture well-disposed toward the contemplative. To the extent that complex aesthetic works such as late-Beethoven quartets resist easy listening, they carve out a social space necessary for their understanding. But to the converse extent that contemplating Beethoven is even possible in today's world, his music can be heard to celebrate that freedom as a performative act—a freedom that *we* perform when we engage with the music. If Beethoven's message is freedom, then the message is the medium. Indeed, it is the continuing possibility of this medium. In its small yet crucial way, listening to late Beethoven can be an act of social affirmation. We do well to bring out this affirmative aspect of Adorno's thought, given his stress on the critical and resistant. This affirmative aspect opens up common ground with thinkers such as Habermas.

The social, then, is intrinsic to music as a quarry of conventions, as we have seen, but also as the precondition for the very understanding of these conventions. Furthermore, there is a way in which the social element inscribed within musical convention kicks back to inspire society at large, and this recalls our discussion of the "allegorical sublime" in chapter 8. By sublimely projecting its enabling conventions, Beethoven's late style teaches us to uphold a social paradigm which makes the reception of this music even possible, indeed, to affirm the paradigm as an act of individual self-fashioning and resistance to nature. Intersubjectivity is thereby subjectively upheld. Wellmer provides the key to such an interpretation, by means of a persuasive reading of Adorno's *Aesthetic Theory* in terms of a theory of communication (Wellmer 1998). Of all the major second-generation critical theorists, Wellmer is the most sensitive to the intersubjective model's bearing on aesthetic questions.

Adorno's theory of the sublime differs from Kant's, as we saw, by collapsing the distinction between the empirical and transcendental self. Adorno demonstrates that even reason partakes of nature, in the shape of the material and the mortal. Since nature is generalized, the key sublime act of "withstanding" (*Standhalten*) thereby changes, from reason transcending nature, to the subject's standing firm against a meaningless, that is, postmetaphysical, universe. Wellmer's important essay "Adorno, Modernity, and the Sublime" (1998: 155–81) takes the concept one step further, updating Adorno's sublime for an intersubjective paradigm. According to Wellmer's "stereoscopic" reading (160), withstanding happens on either side of the art/society divide, in a mutual relationship which unites the aesthetic and intersubjective sublime as two aspects of a single process. On the side of art, a modernist text such as Samuel Beckett's *Endgame* turns the death of metaphysics into aesthetic capital; it is "an aesthetic construction of meaninglessness . . . an act of withstanding the negativity of the world, and therefore a paradigm of the sublime" (170). From this perspective, art continues to intimate the absolute, albeit "veiled in black" (157), thereby securing the possibility of a philosophy of reconciliation. It thus comes as a revelation to grasp that what is being withstood *is the new intersubjective paradigm itself*. Experienced through art, the sublime is a relation between the subjective and intersubjective. On the side of society—the other angle of Wellmer's "stereoscopic" reading—things look quite different. By disclosing "the abyss of meaninglessness *in the midst* of a world of linguistic meaning" (171), the sublime permits us to appreciate the communication model itself as an act of withstanding. The intersubjective paradigm is thus not performative solely on account of its language acts, but because its fragile existence is actively upheld against the abyss of nature. From this perspective, art affords a pragmatic example of how "subjects can have direct experience of their power to articulate, to communicate, to fashion their world" (172). Art affords this example because the three aspects of the aesthetic sublime identified by Wellmer—the "energetic," the "structural," and the "dynamic"—each impact on the communication model; they open up the world to its "borders and abysses," and expand "the frontiers of communicatively shared meaning" (177).

The "energetic" sublime shakes us up with its aesthetic violence; the "structural" makes us open to fragmentation; the "dynamic" heightens our tolerance for the heterogeneous, including aspects of art or society presently deemed to be extrinsic (the mechanical, the sensuously unpleasant, the natural). All in all, sublime art can develop consciousness and help loosen up traditions, fostering what Wellmer, after Habermas, calls "the communicative 'rationalization' of the life world" (166). Echoing Menke's theory of aesthetic sovereignty, Wellmer insists that sublime art can refresh, illuminate, and reenchant the world only by remaining autonomous:

> Only by remaining autonomous can art still generate that surplus by which, for a few moments at a time, a disenchanted world can be reenchanted again, the dried river-

beds of ordinary communication can be flooded, and the structures of meaning we inhabit in our everyday world can be shaken up. (169)

In sum, to adjust the words with which this book started, art puts "feeling" back into "rules." The "allegorical sublime" of Beethoven's late style is the ideal exemplar of the kind of art Wellmer imagines. Actually, his essay ends by singling out a musical tradition which escapes the Austro-German hegemony: the "line of development in modern music [which] links Debussy with Stravinsky, Messiaen, and Ligeti" (179). Wellmer argues that only this tradition shakes off the Austro-German subjectivity model with which Adorno was fixated, a model "rooted in the expressive human voice and its vocal gestures," and the Hegelian notion of "subjective inwardness." By contrast, the tradition of Debussy and Ligeti, Wellmer thinks, is more object-centered, a music in which "things themselves are given acoustic expression, [where] the world is transformed into a realm of sound." It is an authentic recuperation of "natural beauty" (180). Here lies the inconsistency in Wellmer's argument, since its goal is not to deny subjectivity but to reconcile it to the communicative paradigm. The missing link is Beethoven's late style, a music which anticipates the objective, (dialectically) natural, allegorical, quality of these moderns, but crucially mediated by the subjectivity model. Mediation of the subjective and intersubjective paradigms is the Grail of modern philosophy, and only Beethoven discovers it.

Conclusion

This book has explored the extraordinary and inexhaustible series of works which constitute Beethoven's late style. While the focus of my study has been the music in itself, I have also used this music as a platform from which to survey a set of interdependent topics and issues. These bear largely on the question of musical meaning, in particular, on how music signifies by critically miming the spheres of language, subjectivity, and nature. To answer this question, I have adapted some ideas from the writings of Theodor Adorno to an original theory of musical style. I have argued that a theory of Beethoven's late style must be adequate to the context dependence of his musical structures; to their mimesis of language, subjectivity, and nature; and to their conventional, rule-bound, character. In the course of this study, I have foregrounded a number of oppositions, some of which may appear paradoxical. Late Beethoven emerges as a quintessentially Classical composer, yet one who extrapolates the modernism intrinsic to the Classical style. His style is grasped as a mode of cognition—a "music as philosophy"—the ultimate object of which, however, is musical material. Adorno's thought is portrayed as a "tonal philosophy," distinct from the Schoenbergian, "atonal" philosophy that critics such as Susan Buck-Morss have described. Beethoven's tonal modernism becomes the model for a philosophy which mediates idealist subjectivity with the intersubjective paradigm of the linguistic turn. The late style affirms the normative basis of society by stressing rules. At the same time, it transcends the language character of convention through its very medium, by virtue of being *music, and not language*. As a music which projects expression within rules, the subjective within the intersubjective, Beethoven's late style achieves an unmatched aesthetic sovereignty. Let me rehearse the steps of this argument.

Chapter 1 challenged the common assumption that musical expression breaks rules, contending that Beethoven's late music actually emphasizes conventions, in particular, the conventions of the Classical style. Adorno's unfinished Beethoven monograph supplies the key to such an approach; it also suggests that the basis of Adorno's musical philosophy itself might lie in the Classical style, rather than in the Second Viennese School. The chapter ended by recuperating, and expanding, the hermeneutic notion of style as a category which mediates normative and creative perspectives on artworks.

Chapter 2 added a third parameter to these normative and creative aspects, the *natural*. It elaborated the three aspects into a dialectic model of musical style, based on music's mimesis of language, subjectivity, and nature. This broad and dynamic model of style encompassed a dialogue between diverse orientations: a normative music theory (= language), a critical philosophy (= subjectivity), and a foundational cognitive semantics, based on metaphorical image schemata (= nature).

After defining, respectively, Style 1, Style 2, and Style 3, I characterized Style 4 as a model which represents the relationship between Styles 1–3 as harmonious and closed. The preferred Style 5, by contrast, represented their relationship as conflictual and open-ended. I argued that Style 6 attends to the present critical inquiry itself.

Chapter 3 gave an overview of Adorno's position on late Beethoven, explaining his notion of music as a mode of conceptless cognition. I showed how Adorno interprets Beethoven's musical logic as a mimesis of Hegelian logic, and why he thinks late Beethoven critiques this logic. (Indeed, mimesis combines the dual senses of imitation and critique.) With Adorno's analysis of the late style, the chief category proved to be allegory. Adorno uses allegory to describe the conventional, yet dissociated, character of Beethoven's structures. Yet I showed that allegory also has a broader philosophical meaning, in conjunction with the concept of mimesis. I defined allegory and mimesis, and also a set of other central terms in Adorno's aesthetics: *Apparition,* Caesura, Constellation, Dialectic, *Durchbruch, Floskel,* Mediation, Moment, Negative Dialectic, Parataxis, *Rückung,* and *Schein.* The following three chapters gave concrete analytical analogues of these concepts.

Chapters 4, 5, and 6 cut three swathes through Beethoven's late works, beginning with a stylistic overview, continuing to a study of his sonata forms, and ending with whole works considered as multimovement cycles. The survey was generally chronological, progressing from the *Missa Solemnis* through to the "Galitzin" Quartets and the Ninth Symphony. The three chapters amplified Styles 1–3 into three systemic metaphors. Nature became "Landscape"; convention developed into "Invisible Cities"; subjectivity was raised to "Worlds." These three domains suggested various groupings: a lateral overlay, with worlds supervening on cities, on the foundation of landscape; a mobile constellation, with the three domains freely permeating each other; a circular return, worlds doubling back to landscapes, encompassing and sublating the whole.

Chapter 4 organized its overview of Beethoven's late style according to parameters: melody, harmony, texture, and form. Interpreting the music in terms of "motion through a landscape," I detailed the agencies and goals of Beethoven's "journeys." These journeys returned to their beginnings but from a higher vantage point, and they were "natural" in three ways. They engaged the building blocks of Beethoven's landscape; they involved metaphorical image schemata of space and motion; and they foregrounded the materiality of the music by allegorically reversing these schematas' natural affordances. I thereby elaborated my claim that allegorical nature is dialectic in that it critiques the immediacy of image-schematic nature. This is how Beethoven's allegorical style projects nature in the very course of critically resisting it.

Chapter 5 shifted the focus from nature to the large-scale convention of sonata form. It examined the opening sonata-form movements of the last five piano sonatas, and the String Quartets Opp. 127 and 130 (Op. 132 was considered at length in chapter 2). I argued that Beethoven's foregrounding of convention has the paradoxical result of releasing the music's "natural" expressiveness. He achieves this allegorical character through two main devices: parataxis, in the guise of variation and ritornello procedure, and noncongruence, which splits convention into its constituent parameters. A further paradox is that these two devices regenerate sonata form as an abstraction through attacking it as a reality. I gauged this "attack" in relation to a punctuation, or caesura, schema of sonata form. The late style could thus be seen as progressing in two waves. I showed that the first wave (the five piano sonatas) is accommodated within the punctuation schema, and that the second wave (the "Galitzin" Quartets) radically subverts it. Another difference is that the first wave is dominated by the contour model of the dynamic arch, the second wave by the contrapuntal interplay of arches: that is, Beethoven progresses from contour to counterpoint, in line with his increasing archaic, Classicizing tendency. Ironically, this Classicizing tendency is composed out through the subversion of the normative punctuation schema.

Chapter 6 moved from Classical convention to late Beethoven's all-encompassing subjectivity. In this light, every aspect of his compositions was seen to be unified according to a compositional idea. The study thus focused on the cyclic unity of entire works: the last three piano sonatas, the *Diabelli* Variations, the last two quartets, the Ninth Symphony. Paradoxically, we saw that the subjective "idea" projected by the music comprises an aspect of convention or a natural principle, taking us back, cyclically, to the cities and landscapes of the late style, and sublating them to a higher level. For instance, the idea could be the trill as a convention, plus its natural contour of oscillation. It emerged that, by disclosing the nature immanent within convention, Beethoven's ideas remake the musical world by resensitizing us to its materials.

The ideas of works such as the Ninth Symphony opened up the discussion in the last third of the book to the late style's historical and philosophical dimensions. In chapters 7–9 I developed the thesis that Beethoven's heterogeneous and self-reflective meta-style is also a reflection on history. Like his contemporary Hölderlin, Beethoven mourns the past as a means of affirming the world of the present.

Chapter 7 related Beethoven's summatory and retrospective aspects to contemporary debates on stylistic mixture and the rediscovery of early music such as Bach's. I drew a close comparison with the late style of Hölderlin, including an interpretation of the poet's complex theory of genre (this literary perspective complements the focus on Kant and Hegel in chapter 3). I argued that Hölderlin's stylistic system, "The Modulation of Tones," is a poetic analogue for my dialectical theory of musical style.

Chapter 8 explored late Beethoven's roots in the Classical style, making good the claim that his music is an affirmation of Classical principles, and thus musical "rules." Without resorting to organicist teleological models, I charted the development of the Classical style as the unfolding of three "turns." These turns engaged different modes of musical articulation, associated both with Hölderlin's notion of "caesura" and with the modernist concept of "moment." I hereby linked the drama of musical material with a developing aesthetic of *Apparition*. I fleshed out Adorno's claims, discussed in chapter 3, that musical structure mimes concepts and dialectic, with a particular focus on the "Waldstein" sonata. The chapter ended by proposing a theory of the "allegorical sublime." We register this effect in late Beethoven,

I argued, partly in the force by which he affirms conventions, partly in the music's resistance to conceptualization. The sublimity with which Beethoven asserts music's social (i.e., conventional) aspect set up the discussion in the final chapter.

Chapter 9 is the point where my book confronted Adorno and critical theory directly. I defended Adorno's nuanced concept of musical autonomy against two other standpoints: that of postmodern philosophy on the one hand, and on the other hand, that of the intersubjective turn of second-generation critical theory. I proposed that Adorno's model still offers the richest account of the philosophical meaning implicit within Beethoven's late style. Conversely, I claimed that the music stands as a legitimation of the idealist philosophy enshrined within Adorno's thought—moreover, in a way which outlines a rapprochement with more recent philosophical orientations. Music and philosophy, then, complete and reflect on each other as torn halves of a whole. Music *as* philosophy is most encompassing in Beethoven's late style.

Appendix

Example A.1. String Quartet in A minor, Op. 132, first movement, mm. 1–108
Continues on the next page

Example A.1. *Continues on the next page*

Example A.1. String Quartet in A minor, Op. 132, first movement, mm. 1–108
Continues on the next page

Example A.1. *Continues on the next page*

Example A.1. String Quartet in A minor, Op. 132, first movement, mm. 1–108
Continues on the next page

Example A.1. *Continues on the next page*

Example A.1. String Quartet in A minor, Op. 132, first movement, mm. 1–108
Continues on the next page

Example A.1. *Continues on the next page*

Example A.1. String Quartet in A minor, Op. 132, first movement, mm. 1–108
Continues on the next page

Example A.1. *Continued*

Example A.2. String Quartet in E♭, Op. 127, first movement, mm. 1–76
Continues on the next page

Example A.2. *Continues on the next page*

Example A.2. String Quartet in E♭, Op. 127, first movement, mm. 1–76
Continues on the next page

Example A.2. *Continues on the next page*

Example A.2. String Quartet in E♭, Op. 127, first movement, mm. 1–76
Continues on the next page

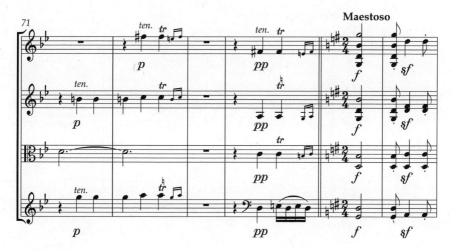

Example A.2. *Continued*

Example A.3. String Quartet in B♭, Op. 130, first movement, mm. 1–25
Continues on the next page

Example A.3. *Continues on the next page*

Example A.3. String Quartet in B♭, Op. 130, first movement, mm. 1–25
Continued

Example A.4. Op. 130, first movement, mm. 92–133
Continues on the next page

Example A.4. Op. 130, first movement, mm. 92–133
Continues on the next page

Example A.4. *Continues on the next page*

Example A.4. Op. 130, first movement, mm. 92–133
Continued

Example A.5. Op. 130, first movement, mm. 52–75
Continues on the next page

Example A.5. Op. 130, first movement, mm. 52–75
Continues on the next page

Example A.5. *Continued*

Example A.6. Op. 131, finale, mm. 1–29
Continues on the next page

Example A.6. *Continues on the next page*

Example A.6. Op. 131, finale, mm. 1–29
Continued

Example A.7. Ninth Symphony, finale, fourth quotation leading to Ode melody
Continues on the next page

Example A.7. Ninth Symphony, finale, fourth quotation leading to Ode melody
Continues on the next page

Example A.7. *Continues on the next page*

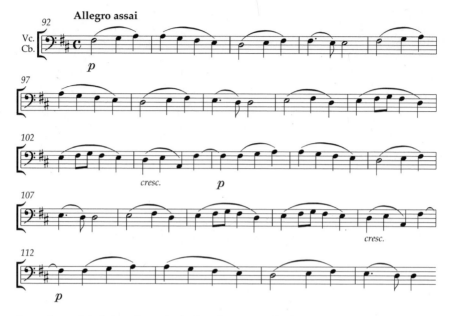

Example A.7. Ninth Symphony, finale, fourth quotation leading to Ode melody
Continued

Example A.8. Ninth Symphony, first movement, mm. 138–50
Continues on the next page

Example A.8. Ninth Symphony, first movement, mm. 138–50
Continues on the next page

Example A.8. *Continues on the next page*

Example A.8. Ninth Symphony, first movement, mm. 138–50
Continued

Example A.9. Haydn, Symphony No. 45 in F♯ minor, first movement, mm. 1–20
Continues on the next page

Example A.9. Haydn, Symphony No. 45 in F♯ minor, first movement, mm. 1–20
Continues on the next page

Example A.9. *Continues on the next page*

Example A.9. Haydn, Symphony No. 45 in F♯ minor, first movement, mm. 1–20
Continued

Example A.10. Haydn, String Quartet in C, Op. 74, no. 1, first movement, mm. 1–54
Continues on the next page

Example A.10. Haydn, String Quartet in C, Op. 74, no. 1, first movement, mm. 1–54
Continues on the next page

Example A.10. *Continues on the next page*

Example A.10. Haydn, String Quartet in C, Op. 74, no. 1, first movement, mm. 1–54
Continues on the next page

Example A.10. *Continues on the next page*

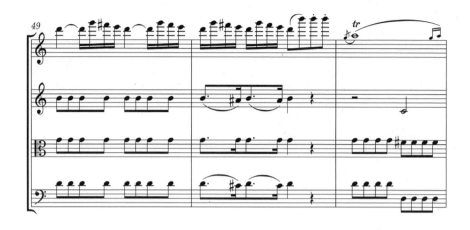

Example A.10. Haydn, String Quartet in C, Op. 74, no. 1, first movement, mm. 1–54
Continued

Example A.11. Piano Sonata in C, Op. 53 ("Waldstein"), first movement, mm. 1–42
Continues on the next page

Example A.11. Piano Sonata in C, Op. 53 ("Waldstein"), first movement, mm. 1–42
Continues on the next page

Example A.11. *Continued*

Notes

1. Away with All Rules?

1. Regarding "family relationships," see also Benjamin's striking example of how "a mother is seen to begin to live in the fullness of her power only when the circle of her children . . . closes around her; so do ideas come to life only when extremes are assembled around them" (1998: 35). Another analogue is George Lakoff's theory of conceptual prototypes, as in his discussion of the "mother" prototype (see Lakoff 1987: 74–76).

2. See, for instance, Habermas (1987); Apel (1998); Wellmer (1998).

3. Context dependence has become a prominent issue in semantics, where "style" tends to be discussed in relation to sociolinguistic issues of code switching and idiolect (see Palmer 1986: 64–66). Context dependence is also closely related to the philosophical topic of holism. "'Only in the context of a sentence does a word have a meaning" says Frege ("On Sense and Reference"), and "to understand a sentence is to understand a language," says Wittgenstein (*Philosophical Investigations,* para. 199, in Fodor and Lepore 1993: ix). The truth of holism at first seems trivial and incontrovertible, but it is rife with problems. If everything is related to everything else, then our experience of tomatoes is constitutive of our concept of the color red, in which case Shakespeare could not have known this color. Similarly, translation across different languages, even on a minimal level, would be impossible, according to the "Sapir-Whorf hypothesis." In reality, however, holism is severely constrained by some variant of the analytic/synthetic distinction, for example, by what Fodor and Lepore call "molecularism." Hence a molecularist "denies that *all* our . . . beliefs have to be shared in order that we should share any of our beliefs" (Fodor and Lepore, 259). But these debates take us far beyond the scope of the present study. It is enough to state that in the rather different contexts of German aesthetics, constraints on holism are effected by notions of artistic originality and the work concept (see Goehr 1992).

4. According to Andrew Bowie: "Underlying Adorno's argument is a vital aspect of Romantic aesthetics . . . the essential model for his conception of aesthetic form is Viennese classical music, itself a product of the period in which the conception of literature at issue here was first articulated" (1997: 25).

5. It is revealing that analytic critics who *do* work on music, such as Peter Kivy and Stephen Davies, concentrate on music's emotional or ontological character, rather than its form (see Kivy 1989; Davies 1994). For notable exceptions, see Debellis (1995); Scruton (1999); and Cumming (2000).

6. As in Lyotard's critique of "meta-narratives" (Lyotard 1984).

7. "On the level of philosophical discourse, any arguer who denies the priority of the consensus-oriented use of language in favor of the strategic-oriented must commit a performative self-contradiction" (Apel 1998: 21).

8. See also Kevin Korsyn's plea for a "decentered disciplinary space" and a "radical pluralism" in contemporary musical research (Korsyn 2003: 188). The moral of Korsyn's book seems to be that "Perhaps we could begin by talking to each other" (189).

2. Styles

1. As in Martin Scorsese's 2002 film *Gangs of New York,* where an elephant (escaped from Barnum's circus) incongruously tramps the streets. Scorsese's elephant pays homage to a famous motif of Federico Fellini's (see his 1969 *Satyricon,* or his 1973 *Amarcord*).

2. For other recent studies of Op. 132, see McClary (2000: 119–33) and Hatten (2004: 267–86). McClary hears the first movement as "an image of shattered subjectivity" (119). Hatten counters her postmodern reading with a highly illuminating semiotic analysis, incorporating his work on markedness and topic theory. He argues convincingly for the work's stylistic coherence: "I would maintain [contra McClary] that Beethoven is not postmodern in his self-conscious play with all the conventions at his disposal; there is too much that is ultimately integrative in his treatment of even the most disparate materials. But there is certainly a link to modernism, in that Beethoven was concerned with expanding the resources of musical expression to the extent of self-conscious awareness of the very conventionality of his language (as Adorno and Rosen, among others, have observed)" (277–78). Hatten's association of Adorno and Rosen is admirable, as is his claim that "Beethoven works quite consistently within the conventions of his extension of Classical principles" (277).

3. I agree with Hatten that the coda "is thematically and expressively integrated as a logical outcome," unlike the "ironic dismissal" in the finale of Op. 95 in F minor (Hatten 2004: 285). Nevertheless, Hatten also talks of our experience of this moment as a "sudden breakthrough" (284), invoking Adorno's notion of *Durchbruch.* It is this modality of suddenness which I hear as significant, rather than its logical mediation.

4. See also my "bidirectional" model of metaphorical mapping in *Metaphor and Musical Thought* (Spitzer 2004), where I model a dialogue between cognitivism and Paul Ricoeur's phenomenological theory of metaphor.

5. The subject of periodization in music history is endlessly controversial. James Webster (2004) proposes that the Baroque era ends in 1720, notwithstanding its persistence especially in the Habsburg dominions, and the death of J. S. Bach at midcentury. He designates the period 1720–1780 "Enlightenment-*galant,*" overlapping the last period of Europian Classicism, 1740–1750 to circa 1815–1830, which he subsumes under the rubric "First Viennese-European Modernism." Webster agrees with Heartz (2003) in designating the period 1720–1780 *galant.*

6. Admittedly, motivation renders Saussure's notion of arbitrariness suspect for all music (see Hatten 1994: 243–44; Spitzer 2004: 14). Nevertheless, this should not level down the differences between historical styles. The Classical style comes closest to the *effect* of arbitrariness, to the illusion of linguistic conventionality.

7. Although apparition is an English word, I prefer to italicize and capitalize it throughout this book to reproduce its appearance as a *Fremdwort* (foreign word)

in Adorno's German. That is, capitalizing the word in English creates the same marked effect as Adorno's lowercase spelling (as *apparition*), since German nouns, of course, begin uppercase. (I am grateful to Berthold Hoeckner for clarifying this point to me.) A separate issue is the complex relationship between *Apparition* and Hegel's *Erscheinung,* to which I will return in chapter 8. Yet another is the likely source of the word in French poetry. Victor Hugo and Stéphane Mallarmé both wrote poems entitled *Apparition,* the latter ending with an image suggestive both of Adornian fireworks and Benjamin's constellations ("laissant toujours de ses mains mal fermées neiger de blancs bouquets d'étoiles parfumées"). It is significant, in this regard, that Mallarmé was the major French Hegelian before Kojève in the twentieth century (see Langan 1986), and that Adorno drew much of his concept of artistic form from Mallarmé's disciple Paul Valéry, who seems to have been the first critic to theorize the connection between apparitions and fireworks: "The phenomenon of fireworks is prototypical for artworks, though because of its fleetingness and status as empty entertainment it has scarcely been acknowledged by theoretical considerations; *only Valéry pursued ideas that are at least related*" (Adorno 1999: 81, my emphasis).

8.   Georg Christian Lichtenberg (1742–1799), a satirist.

9.   See his 1876 *Thematischer Leitfaden durch die Musik zu Richard Wagners Festspiel 'Der Ring des Nibelungen'* (Leipzig: Schloemp).

3. Adorno's Beethoven

1.   Page citations are to this edition unless stated otherwise.

2.   For an extensive discussion of Adorno's concept of mediation, see Paddison (1997: 108–48). For the more traditional concept of mediation as the strategic reconciling of conceptual or syntactic oppositions, see Lidov (2004: 59–77).

3.   This may indeed remind us of how structuralists like Hjelmslev will later explain concepts (of "tree," "wood," etc.) as coordinates within semantic networks.

4.   See also Taussig (1993: 45): "In times past the shamans warded off danger by means of images imitating that danger, and in this sense they used equivalence—mimesis."

5.   See col. 1275 in the *Lexikon.* My thanks to Danuta Mirka for pointing this out to me. The discussion is indebted to her research on *imbroglio.*

6.   This dialectic is neutralized in Jephcott's translation of *Floskel* as "empty phrase" (Adorno 1998a: 126).

4. Late Landscapes

1.   The image of the abyss, or *Abgrund,* was inspired by Baudelaire's common motif of *le gouffre* in poems such as *De profundis clamavi:*

J'implore ta pitié, Toi, l'unique que j'aime,
Du fond du gouffre obscur où mon coeur est tombé.
C'est un univers monre à l'horizon plombé,
Où nagent dans la nuit l'horreur et le blasphème.

5. Invisible Cities

1.   The literature and the attendant issues are enormously complex and cannot be treated here. A fine recent summary is James Hepokoski's "Beyond the Sonata Principle" (2002), an essay heralding Hepokoski and Darcy's much-anticipated book *Elements of Sonata Theory* (Oxford University Press, 2006). Judging from their published writings, the authors shift the orientation of the sonata model from tonality to thematic discourse. Without questioning that sonata forms in which second groups are recapitulated in the tonic are prototypical, Hepokoski (2002) nonetheless argues that this model fails to explain exceptions such as Beethoven's F-minor *Egmont* Overture, Op. 84. Here, "the secondary and closing themes are first sounded in A♭ major but return only in D♭ major in the recapitulation, never to be heard again" (2002: 94). Similarly, the traditional model fails to explain why many recapitulations (especially Haydn's) radically recast the expositional *Anlage* (thematic layout). To account for these apparent deviations, Hepokoski proposes that we replace the tonal model with one based on "a larger narrative purpose or scheme of conceptual organization" (130), a "background idea that is stronger than the sonata principle per se" (131). From this standpoint, given that the *Anlage* of a Haydn exposition is often refractory, then the "background idea" of a recapitulation may be simply to smooth it out and reformulate it in a more normative fashion. I would agree that, with Beethoven's late style, the background idea is indeed discursive, but with the addition of two provisos. First, that his sonata forms are discursive *even when they match the prototypical scheme of the sonata principle.* Second, that "discourse" be understood in the broader, ideational, sense of my Style 2.

2.   I discuss parataxis in relation to the language model of the Classical style in Spitzer (2004, chapter 5). Sisman (1993b) also treats the topic extensively, focusing on Haydn's variation procedure. Whereas Sisman's orienation is rhetorical, I follow Adorno is seeing parataxis as an index of a broad philosophical outlook, whose musical entailments extend beyond variation. Another writer on the subject is Rudolph Klein (1982). Klein associates parataxis with Haydn's tendency to write through-composed monothematic expositions, in which variants of the theme develop additively from each other, hypotaxis with Mozart's preference for thematic contrast integrated within an overarching architecture. I am grateful to Tim Jones for drawing my attention to Klein's work.

3.   For other modern approaches to sonata form in terms of caesura, see Wolfgang Budday (1983), Hepokoski and Darcy (1997), and Hepokoski (2002). Budday's study stands out in its care to ground its punctuation model in historical theory, particularly that of Riepel and Koch. According to Budday, "Koch conceived form in terms of the mutual relationship of melodic phrases (*Sätzen*) from the standpoint of punctuation/rhythm. A network of ending formulas (melodic-harmonic aspects) and phrase lengths (rhythmic aspects) creates the conditions of form." He argues that "The punctuation model can be applied with equal validity to Beethoven's forms" (Budday 1983: 18). For a review of Koch's punctuation model, with particular application to Mozart, see Spitzer (2004: 243–75).

4.   As Rosen points out, Classical and Baroque sequences are opposite in effect. Originally an agent of motoric propulsion, the Baroque sequence loses this energy when absorbed into a Classical periodic syntax: "When the strongly articu-

lated periodic phrase is combined with a sequence, particularly a descending one as most sequences then were, the result is not an increase of energy, but a loss" (1972: 48).

5. Hepokoski and Darcy (1997) explain the Classical three-module exposition (or "tri-modular block") as part of their theory of a "double medial caesura" (for their analysis of Beethoven's Op. 10, no. 3, see p. 150).

6. For a musical interpretation of Bakhtin's concept of heteroglossia, see Hirschkop (1989: 286–88).

7. See Hatten (1994: 137–38) for a contrasting treatment of this section.

6. Ways of World Making

1. The flashback to the Adagio and the Presto codetta are too abbreviated to properly qualify as a double cycle as in Op. 110. Nevertheless, Op. 27, no. 1, is as much a precursor to Op. 110 as the "Moonlight" is to Op. 131, both in C♯ minor. The two "quasi una fantasia" sonatas are a linchpin for the argument that the formal freedom of the late works represents a return to an earlier fantasy style, which either provisionally goes underground in the middle period (see Broyles 1987) or continues into such middle-period works as the "characteristic" sonatas of 1809 (see Sisman 1997).

2. Hatten cites this point as an example of a "monumental" stylistic register (1994: 14).

3. The cobbler conceit is popular in style theory. Kendall Walton couches his essay on style as a critique of the "cobbler model," a model which has a three-part structure: "There is the producer, the product, and the consumer, that is, the *cobbler*, who makes *shoes*, which are worn by *customers*" (Walton 1979: 46–47). Walton's objection is that this model "focuses attention too exclusively on the work of art, the 'object itself,' and not enough on the action of making it" (47). Although Walton's argument is analytic, and hence not strictly pertinent here, it is interesting nonetheless that he invokes a notion of *appearance* (partly after Sircello 1975) which has strong affinities with the Hegelian concept of *Erscheinung*. Walton's account of "appearance" is thus another figure of a possible concordance between the idealist and analytic traditions.

4. I am disregarding the extremely prevalent eighteenth-century genre of three-movement works which end with a minuet or a *Tempo di Menuetto*. This is defined by Dean Sutcliffe as a "countergenre" to the normative practice of ending with a fast and brilliant finale (Sutcliffe 2005). The existence of such countergenres throws the norms into even greater relief, and begs the question why these norms arose in the first place.

5. Op. 131's second-movement Allegro molto vivace, while having sonata-form characteristics, is dancelike.

6. See Hatten (1994: 145–60) for a perspicuous semiotic analysis of the fugue. Hatten focuses on the subject's "noncoincidence between the apex (on C♯) and a crux (*sf*, A) that immediately undermines the apex." Hatten observes that "the structure of the four-note subject head," with its various expressive reversals, "is analogous to the dramatic scheme of tragedy" (152).

7.	Quotation adapted from Edoardo Sanguineti's text for Luciano Berio's *Laborintus II*.

7. Kunstvereinigung

1.	See also Küthen (2002: 278).

2.	See also Reinhold Brinkmann (2000: 9).

3.	Beethoven writes: "I should like you to send me your lectures also and Sebastian Bach's five-part mass as well. I will send you the amount for both from here at once."

4.	"Sie werden eine neue Art der Stimmführung bemerken (hiermit ist die Instrumentirung, die Verheilung der Rollen gemeint) und an Fantasie fehlt's, wenige Gottlob, weniger als je zuvor!" (in Kropfinger 2001: 194). Although Beethoven was referring specifically to Op. 131, his comment applies generally.

5.	The reviewer notes the "zwey überall *obligate,* oder vielmehr durchgängig *selbständige* Flöten" (in Zenck 1986: 298).

6.	Translations of Hölderlin's *Wie wenn am Feiertage* in the preceding paragraph are by Michael Hamburger (see Hamburger 1980: 373–77). Unless otherwise noted, all translations are by the author.

7.	I have elsewhere modeled topical play in Beethoven's Op. 132 as a combinatorial system, on the basis of Greimas's theory of semiotic squares (Spitzer 1998a). By interrelating a series of squares, constructed from diverse cultural standpoints, it was possible to map the music's meaning as a multidimensional grid. In some ways, this Greimassian approach is a structuralist equivalent of Hölderlin's "modulation of tones." The problems with this approach, as I see them now, is that topics engage form only obliquely (being "extroversive" signs, by Agawu's lights), that the designation of topics is rather contingent, and that oppositional systems are somewhat rigid. Nevertheless, I would imagine it possible to create a more nuanced combinatorial model of Op. 132 inspired by the *Schein* of Hölderlin's theory. In fact, such a model is implicit in my analysis of this work in chapter 2.

8.	Gerhard traces the critical prestige of the ode genre to the Berlin philosophical circle of Moses Mendelssohn. Mendelssohn explains, in an essay of 1764, the "apparent disorder ascribed to odes" in terms of "mediating concepts" (*Mittelbegriffe*) which normally unify a poem's structure (Gerhard 2002: 174–75). See also Gerhard's forthcoming monograph *Berlioz, "l'imprévu" und die klassizistische Odentheorie.*

8. Caesura of the Classical Style

1.	In a powerful essay, William Caplin has argued for a far more circumscribed definition of "cadences," constraining their meaning chiefly to formal closure at middleground levels of structure. Following Steven Huebner, Caplin suggests the term "*figurative cadence* to cover the extension of cadence to high structural levels" (Caplin 2004: 66). "Figurative cadence" approximates to my metaphorical model of punctuation.

2.   Hoeckner takes his notion of "Beethoven's star" from Ernst Bloch's discussion in his *The Principle of Hope,* pp. 1102–3. The star is the visual complement to the sonic *Hoffnungssignal* of the trumpet. Debate on how Beethoven's deafness impacted on his work is rather speculative (see Roland Barthes's wonderful essay on Beethoven, "Musica Practica," in Barthes 1977: 152–53). But it is perhaps relevant that the star is the chief natural sign which makes *no* sound.

3.   The story of Haydn's contribution to the Classical style is presented by Webster in three episodes. An initial period of experimentation climaxes with the extraordinary *Sturm und Drang* symphonies of 1768–72. The great turning point is 1772, when Haydn retreats to a more conventionalized and *galant* style, possibly shaped by his new interest in opera (Spitzer 1998b; Webster 1998). This turn initiates a process of consolidation in two phases. First, the language acquires transparency and normativity as a truly "popular" style (Rosen 1972). Second, this popular style is considerably enriched and expanded in the music of the 1780s and 1790s, culminating with the Op. 76 quartets and the "London" Symphonies.

4.   See the striking influence of Jan Ladislav Dusík's E-major Piano Sonata, "The Farewell" (1800), on Beethoven's "*Les Adieux*" Sonata, Op. 81a (Küthen 2002: 265–78).

5.   For the possible influence of Clementi's G-minor Sonata Op. 7 (1783) on Beethoven's *Eroica,* see Küthen (2002: 249–50). The classic study of Beethoven and the London Pianoforte School is Ringer (1970).

6.   See Klein (1982). The *Entwicklung/Fortspinnung* distinction was framed by Friedrich Blume. According to Blume, whereas Haydn submits his material to processive development (*Entwicklung*), Mozart prefers to arrange independent fragments in mosaic-like structures (*Fortspinnung*). Blume's arguments, which where originally presented in his 1929 treatise *Fortspinnung und Entwicklung,* are summarized by Carl Dahlhaus: "*Fortspinnung* means a process of joining together unrelated, independent elements, a series of motifs, which do not need to be substantively related, and which only become related through their placement in connection with one another . . . Development [*Entwicklung*] means a process of gradual transformation of a beginning element into further elements, substantively related to it and joined to it. It is a variety of separate motifs which form a chain of inner connections." Haydn "tends towards the developmental and Mozart towards the *Fortspinnung* principle" (Dahlhaus 1975: 25).

7.   Caplin codifies sets of formal *processes* (repetition, fragmentation, extension, and expansion) and thematic *types* (sentence, period, small ternary). Thematic types are compounded of formal processes according to *functions* such as "presentation, continuation, and cadence" (sentence), "antecedent and consequent" (period), "exposition, contrasting middle, and recapitulation" (ternary). Following Ratz, Caplin regards the sentence and period as opposed theme types, out of which can be generated any number of "hybrid" themes (he actually plots these hybrids along a spectrum, ranging between the extremes of sentence and period). Ratz's definition (which Caplin cites) bears quoting in full, because it so clearly evokes the Hegelian tone of the A. B. Marx tradition:

> In the case of the period we have a symmetrical structure that has a certain "repose in itself" owing to the balance of its two halves, which are more or less equal . . . The eight-measure sentence, however, contains a certain forward-striving character because of the

increased activity and compression in its continuation phrase, making it fundamentally different in construction from the symmetrical organization of the period. (2004: 59)

8. According to Caplin, subordinate themes are usually constructed out of the intra-thematic functions associated with tight-knit main themes, albeit in a significantly looser manner" (2004: 97)—in other words, loose because a chain of cadences; see Agawu (1991: 71).

9. According to Gayatri Spivak, writing *sous rature* is "to write a word, cross it out, and then print both word and deletion" (in Derrida 1976: xiv). The technique avows that a concept is "inaccurate yet necessary." A similar principal is to place long sections of text in brackets, as in Derrida's witty preface to Lacoue-Labarthe (1989). Derrida explores the philosophy of bracketing in his *The Truth in Painting* (1987), in the context of a deconstruction of Kant's framing strategies in the *Critique of Judgment*. Derrida uses the diacritical mark of a half crotchet, to refer to the fifteenth-century device of "lema," an ancestor of our quotation mark. A lema (plural lemata), according to David Wills, "means both an assumed, and therefore accessory proposition on the basis of which an argument, and a similar proposition, is given as a title. It is thus something fundamental to the argument which occupies an accessory or marginal position . . . something like a frame that forms the basis of a conceptual or aesthetic structure while appearing to remain more or less exterior to it" (Wills 2001: 111–12). Although I have not drawn on Derrida's writings significantly, his thought on this occasion follows a parallel track to the German discourse of the sublime, or "abyssal." Moreover, lemata achieve their apotheosis in the allegorical world of seventeenth-century emblems (see Spitzer 2004: 160–70). The "allegorical sublime," as I term it, thus has a French as well as a German complexion.

10. See the ninth of Benjamin's *Theses on the Philosophy of History*: "But a storm is blowing from Paradise; it has got caught in his wings with such violence that the angel can no longer close them. This storm irresistibly propels him to the future to which his back is turned, while the pile of debris before him grows skyward. This storm is what we call progress" (1999: 249).

11. See Harrison (1994). As Harrison points out, "a student of Riemann's system can analyze virtually any chord into any one of the three functions should the occasion demand" (284).

12. For a different interpretation of the sublime in classical music, focusing on Mozart's "Jupiter" Symphony, see Sisman (1993a). Sisman gives a concise account of the Kantian sublime, but also outlines its origins in eighteenth-century theories of rhetoric. Of course, the sublime goes back as far as Pseudo-Longinus's Greek treatise *On the Sublime*, written in the first century. Nevertheless, I have stressed that the sublime comes of age only with Kant's psychological turn, and that the musical analogue for this turn is provided by the cognitive character of Classical form. By internalizing nature into a sensibility for clarity and symmetry, critics such as Johann Mattheson convert form from an objective structure into a subjective faculty: an aspect of imagination, *Einbildungskraft* (see Schleuning 1998: 69–81). Sulzer and Koch complete the project which Mattheson began: their cognitive theory of musical form has close affinities with the Kantian project (see Spitzer 2004).

9. The Persistence of Critical Theory

1. The point is nicely made by Thomas Mann: "All his life this man of remarkable intellect has refused to choose between the professions of philosophy and music. He felt that he was actually pursuing the same thing in both divergent realms" (Mann 1961: 39).

2. See also Hatten's own distinct definition of "methodological dialectic" (Hatten 1994: 29, 56, 299–300). Hatten means the productive interaction between styles and works as "different ontological categories" (29).

3. For example, Brandom (1999) has recently been plowing common ground between his theory of inferential pragmatics, and Hegel's social philosophy. For Brandom, the meaning of a concept depends on its use; for Hegel, on its social context. Once we decant the Hegelian *Geist,* use and context begin to approach each other.

4. In this regard, a good apology for abstract musical discourse as the consensual product of team effort is provided by Keven Korsyn's *Decentering Music* (2003).

5. Habermas is suspicious of precisely such reconcilations, which he ascribes to the category mistakes endemic to metaphorical thinking. Hence Beethoven's apparent utopianism is subject to the same objection Habermas levels against "praxis" philosophers such as Hegel and Marx. Habermas thinks that Hegel and Marx commit the category mistake of metaphorically identifying society with a human subject, or social action (praxis) with individual reflection (352). By their lights, just as consciousness sublates moments of division into unified insight, so society takes up class antagonisms into an overarching ethical totality through revolution. That revolutions rarely succeed is due, according to Habermas, to the fact that abstractions such as "ethical totality" or "spirit" are too fictive to truly assimilate the independent logics of social institutions. This is why Habermas rejects revolution in favor of an incremental tuning of subsystems, a gradual thickening of the social net: "Rationalization of the life world means differentiation and condensation at once—a thickening of the floating web of intersubjective threads that simultaneously holds together the ever more sharply differentiated components of culture, society, and person" (346).

6. Taussig makes a fascinating connection with Freud's theory of the comic: "Freud calmly presents the startling idea of 'ideational mimetics,' in which what I call 'active yielding' as bodily copying of the other is paramount: one tries out the very shape of perception in one's own body; the musculature of the body is physiologically connected to percepts; and even ideational activity, not only perception, involves such embodying—hence 'ideational mimetics.' Just as speech can be understood as thought activating the vocal chords and tongue, so thinking itself involves innervation of all of one's features and sense organs" (Taussig 1993: 46). See also Arnie Cox (2001) for a cognitivist perspective on musical mimesis. Cox's "Mimetic Hypothesis" has two parts: "i) part of how we understand human movement and human-made sounds is in terms of our own experience of making the same or similar movements and sounds, and ii) this process of comparison involves overt and covert imitation of the source of visual and auditory information" (196).

Bibliography

Adler, Guido. 1911. *Der Stil in der Musik.* Leipzig: Breitkopf & Härtel.

Adorno, Theodor W. 1982. "On the Problem of Musical Analysis." Transcribed and translated by Max Paddison. *Music Analysis* 1, no. 2:169–87.

———. 1987. *Philosophy of Modern Music.* Translated by A. G. Mitchell and W. V. Bloomster. London: Sheed & Ward. First published in 1949.

———. 1990. *Negative Dialectics.* Translated by E. B. Ashton. London: Routledge. First published in 1966.

———. 1992a. *Mahler: A Musical Physiognomy.* Translated by Edmund Jephcott. Chicago: University of Chicago Press. First published in 1971.

———. 1992b. "Music and Language: A Fragment." In *Quasi una fantasia: Essays on Modern Music,* 1–6. Translated by Rodney Livingstone. London: Verso. First published in 1963.

———. 1992c. *Notes on Literature.* Vol. 2. Translated by Shierry Weber Nicholsen. New York: Columbia University Press.

———. 1993a. *Beethoven: Philosophie der Musik.* Edited by Rolf Tiedemann. Frankfurt am Main: Suhrkamp.

———. 1993b *Hegel: Three Studies.* Translated by Shierry Weber Nicholsen. Cambridge, Mass.: MIT Press. First published in 1963.

———. 1997. "Notes on Kafka." In *Prisms,* 243–71. Translated by Samuel and Shierry Weber Nicholsen. Cambridge, Mass.: MIT Press. First published in 1967.

———. 1998a. *Beethoven: The Philosophy of Music.* Translated by Edmund Jephcott. Edited by Rolf Tiedemann. Oxford: Polity Press.

———. 1998b. *Gesammelte Schriften.* Edited by Rolf Tiedemann. Darmstadt: Wissenschaftliche Buchgesellschaft.

———. 1999. *Aesthetic Theory.* Translated by Robert Hullor-Kentor. London: Athlone Press. First published in 1970.

———. 2002. *Theodor W. Adorno: Essays on Music.* Selected, with introduction, commentary, and notes by Richard Leppert. Translated by Susan H. Gillespie. Berkeley: University of California Press.

———, with Max Horkheimer. 1989. *Dialectic of Enlightenment.* Translated by John Cumming. London: Verso. First published in 1944.

Agawu, V. Kofi. 1991. *Playing with Signs.* Princeton: Princeton University Press.

Allanbrook, Wye Jamison. 1983. *Rhythmic Gesture in Mozart: Le Nozze di Figaro and Don Giovanni.* Chicago: University of Chicago Press.

Anderson, Emily. 1986. *The Letters of Beethoven.* 3 vols. London: Macmillan. First published in 1961.

Apel, Karlo-Otto. 1998. *From a Transcendental-Semiotic Point of View.* Edited by Marianna Papastephanou. Manchester: Manchester University Press. First published in 1988.

Badura-Skoda, Paul. 1980. "Noch einmal zur Frage Ais oder A in der *Hammerklavier-Sonata* Op. 106 von Beethoven." In Martin Bente, ed., *Musik, Edition, Interpretation: Gedenkschrift Gunther Henle,* 53–81. Munich: Henle Verlag.

Barthes, Roland. 1977. *Image-Music-Text.* Translated by Stephen Heath. Glasgow: Fontana.

Behler, Ernst. 1993. *German Romantic Literary Theory.* Cambridge: Cambridge University Press.

Beissner, Friedrich. 1942. "Klopstock als Erneurer der deutschen Dichtersprache." *Zeitschrift für Deutschkunde* 56:235–40.

Benjamin, Walter. 1989. *Baudelaire: A Lyric Poet in the Era of High Capitalism.* London: Verso.

———. 1998. *The Origin of German Tragic Drama.* Translated by John Osborne. London: Verso. First published in 1925.

———. 1999. *Illuminations.* Translated by Harry Zorn. London: Pimlico.

———. 2002. *Selected Writings.* 2 vols. Edited by Marcus Bullock and Michael Jennings. Cambridge, Mass.: Harvard University Press.

Bent, Ian, ed. 1994. *Music Analysis in the Nineteenth Century.* Vol. 2. Cambridge: Cambridge University Press.

Bergsten, Gunilla. 1969. *Thomas Mann's Doctor Faustus: The Sources and Structure of the Novel.* Edited by Krishna Winston. Chicago: University of Chicago Press.

Birrell, Gordon. 1979. *The Boundless Present: Space and Time in the Literary Fairy Tales of Novalis and Tieck.* Chapel Hill: University of North Carolina Press.

Blackall, Eric A. 1959. *The Emergence of German as a Literary Language.* Cambridge: Cambridge University Press.

Blasius, Leslie David. 1996. *Schenker's Argument and the Claims of Music Theory.* Cambridge: Cambridge University Press.

Bloch, Ernst. 1986. *The Principle of Hope.* Translated by Neville Plaice, Stephen Plaice, and Paul Knight. Oxford: Basil Blackwell. First published in 1959.

Bohrer, Karl Heinz. 1994. *Suddenness: On the Moment of Aesthetic Appearance.* Translated by Ruth Crowley. New York: Columbia University Press.

Bonds, Mark Evan. 1991. *Wordless Rhetoric: Musical Form and the Metaphor of the Oration.* Cambridge: Cambridge University Press.

———. 1997. "The Symphony as Pindaric Ode." In Janet Sisman, ed., *Haydn and His World,* 131–53. Princeton: Princeton University Press.

Bowie, Andrew. 1990. *Aesthetics and Subjectivity: From Kant to Nietzsche.* Manchester: Manchester University Press.

———. 1997. *From Romanticism to Critical Theory.* London: Routledge.

Brandom, Robert. 1999. "Some Pragmatist Themes in Hegel's Idealism: Negotiation and Administration in Hegel's Account of the Structure and Content of Conceptual Norms." *European Journal of Philosophy* 7, no. 2:164–89.

Brinkmann, Reinhold. 2000. "In the Time(s) of the 'Eroica.'" In Scott Burnham and Michael P. Steinberg, eds., *Beethoven and His World,* 1–26. Princeton: Princeton University Press.

Broyles, Michael. 1987. *The Emergence and Evolution of Beethoven's Heroic Style.* New York: Excelsior Music.

Buch, Esteban. 2003. *Beethoven's Ninth: A Political History.* Chicago: University of Chicago Press.

Buck-Morss, Susan. 1977. *The Origin of Negative Dialectics.* Hassocks: Harvester Press.

Bücken, Ernst. 1924. *Der heroische Stil in der Oper.* Reihe 5, Band 1. Leipzig: Veröffentlichung des Fürstlichen Institutes für Musikwissenschaftliche Forschung zu Bückeburg.

Budday, Wolfgang. 1983. *Grundlagen musikalischer Formen der Wiener Klassik: An Hand* der zeitgenössischen Theorie von Joseph Riepel und Heinrich Christoph Koch dargestellt an Menuetten und Sonatensätzen (1750–1790). Basel: Bärenreiter Kassel.

Burnham, Scott. 1990. "Criticism, Faith and the *Idee:* A. B. Marx's Early Reception of Beethoven." *19th-Century Music* 8, no. 3:336–49.

———. 1995. *Beethoven Hero.* Princeton: Princeton University Press.

———. 1997. *Musical Form in the Age of Beethoven: Selected Writings on Theory and Method: A. B. Marx.* Cambridge: Cambridge University Press.

Cahn, Michael. 1984. "Subversive Mimesis: T. W. Adorno and the Modern Impasse of Critique." In Mihai Spariosu, ed., *Mimesis in Contemporary Theory,* vol. 1, 27–64. Philadelphia: John Benjamin.

Caplin, William. 1998. *Classical Form: A Theory of Formal Functions for the Instrumental Music of Haydn, Mozart, and Beethoven.* Oxford: Oxford University Press.

———. 2004. "The Classical Cadence: Conceptions and Misconceptions." *Journal of the American Musicological Society* 57, no. 1:51–117.

Charlton, David, ed. 1989. *E. T. A. Hoffmann's Musical Writings: Kreisleriana, The Poet and the Composer, Music Criticism.* Translated by Martyn Clarke. Cambridge: Cambridge University Press.

Christensen, Thomas. 1993. *Jean-Philippe Rameau: The Science of Music Theory in the Enlightenment.* Cambridge: Cambridge University Press.

Chua, Daniel. 1995. *The "Galitzin" Quartets of Beethoven: Opp. 127, 130, 132.* Princeton: Princeton University Press.

Cook, Nicholas. 2000. *Beethoven: Symphony No. 9.* Cambridge: Cambridge University Press.

Cooke, Deryck. 1963. "The Unity of Beethoven's Late Quartets." *Music Review* 24:30–49.

Cooper, Barry, ed. 1991. *The Beethoven Compendium: A Guide to Beethoven's Life and Music.* London: Thames and Hudson.

Cox, Arnie. 2001. "The Mimetic Hypothesis and Embodied Musical Meaning." *Musicae Scientiae* 5, no. 2:195–212.

Cumming, Naomi. 1991. "Analogy in Leonard B. Meyer's 'Theory of Musical Meaning.'" In Jamie C. Kassler, ed., *Metaphor: A Musical Dimension,* 177–92. Sydney: Currency Press.

———. 2000. *The Sonic Self: Musical Subjectivity and Signification.* Bloomington: Indiana University Press.

Dahlhaus, Carl. 1975. "Some Models of Unity in Musical Form." *Journal of Music Theory* 19:2–30.

———. 1989. *Nineteenth-Century Music.* Translated by J. Bradford Robinson. Berkeley: University of California Press.

———. 1991. *Ludwig van Beethoven: Approaches to His Music.* Translated by Mary Whittall. Oxford: Clarendon Press.

Danto, Arthur. 1981. *The Transfiguration of the Commonplace: A Philosophy of Art.* Cambridge, Mass.: Harvard University Press.

Daverio, John. 2000. "Manner, Tone, and Tendency in Beethoven's Chamber Music for Strings." In Glenn Stanley, ed., *The Cambridge Companion to Beethoven,* 147–64. Cambridge: Cambridge University Press.

Davies, Stephen. 1994. *Musical Meaning and Expression.* Ithaca, N.Y.: Cornell University Press.

Debellis, Mark. 1995. *Music and Conceptualization.* Cambridge: Cambridge University Press.

De Man, Paul. 1984. *The Rhetoric of Romanticism.* New York: Columbia University Press.

DeNora, Tia. 1995. *Beethoven and the Construction of Genius: Musical Politics in Vienna, 1792–1803.* Berkeley: University of California Press.

———. 2003. *After Adorno: Rethinking Music Sociology.* Cambridge: Cambridge University Press.

Derrida, Jacques. 1976. *Of Grammatology.* Translated by Gayatri Chakravorty Spivak. Baltimore: John Hopkins University Press. First published in 1967.

———. 1981. *Writing and Difference.* Translated, with an introduction and additional notes by Alan Bass. London: Routlege and Kegan Paul.

———. 1987. *The Truth in Painting.* Translated by Geoff Bennington and Ian McLeod. Chicago: University of Chicago Press. First published in 1978.

Drabkin, William. 1976. "The Sketches for Beethoven's Piano Sonata in C minor, Opus 111." 2 vols. Ph.D. dissertation, Princeton University.

———. 1991a. *Beethoven: Missa Solemnis.* Cambridge: Cambridge University Press.

———. 1991b. "Beethoven's Understanding of 'Sonata Form': The Evidence of the Sketchbooks." In William Kindeman, ed., *Beethoven's Compositional Process,* 14–19. Lincoln: University of Nebraska Press.

———. 2004. "The Introduction to Beethoven's 'Kreutzer' Sonata: A Historical Perspective." In Lewis Lockwood and Mark Kroll, eds., *The Beethoven Violin Sonatas: History, Criticism, Performance,* 83–109. Urbana: University of Illinois Press.

Dreyfus, Lawrence. 1998. *Bach and the Patterns of Invention.* Cambridge, Mass.: Harvard University Press.

Eagleton, Terry. 1990. *The Ideology of the Aesthetic.* Oxford: Blackwell.

Eggebrecht, Hans Heinrich. 1972. *Zur Geschichte der Beethoven-Rezeption: Beethoven 1970.* Mainz: Verlag der Akademie der Wissenschaften und der Literatur.

Eitan, Zohar, and Roni Granot. 2003. "Motion Imagery and Musical Parameters." Unpublished paper.

Epstein, David. 1987. *Beyond Orpheus: Studies in Musical Structure.* Cambridge, Mass.: MIT Press.

Fink, Robert. 2001. "Going Flat: Post-Hierarchical Music Theory and the Musical Surface." In Nicholas Cook and Mark Everist, eds., *Rethinking Music,* 102–37. Oxford: Oxford University Press.

Fodor, Jerry, and Ernest Lepore. 1993. *Holism.* Oxford: Blackwell.

Frank, Manfred. 1992. *Stil in der Philosophie.* Stuttgart: Reclam.

———. 1997. *The Subject and the Text: Essays on Literary Theory and Philosophy.* Translated by Helen Atkins. Edited by Andrew Bowie. Cambridge: Cambridge University Press. First published in 1989.

Garratt, James. 2002. *Palestrina and the German Romantic Imagination.* Cambridge: Cambridge University Press.

Gerhard, Anselm. 2002. *London und der Klassizismus in der Musik.* Stuttgart: Metzler Verlag.

Geuss, Raymond. 1998. "Art and Criticism in Adorno's Aesthetics." *European Journal of Philosophy* 6, no. 3:297–317.

———. 1999. *The Idea of a Critical Theory: Habermas and the Frankfurt School.* Cambridge: Cambridge University Press.

Gjerdingen, Robert O. 1988. *A Classic Turn of Phrase: Music and the Psychology of Convention.* Philadelphia: University of Pennsylvania Press.

Goehr, Lydia. 1992. *The Imaginary Museum of Musical Works: An Essay in the Philosophy of Music.* Oxford: Clarendon Press.

———. 1998. *The Quest for Voice: On Music, Politics, and the Limits of Philosophy.* Berkeley: University of California Press.

Goethe, Johann Wolfgang von. 1986. "On German Architecture." In *J. W. von Goethe: Essays on Art and Literature*, 3–10. Edited by John Gearey. Translated by Ellen von Nardroff and Ernest von Nardroff. New York: Suhrkamp. First published in 1772.

Goodman, Nelson. 1976. *Languages of Art.* Indianapolis: Hackett.

———. 1978. *Ways of Worldmaking.* Indianapolis: Hackett.

Gossett, Philip. 1989. "Carl Dahlhaus and the 'Ideal Type.'" *19th Century Music* 13, no. 1:49–58.

Habermas, Jürgen. 1987. *The Philosophical Discourse of Modernity.* Translated by Frederick Lawrence. Cambridge: Polity Press. First published in 1985.

Halm, August. 1913. *Von zwei Kulturen der Musik.* Munich: Goerg Müller.

———. 1929. "Über den Wert musikalischer Analysen, I: Der Fremdkörper im ersten Satz der Eroica." *Die Musik* 12, no. 2:481–84.

Hamburger, Michael. 1980. *Friedrich Hölderlin: Poems and Fragments.* Cambridge: Cambridge University Press.

Hanslick, Eduard. 1986. *Vom Musikalisch-Schönen.* Translated by Geoffrey Payzant. Indianapolis: Hackett. First published in 1854.

Harrison, Daniel. 1994. *Harmonic Function in Chromatic Music.* Chicago: University of Chicago Press.

Harvey, David. 1990. *The Condition of Postmodernity.* Oxford: Blackwell.

Hatten, Robert. 1994. *Musical Meaning in Beethoven: Markedness, Correlation, and Interpretation.* Bloomington: Indiana University Press.

———. 2004. *Interpreting Musical Gestures, Topics, and Tropes: Mozart, Beethoven, Schubert.* Bloomington: Indiana University Press.

Haverkamp, Anselm. 1996. *Leaves of Mourning: Hölderlin's Late Work.* Translated by Vernon Chadwick. Albany: State University of New York Press. First published in 1991.

Heartz, Daniel. 2003. *Music in European Capitals: The Galant Style, 1720–1780.* New York: W. W. Norton.

Hegel, G. W. F. 1999. *Science of Logic.* Translated by A. V. Miller. New York: Humanity Books. First published in 1812–1816.

Heidegger, Martin. 1975. *Poetry, Language, Thought.* Translated by Albert Hofstadter. New York: Harper & Row. First published in 1812–1816.

———. 2000. *Elucidations of Hölderlin's Poetry.* Translated by Keith Hoeller. Amherst, N.Y.: Humanity Books. First published in 1937.

Henrich, Dieter. 1997. *The Course of Remembrance and Other Essays.* Stanford, Calif.: Stanford University Press. First published in 1986.

Hepokoski, James. 2002. "Beyond the Sonata Principle." *Journal of the American Musicological Society* 55, no. 1:91–154.

Hepokoski, James, and Warren Darcy. 1997. "The Medial Caesura and Its Role in the Eighteenth-Century Sonata Exposition." *Music Theory Spectrum* 19:115–54.

Hinton, Stephen. 1996. "Adorno's Unfinished *Beethoven.*" *Beethoven Forum* 5, no. 1: 139–53.

Hirschkop, Ken. 1989. "The Classical and the Popular: Musical Form and Social Context." In Christopher Norris, ed., *Music and the Politics of Culture*, 283–304. London: Norris & Wishart.

Hoeckner, Berthold. 2002. *Programming the Absolute: Nineteenth-Century German Music and the Hermeneutics of the Moment.* Princeton: Princeton University Press.

Hölderlin, Friedrich. 1992–1994. *Sämtliche Werke und Briefe.* 2 vols. Edited by Jochen Schmidt. Frankfurt am Main: Deutscher Klassiker Verlag.

Jameson, Frederic. 1990. *Late Marxism: Adorno, or, The Persistence of the Dialectic.* New York: Verso.

———. 1991. *Postmodernism, or The Cultural Logic of Late Capitalism.* New York: Verso.

Jay, Martin. 1973. *The Dialectical Imagination.* London: Heinemann.

Johnson, Julian. 2002. *Who Needs Classical Music?* New York: Oxford University Press.

Kant, Immanuel. 1989. *The Critique of Judgement.* Translated by James Creed Meredith. Oxford: Oxford University Press. First published in 1790.

Kerman, Joseph. 1967. *The Beethoven Quartets.* London: Oxford University Press.

———. 1980. "How We Got into Analysis, and How to Get Out." *Critical Inquiry* 7:311–31.

———. 1985. *Contemplating Musicology: Challenges to Musicology.* Cambridge, Mass.: Harvard University Press.

Kinderman, William. 1985. "Beethoven's Symbol for the Deity in the *Missa Solemnis* and the Ninth Symphony." *19th-Century Music* 9, no. 2:102–18.

———. 1987. *Beethoven's Diabelli Variations.* Oxford: Clarendon Press.

———. 1995. *Beethoven.* Oxford: Oxford University Press.

———. 2003. *Artaria 195: Beethoven's Sketchbook for the Missa Solemnis and the Piano Sonata in E Major, Opus 109.* Urbana: University of Illinois Press.

Kirkendale, Warren. 1970. "New Roads to Old Ideas in Beethoven's *Missa Solemnis.*" *Musical Quarterly* 56:665–701.

Kivy, Peter. 1989. *Sound Sentiment.* Philadelphia: Temple University Press.

Klein, Rudolph. 1982. "Wo kann die Analyse von Haydns Symphonik ansetzen?" *Österreichische Musikzeitschrift* 37:234–41.

Klumpenhouwer, Henry. 2001. "Late Capitalism, Late Marxism and the Study of Music." *Music Analysis* 20, no. 3:367–405.

Koch, Heinrich. 1782–1794. *Versuch einer Anleitung zur Composition.* Rudolstadt and Leipzig. Partial English translation in Nancy Baker, *Heinrich Koch: Introductory Essay on Composition.* New Haven, Conn.: Yale University Press, 1983.

———. 1802. *Musikalisches Lexikon.* Frankfurt am Main.

Korsyn, Kevin. 2003. *Decentering Music: A Critique of Contemporary Musical Research.* New York: Oxford University Press.

Koselleck, Reinhart. 1985. *Futures Past: On the Semantics of Historical Time.* Translated by Keith Tribe. Cambridge, Mass.: MIT Press.

———. 2002. *The Practice of Conceptual History: Timing History, Spacing Concepts.* Translated by Todd Samuel Presner, with a foreword by Hayden White. Stanford, Calif.: Stanford University Press.

Kramer, Lawrence. 1995. *Classical Music and Postmodern Knowledge.* Berkeley: University of California Press.

Kropfinger, Klaus. 2001. *Beethoven.* Weimar: Bärenreiter.

———. 2003. "Denn was schwer ist, ist auch schön, gut, gross." *Bonner Beethoven-Studien* 3:81–100.

Küthen, Hans-Werner. 1980. "Quaerendo inventietis: Die Exegese eines Beethoven-Briefes an Haslinger vom 5. September 1823." In Marin Bente, ed., *Gedenkenschrift Günter Henle,* 296–313. Munich: Henle.

———. 2002. "'Szene am Bach' oder Der Einfluss durch die Hintertür: Die Bach-Rezeption der anderen als Impuls für Beethoven." In Hans-Werner Küthen, ed.,

Beethoven und die Rezeption der Alten Musik, 243–80. Bonn: Verlag Beethoven-Haus.

———. 2003. "Beethovens 'Kunstvereinigung': Die Fusion von Wiener Avantgarde und Barocker Tradition." In *Internationale Konferenzbeiträge zu den Ludwig van Beethoven Osterfestivals.* Kraków, 2003.

Lacoue-Labarthe, Philippe. 1989. *Typography: Mimesis, Philosophy, Politics.* Translated by Christopher Fynsk. Stanford, Calif.: Stanford University Press.

———, and Jean-Luc Nancy. 1988. *The Literary Absolute: The Theory of Literature in German Romanticism.* Translated by Philip Barnard and Cheryl Lester. Albany: State University of New York Press. First published in 1978.

Lakoff, George. 1987. *Women, Fire, and Dangerous Things: What Categories Reveal about the Mind.* Chicago: University of Chicago Press.

Langan, Janine D. 1986. *Hegel and Mallarmé.* New York: University Press of America.

Lenz, Wilhelm von. 1852–1853. *Beethoven et ses trois styles.* St. Petersburg.

Lerdahl, Fred. 1996. "Issues in Prolongational Theory: A Response to Larson." *Music Perception* 13, no. 3:141–55.

———. 2001. *Tonal Pitch Space.* Oxford: Oxford University Press.

Lerdahl, Fred, and Ray Jackendoff. 1985. *A Generative Theory of Tonal Music.* Cambridge, Mass.: Harvard University Press.

Lester, Joel. 1970. "Revisions in the Autograph of the *Missa Solemnis Kyrie.*" *Journal of the American Musicological Society* 23:420–38.

Lewin, David. 1984. "Amfortas's Prayer to Titurel and the Role of D in Parsifal: The Tonal Spaces of the Drama and the Enharmonic C♭/B." *19th-Century Music* 7, no. 3:336–49.

Lidov, David. 2004. *Is Language a Music? Writings on Musical Form and Signification.* Bloomington: Indiana University Press.

Lockwood, Lewis. 2002. "Recent Writings on Beethoven's Late Quartets." *Beethoven Forum* 9, no. 1:84–99.

———. 2003. *Beethoven: The Music and the Life.* New York: W. W. Norton.

Lodes, Birgit. 1998. " 'When I try, now and then, to give musical form to my turbulent Feelings': The Human and the Divine in the Gloria of Beethoven's *Missa Solemnis.*" *Beethoven Forum* 6, no. 1:143–79.

Longyear, Ray. 1970. "Beethoven and Romantic Irony." *Musical Quarterly* 56, no. 4:647–64.

Lukács, Georg. 1988. *The Theory of the Novel: A Historical-Philosophical Essay on the Forms of the Great Epic Literature.* Translated by Anna Bostock. London: Merlin Press. First published in 1963.

Lyotard, Jean-François. 1984. *The Postmodern Condition: A Report on Knowledge.* Translated by G. Bennington and B. Massumi. Manchester: Manchester University Press.

Mann, Thomas. 1961. *The Genesis of a Novel.* Translated by Richard and Clara Winston. London: Secker & Warburg. First published in 1949 as *Die Enstehung des Doktor Faustus: Roman eines Romans.* Frankfurt am Main: Fischer.

———. 1980. *Doktor Faustus: Das Leben des deutschen Tonsetzers Adrian Leverkühn erzählt von einem Freunde.* Frankfurt am Main: Fischer. First published in 1947. Translated by H. T. Lowe-Porter as *Doctor Faustus: The Life of the German Composer Adrian Leverkühn as Told by a Friend.* New York: Alfred A. Knopf, 1948.

Marpurg, Friedrich Wilhelm. 1753. *Abhandlung von der Fuge.* Berlin.

Marston, Nicholas. 1989. "Analysing Variations: The Finale of Beethoven's String Quartet Op. 74." *Music Analysis* 8:303–24.

———. 1995. *Beethoven's Sonata in E, Op. 109.* Oxford: Oxford University Press.

———. 1998. "From A to B: The History of an Idea in the '*Hammerklavier*' Sonata." *Beethoven Forum* 6, no. 1:97–127.

Marx, Adolph Bernhard. 1884. *Ludwig van Beethoven, Leben und Schaffen.* 4th edition. Berlin: Verlag von Otto Janker. First published in 1859.

Maurer Zenck, Claudia. 2001. *Überlegungen zur Theorie und kompositorischen Praxis im ausgehenden 18. und beginnenden 19. Jahrhundert.* Weimar: Böhlau.

McClary, Susan. 2000. *Conventional Wisdom: The Content of Musical Form.* Berkeley: University of California Press.

McGrann, Jeremiah. 2003. "Der Hintergrund zu Beethovens Messen." *Bonner Beethoven-Studien* 3:119–38.

Menke, Christoph. 1999. *The Sovereignty of Art: Aesthetic Negativity in Adorno and Derrida.* Translated by Neil Solomon. Cambridge, Mass.: MIT Press. First published in 1988.

Meyer, Leonard B. 1973. *Explaining Music.* Chicago: University of Chicago Press.

———. 1997. *Style and Music.* Chicago: University of Chicago Press. First published in 1989.

———. 2000. *The Spheres of Music: A Gathering of Essays.* Chicago: University of Chicago Press.

Michaelis, Christian Friedrich. 1795. *Ueber den Geist der Tonkunst. Mit Rücksicht auf Kants Kritik der ästhetischen Urtheilskraft.* Leipzig.

Miller, R. D. 1970. *Schiller and the Ideal of Freedom.* Oxford: Clarendon Press.

Narmour, Eugene. 1992. *The Analysis and Cognition of Melodic Complexity: The Implication-Realization Model.* Chicago: University of Chicago Press.

Neubauer, John. 1986. *The Emancipation of Music from Language: Departure from Mimesis in Eighteenth-Century Aesthetics.* New Haven, Conn.: Yale University Press.

Nicholsen, Shierry Weber. 1997. *Exact Imagination, Late Work: On Adorno's Aesthetics.* Cambridge, Mass.: MIT Press.

Nottebohm, Gustav. 1970. *Zweite Beethoveniana: nachgelassene Aufsätze.* New York: Johnson Reprint. First published in 1987.

Paddison, Max. 1996. *Adorno, Modernism and Mass Culture: Essays on Critical Theory and Music.* London: Kahn and Averill.

———. 1997. *Adorno's Aesthetics of Music.* Cambridge: Cambridge University Press.

———. 1998. "The Language-Character of Music: Some Motifs in Adorno." In Richard Klein and Claus-Steffen Mahnkopf, eds., *Mit den Ohren denken: Adornos Philosophie der Musik,* 71–91. Frankfurt am Main: Suhrkamp.

Palmer, F. R. 1986. *Semantics.* Cambridge: Cambridge University Press.

Porter, David. 1970. "The Structure of Beethoven's Diabelli Variations, Op. 120." *Music Review* 31:295–97.

Ratner, Leonard G. 1980. *Classic Music: Expression, Form, and Style.* New York: Schirmer.

Réti, Rudolph. 1967. *Thematic Patterns in Sonatas of Beethoven.* London: Faber.

Reynolds, Christopher. 1988. "The Representational Impulse in Late Beethoven, II: String Quartet in F Major, Op. 135." *Acta Musicologica* 60:180–94.

Riezler, Walter. 1936. *Beethoven.* Berlin: Atlantis Verlag.

Ringer, Alexander. 1970. "Beethoven and the London Pianoforte School." *Musical Quarterly* 56:742–58.

Rochlitz, Rainer. 1996. *The Disenchantment of Art: The Philosophy of Walter Benjamin.* Translated by Jane Marie Todd. New York: Guilford Press. First published in 1992.

Rorty, Richard. 1989. *Contingency, Irony, Solidarity.* Cambridge: Cambridge University Press.

———. 1991. *Essays on Heidegger and Others. Philosophical Papers, Volume 2.* Cambridge: Cambridge University Press.

Rosen, Charles. 1972. *The Classical Style.* London: Faber.

———. 1988. *Sonata Forms.* Revised edition. New York: W. W. Norton.

———. 1996. *The Romantic Generation.* London: HarperCollins.

———. 2002. *Beethoven's Piano Sonatas: A Short Companion.* New Haven: Yale University Press.

Ross, Stephanie. 2003. "Style in Art." In Jerrold Levinson, ed., *The Oxford Handbook of Aesthetics,* 28–44. New York: Oxford University Press.

Rumph, Stephen. 2004. *Beethoven after Napoleon: Political Romanticism in the Late Works.* Berkeley: University of California Press.

Ryan, Lawrence. 1960. *Hölderlin's Lehre vom Wechsel der Töne.* Stuttgart: W. Kohlhammer.

Scaglione, Aldo. 1981. *The Theory of German Word Order.* Minneapolis: University of Minnesota Press.

Schama, Simon. 1999. *Rembrandt's Eyes.* New York: Alfred A. Knopf.

Schenker, Heinrich. 1971–1972. *Beethoven: Die letzten Sonaten: Sonate in A, Op. 101; Sonata in As, Op. 110; Sonata in C Moll, Op. 111, Kritische Ausgabe mit Einführung und Erläuterung.* Edited by Oswald Jonas. Vienna: Universal Edition. First published 1913–1921.

———. 1992. *Beethoven's Ninth Symphony: A Portrayal of Its Musical Content, with Running Commentary on Performance and Literature as Well.* Edited and translated by John Rothgeb. New Haven, Conn.: Yale University Press. First published in 1913.

Schleiermacher, Friedrich. 1977. *Hermeneutik und Kritik: Mit einem Anhang sprachphilosophischer Texte Schleiermachers.* Edited by Manfred Frank. Frankfurt am Main: Suhrkamp.

Schleuning, Peter. 1998. *Die Sprache der Natur: Natur in der Musik des 18. Jahrhunderts.* Weimar: Verlag J. B. Metzler.

Schleuning, Peter, and Martin Geck. 1989. *"Geschrieben auf Bonaparte": Beethovens "Eroica": Revolution, Reaktion, Rezeption.* Reinbek: Rowohlt.

Schmalfeldt, Janet. 1995. "Form as the Process of Becoming: The Beethoven-Hegelian Tradition and the 'Tempest' Sonata." *Beethoven Forum* 4, no. 1:37–71.

Schmitz, Arnold. 1927. *Das romantische Beethovenbild. Darstellung und Kritik.* Berlin: Dunnler.

Schoenberg, Arnold. 1969. *Structural Functions of Harmony.* London: Faber and Faber. First published in 1954.

———. 1984. *Style and Idea: Selected Writings of Arnold Schoenberg.* Edited by Leonard Stein. Translated by Leo Black. London: Faber and Faber.

Scruton, Roger. 1999. *The Aesthetics of Music.* Oxford: Oxford University Press.

Simpson, David, ed. 1988. *The Origins of Modern Critical Thought: German Aesthetic and Literary Criticism from Lessing to Hegel.* Cambridge: Cambridge University Press.

Singer, Peter. 2001. *Hegel.* Oxford: Oxford University Press.

Sipe, Thomas. 1992. "Interpreting Beethoven: History, Aesthetics, and Critical Reception." Ph.D. dissertation, University of Pennsylvania.

———. 1998. *Beethoven: Eroica Symphony.* Cambridge: Cambridge University Press.

Sircello, Guy. 1975. *A New Theory of Beauty.* Princeton: Princeton University Press.

Sisman, Elaine. 1993a. *Mozart, the "Jupiter" Symphony, No. 41 in C Major, K. 551.* Cambridge: Cambridge University Press.

——. 1993b. *Haydn and the Classical Variation.* Cambridge, Mass.: Harvard University Press.

——. 1997. "After the Heroic Style: *Fantasia* and the 'Characteristic' Sonatas of 1809." *Beethoven Forum* 6, no. 1:67–96.

——. 2000. "Memory and Invention at the Threshold of Beethoven's Late Style." In Scott Burnham and Michael P. Steinberg, eds., *Beethoven and His World,* 51–87. Princeton: Princeton University Press.

Solomon, Maynard. 1980. *Beethoven.* London: Granada.

——. 1986. "Beethoven's Ninth Symphony: A Search for Order." *19th-Century Music* 10, no. 1:3–23.

——. 1990. "Beethoven's Ninth Symphony: The Sense of an Ending." In Siegfried Kross, ed., *Probleme der Symphonischen Tradition im 19. Jahrhundert,* 145–56. Tutzing: Hans Schneider.

——. 2003. *Late Beethoven: Music, Thought, Imagination.* Berkeley: University of California Press.

Spitzer, Leo. 1948. *Linguistics and Literary History.* Princeton: Princeton University Press.

Spitzer, Michael. 1996. "The Significance of Recapitulation in Beethoven's *Waldstein* Sonata." *Beethoven Forum* 5, no. 1 103–17.

——. 1997. "Meditations on Meyer's Hobby Horses: Levels of Motivation in Musical Signs." *Applied Semiotics* 4:201–7. www.chass.utoronto.ca/french/as-sa/ASSA-No4/index.htm.

——. 1998a. "Inside Beethoven's Magic Square: The Structural Semantics of Opus 132." In Costin Miereanu and Xavier Hascher, eds., *Musique et Signification: les Universaux en Musique,* 87–126. Paris: Publications de la Sorbonne.

——. 1998b. "Haydn's Reversals: Style Change, Gesture, and the Implication-Realization Model." In Dean Sutcliffe, ed., *Haydn Studies,* 170–217. Cambridge: Cambridge University Press.

——. 2004. *Metaphor and Musical Thought.* Chicago: University of Chicago Press.

Strunk, Oliver. 1974. "Haydn's Divertimenti for Baryton." In *Essays on Music in the Western World,* 126–70. New York: W. W. Norton.

Subotnik, Rose Rosengard. 1976. "Adorno's Diagnosis of Beethoven's Late Style." *Journal of the American Musicological Society* 29, no. 2:242–75.

——. 1978. "The Historical Structure: Adorno's French Model for Criticism of 19th-Century Music." *19th-Century Music* 2, no. 1:36–60.

——. 1991. *Developing Variations: Style and Ideology in Western Music.* Minneapolis: University of Minnesota Press.

Sulzer, Johann Georg. 1771–1774. *Allgemeine Theorie der schönen Künste.* Leipzig.

Sutcliffe, W. Dean. 2005. "A Dying Art: Haydn and the Tempo di Menuetto Finale." Unpublished paper presented at the conference "Communicative Strategies in the Music of the Late Eighteenth Century," Freiburg, Germany.

Szondi, Peter. 1970. *Hölderlin Studien.* Frankfurt am Main: Suhrkamp.

——. 1986. *On Textual Understanding and Other Essays.* Translated by Harvey Mendelsohn. Minneapolis: University of Minnesota Press. First published in 1978.

——. 2003. *Introduction to Literary Hermeneutics.* Translated by Martha Woodmansee. Cambridge: Cambridge University Press.

Taussig, Michael. 1993. *Mimesis and Alterity: A Particular History of the Senses.* New York: Routledge.

Taylor, Charles. 1999. *Hegel.* Cambridge: Cambridge University Press.

Thayer, A. W. 1964. *The Life of Ludwig van Beethoven.* Revised and edited by Elliot Forbes. Princeton: Princeton University Press.

Todorov, Tzvetan. 1982. *Theories of the Symbol.* Translated by Catherine Porter. Ithaca, N.Y.: Cornell University Press. First published in 1977.

Toorn, Pieter C. Van den. 1995. *Music, Politics, and the Academy.* Berkeley: University of California Press.

Tovey, Donald Francis. 1944. *Beethoven.* Oxford: Oxford University Press.

———. 1989. *Symphonies and Other Orchestral Works.* Oxford: Oxford University Press.

Treitler, Leo. 1989. *Music and the Historical Imagination.* Cambridge, Mass.: Harvard University Press.

Uelein, Friedrich A. 1998. "Beethovens Musik ist die Hegelsche Philosophie: sie ist aber zugleich wahrer." In Richard Klein and Claus-Steffen Mahnkopf, eds., *Mit den Ohren denken: Adornos Philosophie der Musik,* 206–28. Frankfurt am Main: Suhrkamp.

Wagner, Richard. 1993–1995. *Richard Wagner's Prose Works.* Translated by William Ashton Ellis. Lincoln: University of Nebraska Press.

Walton, Kendall. 1979. "Style and the Products and Processes of Art." In Berel Lang, ed., *The Concept of Style,* 45–66. Ithaca, N.Y.: Cornell University Press.

Webster, James. 1978. "Schubert's Sonata Form and Brahms's First Maturity." *19th-Century Music* 2, no. 1:18–35.

———. 1991. *Haydn's 'Farewell' Symphony and the Idea of the Classical Style: Through-Composition and Cyclic Integration in His Instrumental Music.* Cambridge: Cambridge University Press.

———. 1997. "The *Creation,* Haydn's Late Vocal Music, and the Musical Sublime." In Elaine Sisman, ed., *Haydn and His World,* 57–102. Princeton: Princeton University Press.

———. 1998. "Haydn's Symphonies between *Sturm und Drang* and 'Classical Style': Art and Entertainment." In W. Dean Sutcliffe, ed., *Haydn Studies,* 218–45. Cambridge: Cambridge University Press.

———. 2004. "The Eighteenth Century as a Music-Historical Period?" *Eighteenth-Century Music* 1, no. 1:47–60.

Wellbery, David E. 1984. *Lessing's Laocoon: Semiotics and Aesthetics in the Age of Reason.* Cambridge: Cambridge University Press.

Wellmer, Albrecht. 1998. *Endgames.* Translated by David Midgley. Cambridge, Mass.: MIT Press. First published in 1993.

Wheelock, Gretchen. 1992. *Haydn's Ingenious Jesting with Art: Contexts of Musical Wit and Humor.* New York: Schirmer.

Williams, Alastair. 1997. *New Music and the Claims of Modernity.* Aldershot: Ashgate.

———. 1998. "Torn Halves: Structure and Subjectivity in Analysis." *Music Analysis* 17, no. 3:281–93.

Wills, David. 2001. "Derrida and Aesthetics: Lemming (Reframing the Abyss)." In Tom Cohen, ed., *Jacques Derrida and the Humanities: A Critical Reader,* 108–31. Cambridge: Cambridge University Press.

Winter, Robert. 1977. "Plans for the Structure of the String Quartet in C Sharp Minor, Op. 131." In Alan Tyson, ed., *Beethoven Studies.* Vol. 2, 106–37. Oxford: Oxford University Press, 106–37.

Wittgenstein, Ludwig. 1984. *Philosophical Investigations.* Translated by G. E. M. Anscombe. Oxford: Basil Blackwell. First published in 1958.

Wollheim, Richard. 1979. "Pictorial Style: Two Views." In Berel Lang, ed., *The Concept of Style*, 129–45. Ithaca, N.Y.: Cornell University Press.

——. 1995. "Style in Painting." In Caroline van Eck, James McAllister, and René van Vall, eds., *The Question of Style in Philosophy and the Arts*, 37–49. Cambridge: Cambridge University Press.

Wolff, Christoph. 2001. *Johann Sebastian Bach: The Learned Musician*. New York: W. W. Norton.

Zbikowski, Lawrence. 2002. *Conceptualizing Music: Cognitive Structure, Theory, and Analysis*. New York: Oxford University Press.

Zenck, Martin. 1986. *Die Bach-Rezeption des späten Beethoven: Zum Verhältnis von Musikhistoriographie und Rezeptionsgeschichtsschreibung der "Klassik."* In *Beihefte zum AfMw* 24. Stuttgart: Franz Steiner Verlag.

——. 1995. "Musik über Musik in Adornos Ästhetischer Theorie." In Annegrit Laubenthal and Kara Kusan-Windweh, eds., *Studien zur Musikgeschichte. Eine Festschrift für Ludwig Finscher*, 736–49. Kassel: Bärenreiter.

——. 2002. "Geschichtsreflexion und Historismus im Musikdenken Beethovens." In Hans-Werner Küthen, ed., *Beethoven und die Rezeption der Alten Musik*, 1–24. Bonn: Verlag Beethoven-Haus.

Zuidervaart, Lambert. 1994. *Adorno's Aesthetic Theory: The Redemption of Illusion*. Cambridge, Mass.: MIT Press.

Index of Names and Concepts

Note: The index of works includes Adorno's references to Beethoven's music.

Derrida, Jacques, 3, 275; on framing, 344n9; on Hegelian teleology, 183, 251; poststructuralist philosophy of, 264, 272. *See also* deconstruction

developing variation, 116, 208; as Hegelian, 242, 246

development, 129–32. *See also* core

Dewey, John, 12, 49

Diabelli, Anton, 1

dialectic, 47, 51; definition of, 49, 69, 269; and developing variation, 242–44; dialectical sublime, 143–47. *See also* Hegel; negative dialectic

Dichtarten. See genre, poetic

Diderot, Denis, 9

Dilthey, Wilhelm, 10

Drabkin, William, 2, 101, 109, 136, 165

"dual character," music's, 263

Durchbrochene Arbeit, 206–208. *See also* Adler

Durchbruch, 6, 18, 20, 22, 63, 72, 85, 169, 193, 229; definition of, 21, 32, 69, 71, 206; and Hegel, 240–41; of historical styles, 201, 223; in Hölderlin's system, 220; as revolution, 208, 211; and SURFACE-DEPTH schema, 73

Dusík, Jan Ladislav, 239, 343

Dürer, Albrecht, 203

Eagleton, Terry, 196

Eco, Umberto, 190

Eggebrecht, Hans Heinrich, 33

Einschnitt. See caesura; punctuation

Eitan, Zohar, 79

Enlightenment, 6, 262, 264, 265; dialectic of, 272–75; as interregnum, 66; and rationalization of space, 113

Entwicklung. See Fortspinnung

epic. *See* genre, poetic

Episierung, 217, 220, 224

Epstein, David, 29, 149

Erscheinung, 4, 32, 78; as *Apparition*, 240; definition of, 51, 240, 338n7, 341n3

Euler, Leonhard, 85

exact imagination (*exakte Phantasie*), 277–78

extensive temporality, 55. *See also* intensive temporality

extraterritoriality, 20

false consciousness, 263

false reprise, 19, 20, 37, 123, 145; as formal non-congruence, 114, 142; origin of, 141–42

fanfare. *See* topic theory, fanfare

fantasy, 341

Fichte, Johann Gottlieb, 215

figurative cadence, 342n1

finale, 167–69

Finscher, Ludwig, 204

fireworks, artworks as, 338n7

Fischer, Wilhelm, 204

Floskel: definition of, 60, 69, 122, 339n6; as trill, 149–150, 156,161

Fodor, Jerry, 337n3

formalism, 8, 266, 267

Forte, Allan, 79

Fortspinnung, 95, 97–99; definition of, 204, 235; vs. *Entwicklung*, 343n6; as lyrical trajectory, 170–74, 178

Foucault, Michel, 264

fragment, Romantic, 230

Frank, Manfred, 10, 14

Franklin, Benjamin, 252

freedom, 195

Frege, Gottlob, 337n3

French revolution, 209, 211

Freud, Sigmund, 263, 278, 345n6

fugue, 83, 84, 85, 95, 97–99, 169–74, 178; in classical finale, 41; figurative logicality of, 57; homophonic turn of, 106. *See also* counterpoint; *Fortspinnung*

functional multitasking, 108, 109, 112

functional rubato, 108, 116, 160–61, 163

future, memory of (Bloch), 210

"futures past" (Koselleck), 210–13

Gadamer, Hans-Georg, 10, 35

galant: contrasted with Classical, 26–29, 203; conventionalization of, 139, 142; as metropolitan style, 113; periodization of, 204–205, 343n3; and rhythmic paradigm, 231–32

Galitzin, Prince Nikolaus, 1, 31

genre, poetic, 216–25

Gerhard, Anselm, 224, 239, 342n8

Gervinus, Georg Gottfried, 212

gesture, 12, 13, 24, 54

Geuss, Raymond, 68, 263, 267, 269

Gjerdingen, Robert O, 26, 27

Goehr, Lydia, 266, 268, 337n3

Goethe, Johann Wolfgang von, 36, 64, 71, 78, 227, 229; *Goethezeit*, 224; and the Gothic, 202

Gogh, Vincent van, 3, 148, 167

Gombrich, Ernst, 12

Goodman, Nelson, 11, 13, 23

Gossett, Philip, 239

Greimas, Algirdas, 342n7

Grétry, André Ernest, 209–10

Grimm, Friedrich Melchior, 211

Grund (Hölderlin), 220–22

Grundgestalt. See Schoenberg, *Grundgestalt*

Habermas, Jürgen, 6, 14, 54; and dialectic of Enlightenment, 265, 272–75; and intersubjectivity paradigm, 275–77; against metaphorical thinking, 345n5

Halm, August, 36, 204, 209, 241

Handel, George Frederic, 34, 182; revival of, 198, 202

Hanslick, Eduard, 36, 266, 268

harmony: aesthetic of, 35, 40, 57, 59, 64, 213; complementary, 64–65; definition of, 63; "universal," 257

Harrison, Daniel, 76, 82

Harvey, David, 113, 264, 265

Hatten, Robert, 28, 117, 174, 223, 338n3, 341n7; on markedness, 23; on methodological dialectic, 18, 345n2

Haydn, Joseph, 17, 19, 99; and cadential openings, 108, 153, 237–38; and classical texture, 95; and critique of harmony, 58; and *Entwicklung/Fortspinnung* distinction, 343n6; influence on Beethoven, 17, 24, 26, 46, 47, 230, 238–39, 247; and *Neuzeit,* 212; "new and special way" of, 199; periodic style of, 66; and periodization, 204–205, 208, 343n3; and sonata form, 116, 123, 126, 129, 340n1; and *Sturm und Drang,* 234–36; and symphony as ode, 224; and variation, 116, 153, 340n2. *See also* false reprise

Haverkamp, Anselm, 222, 226

"hearing as," 78

Heartz, Daniel, 205

Hegel, G. W. F., 4, 46, 183; Beethoven, analogy with, 53, 213, 274–75; and genre, 220; Hegelian logic, 45, 48–53, 56, 78, 240–42, 247; Hölderlin's critique of, 215–16, 225, 228; and Kant, critique of, 273–74; "left" vs. "right," 49, 241–46; and mediation, 47, 50, 213; positing, 50–51, 52, 56, 159; and subject, 50, 57

Heidegger, Martin: and clearing, 18; and Hölderlin, 215; and materiality, 3, 148–49; and ontology, 60, 61

Helm, Theodor, 36–38, 40

Henrich, Dieter, 215–16

Hepokoski, James, 340n1, 341n5

Herder, Johann Gottfried, 232

hermeneutics, 10, 17, 197, 266. *See also* Schleiermacher

vs. critical theory, 6–7, 68

hermeneutic circle, 9; Adorno's, 10–11; of Beethoven reception, 33–34

imperative of, 250

and Style 4, 35, 36–41

heroic style, 76, 120, 122, 131, 201; deconstruction of, 248–49; and historical consciousness, 208–13; and Hölderlin's "striving," 219

Hinton, Stephen, 168

Hirschkop, Ken, 341n6

history, theories of, 198–213; and dialectic, 270. *See also* periodization; time consciousness

Hjelmslev, Louis, 339

Hoeckner, Berthold, 21, 71, 229, 338n7, 343n2; on hermeneutics of moment, 230–31

Hoffmann, E. T. A., 203, 241

Hoffmeister, Franz Anton, 203, 205

Hölderlin, Friedrich, 8, 33, 56, 114, 186, 202, 213–25, 251; *Andenken,* 216; *Anmerkungen zum Ödipus,* 214; *Das fröhliche Leben,* 226; *Hälfte des Lebens,* 213; *Mnemosyne,* 216–17; and modulation *(Wechsel),* 196, 201, 216, 217–25, 342n6; *Wie wenn am Feiertage,* 214–15, 219; *Der Winkel von Hahrdt,* 220–22, 227. *See also* caesura; *Grund*

Holz, Karl, 205

Horkheimer, Max, 10, 262, 272

Huebner, Steven, 342n1

Hugo, Victor, 115, 338n7

Husserl, Edmund, 260, 262

Hüttenbrenner, Anselm, 249

hypotaxis: definition of, 114–115, 120; and Mozart, 239. *See also* parataxis

idea, 148–49, 270

ideal type (Weber), 239

image schema, 12, 13, 20, 107, 189–90; definition of, 22, 31; and landscape metaphor, 73; schematic reversals, 78

imbroglio, 55

intensive temporality, 55. *See also* extensive temporality; time consciousness

intersubjectivity paradigm, 261, 275–80

interval cycles, 77, 82–85

introduction, 125, 133, 199

Jameson, Frederic, 43, 54, 67, 264, 265

jazz, 8

Kafka, Franz, 58, 64, 271

Kant, Immanuel, 15, 51, 215, 221, 232, 240; and aesthetic beauty, 232, 256, 257–59; and autonomy, 266; and concepts, 46, 258, 260; and counter-Enlightenment, 67; and Enlightenment rationality, 273–74; and musicoanalytical tradition, 231–34; three critical domains of, 265, 277. *See also* sublime

Keller, Hans, 84

Kerman, Joseph, 59, 117, 141, 142, 251; and criticism, 266

Kinderman, William, 72–73, 77, 166. *See also* parenthetical enclosure
Kirkendale, Warren, 73
Kivy, Peter, 337n5
Klein, Rudolph, 340n2
Klopstock, Friedrich Gottlieb, 224
Koch, Heinrich, 116, 204, 231, 258, 116, 340n3; on generic fusion, 224; on *Rückung,* 55; theory of lyric forms, 167–68. *See also* caesura; punctuation
Kojéve, Alexandre, 338n7
Kolisch, Rudolph, 45, 48
Korsyn, Kevin, 338n8, 345n4
Koselleck, Reinhart, 199, 210–13
Kramer, Lawrence, 265, 266, 267. *See also* New Musicology
Kraus, Joseph Martin, 239
Kreutzer, Rodolphe, 209
Kropfinger, Klaus, 17, 208
Krypt. *See* allegory, mourning
Kurth, Ernst, 95
Küthen, Hans-Werner, 97, 198, 342n1

Lacan, Jacques, 227, 264
Lacoue-Labarthe, Philippe, 215, 217, 228
Lakoff, George (and Mark Johnson), 107, 337n1. *See also* image schema
landscape, 59, 64, 71–72, 115. *See also* abyss
Langer, Susan, 197
language character, 6, 16, 21, 269–70; and Hölderlin's system, 224; intrinsic to Classical material, 228, 236–37, 268
lateness, 43, 54, 58–70, 71; definition of, 62–63, 213; "late work without late style" (Adorno), 62, 72
Leibniz, Gottfried Wilhelm Freiherr von, 231, 257
Lenz, Wilhelm von, 35, 209
Leppert, Richard, 8, 43
Lerdahl, Fred, 21, 85, 116, 267
Lessing, Gotthold, 232
Lester, Joel, 85
Lewin, David, 87
Lichtenberg, Georg Christoph, 34, 339n8
Lidov, David, 339n2
Ligeti, Gyorgy, 280
liquidation. *See* Schoenberg, liquidation
Liszt, Franz, 72, 84, 271
Lockwood, Lewis, 1
Lodes, Birgit, 73, 77
Longinus, 257, 344n12. *See also* sublime
Lukács, Georg, 269, 275
Luther, Martin, 209
Lyotard, Jean-François, 265, 337n6

lyric, 124, 128, 170–79; as archaic, 114; vs. dynamic, 125; and junctures of sonata form, 116; levelling effect of, 119; movements, 167–69; as "natural," 24; as pole of style, 117. *See also Fortspinnung,* as lyrical trajectory; genre, poetic

Mahler, Gustav, 21, 43, 63, 271
Mallarmé, Stéphane, 338n7
Mann, Thomas, 156–57, 165, 271, 345n1
Marcuse, Herbert, 262
markedness. *See* Hatten
Marpurg, Friedrich Wilhelm, 202
Marston, Nicholas, 79–80, 161
Marx, Adolph Bernhard, 36–37, 107, 209, 241, 266; on *Idee,* 242
Marxism, 4, 49, 263; and musical form, 268–69, 345n5
mass culture, 264
material: disclosing of, 3, 148–49; Hölderlin's theory of *(Stoff),* 218; and landscape, 72; reflection on, 149, 166, 190; as style, 36–39. *See also* Schiller, sense and formal drives
Matthesohn, Johann, 258, 344n12
Mead, George Herbert, 12
mediation, 6, 7, 22, 196; definition of, 44, 69, 339n2; and harmony, 63. *See also* context dependence; Hegel, mediation
Mendelssohn, Moses, 232, 342n8
Menke, Christoph: on aesthetic negativity, 59–60, 266, 277, 278; on allegory, 64; on autonomy vs. sovereignty, 265–266, 279; on exact imagination, 278
Messiaen, Olivier, 280
metaphor, 5–6, 12, 338n4; as caesura, 229; definition of, 22–23; Enlightenment theory of, 231–32, 237; Hölderlin's theory of *(Metapher),* 219
metre: baroque, 160–61; metrical pattern, 185–86. *See also* rhythmic paradigm
Meyer, Leonard B., 5, 21, 29, 76, 82, 94, 228; critique of, 12–13; and Kantian aesthetics, 232–33; and statistical climax, 79
Michaelis, Christian Friedrich, 202–204; on sublime, 257, 258–59
mimesis, 6, 31, 45, 61; as critique, 274; definition of, 16, 21–23, 31, 53–55, 69; and exact imagination, 278; ideational, 345n6; as withstanding, 53–54, 185
minuet. *See* dance
Mirka, Danuta, 339n5
modernism (modernity), 3–4, 8, 22, 35, 211, 256; and alienation, 270; and Enlightenment, 272–75; vs. postmodernism, 264. *See also Neuzeit*

Index of Names and Concepts 363

modulation *(Wechsel)* of tones. *See* Hölderlin, and modulation

moment *(Augenblick),* 21; definition of, 69; hermeneutics of, 230–31. *See also* Hoeckner

Monteverdi, Claudio, 206

mourning. *See* allegory, mourning

Mozart, Wolfgang Amadeus, 193, 204; and *Apparition* of material, 233–34; and classical texture, 95; and developments, 129; and *Entwicklung/Fortspinnung* distinction, 343n6; and *galant* schema, 26; influence on Beethoven, 17, 24, 46, 47, 230, 238–40, 247; periodic style of, 66; reception of, 34; and thematic contrast, 340n2

Nägeli, Hans Georg, 202

Narmour, Eugene, 5, 7, 21, 228, 267

nature, 20–21, 24–28, 31–33; beauty of, 260, 280; Beethoven's views on, 249; vs. culture, 12–13; and death, 256; domination of, 272–73; and drones, 251; and history, 260; and landscape, 73; and lyric movements, 167–69; as music psychology, 12, 21; resistance to, 156, 279. *See also* anamnesis

Nazis, 265

Neefe, Christian Gottlob, 204

negation (negativity), 47, 259, 269; classical articulation as, 230; definition of, 50, 273–74; negation of the negation, 50, 51. *See also* Hegel

negative dialectic, 60, 61, 260; caesura as, 240; definition of, 69–70

Neubauer, John, 269

Neuzeit, 211. *See also* modernism

New Musicology, 6, 267. *See also* Kramer

Nichelmann, Christoph, 206

Nicholsen, Shierry Weber, 43, 278

noncongruence. *See* congruence

Novalis (Friedrich von Hardenberg), 62, 78, 266

novel, theory of, 217

obbligato, 94, 199, 204–208

ode, 203, 224, 342n8. *See also Episierung*

ontology, 61, 66–67, 149. *see also* Heidegger

orchestration, 195. *See also* timbre

organicism, 64; ideology of, 266

Oulibicheff, Aléxandre, 209

Paddison, Max, 7, 36, 38–39, 43, 53, 262–63, 339n2

Palestrina, Giovanni Pierluigi da, 72

parenthetical enclosure: and ABA forms, 76, 143; and IN-OUT schema, 20, 73; and land-scape metaphor, 72–73; as lyrical interlude, 107, 108, 126–28; reversal of, 78, 150–51

parataxis: and canon, 178, 181; definition of, 32, 70; and Haydn, 239, 340n2; in Hölderlin, 214; and repetition, 181; and sonata form, 114–15, 116, 120, 129, 144, 168. *See also* hypotaxis

pastoral: as Baroque topos, 117–19; and Enlightenment metaphor, 238; as quest for Elysium, 167; violence of, 250–51. *See also* nature

Peirce, Charles Sanders, 49

performativity, 275–78

periodicity, classical, 115, 228, 235, 343n7

periodization, 224, 338n5. *See also* Webster

phantasmagoria, 4

Pindar, 214, 224

Piranesi, Giambattista, 115

Plato, 23

play: classical, 59, 237, 239; of Kantian faculties, 257. *See also* comic; Schiller, play

polyphony. *See* counterpoint

positing. *See* Hegel, positing

postmodernism, 6, 28, 264, 265, 267, 338n2

poststructuralism, 13, 264

punctuation: schema, 116, 133, 235–36, 340n3 (*see also* sonata schema); theory of, 228. *See also* caesura; Koch

Rameau, Jean-Philippe, 85, 87

ratio (construction), 6, 54, 58, 61

Ratner, Leonard G., 5, 236, 270

Ratz, Erwin, 241, 242, 244, 343n7

reception history, 35

Rembrandt, van Rijn, 230

Réti, Rudolph, 29, 84, 149

retransition, 122–23, 131

Reynolds, Christopher, 180

rhythmic paradigm, 185, 231–32; and dramatic caesura, 227, 230; properties of, 229. *See also* metre

Richter, Jean Paul, 199

Riemann, Hugo, 36, 207

Riezler, Walter, 85, 181, 189, 249–50, 251

Rochlitz, Friedrich, 33–35, 202–203

rondo, 169, 195

Rosen, Charles, 7, 67, 125, 238; on *Arietta,* 156–57; on Clementi, 239; convergence with Adorno, 7, 338n2; on false reprise, 141–42; on Romantic harmony, 255; on sequences, 340n4

Ross, Stephanie, 11

Rossini, Giacchino, 203

Rousseau, Jean-Jacques, 23

Rückung, 126, 248; definition of, 70; in *Hammerklavier,* 120–22; history of term, 55–56

Rudolph, Archduke, 198, 202
ruin, 114–15
Rumph, Stephen, 7–8, 190, 210
Ryan, Lawrence, 217–18, 220

Sandberger, Adolf, 204–205
Sanguinetti, Eduardo, 342n7
Saussure, Ferdinand de, 338n6
Scarlatti, Domenico, 239
Schein, 6, 60, 139, 156, 195; and bifocality, 95,
    101; and caesura, 230; as "cognitive trill,"
    159; and creative alternative, 179–82, 119;
    definition of, 1, 4–5, 32, 57, 70, 241; and
    "false" polyphony, 40–41, 208; and harmony,
    63, 255; Hölderlin's theory of, 219, 220; and
    reconcilation, 229; *Scheincharakter*, 57, 63, 65;
    and SURFACE-DEPTH schema, 175–76, 179;
    and vibration of dynamic sublime, 258
Schelling, F. W. J., 215, 266
schemata, melodic, 26, 27, 233–34. *See also*
    image schema
Schenker, Heinrich, 185, 241, 245; and Adorno,
    64–65; and hermeneutic analysis, 156, 157;
    ideology of, 266–67; and *Steigerung*, 79; syn-
    chronicity of graphs, 2, 52; and voice-leading
    contour, 132–33
Schering, Arnold, 209
scherzo. *See* dance
Schiller, Friedrich von, 182, 190, 215; Adorno
    and, 269; form, theory of, 257, 259; naïve vs.
    sentimental, 202, 204; *Ode to Joy*, 226; play,
    theory of, 216; sense and formal drives, 190,
    196, 216, 259
Schindler, Anton, 35
Schlegel, August, 202
Schlegel, Friedrich, 266; on music as philoso-
    phy, 241; and Romantic irony, 78; on style,
    217, 223
Schleuning, Peter, 20, 117, 209, 259, 344
Schleiermacher, Friedrich, 14, 21, 35; and her-
    meneutic circle, 9, 11; on style, 10, 21, 18,
    183, 250
Schlösser, Louis, 29, 241
Schmalfeldt, Janet, 241–42
Schmitz, Arnold, 7, 204, 209
Schoenberg, Arnold, 84, 107, 149, 241; and
    death of style, 38; and *Entrückung*, 56; on
    German music, 66; on *Grundgestalt*, 29, 242;
    and ideal counterpoint, 207; influence on
    Adorno, 7, 262; on liquidation, 245; and mod-
    ernist antinomies, 270–71; and monotonality,
    89; surface/depth model of serialism, 65. *See
    also* sentence

Schopenhauer, Arthur, 23
Schubert, Franz, 43, 55, 136, 166; and land-
    scape, 71
Schumann, Robert, 72, 94
Scorsese, Martin, 338n1
Scruton, Roger, 266, 337n5
Second Viennese School, 5. *See also* Berg;
    Schoenberg
semiotics, 9; semiotic squares, 342n7
sentence, 26, 242, 343n7
Seyfried, Ignaz von, 149
Singer, Peter, 274
Sipe, Thomas, 33
Sircello, Guy, 11, 341n3
Sisman, Elaine, 116, 169, 340, 341n1
sketches, 2–3, 44, 79, 97, 115, 165, 171. *See also*
    compositional process
sociology, 8
Solomon, Maynard, 7, 92, 166–67, 180, 190
sonata form, 37; Beethoven's conception of, 115;
    binary vs. ternary, 107–108, 109–110, 115–
    117; as "city," 113–115; sonata schema, punc-
    tuated, 116; and sonata theory, 340n1
song. *See* lyric
Sophocles, 214, 227
sovereignty. *See* autonomy
Spitta, Philipp, 36
Spitzer, Leo, 9–10
Spivak, Gayatri Chakravorty, 344n9
Spontini, Gaspare, 209
Staiger, Emil, 9
Star, 6, 157, 181, 229, 343n2
statistical climax. *See* Meyer, and statistical
    climax
Steigerung, 78–79, 95
Stravinsky, Igor, 2, 8, 61, 67, 280
structural listening, 8
structuralism, 9
Strunk, Oliver, 142
Stumpf, Johann Andreas, 249
style, 5, 8
    literary, 9–11; history of, 224
    mixture, theories of, 217, 224
    painterly, 11–12
    style 1, 18, 20–21, 24, 25–28, 277
    style 2, 18, 20–21, 24, 28–31, 277
    style 3, 20–21, 24, 31–33, 277
    style 4, 35–39
    style 5, 35, 36, 39–41
    style 6, 41–43
stylization, 10, 71, 107
subdominant, 77, 83, 171, 174, 179; as domi-
    nant substitute, 255

Index of Names and Concepts 365

Index of Works

Mozart, Wolfgang Amadeus

MUSICAL MEANING AND INTERPRETATION
Robert S. Hatten, editor

MICHAEL SPITZER is Reader in Music at Durham University, United Kingdom. He has written widely on aspects of music theory and semiotics and is author of *Metaphor and Musical Thought*.